RAOUL SMITH is a professor of computer science at Northeastern University in Boston, Massachusetts and a consultant to over a dozen firms and organizations including the National Science Foundation, the American Psychoanalytic Association, and the Ministry of Machine Building in the People's Republic of China. He lectures and publishes widely on computer science topics; he is the author of over 40 papers and articles and his other books include *Lexical-Semantic Relations*, *Probabilistic Performance Models of Language* and *Knowledge Representation*.

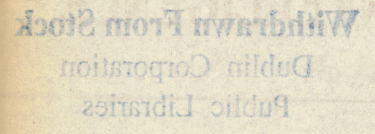

# COLLINS

## DICTIONARY OF

# ARTIFICIAL
# INTELLIGENCE

# COLLINS

## DICTIONARY OF

# ARTIFICIAL INTELLIGENCE

### *Raoul Smith*

**COLLINS**
*London and Glasgow*

Published in hardback as *The Facts on File Dictionary of Artificial Intelligence* by Facts on File Publications, New York and Oxford, 1989

First published by Harper Collins Publishers 1990

Reprint 10 9 8 7 6 5 4 3 2 1 0

ISBN 0 00 434366 2

**British Library Cataloguing in Publication Data**
Smith, Raoul
   Collins dictionary of artificial intelligence. – (Collins
   subject dictionaries)
   1. Artificial intelligence
   I. Title
   006.3

Printed in Great Britain by Collins, Glasgow

# PREFACE

This dictionary is a compendium of concepts from all of the subfields of artificial intelligence. This includes search, logic, vision, and natural language processing. The attempt has been made to make each entry as encyclopedic as possible; definitions go beyond just the traditional Aristotelian form found in standard dictionaries and most are elaborated upon extensively. This is useful for all classes of readers, be they interested lay people or dedicated specialists. The most basic concepts are given extended definitions in a simple language for the novice and require little cross-referencing; these entries are as self-contained as possible. For the specialist, the most technical definitions presuppose some prior knowledge. However, even these definitions are accessible to the novice because all the technical terms they use are themselves defined. Words used in entries that occur as entries themselves appear in the text in **bold** type.

I want to thank Eric Schuster who did much of the writing of the entries from the citation slips that were compiled. His diligence helped bring the project to fruition.

I want to dedicate this book to my two sons, Stephen and Timothy.

Raoul Smith

# A

**A\* algorithm,** *n.* a form of HEURISTIC SEARCH that attempts to determine the cheapest path from the initial state to the goal. The heuristic power of this method depends on the properties of the EVALUATION FUNCTION. Serving as the distinctive feature of the A\* algorithm, the evaluation function is the sum of two components: the estimated MINIMAL COST of a path from the initial state to the current state, and the estimated cost from the current state to the GOAL. The first component can be calculated if the search space is a tree, or it can be approximated by the cheapest known path if the search space is a graph. As with any evaluation function, the second component must be defined with respect to the DOMAIN.

**A\*, admissibility of,** *n.* that quality of a SEARCH ALGORITHM that, for any GRAPH, always terminates in an optimal path from s to a goal NODE whenever a path from s to a GOAL node exists.

**AALPS,** *n.* an expert system developed by Quintis Computer Systems for internal use by the U.S. Army. It helps to plan optimal loading of equipment on an aircraft. Quintus Prolog is the development software.

**abduction,** *n.* an INFERENCE process that generates explanations. To a first approximation, abduction has the following PARADIGM:

> From: *b*
> *(if a b)*
>
> Infer: *a*

Unlike deduction, abduction is not a legal inference. Abduction permits false conclusions, as in:

> From: *(feels-weak Jack)*
> *(for all (x) (if(has-AIDS x)*
> *(feels-weak x)))*
>
> Infer: *(has-AIDS Jack)*

Assuming that Jack feels weak, then the two premises are true, yet the conclusion we have drawn may be false or exaggerated. Although abduction can lead to wrong conclusions, it is useful and often necessary.

**ABEL,** *n.* a program for Acid-Base and Electrolyte disturbances; an expert system that uses KNOWLEDGE about the diseases and symptoms acid-base and electrolyte disorders produce in patients. Using a causal model of a patient's possible diseases, ABEL helps the clinician arrive at a diagnosis. The program organizes queries to the clinician using data about the patient and knowledge about the relations between various disease states. ABEL also tests for erroneous data by comparing the clinician's responses to the queries against responses it expects based on the causal model. The program accounts for cause-effect relations between diseases and the clinician's findings by representing its knowledge within a CAUSAL NETWORK. The causal network is a type of SEMANTIC NETWORK that specifies cause-effect relations. ABEL was developed at MIT.

**abstract individual,** *n.* the CONCEPT representing a class of items.

**abstract operator,** *n.* or a HIERARCHY of SUBGOALS. Such an operator specifies abstract actions that the planner would like to execute but that it cannot execute until it is expanded to subgoals attainable by problem-solving operators. NOAH, for example, plans by developing a hierarchy of subgoals (that is, abstract operators). There is a notable distinction between the simple problem-solving operators specified in the problem space and abstract operators that will eventually be expanded to PROBLEM-SOLVING operators. The latter are GOALS expanded to subgoals attainable by the former.

**abstraction space,** *n.* an approach to PROBLEM REPRESENTATION that abstracts less detailed levels of a problem obtained from a fully detailed version of the problem. The detailed version appears in the GROUND SPACE, and subsequent abstract versions occupy higher-level PROBLEM SPACES. The represented levels of detail result in a HIERARCHY of problem spaces. In effect, each space in the hierarchy functions as both an abstraction space for the more detailed space below and as a ground space with respect to the less-detailed space above. ABSTRIPS, for example, plans in a hierarchy of abstraction spaces. An ABSTRIPS abstraction space contains all of the objects and operators given in the initial specification of the problem (the ground space), but some preconditions of some OPERATORS are judged to be more important than others. For example, 'Have boiling water' is a rather unimportant precondition to making tea because it is so easy to accomplish. The advantage of considering the critical SUBGOALS before detailed ones is that it reduces search: by ignoring details, one effectively reduces the number of subgoals to be accomplished in some given abstraction space.

**ABSTRIPS,** *n.* a modification of STRIPS. Using HIERARCHICAL PLANNING, ABSTRIPS is an extension of the relatively straightforward patching process of a STRIPS-type PROBLEM-SOLVER. Hierarchical planning is achieved by constructing a plan in levels, using some single-level methods. During each level, certain conditions are regarded as details and are thereby postponed until a subsequent level. A condition considered a detail at a certain level is then effectively invisible at that level. When details become visible at a lower level, the higher-level plans are patched in in order to achieve them.

**access–oriented methods,** *n.* programming methods that use probes to execute new computations when data are changed or read.

**ACE,** *n.* an expert system developed at Bell Labs (AT&T) for internal use. ACE troubleshoots cable systems and recommends maintenance. OPS4 is the development software.

**ACE,** *n. acronym for* Automated Cable Expertise, an expert system that operates independently to troubleshoot telephone cable networks and recommend appropriate repair and maintenance strategies. Without human input, ACE analyses maintenance reports on a daily basis generated from the cable repair administration program CRAS. When ACE discovers defective telephone cables, it decides if the cables need maintenance and selects the potentially most effective maintenance procedure. ACE also stores its recommendations in a data base users can access. To make decisions, ACE uses a rule-based KNOWLEDGE REPRESENTATION scheme controlled by FORWARD CHAINING in order to apply knowledge about CRAS maintenance reports, wire centres, and network analysis strategies. ACE is implemented in OPS4 and FRANZ LISP and runs on AT&T 3B-2 microcomputers located in the cable analysts' offices. Bell Laboratories developed ACE at Whippany, New Jersey.

**ACES,** *n. acronym for* AI Cartographic Expert System, an expert system that acts as a cartographer to label maps. To label a map, the program aesthetically positions labels next to symbols without overlap. It decides where to position symbols and how best to describe them. In addition, ACES selects appropriate type fonts and label sizes for a given design. As input, the program takes an unlabelled map, as well as the data describing the points where objects are located, and the text string and symbol type associated with each point. ACES applies an object–oriented KNOWLEDGE REPRESENTATION scheme implemented in LOOPS and runs on the Xerox Dolphin workstation. ESL developed the program that reached the stage of a research prototype.

**ACLS,** *abbrev. for* Analog Concept Learning System, a tool knowledge engineers can use to induce rules for an expert system. It acts as a system-building aid by inducing rules from examples of decisions provided by a DOMAIN EXPERT. The set of attributes of a problem relevant to a decision, and the possible decision classes, constitutes an example of a domain expert decision–maker. From a further specification of the examples into situation-decision pairs, ACLS constructs general rules that classify the examples in terms of their attributes. In addition, ACLS allows users to supply examples and counterexamples interactively so users can correct or refine rules continuously. ACLS can print out the resulting rules as either a decision tree or a PASCAL program. Rule induction derives from Ross Quinlan's ID3 inductive learning algorithm. ACLS is implemented in UCSD-PASCAL and runs on the APPLE II+ and the IBM PC. It was developed at the University of Edinburgh.

**ACRONYM,** *n.* a system wherein the user specifies parametric models of objects in the world in order to help in IMAGE UNDERSTANDING. See MODEL IN VISION SYSTEMS.

**ACT,** *n.* a system built by John Anderson following his work on HAM. ACT is intended as a general model of cognition whereas HAM is a model of human memory. ACT and HAM overlap in many ways but also fundamentally differ. ACT does more because it can be programmed to perform a wide variety of cognitive tasks. In addition to long-term memory, ACT has a short-term working memory of active concepts and a programmable PRODUCTION SYSTEM that gives rise to changes in working and long-term memories. Certain features of long-term memory are common to ACT and HAM. Strategy invariance has been incorporated into ACT, along with PROPOSITIONAL KNOWLEDGE REPRESENTATION, although modified in some details. ACT contains a long-term memory component and a user-programmable procedural component. The memory, which is similar to HAM's, is an associative network. A noteworthy feature of ACT's memory is that only parts of it are active at a given time. Activation can spread through the network as nodes activate adjacent nodes. The required time in activating the neighbours of an active node depends on its fan-out, that is, the number of nodes connected to it.

**action clause of production rule,** *n.* the second half of a PRODUCTION RULE. The premise, or first half, of each rule is a Boolean combination of one or more clauses, each of which is constructed from a predicate function with an associative triple of attribute, object, and value as its argument. The premise is always a conjunction of clauses that may contain arbitrarily complex conjunctions or disjunctions nested within each clause. (This distinguishes them from writing rules whose premise is a disjunction of clauses, where a separate rule is written for each clause.) The action part indicates one or more conclusions that can be drawn, or actions to be taken, if the premises are satisfied. This makes the rules purely inferential.

**actional predicate,** *n.* a PREDICATE in the MEMOD model of long-term memory. In this model semantic decomposition of words is accomplished through the use of primitives called predicates. One of these is actional. Semantic decomposition is a representational tool that guarantees that similar meanings have similar structures. Some structures are common to several verbs with overlapping meanings: push, shove, carry, pull, transport, and so on. The actional predicate achieved through decomposition is instrumental in making finer distinctions in meaning. Little work has been done however, and with actionals, generally, the primitive predicate DO is used.

**activation,** *n.* the output of a CELL in a NEURAL NETWORK.

## ACTIVE INSTANCE SELECTION

**active instance selection,** *n.* the process of choosing active instances. In learning from examples a program must reason from specific instances to general rules. The space of possible training instances is called the INSTANCE SPACE. Programs that explicitly search the instance space are then said to perform active instance selection.

**active structural network,** *n.* a part of a semantic network-based computer program called MEMOD. The active structural network, or ASN, is the node space containing a semantic net representation of world knowledge. It represents both DECLARATIVE and PROCEDURAL KNOWLEDGE and is therefore called an active structural network.

**active value,** *n.* a procedure invoked when programs are changed or read. This procedure often drives graphical displays of gauges that show the values of the program variables. These values can be changed in the course of a consultation, permitting users to change the values in a system by simply altering an image on the computer screen.

**actor,** *n.* within the actor model of computation, objects that both know about other actors and can receive messages from other actors. The actor model of computation was developed by Hewitt (1977) for the purpose of exploring the fundamental issues involved with computation via message-passing. Each actor is specified by detailing what kind of messages it will receive and its sequence of actions, should it be sent one of these messages. Everything in an actor-based programming system is an actor. For instance, to increment a value, a message would be sent to the actor representing the number, asking the actor to increment itself. The central difference between the actor model of computation and the SMALLTALK-80 language lies in the sequencing of computations by actors. The computations depend critically on the concept of continuation. A continuation is an actor that is prepared to accept an intermediate value as a message and continue the computation. In SmallTalk-80, an object (or actor) will instead return a message to the object that instigated the computation, in much the same way that a Pascal function will return a value to the routine that called it.

**actor formalism,** *n.* a type of communication protocol available to the designer of a community of systems. Designed to communicate among a community of systems in order to solve problems cooperatively, each of the systems involved could be a production or a system of some different style, with internal processes that are either serial or parallel. If each of the component systems is relatively simple, the communication protocols and the procedures for control and cooperation must be specified in precise detail by the designer of the community. On the other hand, if each of the systems is itself a complex AI system, then the situation is analogous to a society of humans who must plan their communication and cooperation strategies.

**ACUMEN,** *n.* an expert system developed by the Human Factors Advanced Technology Group for commercial use. The program evaluates psychological characteristics in terms of management theory.

**ad hoc parser,** *n.* any of the early special purpose natural language parsers. None of these systems dealt with the syntax of language in any sophisticated way. In these programs, the semantic knowledge needed to respond to the user was implicit in the patterns and the ad hoc rules used for PARSING. More recent natural language programs maintain large data bases of explicit WORLD KNOWLEDGE that they use to assist in parsing the sentence as well as in interpreting it.

**adaptive learning,** *n.* a form of learning developed where environments are extremely noisy (see NOISE) or rapidly changing. Learning systems developed for these environments have centred on the problems of control and pattern recognition. Basically, the approach is to construct a model by observing the system in operation and finding an empirical relationship between the inputs and the outputs. Four methods of adaptive learning are in use: STATISTICAL ALGORITHMS, PARAMETER LEARNING, AUTOMATA (as MODELS of learning), and STRUCTURAL LEARNING.

**adaptive production system,** *n.* a system that can automatically change the productions in its RULE BASE. For example, a program for playing poker might start with a set of fairly simple HEURISTICS for playing poker, such as when to raise, when to bluff, etc., and extend and improve these rules as it gains experience in actually playing the game. The constrained, modular fashion in which knowledge in PRODUCTION

# ADAPTIVE SYSTEM

SYSTEMS is represented helps to aid the learning component of the system, because the program analyses and manipulates its own representation.

**adaptive system,** *n.* a system where learning methods developed by researchers in electrical engineering and systems theory represent acquired knowledge in the form of polynomials and matrices. The learning systems, usually called adaptive systems, typically perform tasks such as pattern classification, adaptive control, and adaptive filtering. Adaptive systems are useful in noisy environments, in environments whose properties change rapidly, and in situations where analytic solutions based on classical systems theory are unavailable.

**add formula,** *n.* the third component of a STRIPS-form F-rule. The add formula consists of a conjunction of literals, which possibly contain free variables, and is like the CONSEQUENT of an implicational F-rule. When an F-rule is applied to a state description, the MATCH substitution is applied to the add formula and the resulting match instance is added to the old state description (after the literals in the delete list are deleted) as the final step in constructing the new state description. All of the free variables in the add formula occur in the PRECONDITION formula so that any match instance of an add formula will be a conjunction of ground literals. It is possible to lift some of these restrictions on F-rule components. They are used to make the presentation simpler.

**add list,** *n.* a list of formulas that will become true. The list should be added to the WORLD MODEL when the OPERATOR is applied.

**adder,** *n.* a condition in a system for dealing with interactive goals, $A_{ij}$, computed for the condition $C_{ij}$, is the set of F-rules specified by the graph that add condition $C_{ij}$, and are not ancestors of rule j in the graph nor j itself.

**ADEPT,** *n.* an expert system using military knowledge and expertise to assess battlefield situations. It provides tactical interpretations of intelligence sensor reports. Rules concerning how and why enemy forces operate, and the tactical significance of situation interpretations, account for the program's knowledge. The program uses intelligence sensor reports to construct a display of combat locations on a battlefield and to explain the reasoning behind its battlefield assessments. ADEPT is implemented in ROSIE and uses a Chromatics CGC 7900 colour graphics system to display maps and military symbology. TRW developed the system.

**admissibility condition,** *n.* a condition that states: For the properties of the A* ALGORITHM to hold, h* should be non-negative and never overestimate the cost of reaching a GOAL node from the NODE being evaluated. That is, for any such node n, it should always hold that h*(n) is less than or equal to h(n), the actual cost of an optimal path from n to a goal node.

**admissible,** *adj.* that quality of an algorithm if it can find a MINIMAL-COST solution tree if any such solution exists. In particular it is the property of a condition that states: If h* in the A* ALGORITHM satisfies the ADMISSIBILITY CONDITION, and in addition, all arc costs are positive and can be bounded from below by a positive number, then A* is guaranteed to find a SOLUTION path of minimal cost if any solution path exists.

**advice appended to rules,** *n.* a technique for specifying useful control information. In order to minimize combinatorial difficulties, rule applications must be guided by an intelligent control strategy. Advice appended to rules proceeds by adding advice to delineations about rule applications. Two forms exist for such advice: the 'to-fill' form and the 'when-filled' form. The to-fill form gives advice about the manner in which rules should be used in the backward direction when attempting to match existential variables in GOALS. The when-filled form gives advice about which rules should be used in the forward direction to create new fact units.

**advice taker,** *n.* a program that can learn from a helpful teacher.

**ADVISE,** *n.* an integrated set of development tools to aid KNOWLEDGE ENGINEERS. The development tools include the following utilities: support for such multiple forms of KNOWLEDGE REPRESENTATION as RULES, semantic networks, and relational data bases; support for several CERTAINTY propagation schemes, including probabilistic, approximate Bayesian, min/max logic, and weighting evidence; support for such various control strategies as utility optimization, probabilistic network traversal, and forward and backward rule-chaining. ADVISE also supplies the inductive learning programs GEM and CLUSTER for deriving decision rules and control information from examples. GEM creates formal logic rules for recognizing general properties present among examples of different concepts. CLUSTER uses a conceptual clustering approach to construct a classification of given entities. An explanation mode enables ADVISE to paraphrase decision rules and display its reasoning steps, and to allow the user to query the knowledge base. Implemented in PASCAL, ADVISE operates on DEC VAX computers under the UNIX operating system. ADVISE was developed as a research system at the University of Illinois.

**ADVISOR,** *n*. an expert system that advises novice users of MACSYMA about their failure to understand a particular problem they are working on. The program diagnoses a user's misconceptions in a given instance and provides advice to correct the user's reasoning. ADVISOR takes a sequence of user-entered MACSYMA commands as input along with a statement of the overall goal not achieved by the command sequence. It then returns advice based on its ability to infer the user's plan for achieving the goal. When ADVISOR recognizes the problem, it verifies its conclusions with the user before delivering advice. ADVISOR applies a model of novice user behaviour of MACSYMA to help recognize a user's planning strategies, goals, and the source of any misconceptions. The program relies on data-flow graphs and goal trees to represent user plans and goals. ADVISOR is written in MACLISP and was developed at MIT.

**AGE,** *n. acronym for* Attempt to GEneralize, a system-building aid for knowledge engineers experienced as INTERLISP programmers. It helps users select a framework, construct a rule language, and form a complete expert system. A set of INTERLISP functions serves as tools called building blocks, which apply to various expert system ARCHITECTURES. The building blocks include INFERENCE ENGINES for FORWARD CHAINING and BACK-CHAINING and structures for representing a BLACKBOARD ARCHITECTURE. Implemented in INTERLISP, AGE was developed at Stanford University as a research system.

**agenda,** *n*. an ordered list of actions that can be stored and reasoned about by some KNOWLEDGE SYSTEMS. Often ordered to reflect priority, such a list structure can enable a knowledge system to decide whether or not to pursue a particular line of reasoning. It is a mechanism that must decide, based on some CONTROL STRATEGY, what to do next every time the processor (or one of the processors, if there are several) is free. HEARSAY uses agenda–based control.

**agent,** *n.* a deep case in CASE GRAMMAR that indicates the instigator of the event.

**AI languages,** *n.* programming languages predominantly used in implementations of AI systems. These include LISP, PROLOG, and derivatives from these, such as SCHEME, PLANNER, and CONNIVER.

**AI/COAG,** *n.* an expert system that analyses and interprets clinical blood coagulation tests to help physicians diagnose diseases of homeostasis. The program administers six types of screening test, including tests for platelet count and urea clot solubility. To confirm a diagnosis suggested by the screening tests, the program also evaluates a clinical homeostasis history of the patient. Implemented on a DEC LSI-11 microcomputer, AI/COAG was developed at the University of Missouri School of Medicine.

**AIMIDS,** *n.* a knowledge engineering language for frame-based REPRESENTATION, which also permits procedure–oriented representation (see PROCEDURE-ORIENTED METHODS). It features deductive and nondeductive reasoning, multiple INHERITANCE, maintenance of BELIEF contexts, automatic deduction of KNOWLEDGE BASE inconsistencies, reasoning about hypothetical worlds, PROCEDURAL ATTACHMENT, and use of expectations to guide actions and perform analogical inference. AIMIDS is implemented in FUZZY. FUZZY, implemented in UCI-LISP, supplies all the features and tools of both the LISP and FUZZY ENVIRONMENTS. AIMIDS was developed at Rutgers University.

**AI/MM,** *abbrev. for* Artificial Intelligence/Mathematical Modelling system, an expert system that applies knowledge of the laws of physics and anatomy, fundamental principles of physiology, and empirical knowledge of physiological processes to analyse behaviour in the renal physiology domain. It also explains the rationale for its analyses. Users can pose questions about the values of various parameters such as the volume of body water. The program also interprets user observations such as abnormally high water intake. Rules comprising a complex causal model provide the program's KNOWLEDGE REPRESENTATION scheme. To enable AI/MM to explain the rationale for its analysis in a given case, each rule includes a description of its underlying principle. AI/MM is implemented in MRS and was developed at Stanford University.

**AIRCRAFT FINISH ADVISOR,** *n.* an expert system developed at McDonnell Aircraft for internal use. The program helps select aircraft finishing specifications. Insight 2 is the development software.

**AI/RHEUM,** *n.* an expert system that applies formal diagnostic criteria acquired from rheumatology experts. It helps physicians diagnose connective tissue diseases of clinical rheumatology. Patient symptoms and laboratory findings provide the basis for AI/RHEUM to consider seven diseases, including rheumatoid arthritis, progressive, systemic sclerosis, and Sjoegren's disease. The program uses a rule–based KNOWLEDGE REPRESENTATION scheme controlled by FORWARD CHAINING. Implemented in EXPERT, AI/RHEUM was developed at the University of Missouri School of Medicine.

**AIRID,** *n. acronym for* AIRcraft IDentifier, an expert system that determines the identity of target aircraft based on the user's visual observations. The user enters observations such as wing shape, engine configuration (number and mounting position), fuselage shape, and tail shape. In addition, AIRID can consider features of the conditions under which an observation occurs, such as bad weather conditions. AIRID derives its knowledge of an aircraft's physical characteristics from Jane's *All the World's Aircraft 1982-83*. Combining a rule–based and SEMANTIC NETWORK representation technique, AIRID assumes it has successfully identified a target when the certainty level in its network reaches 98% confidence. Implemented in KAS, AIRID was developed at Los Alamos National Laboratories.

**AIRLINE SEAT ADVISOR,** *n.* an expert system developed at Sperry (Intellicorp) for commercial use. The program allots discount fares to flights. KEE is the development software.

**AIRPLAN,** *n.* an expert system that assists air operations officers with the launch and recovery of aircraft on a carrier. The program analyses current information, such as the aircraft's fuel level and the weather conditions at a possible divert site, and then alerts the air operations officer of possible impending problems. AIRPLAN assesses the seriousness of a situation and manages its use of time by attending first to the most significant aspects of a problem. If time permits, the program extends the analysis based on its initial conclusions. The program is rule-based. It interfaces with the ship's officers through ZOG, a rapid-response, large network, menu-selection system for human–machine communication. Implemented in OPS5, AIRPLAN was developed at Carnegie-Mellon University.

**AISPEAK,** *n.* an expert system developed for Digital Equipment Corporation for tape-drive diagnostics.

**ALCHEM,** *n.* a language enabling chemists to enter new TRANSFORMS into the KNOWLEDGE BASE of the SECS program. Each of the SECS transforms is stored external to the SECS program, permitting the knowledge base to be tailored to a specific problem domain. In addition, the external storage reduces limitations otherwise placed on the number and complexity of the transforms. ALCHEM constitutes a model of what information is needed in order to describe a reaction adequately.

**algorithm,** *n.* a formal procedure that always produces a correct or optimal result. An algorithm applies a step-by-step procedure that guarantees a specific outcome or solves a specific problem. The procedure of an algorithm performs a computation in a finite amount of time. Programmers specify the algorithm the program will follow when they develop a conventional program.

**ALICE,** *n. acronym for* A Language for Intelligent Combinatorial Exploration, a KNOWLEDGE ENGINEERING language for logic-based representation (see LOGIC-BASED METHODS). It features an extensive vocabulary for describing COMBINATORIAL PROBLEMS in operations research. It also supplies a routine for setting and achieving GOALS. The program determines a workable solution and revises the solution, providing proof of its selection of the most favourable solutions to choose from. ALICE was developed at the Institut de Programmation, Paris.

**allophone,** *n.* a unit of speech that designates a sound as it occurs in a word.

**alpha/beta pruning,** *n.* a refinement of MINIMAX PROCEDURE for the purpose of determining the optimal move in a game whereby NODES that are not needed to evaluate the possible moves of the top nodes are 'pruned.' For example, say MAX is to move at parent node P, and it is known from previous calculations that the daughter D1 guarantees a minimum gain of +20 for MAX. Then we start exploring D2 and discover that the opponent can force a maximal gain of +10 by reacting D2 with D2.1. In this case there is no need to explore other daughters of D2, because MAX can never gain more than +10 and therefore will always prefer D1. Following this line of reasoning, both from the point of view of MAX and of MIN, large parts of the TREE need not be explored and an OPTIMAL SOLUTION will still be found.

**alphabetic variant,** *n.* a variant of a formula where the original LITERALS are substituted by different variables for the variables appearing in the formula. This is often of importance in RESOLUTION THEOREM PROVING.

**alternative dialogue,** *n.* one of a set of possible scenarios in GUIDON, which requires the student to determine what he could have inferred from previous interactions and the current situation. When the student using GUIDON asserts that he has determined some subgoal, the TUTOR needs to determine what response makes sense, basing its response on what it knows about the student's knowledge and shared GOALS for the tutorial session (topics or rules to discuss). In this case, the tutor may want to suspend a detailed response and simply acknowledge the student's remark, or probe the student to uncover evidence that the student actually knows the fact in question.

**AL/X,** *abbrev. for* Advice Language X, a KNOWLEDGE ENGINEERING language for rule-based representation, which also supports FRAME-BASED METHODS of representation. This language closely resembles the KAS system. The KAS system is PROSPECTOR with its knowledge of geology eliminated. AL/X features include a combination BACK-CHAINING and FORWARD CHAINING control scheme, a SEMANTIC NETWORK that links rule components, certainty-handling mechanisms, and automatic user querying. A support environment provides facilities to explain the system's reasoning. Implemented in PASCAL, AL/X operates on a PDP-11/34 and runs under UNIX. It was developed by Intelligent Terminals Ltd.

**AM,** *n.* a system that uses a collection of primitive concepts in mathematics and discovers concepts, such as prime numbers. .

**ambiguity,** *n.* that quality of a word or sentence that allows it to have more than one interpretation. 'Bill caught cold and Tom caught a ball.' is an example of word-sense ambiguity because the word 'caught' in English has more than one meaning.

**AMORD,** *n. acronym for* A Miracle Of Rare Device, a name taken from S.T. Coleridge's poem 'Kubla Khan'; a KNOWLEDGE ENGINEERING language for rule-based representation. It features DISCRIMINATION NETWORKS for assertions and rules, a FORWARD CHAINING control scheme, and a TRUTH MAINTENANCE SYSTEM (TMS) for maintaining justifications and program BELIEFS. A TMS NODE accompanies every AMORD fact or rule. To preserve the logical grounds for belief in assertions, the TMS applies a nonmonotonic DEPENDENCY system. The program also explains and proves how it can justify its belief in specific facts. Implemented in MACLISP, AMORD was developed at MIT.

**AMUID,** *n. acronym for* Automated Multisensor Unit IDentification system, an expert system that uses information from intelligence reports, infrared and visual imaging sensors, and MTI (moving target indicator) radar to help military commanders analyse land battlefield situations. The program first classifies targets and then organizes them into units such as battalions and regiments. In real time, it continuously updates an analysis of a situation according to the most recent entered data. Encoded rules structured into a SEMANTIC NETWORK account for AMUID's knowledge and expertise. The rules operate on DOMAIN KNOWLEDGE such as types of military equipment, deployment patterns for military units, and tactics. In addition, AMUID applies CERTAINTY FACTORS to compensate for uncertainty typical to the analysis of sensor data. The CONTROL structure is EVENT-DRIVEN. Events include new sensor reports, major decisions made by the system itself, and user queries. Advanced Information & Decision Systems developed AMUID.

**analogical knowledge representation,** see DIRECT KNOWLEDGE REPRESENTATION.

**analogical problem solving,** *n.* a technique for solving a current problem by retrieving from memory a similar problem that has previously been solved, and then appropriately adapting that problem's solution to the current problem. For example, when asking a question like 'Can eagles fly?' the system might reason that since eagles are like sparrows, and it knows that sparrows can fly, so eagles probably can fly also.

**ANALYST,** *n.* an expert system with military applications that obtains information from multiple sensor sources to generate displays of enemy combat unit deployment. ANALYST can locate and classify enemy battlefield units by echelon, general function, and relative location as well as detect any force movement. The program combines frames and rules to represent its knowledge. Implemented in FRANZ LISP, ANALYST was developed at the Mitre Corporation.

**anaphoric reference,** *n.* reference, usually pronominal, to a previous word or phrase.

**AND/OR graph,** a special graph used with problem-solving methods involving problem reduction. In addition to conventional trees and graphs used for STATE-SPACE REPRESENTATIONS, AND/OR graphs apply to problems for which the GOAL can be reduced to sets of subgoals. The and/or graphs reflect which subgoals have been attempted and which combinations of subgoals are sufficient to achieve the goal. Tree notation must be generalized if it is to represent the full variety of situations that may occur in problem reduction. In one common formulation an AND/OR graph is constructed according to the following rules:

(a) Each NODE represents either a single problem or a set of problems to be solved. The graph contains a start node corresponding to the original problem.

(b) A node representing a PRIMITIVE PROBLEM, called a terminal node, has no descendants.

(c) For each possible application of an operator to some problem P, transforming it to a set of subproblems, there is a directed arc from P to a node representing the resulting subproblem set. For example, figure (a) below illustrates the reduction of P to three different sub-problem sets: A, B, and C. Since P can be solved if any one of sets A, B, or C, can be solved, A, B, and C are called OR nodes.

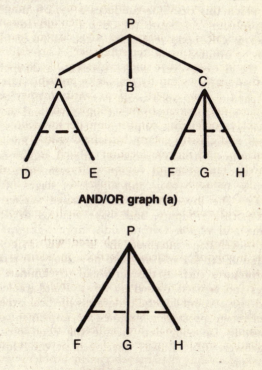

**AND/OR graph (a)**

**AND/OR graph (b)**

(d) Figure (a) above further illustrates the composition of sets A, B, and C. Here, A={D,E}, B consists of a single (unnamed) problem, and C={F,G,H}. In general, for each node representing a set of two or more sub-problems, there are directed arcs from the node for the set to individual nodes for each subproblem. Since a set of subproblems can be solved, the subproblem nodes are called AND nodes. To distinguish them from OR nodes,

17

the arcs leading to AND-node successors of a common parent are joined by a horizontal line.

(e) A simplification of the graph produced by rules (c) and (d) may be made in the special case in which only one application of an operator is possible for problem P and in which this operator produces a set of more than one subproblem. As figure (b) on p.17 illustrates, the intermediate OR node representing the subproblem set may then be omitted.

In both the figures, every node represents a distinct problem or set of problems. Since each node except the start node has just one parent, the graphs are in fact AND/OR trees.

**ANGY,** *n.* an expert system that identifies and isolates coronary vessels in angiograms to help physicians diagnose narrowing coronary vessels. In order to extract initial line and region features, ANGY processes digital angiograms first. ANGY's knowledge-based expert subsystem uses the angiograms to relate both low- and high-level stages of its vision processing. The low-level processing stage applies rules for SEGMENTATION, grouping, and shape analysis to develop the initial line and region features into more significant images. The high-level stage interprets the low-level images applying knowledge of cardiac anatomy and physiology to recognize relevant structures such as the aorta and to eliminate irrelevant structures and artifacts caused by noise. Rules implemented in OPS5 and LISP account for the program's medical expertise. The low-level image processing routines are implemented in the C programming language and include the edge protector and image grower. ANGY was developed at the University of Pennsylvania.

**ANNA,** *n.* an expert system that uses patient symptoms and history to help physicians administer the drug digitalis. For patients with heart problems such as arrhythmia and congestive heart failure, ANNA determines the appropriate dosage regimen, including the amount to administer and the rate at which a patient should take the medication. After ANNA prescribes the initial dosage, the program monitors the patient's response to the drug and adjusts the dosage appropriately when the patient's response diverges from the response ANNA expects. Implemented in LISP, ANNA was developed at MIT.

**answer statement,** *n.* the clause at the root in resolution refutation.

**antecedent,** *n.* the left-hand side of an implication.

**antecedent theorem,** *n.* a theorem in MICRO-PLANNER that is called when its pattern matches an assertion added to the data base. The other type of procedure is called the consequent theorem.

**APES,** *n. acronym for* A Prolog Expert system Shell, a KNOWLEDGE ENGINEERING language for logic-based representation that supplies a user interface for writing expert systems in the Micro-PROLOG logic programming language. Users express rules and facts in the knowledge base as PROLOG clauses and can implement MYCIN-style, Bayesian-style, and user-defined certainty-handling modules. APES features include handling uncertain information, extensions to PROLOG that provide interactive procedures for user interfaces, and an explanation facility. Implemented in Micro-PROLOG, APES operates on microcomputers and was developed as a commercial system at Imperial College, London.

**APLICOT,** *n.* a KNOWLEDGE ENGINEERING language for logic-based representation. It features CERTAINTY FACTOR handling, a control scheme for FORWARD CHAINING and BACK-CHAINING, an explanation facility, and supplies PROLOG utility packages such as an interactive clause and rule editor. Implemented in DEC-10 PROLOG, APLICOT operates on an ICOT DEC-2060 computer and was developed at the University of Tokyo.

**application language,** *n.* a subset of English in LIFER, which is appropriate for interacting with an application system. An INFERENCE builder uses the language specification functions in order to define an application language. The LIFER system then uses the language specification to interpret natural language inputs as commands for the application system.

**applicative language,** *n.* a programming language that uses nested function calls to perform computations instead of using sequences of statements. LISP is a well-known applicative language. Applicative languages typically do not have a program counter and may not allow side effects.

**Apprentice in MACSYMA,** *n.* a part of the MACSYMA system. MACSYMA is used mostly as a 'symbolic calculator,' with the user directing its actions line by line and keeping track of the meaning of each result. The apprentice relieves the user of much of this bookkeeping. The approach involves two components, namely, knowledge about the user's DOMAIN and the use of a high-level, problem-solving PLAN formalism.

**Aq algorithm,** *n.* an algorithm for use with an extended propositional calculus representation. The algorithm selects as a 'seed' positive TRAINING INSTANCE one that has not been covered by any description in any previous G SET. This has the effect of choosing training instances that are 'far apart' in the INSTANCE SPACE.

**AQ11,** *n.* a learning program that seeks to find the most general RULE in the RULE SPACE that discriminates training instances in class $c_i$ from all TRAINING INSTANCES in all other classes $c_j$ ($i \neq j$). The performance that applies these rules is a PATTERN classifier that takes an unknown pattern and classifies it into one of n classes. Many performance tasks have this form, such as optical character recognition and disease diagnosis. The classification rules are learned from training instances consisting of sample patterns and their correct classification. The classification rules should test as few features of the input pattern as is necessary to classify it reliably, in order for the classifier to work as efficiently as possible. This is particularly true for areas like medicine, where the measurement of each additional feature of the input pattern may be very costly and dangerous.

**ARAMIS,** *n. acronym for* American Rheumatism Association Medical Information System, an expert system that helps physicians assess new patients with rheumatic diseases by analysing their symptoms. The program collects data about previous patients with rheumatic diseases and performs statistical analyses on the data. It then produces a prognostic analysis of various endpoints such as death and pleurisy, recommends therapy, and generates a prose case analysis. A collection of statistical analysis methods and a number of data bases containing detailed patient records constitute ARAMIS's knowledge base. Patient data are stored in a tabular data base using TOD (Time Oriented Databank system), a system that can follow relevant clinical parameters over time. Implemented in PL/X, a specialized form of PL/1, ARAMIS was developed at Stanford University.

**ARBY,** *n.* a KNOWLEDGE ENGINEERING language for RULE-BASED REPRESENTATION. It features PREDICATE CALCULUS for expressing rules, a BACK-CHAINING facility (HYPO) for generating hypotheses, and a human interface subsystem (IFM) to manage a set of interaction frames (IFs). IFs apply when the HYPO component requires information not contained in the data base yet obtainable through asking the user. ARBY also provides for IF and rule editing, and has an ability to explain why it is asking a certain question and why it currently believes a certain fact. ARBY is implemented in FRANZ LISP and uses the DUCK general-purpose retrieval system. It was developed at Yale University.

**arc,** *n.* a line connecting two points in a GRAPH. This is used, for example, in SEMANTIC NETWORKS to connect CONCEPTS but is also used in other graph–like structures.

**architecture,** *n.* **1.** the framework that organizes knowledge applications and problem–solving processes.
**2.** The KNOWLEDGE ENGINEERING principles that control selecting an appropriate structure with which to organize a specific expert system.

**areal feature,** *n.* an IMAGE FEATURE appropriate to a region.

**ARPA,** *n. acronym for* the Advanced Research Projects Agency of the U.S. Department of Defense.

**array,** *n.* an arrangement of OBJECTS in one or more dimensions. A one–dimensional array is a vector. An example of a two–dimensional array is a table.

**ARS,** *abbrev. for* Antecedent Reasoning System, a KNOWLEDGE ENGINEERING language for RULE-BASED REPRESENTATION. It features FORWARD CHAINING with DEPENDENCY-DIRECTED BACKTRACKING, an ability to represent problem–solving rules as DEMONS with pattern–directed calls, and an associative data base for issuing assertions. To explain its reasoning, and to process contradictions that occur during backtracking, the program keeps records of all deductions it makes. Implemented in MACLISP, ARS runs under the MULTICS TOPS-10 and ITS computer operating systems. ARS was developed at MIT.

**ART,** *n. acronym for* Advanced Reasoning Tool, a KNOWLEDGE ENGINEERING language for RULE-BASED REPRESENTATION, which also permits FRAME-BASED METHODS and PROCEDURE-ORIENTED methods of representation. It features FORWARD CHAINING and

BACK-CHAINING control-schemes, certainty handling routines, and hypothetical worlds. ART provides DEBUGGING aids, including trace facilities and BREAK PACKAGES that incorporate graphics. Implemented in LISP, ART operates on CADR machines and the Symbolics 3600. It was developed by Inference Corporation.

**articulate expert,** *n.* the expert component of an ICAI system that can explain each problem-solving decision in terms that correspond (at some level of abstraction) to those of a human problem-solver.

**artificial intelligence** or **AI,** *n.* the field of computer science that seeks to understand and implement computer-based technology that can simulate characteristics of human intelligence. A common goal of artificial intelligence work involves developing computer programs capable of learning from experience in order to solve problems. Other noteworthy pursuits of the field include programs that understand NATURAL LANGUAGE and programs that interpret visual scenes. Methods of symbolically representing KNOWLEDGE, in a way that the computer can use the symbols to make INFERENCES, is a central task of any artificial intelligence project. Specific examples of programs that simulate a form of human intelligence include programs that can diagnose diseases, plan the synthesis of complex chemical compounds, solve differential equations in symbolic form, analyse electronic circuits, understand limited amounts of human speech or natural language text, or write small computer programs to meet formal specifications. Work on building AI systems proceeds from a growing body of computation techniques that have become widely applied AI principles. A larger scientific goal to establish an information-processing theory of intelligence underlies much AI research. The benefits of such a science of intelligence include guidelines for designing intelligent machines and models of human or other animal's intelligent behaviour. A general theory of intelligence remains a goal of AI and the field therefore often interests other researchers such as cognitive psychologists who are attempting to understand natural intelligence. Currently, much AI research is focused on the engineering goal of building intelligent machines.

**ASH MIXER,** *n.* an expert system developed at Dupont for internal use. It controls mixing of radioactive ash with concrete for disposal. EXSYS is the development software.

**askable versus unaskable questions,** *n*. a classification of questions in PROSPECTOR, in which, if the current GOAL is askable and has not been asked before, the user is asked about it. The effects of the answer are then propagated through the INFERENCE NETWORK, and the process is repeated. If it is unaskable, it must be either the consequence of one or more INFERENCE RULES or a logical combination of one or more other spaces. In the former case, the rules are scored to determine their potential effectiveness in influencing H, and the ANTECEDENT of the best-scoring RULE becomes the next goal. In the latter case, a predetermined supporting space becomes the next goal. In either case, the same procedure is repeated until: (a) the top-level goal becomes so unlikely that another top-level goal is selected, (b) all of the askable spaces have been asked, or (c) the user interrupts with new volunteered information.

**assertion,** *n*. an English statement that translates into one piece of internal representation. These pieces of internal representation are called FORMULAS. When they are stored in some data base, they are called assertions.

**associated pair,** *n*. a pair of PATTERNS found in the process of ROTE LEARNING. It is achieved by taking problems that the PERFORMANCE ELEMENT has solved and memorizing the problem and its solution. Viewed abstractly, the performance element can be thought of as some function, f, that takes an input pattern $(X_1, \ldots, X_n)$ and computes an output value $(Y_1, \ldots, Y_p)$. A rote memory for f simply stores the associated pair $[(X_1, \ldots X_n),(Y_1, \ldots, Y_p)]$ in memory.

**association,** *n*. a characteristic of pairs of symbols. Many AI programming languages were created for problem-solving. Their design was guided by ideas from psychology, especially the intuitive notion of association. The primary elements of the languages are SYMBOLS, as opposed to numbers. To form associations of these symbols, list processing is used, allowing programs to conveniently build data structures of unpredictable shape and size. The idea of associations of symbols, a central motivation of IPL, was implemented in LISP in a simple and elegant mechanism called property lists (see ATOM).

Property lists are thus a very general way of associating symbols.

**ASTA,** *n. acronym for* Assistant for Science and Technology Analysis, an expert system that uses general knowledge of the physics of radar and specific knowledge about types of radar systems to help analysts identify the type of radar that generated an intercepted signal. It can provide explanations for the conclusions it reaches as well as access to relevant data bases. ASTA's knowledge is represented in the form of rules. It was developed by Advanced Information & Decision Systems.

**ATN,** see AUGMENTED TRANSITION NETWORK.

**atom,** *n.* a SYMBOL in LISP that can have several properties associated with it. LISP programmers can define the properties associated with each atom. For instance, with each atom that represents a person in an IMPLEMENTATION, the programmer can associate a property of the atom called HEIGHT, with the symbols for TALL and SHORT as values. Further, there may be other properties of each person called BROTHER and SISTER whose values are the symbols for other people. These property lists are therefore a very general way of associating symbols.

**atomic formula,** *n.* a formula composed of PREDICATE SYMBOLS and terms. The elementary components of the PREDICATE CALCULUS language include such predicate symbols, variable symbols, function symbols, and constant symbols. A predicate symbol is used to represent a relation in a DOMAIN of discourse. For instance, if we want to represent the fact that someone wrote something, we can use the predicate symbol WRITE to denote a relationship between a person doing the writing and a thing written. To do so, we can compose a simple atomic formula using WRITE and two terms, denoting the writer and what is written.

**ATR,** *abbrev. for* Automatic Target Recognizer, an expert system that uses information from sensor images to detect and classify military targets. To detect and identify the objects, it unites low-level image processing with high-level, DOMAIN-specific RULES. To form hypotheses about the existence of certain OBJECTS of an image, ATR accounts for contextual data such as the structure of the object and time. Applying FRAMES and CERTAINTY FACTORS together with an object-oriented CONTROL scheme to represent and access its knowledge, the program searches for evidence to satisfy its hypotheses. ATR's model-driven processing serves to redirect the low-level image-processing ALGORITHMS to gain new information from the image and generate further hypotheses. ATR is implemented in ZETALISP, and was developed by the Hughes Aircraft Company.

**ATRANS,** *n.* a primitive act in CONCEPTUAL DEPENDENCY that signifies the transfer of an abstract relationship. To 'give' is to ATRANS the relationship of possession or ownership.

**ATTENDING,** *n.* an expert system that acts as an instructional aid for medical students of anaesthesiology. The program presents the student with a hypothetical patient about to undergo surgery and then requires the student to plan the anaesthetic management. ATTENDING then analyses and critiques the plan the student devised. In order to analyse the student's work, the program draws on knowledge of the risks involved with the plan in the context of the patient's medical problems. The critique the program produces appears as a prose commentary averaging four to five paragraphs of text. It was developed at Yale University School of Medicine.

**attribute,** *n.* a property of an OBJECT. For example, Grade Point Average is an attribute of a student. In addition, the value of an attribute reflects a specific case, for example, where Tim Smith's Grade Point Average is 4.0.

**AUDITOR,** *n.* an expert system that uses information about a client's financial background to help an auditor evaluate the client's likelihood of defaulting on a loan. The client's payment history, economic status, credit standing, and any other important information help AUDITOR to decide if money should be held in reserve to cover the client's possible loan default. The program applies a RULE-based KNOWLEDGE REPRESENTATION scheme implemented in AL/X, a derivative of KAS. The version of AL/X is adapted for use in PASCAL systems in microcomputers. It was developed at the University of Illinois, Champaign-Urbana.

**augmented transition network** or **ATN,** *n.* a representation scheme for grammars that is developed from simple finite-state transition networks by allowing RECURSION and augmentation – augmentation being the use of arbitrary tests and actions on arcs – thus giving full TURING MACHINE power. ATNs were first developed as a versatile representation of grammars for NATURAL LANGUAGES. ATN involves the use of registers for strong constituents, and the use of tests and actions on register contents giving way to powerful flexibility in PARSING, and in particular, permitting the construction of sentence representations that are quite distinct from the surface text (e.g., DEEP STRUCTURES as opposed to surface syntactic structures). The form of grammar representation is procedure-oriented, but the grammar itself is separated from the interpretive parser, which is a TOP-DOWN PARSER and usually depth-first. A popular FORMALISM, ATNs can be adapted for purposes such as guiding parsing by explicit ordering.

**automata (as models of learning),** *n.* systems that can be used for MACHINE LEARNING. The goal is to find a finite-state automaton whose behaviour imitates that of the unknown system. Two approaches have been pursued. One models the unknown system as a deterministic finite-state machine with randomly perturbed inputs. The learning program is given an initial state transition probability matrix, M, which tells overall for each state, $q_i$, what the probability is that the next state will be $q_i$. From M, an equivalent deterministic machine can be derived, and the probability distribution of the input symbols can be determined. This approach requires that the internal states of the unknown system can be precisely observed and measured. A second approach models the unknown system as a stochastic machine with a random transition matrix for each possible input symbol. REINFORCEMENT techniques are applied to adjust the transition probabilities. Both methods have the advantage over parameter-learning methods in that they do not require that there be a performance criterion with a unique minimum point. In addition, automata provide a more expressive representation for describing the unknown system. The principal disadvantage of automata learning methods is that they are relatively slow compared to parameter learning techniques.

**automatic backtracking,** *n.* a system that takes a GOAL to be achieved along with a collection of THEOREMS, and then attempts to find a theorem with which to achieve the goal. If the first theorem that matches the goal must itself be proved (e.g., proving that cows are mammals, so that one can conclude that Bessie is mortal), the system attempts to prove this goal in the same way, that is, by matching it against the knowledge base of theorems. This process continues, recursively, until either it succeeds in finding a fact that proves some goal or the line of attack fails. In this case, the system automatically backtracks to the most recent point of deciding between several alternative theorems for proving a goal and then tries another theorem.

**automatic coding,** see AUTOMATIC PROGRAMMING.

**automatic deduction,** *n.* a method for drawing conclusions automatically from bodies of facts. This problem requires choosing an application, a representation for bodies of facts, and methods for deriving conclusions. The issues involve drawing conclusions by means of DEDUCTIVE INFERENCE from bodies of commonsense knowledge represented by logical formulas. Deductive methods are necessary to solve problems that involve certain types of incomplete information. Also, supplying domain-specific control information offers a solution to the difficulties that previously led to disillusionment with automatic deduction. A relationship exists between automatic deduction and the field of LOGIC PROGRAMMING. Some of the issues that arise in automatic deduction techniques have led to nonstandard logics.

**automatic derivation of natural-language front-ends,** *n.* the process by which front ends can be produced procedurally. This method explores the usefulness of capturing specific NATURAL LANGUAGE (NL) features in the front end rather than providing a general NL interface. For instance, the TED system functions in a similar manner to LADDER, but TED's NL front end is derived semi-automatically. Instead of requiring extensive programming to build the NL interface, TED uses the data base schema and a dialogue it conducts with the user; the result of this process is a grammar similar to the one used by LADDER.

**automatic programming,** *n.* a process that can automate many aspects of computer programming. Current development projects aim at producing 'high-level' computer programs capable of writing other computer programs. Conventional COMPILERS accomplish a form of automatic programming. They accept as input a complete source code specifying the performance of the program and then write an OBJECT code that runs it. Automatic programming extends beyond mere compilers by processing high-level descriptions of a program's function into a complete program. High-level descriptions may take the form of precise statements in a formal language such as the PREDICATE CALCULUS, or an English statement that requires a dialogue between the system and the user to clarify any ambiguities of the statement. The common task of program verification, that of proving a given program's success, reflects the task of automatically writing a program to achieve a stated result. A feature of automatic programming systems should be their ability to verify the accuracy of the output program they produce. Methods used by existing systems include theorem proving, program formation, KNOWLEDGE ENGINEERING, automatic data selection, traditional problem-solving, and INDUCTION.

**automatic theory formation,** *n.* a technique for handcrafting KNOWLEDGE BASES that developed out of a need to decrease the time-consuming consultation process involved in deriving the DOMAIN-specific RULES that constitute DENDRAL. Meta-DENDRAL is a program that applies such automatic theory formation. The rule-formation task that Meta-DENDRAL performs is similar to grammatical inference, sequence extrapolation, and concept formation; it is classified in AI as learning. Because these programs formulate general rules (or concepts, or patterns) from examples, they can be viewed as 'induction' programs.

**AUTONOMOUS VEHICLE CONTROL (Robot),** *n.* an expert system developed at Oakridge National Labs for commercial use. The program provides autonomous vehicle control. The development software is PICON.

**average branching factor,** *n.* the average of the number of words that might come next after each word in a sentence.

**axiom,** *n.* the initial facts that drive the deductions in the PREDICATE CALCULUS. Axioms are the things that we assume and are distinguished from THEOREMS, which are the things we deduce using the axioms. (See THEOREM PROVING.)

**axiomatization,** *n.* the formal expression of a problem in the form of sentences of FIRST-ORDER LOGIC.

28

**axiomatization of operations,** *n.* the process of stating all the possible primitive operations that can be applied to the data structures of an inductive INFERENCE system so it can construct, by composition of these primitives, the desired program.

# B

**B\* algorithm,** *n.* a method of HEURISTIC SEARCH that can be applied, in games, for example, to both adversary and non-adversary problems. It can only apply when the search has an iterative character. The search works to compute the best next step toward the solution on the basis of an EVALUATION FUNCTION. An evaluation function assigns two values to each NODE, a pessimistic value and an optimistic value, on the basis of evaluation of the descendants. In non-adversary search, this is done according to the following rules:

    (a) Evaluate the descendants of a node in arbitrary order. If one of the descendants of a node has a pessimistic value greater than the pessimistic value of its parent, then raise the pessimistic value of the parent to the value of this daughter.

    (b) Terminate when a daughter of the root of the search tree has a pessimistic value that is not lower than the optimistic value of all other daughters. The ARC to that daughter is the best step to do.

In the case of adversary search (game playing), B\* is the same as Alpha/Beta search except that it stops once it has found the best next move. Heuristic or BEST-FIRST SEARCH may be implemented in this manner.

**BABEL,** *n.* the text-generation subsystem of MARGIE.

**BABY,** *n.* an expert system that uses knowledge of neonatology to monitor patients in a newborn intensive care unit (NICU). In an attempt to find clinically important medical and demographic data about NICU patients, BABY monitors all on-line data in the NICU, keeps track of the clinical states of the patients, suggests further evaluation for important findings, and answers clinicians' questions about the patients. The program applies a FORWARD CHAINING, rule-based control scheme that uses rules embedded in a PROSPECTOR-like network, and handles certainty using a Bayesian probabilistic method similar to that used in PROSPECTOR. Implemented in PASCAL, BABY operates within the ADVISE system, which is an integrated, RULE-based software environment. It was developed at the University of Illinois, Champaign-Urbana.

**back–chaining,** *n.* a CONTROL procedure applied to achieve GOALS recursively. Antecedent steps adequate to achieve the goal are first cited in a list. Then each of the steps toward the major goal becomes a goal in itself to be achieved; the procedure establishes a backward–chain of antecedent goals inferred from the originally cited goal. In a rule-based implementation, for example, a goal rule initiates a back-chaining procedure. To determine if the goal rule is correct, the system checks the if-clauses of the rule. The system can equally consider other rules that confirm the original if-clauses. A typical case exists in which the system starts with a conjecture (Z) that it wants to prove. To prove (Z), it needs to establish the facts that do so. Facts are typically expressed in rule form such as IF A & B, THEN Z. However, if A and B are unknown, not available as data, the system tries to prove (Z) by applying other rules to establish any additional facts necessary to prove A and B. Since the additional facts are established the same way as A and B, the process can continue until it establishes all the necessary facts to prove (Z); or else the system quits without success. Back-chaining thus admits other rules that confirm the if-clauses of the original facts. In effect, the system backs into its rules.

**backed–up value,** *n.* VALUE assigned to the ancestor of a TIP NODE in partial GAME TREES. We assume that were MAX to choose among tip nodes, it would choose that node having the largest EVALUATION. Therefore, the (MAX node) parent of MIN tip nodes is assigned a backed–up value equal to the maximum of the evaluations of the tip nodes. On the other hand, if MIN were to choose among tip nodes, it would presumably choose that node having the smallest evaluation, which would be the most negative.

**backward production system,** *n.* a CONTROL procedure in which the problem GOAL description becomes the global data base.

**backward reasoning,** *n.* an alternative strategy involving a type of OPERATOR, which is applied to the GOAL instead of to the current task-domain situation. First, the goal statement, or problem statement, is converted to one or more subgoals that are hopefully easier to solve and whose solutions are sufficient to solve the original problem. These subgoals may in turn be reduced to subgoals, and so on, until each of them is accepted to be a trivial problem or its subproblems have been solved.

**BACON,** *n.* a set of concept-learning programs that solves a variety of single-concept learning tasks, including 'rediscovering' such classical scientific laws as Ohm's law, Newton's law of universal gravitation, and Kepler's laws.

**bag,** *n.* an unordered group of elements. A bag can be taken as a single argument of a FUNCTION.

**BAIL,** *n.* the interactive DEBUGGING facility in SAIL.

**bandwidth condition,** see BANDWIDTH SEARCH.

**bandwidth search,** *n.* a search strategy in an ordered STATE-SPACE SEARCH, where it is assumed that no good h★ function satisfying the ADMISSIBILITY CONDITION is available. In its place is introduced the bandwidth condition, which requires that for all nongoal nodes n,

(a) $h \star (n) i \leqslant h(n) + e$

and

(b) $h(n) - d \leqslant h \star (n)$.

It is assumed that h★ satisfies the CONSISTENCY ASSUMPTION.

**bare template,** *n.* a built-in set of element triples in ACTOR-action–OBJECT format used in some machine translation systems. Examples of such triples are MAN–CAUSE–MAN. The system first fragments the input text into substrings of words. It then replaces each word in the text fragments with the internal formulas representing the word's meanings and matches the resulting string of formulas against a set of standard forms, which are bare templates. The output of this stage is a first approximation to a SEMANTIC REPRESENTATION of each of these fragments.

**base, grammar,** see GRAMMAR BASE.

**base set,** *n.* a set of clauses used in a RESOLUTION production system.

**BASEBALL,** *n.* an information retrieval program developed in the early 1960s at Lincoln Laboratories. It is an information retrieval program, since its data base of facts about all of the American League games during one year is not modified by the program. BASEBALL was written using the IPL-V programming language.

**BATTLE,** *n.* an expert system that furnishes well-timed recommendations to military commanders in combat situations on how to best allocate a set of weapons to a set of targets. The program improves the performance of the US Marine Corps' Marine Integrated Fire and Air Support System. During consultations, BATTLE applies a best-first strategy in order to compensate for the critical timing of real battle situations. It considers first those propositions (battle conditions) likely to have the most cost effective influence on higher-level propositions. BATTLE represents its knowledge as RULES with associated PROSPECTOR-like certainty values. It was developed at the Naval Research Laboratory.

**Bayesian inference** or **statistical inference,** *n.* one means by which KNOWLEDGE-BASED systems can reason when UNCERTAINTY is involved. PROSPECTOR is a system that provides an example of the use of Bayesian inference. Given a hypothesis event H and an evidence event E, we obtain from an expert estimates of the prior probabilities P(H) and P(E), and the conditional probability P(E|H). From Bayes's Rule we obtain the probability of H given evidence E. This is calculated as:

$$P(H|E) = P(E)|P(E|H).P(H)$$

In practical problems E may be any subset of all possible evidence events and H may be any subset of the set of all possible hypotheses. This tends to require a vast number of conditional probabilities to be calculated. An alternative approach is therefore to combine with a RULE-BASED SYSTEM where conditional probabilities are given only for each rule. This approach is adequate until one considers the local updating problem that arises when two or more INFERENCE RULES make a conclusion about the same hypothesis. This problem has only been solved by various ad hoc means.

**Bayes's theorem,** *n.* a theorem of probability that says if you know, for example, how many patients with a given disease show a particular symptom, as well as the likelihood of the disease and the symptom, then you can calculate the conditional probability of the disease given the symptom. Bayes's theorem is written:

$$P(d|s) = \frac{P(d)P(s|d)}{P(s)}$$

Most doctors know, if only informally, how many of the patients with a given disease show a particular symptom. A doctor will know that, say, 'virtually all' of the cardiac arrest patients show chest pain, while 'the majority' have redness of the skin, but 'hardly any' have puffy eyelids. In a crude way, doctors know the following:

P(puffy eyelids|cardiac arrest)≈1%
P(redness of skin|cardiac arrest)≈60%
P(chest pain|cardiac arrest)≈90%

Although Bayes's theorem may look mysterious, it is very easy to prove. Substitute in the definitions for each probability, and we get the following:

$$\frac{|d \cap s|}{|s|} = \frac{|d|}{|\text{people}|} \times \frac{\dfrac{|s \cap d|}{|d|}}{\dfrac{|s|}{|\text{people}|}}$$

Multiplying out the right-hand side, while recognizing that $|d \cap s| = |s \cap d|$, results in the left-hand side. Bayes's theorem points out that the numbers on the right-hand side are easily available, at least by comparison to the quantity on the left-hand side. Moreover, for the simple case of the conditional probabilities for a single disease given a single symptom, relatively few numbers are needed. So, if we have m diseases and n symptoms, then we will need about n x m numbers.

(mm conditional probabilities)+
(m disease probabilities)+
(n symptom probabilities)=mm+m+n≈mn

This last approximation is reasonable, since in a realistic diagnosis system one could have several hundred diseases and several thousand symptoms, so for

$m = 500$

$n = 3000$

$mn + m + n = 1\ 503\ 500$

$mn = 1\ 500\ 000$

1 500 000 is not insignificant, but many of these diseases and symptoms will be unrelated to each other. In such cases, it should not be necessary to store any numbers.

**BDS,** *abbrev. for* Baseband Distribution Subsystem, an expert system that identifies defective modules in a baseband distribution subsystem (a large signal-switching network). It employs the strategies of the expert diagnostician and uses knowledge about the structure and function of the device, and causal relations of the components in the network circuitry. The program analyses results of equipment tests to isolate the flawed printed boards or other chassis-mounted parts that could have caused a failure. BDS applies a rule-based KNOWLEDGE REPRESENTATION scheme with BACK-CHAINING. Implemented in the LES (Lockheed Expert System) language, BDS was developed at the Lockheed Palo Alto Research Laboratory.

**BEACON,** *n.* an expert system developed by Burroughs Company for configuring Burroughs Computer hardware. Quintus PROLOG is the development software.

**beam search,** *n.* a SEARCH scheme used in SPEECH UNDERSTANDING systems such as HARPY, DRAGON, and INDUCE. The beam search process involves the following steps:

Step (a) Initialize. Set *H* to contain a randomly chosen subset of size W of the TRAINING INSTANCES (W is a constant called the beam width).

Step (b) Generate. Generalize each concept in *H* by dropping single conditions. This produces all the concept descriptions that are minimally more general than those in *H* and forms the new *H*.

Step (c) Prune implausible hypotheses. Remove all but W of the concept descriptions from *H*. This pruning is based on syntactic characteristics of the concept description, such as the number of terms and the user-defined COST of the terms. Another criterion is to maximize the number of training instances covered by each element of *H*.

## BEHAVIOURAL SPECIFICATION OF PROGRAMS

Step (d) Test. From the information obtained in step (c), check
each concept description in *H* to see if it covers all of
the training instances. If any concept does, remove it
from *H* and place it in a set *C* of output concepts.

Repeat steps (b), (c), and (d) until *C* reaches a prespecified size
limit or *H* becomes empty. The illustration below depicts the
beam search process.

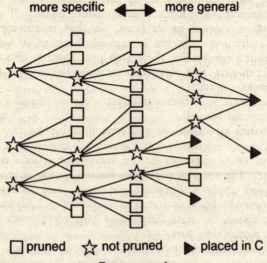

more specific ◄──────► more general

☐ pruned ☆ not pruned ▶ placed in C

**Beam search**

**behavioural specification of programs,** *n*. an approach in
AUTOMATIC PROGRAMMING that takes as input a description of
the desired behaviour of a program and produces as output a
program. An example of such a system is SAFE.

**belief,** *n*. a hypothesis about an unobservable subject. A belief
is also the measure of the believer's confidence in an uncertain
proposition. The degree of confidence may be indexed by a
certainty or CONFIDENCE FACTOR.

**belief revision,** see TRUTH MAINTENANCE.

**belief system,** *n*. what distinguishes an objective fact from its
interpretation by an individual. Unlike 'facts,' beliefs are non-
consensual, have associated effects, and have associated confidences or credibilites. Humans do not reason entirely from

facts with consistent inference rules, but also from prejudices, biases, episodic memory, confidences, and emotional states integrated into 'rational' reasoning. Much of the research in this area has been conducted within the CONCEPTUAL DEPENDENCY paradigm.

**best–first search,** *n.* a SEARCH method whereby the move considered next (or the position to which it leads) is on some estimate the most promising in the entire SEARCH TREE generated so far, subject to whatever depth limit exists. If DYNAMIC ORDERING is carried to its limit, so that reordering is considered every time a NODE is expanded instead of only under more limited conditions, the search procedure in effect changes from depth-first (see DEPTH-FIRST SEARCH) to best-first. See also ORDERED SEARCH.

**beta structure,** *n.* structured OBJECT representations proposed by Moore and Newell.

**bidirectional production system,** *n.* a system that searches forward and backward simultaneously. Both STATE descriptions and GOAL descriptions are incorporated into the global data base. The CONTROL system has to decide at every stage whether to apply a Forward-rule or a Backward-rule. The termination condition is stated as some type of matching condition between the state description part of the data base and the goal description part.

**bidirectional search,** *n.* a STATE-SPACE SEARCH that proceeds both backwards and forwards. The program terminates when a common state is reached because a path has been found from the initial state to the goal state.

**binary image,** *n.* an image with just two 'grey levels,' 0 and 1.

**BIP,** *n. acronym for* Basic Instructional Program, an ICAI program used to help teach the programming language BASIC.

**blackboard,** *n.* a DATA BASE that is globally accessible to problem-solving applications. Originally used in HEARSAY-II and other independent KNOWLEDGE SOURCES, blackboard records intermediate, partial results during problem-solving. A blackboard is normally partitioned to represent hypotheses at different levels of abstraction. It serves to structure communication among multiple independent knowledge sources according to an established protocol. An architectural

# BLACKBOARD APPROACH

(see ARCHITECTURE) technique developed principally for continuous reasoning 'real time' systems, the concept of blackboard is based on the idea of 'experts' sitting around a blackboard. Blackboard attempts to coordinate the activities of a number of different knowledge sources by providing a global data base among them, to which partial solutions to the problem in question are posted.

**blackboard approach,** *n.* a strategy for solving problems in which the various system elements communicate with each other. A BLACKBOARD supplying a common working data storage provides the medium the system elements use to communicate.

**blackboard architecture,** *n.* an expert system design where several independent knowledge bases examine a central data base called a BLACKBOARD. The blackboard acts as working memory for an AGENDA-based control system to choose an action from among all possible actions. Blackboard architecture enables communication between independent KNOWLEDGE SOURCES.

**blind search,** *n.* an algorithm that treats the SEARCH SPACE syntactically, as contrasted with heuristic methods, which use information about the nature and structure of the problem DOMAIN in order to limit the search. The search for a solution in STATE-SPACE SEARCH is done by making explicit just enough of the state-space graph to contain a solution path. If the order in which potential solution paths are considered is arbitrary, using no domain-specific information to judge where the solution is likely to lie, the search is called blind search.

**blocks world,** *n.* an application DOMAIN of systems such as SHRDLU. Their function was to allow the system to answer questions about both the state of a set of blocks in their tabletop domain and certain of the system's internal states.

**BLUE BOX,** *n.* an expert system that uses knowledge about patients complaining of depression in order to advise the physician on an appropriate therapy selection. The program diagnoses the type and extent of depression and suggests a management plan to control the depression, which can include decisions about hospitalization and drug treatments. It takes into account the patient's symptoms along with details about the patient's medical, psychiatric, drug, and family histories.

BLUE BOX is a RULE-BASED SYSTEM. Implemented in EMYCIN, it was developed at Stanford University and was tested at the Palo Alto VA Mental Health Clinical Research Center.

**bottom-up,** see FORWARD REASONING.

**bottom-up parser,** *n*. a parser that looks first for rules in the grammar for combining the words of the input sentence into constituents of larger structures (phrases and clauses) and then continues to try to recombine these in order to show how all the input words of syntactic constituents form a legal sentence in the grammar.

**boundary detection,** *n*. In early visual processing, a process for identifying an object's outlines that refines on and follows EDGE DETECTION, the conventional approach to image segmentation. Edge detection serves to produce PRIMITIVE edge elements, possibly with properties of magnitude and/or direction, at places in the image where the edge operator has 'fired.' The boundary detection process then works to produce a set of boundaries by appropriately linking up the primitive edge elements according to one of two main methods: boundary tracking or the generalized HOUGH TRANSFORM. A boundary is by definition a connected set of edge elements. Boundary detection therefore takes an obvious approach by first choosing any edge element and then looking for its neighbours, which are then connected to the initial element in order to form a boundary. This search process involved in boundary detection is then continually repeated for the elements at the ends of the boundary until some termination criterion is met, such as not being able to find any neighbours. In the Hough transform technique, each primitive edge element is transformed into a curve in a transform space representing all the possible boundaries the edge element could be a part of. The transform space curves produced by edge elements on the same image boundary should all intersect at the same point in transform space, which can be subjected to the inverse transform in order to characterize the boundary in the image. Although originally applicable only to straight boundaries, the boundary detection method described here has been generalized to deal with any curve describable in an analytic or tabular form. (See also LINE FINDING.)

**boundary line,** *n.* a line on the borders of an object, including all CONTOUR LINES. Boundary lines are the contour lines plus the lines on the boundaries between objects.

**box notations,** see CELL.

**Boyer–Moore theorem prover,** *n.* an automatic theorem-proving program, whose underlying formalism is recursive function theory. Designed to prove theorems via continuous application of REWRITE RULES and structural INDUCTION, the central feature of the program is the heuristics it uses in order to guide the search. Included are powerful heuristics for the automatic use of induction. Users must provide some guidance by specifying which lemmas must be known before the goal theorem is attempted. The system must prove the lemmas before they are automatically used in order to assure the validity of the proof of the final theorem. However, because some heuristics generalize the theorem, the system is not complete. The system's standard set consists of 400 theorems, including the soundness and completeness of a tautology checker for propositional calculus, the equivalence of interpreted and optimized compiled code for a simple arithmetic language, the correctness of a fast string-searching algorithm, the prime-factorization theorem, and the unsolvability of the halting problem.

**branch–and–bound algorithm,** *n.* a type of ALGORITHM similar to A* ALGORITHM used in operations research. It is a solution technique that is widely used outside AI for solving discrete optimization problems. The task is to find the optimally valued tip of a walkable SEARCH TREE. A subtree of the search tree does not need to be searched if a computation at its root yields a bound for its set of tip values implying that none of them can be optimal.

**branching factor of a tree,** *n.* a measure of the number of branches at a NODE in a GAME TREE. It is a controlling fact about search depth in terms of COMBINATORIAL EXPLOSION. For example, if the average number of legal moves from a position, the branching factor, is b, the game tree will have about $b^d$ nodes at depth d. (See also DEGREE OF A TREE.)

**breadth–first parsing,** *n.* a form of parsing where essentially breadth-first searching of the tree of alternatives is accomplished first.

**breadth-first search,** *n.* a SEARCH strategy applicable to a hierarchy of rules or objects. All rules or objects on the same level of the hierarchy are evaluated before any of the rules or objects on the next lower level can be evaluated. An uninformed graph-searching strategy in which each level is searched before going to the next deeper level. The strategy guarantees finding the shortest path to the NODE sought first such that any path to the solution that is of length n will be found when the search reaches depth n, and this is guaranteed to be before any node of depth $>$ n is searched.

**break package,** *n.* a procedure contained in a programming or KNOWLEDGE ENGINEERING language that tells the program where to stop so the programmer can inspect the values of variables at that point.

**British Museum algorithm,** *n.* the simple approach of scanning the entire data base and testing each item against the pattern. This approach is insufficient for large data bases.

**Brush Designer,** *n.* an expert system developed by the General Motors/Delco Products Division to assist the design of brushes for DC motors. The development software is S.1.

**bug,** *n.* an approach to modelling a student's knowledge not as a subset of the expert's knowledge, but rather as a perturbation of or a deviation from the expert's knowledge. (For examples, see the SOPHIE and BUGGY systems.) In contrast to the overlay approach to modelling a student, the bug approach does not simply assume that the student reasons as the expert does, except for knowing less; in the bug approach, student reasoning can be substantially different from expert reasoning.

**BUGGY,** *n.* a program that can accurately determine a student's misconceptions (BUGS) about basic arithmetic skills. The system provides a mechanism that extends beyond simply identifying a student's mistake to explaining why a student is making a mistake in the arithmetic. For successful tutoring, a detailed model of a student's knowledge indicating the student's misconceptions is necessary. BUGGY was developed at Bolt Baranek and Newman, Inc.

**Business Classifier,** *n.* an expert system developed by L. Johnson Creighton Companies Inc. for classifying incoming business at Norkinons Corp. Center. The development software is EXSYS.

# C

**C,** *n.* a programming language originally designed for use with the UNIX operating system and to run on a wide variety of computers. As a general-purpose programming language, C provides an ENVIRONMENT for relatively low-level system programming and is often used for writing operating systems. The language permits users to directly manipulate characters, numbers, and addresses instead of the character-strings, sets, lists, or arrays of higher-level programming languages like PASCAL. C features straightforward tests, loops, and subprograms but does not feature exceptional CONTROL mechanisms such as parallel operations or co-routines. The language was developed by Bell Laboratories.

**C-13,** *abbrev. for* Carbon-13, an expert system which helps chemists determine the structure of newly isolated, naturally occurring compounds. Based on its knowledge of rules relating substructural (bonding) and spectral (resonance) features, derived from data for known structures, C-13 helps chemists analyse carbon-13 nuclear magnetic resonance spectra. The program uses a CONSTRAINT refinement search to determine the arrangement of atoms and bonds in complex organic molecules. C-13 was developed as part of the DENDRAL project and follows DENDRAL's PLAN-GENERATE-TEST PARADIGM. Implemented in INTERLISP, C-13 was developed at Stanford University.

**caching,** see ROTE LEARNING.

**CAD,** *n. acronym for* computer-aided design, the application of computer technology to assist in the graphics design process.

**CADHELP,** *n. acronym for* Computer-Aided Design HELP, an expert system that demonstrates how to best operate graphical features of a computer-aided design (CAD) subsystem for designing digital logic circuits. The program generates explanations in English when the user asks for help or makes an error. The text of the explanations conforms to the level of experience the user has with the CAD subsystem. Novices receive more detailed feedback from CADHELP than the more concise feedback that experts normally desire. As the user becomes more adept with the CAD subsystem, CADHELP's explanations become more concise. The program relies on scripts associated with the different features of the CAD subsystem. Controlled by a higher-level task manager program, CADHELP's knowledge is organized as a set of expert subsystems. Implemented in FRANZ LISP, CADHELP runs on a DEC VAX 11/780 under UNIX. The program was developed at the University of Connecticut.

**CAI/CBI,** *abbrev. for* Computer-Assisted Instruction/ Computer-Based Instruction, the application of computer technology to presenting educational instruction programs. A CAI program directs the student's learning process via the program's instructional format, monitoring both the student's responses to the instruction and the student's progress. Conventional forms of CAI involve statements the computer issues to the student followed by questions to test the student's learning and a presentation of answers to summarize the CAI program's teaching goals. Additional CAI formats include simulations of topics, and games that teach the students to infer patterns. Presentations may branch according to student responses in order to correct a student's thinking or to provide a review of previously covered material. CAI programs are generally not intelligent. They do not develop a model of how a student conceptualizes the subject matter and cannot tailor presentation to a particular student.

**calling sequence,** *n.* a set of instructions to programmers used to begin, initialize, or transfer control to a subroutine and then to return from the subroutine.

**CAM,** *n. acronym for* Computer-Aided Manufacturing, the application of computer technology to assist in the manufacturing process.

**camera calibration,** see CAMERA MODEL.

**camera model** or **camera calibration,** *n* a step in the interpretation process of aerial photographs in stereo vision. In order for the translation of the lens position to occur, the process consists of the transformation of the camera centre from the origin and its rotation about the camera centre.

**Can Am Treaty,** *n.* an expert system that interprets legal and financial differences between US and Canadian practice. GURU is the development software.

**candidate solution graph,** *n.* in a backward deduction system, any SOLUTION GRAPH that is checked for consistency in the search for a consistent solution graph. A sophisticated CONTROL STRATEGY would make it possible to evaluate partial candidate solution graphs as they are developing and thus reduce the amount of search effort.

**candidate–elimination algorithm,** *n.* a learning ALGORITHM that takes advantage of the boundary-set representation for the set H of plausible HYPOTHESES. The H set of all plausible hypotheses is called the VERSION SPACE. Mitchell defines a plausible hypothesis as any hypothesis that has not yet been ruled out by the data. The version space H is thus the set of all concept descriptions that are consistent with all of the TRAINING INSTANCES seen so far. The version space initially constitutes the complete RULE SPACE of possible concepts. As training instances are presented to the program, candidate concepts are eliminated from the version space. When the version space contains only one candidate concept, the desired concept has been found. Since the candidate–elimination algorithm does not modify the set H until the algorithm is forced to do so by the training information, the candidate–elimination algorithm is a least-commitment algorithm.

**Capital Asset Process Advisor,** *n.* an expert system developed at IBM for internal use. It helps develop procedures for moving capital equipment. ES Environment/VM is the development software.

**CAPS,** *n.* a chess-playing program. Its basic search ALGORITHM is DEPTH-FIRST SEARCH, with mini-maxing and ALPHA/BETA PRUNING.

**car,** *n.* a LISP function that returns as its value the first element of a list.

**CARGuide,** *n. acronym for* Computer for Automobile Route Guidance, an expert system that uses starting and destination locations to calculate the most efficient driving routes in city streets. Using map information, CARGuide helps drivers find and navigate the routes. A streetmap data base contains the information relating street names to intersections and intersections to routes; it also contains graphic information to display the information in pictures. The program calculates an optimum route combining a DIVIDE-AND-CONQUER method, precomputed routes, and Dijkstra's shortest-path algorithm. CARGuide displays and highlights the preferred route graphically as a streetmap. The program also updates and displays the car's position along the route during the trip. At each intersection, the program instructs the user to take a direction (straight, left, or right) and cites the correct street name. It was developed at Carnegie–Mellon University.

**Cascaded Augmented Transition Network (CATN),** *n*. an extension of AUGMENTED TRANSITION NETWORK (ATN) parsing. It permits the use of a sequence of ordinary ATNs that include among the actions on their ARCS a special operation for the purpose of transmitting an element to the next ATN 'machine' in the sequence, with the first machine in the cascade taking its input from the output string.

**case,** *n*. a semantic aspect of a CONCEPT that specifies its role with respect to an action. Typical cases include AGENT, OBJECT, and INSTRUMENT.

**case ambiguity,** *n*. the ambiguity in CASE assignment that arises from SURFACE STRUCTURE interpretations of such things as prepositional phrases and pronominal reference.

**case analysis,** *n*. the reformulating of a single CONCEPT as several disjoint expressions each of which can be evaluated separately.

**case frames,** *n*. a widely used device for determining and representing text meaning based upon CASE roles (e.g., AGENT, INSTRUMENT, LOCATION), which express the organization of information that verbs or actions contain. Case representations extend the basic notions of SEMANTIC NETS with the idea of a case frame, the cluster of the properties of an object or event into a single concept. In contrast to the typical large-scale structures adapted for WORLD KNOWLEDGE represented by FRAMES, case frames are ordinarily small-scale structures adapted for linguistic units like sentences. The cases for any particular verb form an ordered set, a case frame. For example, the verb *open* has the case frame indicating that the object is obligatory in the DEEP STRUCTURE of the sentence, whereas it is permissible to omit the instrument (John opened the door) or the agent (the key opened the door) or both (the

45

door opened). Noteworthy variations in the treatment of every aspect of case frames exists even though Fillmore's linguistically motivated ideas are the conventional ones. For example, when considering the case frame's relation to surface text features (see SURFACE STRUCTURE) (e.g., Is the sentence subject the Agent?), or when considering the constraints on the case frame's fillers (Is the Agent HUMAN?). CONCEPTUAL DEPENDENCY, for example, uses a small number of deep cases referring primarily to underlying rather than surface relations.

**case grammar,** *n.* a model of grammar developed by Fillmore as a revision to the framework of TRANSFORMATIONAL GRAMMAR. The principal notion implied in the grammar is that the proposition embodied in a simple sentence has a DEEP STRUCTURE consisting of a verb, which is the central component, and one or more noun phrases. Each noun phrase is associated with the verb in a particular relationship. Fillmore characterized these relationships as 'semantically relevant syntactic relationships,' and he called these relationships 'CASES'. For example, in the sentence: *John opened the door with the key*, John would be the AGENT of the verb opened, the door would be the OBJECT, and the key would be the INSTRUMENT. For the sentence: *The door was opened by John with the key*, the case assignments would be the same, even though the SURFACE STRUCTURE has changed.

**case-method tutor,** *n.* a type of ICAI system that attempts to replicate the teaching style of Socratic dialogue. This style is especially effective for tutoring complex subjects in which factors interact and this very interaction accounts for the phenomenon being studied.

**CASNET,** *n. acronym for* Causal ASsociational NETwork, a computer system developed at Rutgers University for performing medical diagnosis. The primary application of CASNET has been in the domain of glaucoma. A disease is represented not as a static state but as a dynamic process that can be modelled as a network of causally linked pathophysiological states. By determining the pattern of pathophysiological causal pathways present in the patient, the system diagnoses a patient by identifying this pattern with a disease category. The most appropriate treatments can be prescribed once the disease category is explicitly identified. The causal model also makes possible a prediction of the likely course of disease both if treated and if untreated.

**CASNET/GLAUCOMA,** *n. acronym for* Causal-ASsociation NETwork/GLAUCOMA, an expert system that uses clinical data to base its diagnoses of disease states related to glaucoma, and to prescribe treatment plans and therapies for such diseases. Relationships among patient symptoms, test results, internal abnormal conditions, disease states, and treatment plans account for the knowledge the program uses to make decisions. The program generates a narrative interpretation of a case. In addition, the program can support its conclusions by retrieving related references from literature on the topic. A SEMANTIC NETWORK known as a causal-association network supplies the program's KNOWLEDGE REPRESENTATION scheme. Implemented in FORTRAN, CASNET/GLAUCOMA was developed at Rutgers University.

**categorical reasoning,** *n.* in PIP, the system uses two types of reasoning, categorical and probabilistic (see PROBABILISTIC REASONING). Using the former the relevance of a hypothesis is achieved using the logical decision criteria (the IS-SUFFICIENT, MUST-HAVE, and MUST-NOT-HAVE rules) that a physician applies.

**CATS (DELTA),** *n.* an expert system developed by General Electric for commercial use. It troubleshoots problems with diesel-electric locomotives. The program was developed in LISP and implemented in Forth.

**causal chains,** *n.* a representation of knowledge about the world connected by the concept of causality. For example, in CONCEPTUAL DEPENDENCY theory five important rules hold:

  (a) Actions can result in state changes.
  (b) States can enable actions.
  (c) States can disable actions.
  (d) States (or acts) can initiate mental events.
  (e) Mental events can be reasons for actions.

Conceptual dependency includes a shorthand representation of each rule, along with combinations of some, to produce causal links.

**causality,** *n.* one of the principal methods of explanation in AI. It is particularly popular in systems based on CONCEPTUAL DEPENDENCY.

**CBT Advisor,** *n.* an expert system developed for Courseware Inc.'s internal use. It helps judge how appropriate the organization of an instructional unit is to Computer Based Training formats.

**CDR,** *abbrev. for* a LISP function that returns a list with everything but the first element, that is, the rest of the list.

**CDX,** *n.* an expert system developed for Digital Equipment Corp. for VMS system crash analysis.

**cell,** *n.* **1.** a structure depicted graphically in cell notation (or box notation). In cell notation, the LIST (A B) would be represented as two rectangles, with each rectangle containing two parts. The rectangles are called CONS cells. The two parts of a cons cell are used to store pointers to the CAR and CDR respectively. They are called cons cells because the function cons works by grabbing one and filling in the cell's left and right parts with its two arguments.
**2.** a NODE in a NEURAL NETWORK.

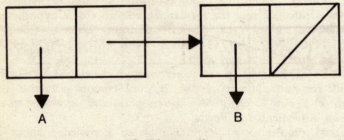

**Cell (sense 1)**

**CENTAUR,** *n.* an expert system that uses knowledge of pulmonary physiology and prototypical lung tests for each pulmonary disease or subtype to help pulmonary physiologists interpret pulmonary function tests. To determine the presence and severity of lung disease in a patient, the program interprets measurements of the amount of gas in the lungs and the rates of flow of gases into and out of the lungs. CENTAUR can explain and justify its findings based on its use of an underlying model of pulmonary physiology. The program uses a combination of FRAMES and RULES to represent its knowledge, and CERTAINTY measures similar to EMYCIN's CERTAINTY FACTORS to discern how closely the actual patient data agrees with the expected values of the prototype. Implemented in INTERLISP, CENTAUR was developed at Stanford University.

**central projection,** *n*. a REPRESENTATION of the picture-taking process where the image plane is located in front of the pinhole by a distance f, as shown in the figure below. For simplicity, the centre of the image plane is defined as the origin, and the z-axis is defined as the line intersecting the pinhole and the origin. The pinhole is thus at $(0,0,f)$ and the points of the image plane are at $(x_p, y_p, 0)$. The subscript p is used to denote points on the image plane.

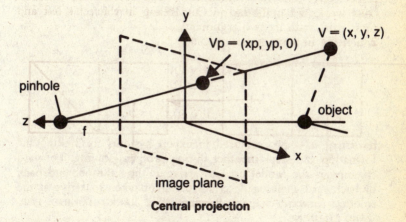

**Central projection**

**certainty,** *n*. the measure of confidence a person or expert system has in the validity of a fact or relationship (proposition, hypothesis, or INFERENTIAL RULE). In AI, certainty is used in contrast to PROBABILITY, which measures the likelihood that an event will occur.

**certainty factor,** *n*. a numerical weight assigned to a given fact or relationship that indicates the confidence a person has in the fact or relationship. Most RULE-BASED SYSTEMS use certainty factors. In contrast to probability coefficients, the methods for manipulating certainty factors are generally less formal than the approaches for combining probabilities.

**certainty in probabilistic relaxation,** *n.* a significant characteristic of RELAXATION ALGORITHMS where discrete labels are assigned to the OBJECTS. This notion can be generalized by attaching a level of CERTAINTY to each label. For example, a region may be a wall with a certainty of 0.3 and a door with a certainty of 0.7.

**chain rule,** *n.* an extension of MODUS PONENS, namely:

$$((P \rightarrow Q) \text{ and } (Q \rightarrow R) \vdash (P \rightarrow R)).$$

When the implications in the chain rule are rewritten in their logically equivalent form ($\neg P \vee Q$), the chain rule becomes

$$(\neg P \vee Q) \text{ and } (\neg Q \vee R) \vdash (\neg P \vee R),$$

which can be written as:

$$\frac{(\neg P \vee Q)}{(\neg Q \vee R)}$$
$$(\neg P \vee R).$$

**chaining,** *n.* a process used in expert systems for linking information and steps together during problem-solving. Forward chaining is the model used to arrive at the solution, and back or backward chaining describes the steps taken to arrive at the solution forward chaining specifies. (See BACK-CHAINING, FORWARD CHAINING.)

**chart,** *n.* a data structure in Kaplan's GENERAL SYNTACTIC PROCESSOR (GSP) used to represent both the grammar and the input sentence. A chart can be described in terms of a modified TREE, which, in turn, is commonly defined as a set of NODES that can be partitioned into a root and a set of disjoint subtrees. Trees encode two kinds of RELATION between nodes: DOMINANCE, which is the relation between a parent and a daughter node, and PRECEDENCE, which is the relation between a node and its right-hand sister node. The following diagram depicts a tree that represents a particular noun phrase.

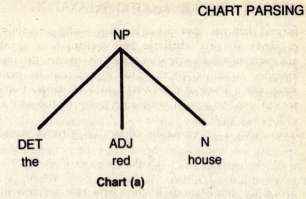

**Chart (a)**

A chart is essentially a tree modified in the following two ways:

(a) The ARCS of the tree have been rearranged to produce a binary tree, that is, a tree in which each node has at most two dangling nodes. This arrangement captures a 'natural correspondence' between trees and binary trees.

(b) The nodes and arcs have been interchanged; what were previously nodes are now arcs, and vice versa.

An example is the chart representation for the tree representing the noun phrase below:

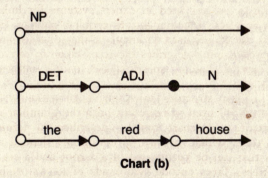

**Chart (b)**

**chart parsing,** *n.* an approach to non-deterministic PARSING developed by Kay and Kaplan based on earlier work by Earley, Kay and Colmerauer. In contrast to the earlier work, in which the chart was a well-formed substring table (in some cases enriched) for recording intermediate results, the later systems use the chart as the active agent in the parsing process. The chart is a directed graph having two sorts of edges – active and inactive. Inactive edges serve to record the existence of complete constituents. Active edges record hypothesized incomplete constituents. The parsing process involves adding new edges as a response to the meeting of active with inactive edges. As a record of an incomplete constituent, an active edge must carry some indication of how it could be extended (e.g., a dotted CONTEXT-free rule or a state in a network grammar [RTN or ATN]). When an active edge or an inactive edge meet for the first time, if the inactive edge satisfies the active edge's conditions for extension, then a new edge will be constructed. Parsing will be TOP-DOWN if initial hypotheses about constituents are keyed by active edges and their needs. Conversely, parsing will be BOTTOM-UP if the hypotheses are keyed by inactive edges. One of the principle advantages of the chart parsing methodology is that it easily supports a variety of grammatical formalisms, rule invocation strategies, and control regimes.

**Chemical Process Simulator,** *n.* an expert system developed at Eastman Kodak (LMI) for internal use. It displays simulations of complex chemical processes. The development software is PICON.

**Chest Pain,** *n.* an expert system that helps emergency room staff diagnose chest pains. The development software is First Class (GC LISP).

**CHI,** *n.* an integrated ENVIRONMENT of KNOWLEDGE-based TOOLS for assisting with various aspects of building computer systems. Included is a very high level, wide spectrum language called V, which is used for expressing not only software specifications but also programming knowledge; a PROGRAM TRANSFORMATION component; and a set of RULES (in V) for PROGRAM SYNTHESIS, including a data structure generation, a CONSTRAINT maintenance system, and a program/knowledge editor and DEBUGGER. Design also includes support for project management and integrated communication facilities for documentation, bug reports, message sending, etc.

**CHINA,** *n.* an expert system developed by the Federal Highway Administration for internal use. It acts as a front-end (for human interaction) to help engineers create queries for a FOR-TRAN system that designs highway noise barriers. GENIE (FRANZ LISP) is the development software.

**chronological backtracking,** *n.* a form of backtracking where the decision about where to backtrack is based upon the time when the decisions occurred; the last decision being the first one to redo.

**chunk,** *n.* a set of facts which are stored and retrieved as a single unit. The number of chunks that can be simultaneously manipulated in working memory provides the normal measure of functional working memory.

**Church–Rosser theorems,** *n.* theorems of abstract algebra that explain why rule application order is unimportant in commutative and decomposable production systems. (See COMMUTATIVE PRODUCTION SYSTEMS.)

**circumscription,** *n.* a form of NONMONOTONIC REASONING that overlaps DEFAULTS in some (or even all) cases. In reasoning about some problem, one often assumes that the problem involves only those OBJECTS and relationships that it mentions and no others. For example, INHERITANCE procedures may make an assumption (the CLOSED-WORLD ASSUMPTION) about the nonexistence of unlisted GENERALIZATION links and generalizing FRAMES. As another example, in the well-known missionaries-and-cannibals problem of traversing a river un-eaten, one typically does not think of solutions involving bridges, rocket ships, handcuffs, murder of the cannibals, or holes in the boat. Another way of viewing the circumscription principle is the assumption that all qualifications to the problem have been stated explicitly.

**clarification dialogue,** *n.* a dialogue for resolving parts of a query to a DATA BASE that were ambiguous or unclear.

**CLASS,** *n.* an expert system that determines secrecy status of sensitive information. EXSYS is the development software.

**classification (ID3),** *n.* the problem of assigning class membership to a set of OBJECTS. This is especially helpful for the purposes of building a DISCRIMINATION NET. Repeatedly split items into subsets by the value of a PREDICATE, until each subset contains members of one class only; the series of splits serve to define the discrimination set. In order to increase the efficiency of the resulting discrimination net, the predicates on which the items are split are chosen using information theoretic techniques so that they make the number of instances in each subset as similar as possible. This technique has been successfully applied to the problem of classifying chess positions as won or drawn.

**classification system,** *n.* in LEARNING FROM EXAMPLES, the task of predicting membership based on a single CONCEPT or RULE.

**classification table,** *n.* a method of defining a disease as a set of confirmed and denied pathophysiological states. It also contains a set of treatment statements for the disease. In CASNET, the third PLANE contains the classification tables for the disease.

**clausal form,** *n.* in automatic theorem-proving, a widely used normal form for predicate calculus formulae borrowed from mathematical logic. Consisting of applying prenex normal form, SKOLEMIZATION, and CONJUNCTIVE NORMAL FORM, in succession, the resulting formula has a model if and only if the original formula has a model. A formula that is in clausal form consists of a conjunction of clauses. Each clause is a disjunction of LITERALS and each literal is a predicate applied to some terms.

**cleavage rule,** *n.* a rule used in META-DENDRAL to predict which bonds in the proposed structure will be broken.

**CLISP,** *n. acronym for* Conversational LISP, in INTERLISP, an alternative, extensible, expression SYNTAX; a set of convenient surface syntax constructs that are translated into ordinary LISP. Features of CLISP include various abbreviations, a record package, a pattern match compiler, and algebraic notation. Via the error-catching mechanism of INTERLISP, any input not recognised as LISP is analysed to see if it is valid CLISP before the system indicates that an error has been made.

**closed-world assumption,** *n.* the assumption of a system that there are no external VARIABLES to affect its operation. For example, if we first assume that there is no uncertainty about the state of the WORLD before any tasks are executed, and q is an ATOMIC FORMULA with no free variables, then it is assumed that q's current TRUTH VALUE (before any execution) is known to the planner. Conventionally, the way this assumption is implemented is to stipulate that if q cannot be proven true, it will be assumed false. This is an example of the closed–world assumption. For instance, if (on a b) is not explicitly known, (not(on a b)) will be assumed to be true. What will be assumed is that initially every block is ON exactly one thing.

**CLOT,** *n.* an expert system that helps physicians evaluate evidence for blood–coagulation system disorders. The program looks to the two coagulation subsystems, the platelet-vascular or the coagulative, in order to diagnose a bleeding defect. CLOT was developed primarily to study knowledge acquisition tools and techniques. Its medical expertise was therefore not refined or fully tested. The program is a RULE-BASED PROGRAM and controlled by BACK-CHAINING. Implemented in EMYCIN, CLOT makes use of EMYCIN features including KNOWLEDGE ACQUISITION, CERTAINTY FACTORS, and EXPLANATION mechanisms. It was developed at Stanford University.

**CLS,** *n.* a refinement-operator system for learning.

**clustering,** *n.* the techniques for developing the distribution of FEATURE-VALUES in a multidimensional space. Clustering is a practice commonly applied in the fields of statistical data analysis and statistical pattern recognition.

**coaching,** *n.* a teaching strategy in which the coaching activity engages the student in a fun, playful manner, and promotes skill acquisition as an indirect consequence. Coaching programs are not oriented to covering a predetermined lesson plan within a fixed time (in contrast to SCHOLAR). Instead, the goal of coaching is to encourage skill acquisition and general problem-solving abilities by engaging the student in some activity like a computer game. Tutoring results as the computer coach 'observes' the student's play of the game, interrupts the student, and offers new information or suggests new strategies. To achieve successful results, the computer coach must be able to discern what skills or knowledge the student might acquire, based on his or her playing style, and to judge effective ways to intercede in the game and offer advice. WEST and WUMPUS are both coaching programs.

**COCOMO1,** *n.* an expert system developed by Level Five Research. It assists planning and scheduling software development projects. The development software is Insight 2.

**code generation in automatic programming,** see PRO-GRAM SYNTHESIS.

**CODES,** *n. acronym for* COnceptual DESign system, an expert system that uses knowledge of IDEF1 rules and heuristics to generate a conceptual schema of a data base. The program helps data base developers exercising the IDEF1 approach to cope with the intricate rules involved in applying IDEF1. An interactive front-end (for human interaction) enables developers to describe the features and relationships they want to include in the data base. Rules that use a BACK-CHAINING control strategy provide the KNOWLEDGE REPRESENTATION scheme for the program. Implemented in UCI LISP, CODES was developed at the University of Southern California.

**codification of programming knowledge,** see REPRESENTA-TION OF PROGRAMMING KNOWLEDGE.

**cognitive science,** *n.* the field that studies the mechanics of human intelligence. Cognitive science also involves the invest-igation of the processes involved in producing intelligence in a given situation.

**cohesiveness,** *n.* that property of matter such that the distance from the camera to objects that appear near to each other in the image tends to be approximately the same.

**COMAX,** *n.* an expert system developed by the US Depart-ment of Agriculture, Mississippi for commercial use. It advises farmers on irrigation, fertilization, and when to harvest.

**combinatorial explosion,** *n.* a phenomenon that occurs in the search for optimal solutions in a search. In most cases, the domain of possible combinations is so large that the time re-quired to find the optimum solution increases exponentially and exceeds the capacity of the computer system. As suggested by applications in games such as chess and draughts, exhaustive search is rarely feasible for nontrivial problems. Examining all sequences of n moves, for example, would re-quire operating in search space in which the number of NODES grows exponentially with n. This is combinatorial explosion.

**combinatorial problems,** *n.* problems that require sophisticated strategies to delay or moderate the effects of COMBINATORIAL EXPLOSION. Such strategies usually rely on knowledge about the problem DOMAIN to temper these effects.

**COMMON LISP,** *n.* a dialect of the LISP programming

language that is intended to serve as a standard version of LISP. Common LISP is a portable system designed to run on a wide range of computers. It is a common subset of LISP functions that can be supported efficiently in a wide variety of hardware and software environments, and within which large amounts of software can be written and shared among several applications. Common LISP provides for extensive and complex data types and control structures. The dialect supplies most of the facilities provided by any 'modern' LISP such as MACLISP or INTERLISP. Common LISP features include fully lexically scoped variables, a rich set of numerical data types, strings, arrays and vectors, bit and field manipulation, non-local exits and user controllable error handling, a hash facility, user-defined data types (Defstruct), stream-based I/O, and formatting and pretty-printing facilities. Common LISP does not provide graphic primitives, multiprocessing, or object-oriented programming. However, it is expected that any given implementation will provide a superset of Common LISP, which may provide these facilities. As these facilities become more standardized, Common LISP is expected to evolve in a manner to include them. Developed at Carnegie-Mellon University, Common LISP is commercially available from a number of companies including Gold Hill Computers (GCLISP) and Digital Equipment Corporation (VAX LISP).

**commonsense physics,** *n*. commonsense knowledge about the everyday physical world as opposed to more precise mathematical models of our environment. Many AI applications require this kind of fundamental knowledge about space, time or objects, although it is difficult to formalize.

**commonsense reasoning,** *n*. the method of arriving at useful conclusions about everyday matters or even about technical matters such as medicine by applying everyday or uncertain facts and rules. The conclusions arrived at by such approximate reasoning are tenuous, especially when the facts and rules are not independent, or when they involve quantified variables. Nevertheless, commonsense reasoning may be useful in many AI applications, so many AI researchers have begun to identify various components of commonsense reasoning, such as the interaction between action and knowledge and fuzzy sets. (see FUZZY LOGIC).

**commutative production system,** *n*. a PRODUCTION SYSTEM whose set of applicable RULES can be applied in any order. This set of applicable rules includes only the rules that are initially applicable to the DATA BASE and does not include those that become applicable after the application of a rule. More specifically, a commutative production system has three essential characteristics. Each member of the set of rules that can be applied to the data base can also be applied to any data base generated by the application of a rule to the original data base. If the original data base satisfies the GOAL condition, then any data base generated by the application of a rule also satisfies the goal condition. The data base that is generated by the application of a sequence of rules to the original data base does not vary, even if the order of the application of the rules varies. Commutativity improves the efficiency of a production system because it is possible to avoid the exploration of solutions that are equivalent except for the sequence of rules. Mechanisms to revoke the application of a rule or to apply alternative sequences of rules are not necessary. It is possible to transform any production system into a commutative system.

**COMPASS,** *n*. an expert system that applies the knowledge of a switch expert and of individual switch structure, switch faults, maintenance messages, and appropriate maintenance procedures to troubleshoot GTE's No. 2 EAX Switch. The program analyses telephone switching-system maintenance messages. To do so, it describes error situations that occurred during the telephone call-processing operation of the switch. Then, in order to determine potential specific faults in the switch, it identifies groups of messages most likely to occur from such error situations. Finally, the program then proposes maintenance procedures to confirm and correct the faults. Implemented in KEE and INTERLISP-D, COMPASS runs on Xerox 1108 workstations. It was developed by GTE Laboratories, Inc.

**competence,** *n*. the communal KNOWLEDGE of a group of speakers of a language. As a model of abstract knowledge and not of human behavior, GENERATIVE GRAMMAR is said to be concerned with competence, as opposed to performance, which accounts for how this communal knowledge is actually used.

**compiled knowledge,** *n.* the level of KNOWLEDGE that a person obtains from acquiring and organizing knowledge into CHUNKS and networks. Knowledge becomes compiled in the form of DEEP KNOWLEDGE and in the form of SURFACE KNOWLEDGE. Deep knowledge results from organizing knowledge into increasingly more abstract and theoretical patterns. Surface knowledge results from practical experience (practical HEURISTICS). EXPERTISE results from large amounts of compiled knowledge stemming from deep and surface knowledge.

**compiler,** *n.* a program that translates a source program written in a HIGH-LEVEL LANGUAGE into an object program in a lower-level machine language. When a source program is compiled, the program usually runs faster than when the same program is interpreted (see INTERPRETATION).

**completeness,** *n.* that property of a LOGIC SYSTEM in which any true statement has a proof. In cases where a system, like PLANNER, could know all the facts necessary to reach a particular conclusion, yet be incapable of making the required deduction, the system is not complete. In this sense, many PROCEDURAL SYSTEMS are not complete. Completeness is not always a desirable feature in a system. In cases where a system should work quickly and spend as little time as possible finding a particular answer, or concluding it cannot find the answer, completeness would slow the system.

**completeness of a knowledge representation,** *n.* that characteristic of a KNOWLEDGE REPRESENTATION scheme in which a system could know all the facts required to reach a certain conclusion but not be powerful enough to make the required deductions. Completeness, however, is not necessarily always desirable. There are cases when the system should work quickly and not spend a long time finding a particular answer or concluding that it cannot find the answer.

**completeness of a program specification,** *n.* the specification that completely and precisely indicates what it is that the program is to accomplish.

**completeness of resolution refutation strategies,** *n.* that characteristic of a resolution refutation system that eventually finds any existing contradiction. However, in AI applications, the efficiency of a CONTROL STRATEGY is often more important than its completeness.

**completeness of rules of inference,** *n.* a system of rules of INFERENCE whereby all well-founded formulas that can be derived from any set are also theorems that follow from that set.

**COMPONENT IMPACT ANALYSIS SYSTEM,** *n.* an expert system developed by Argonne National Labs for internal use. It advises nuclear power plant operators on value and switch settings. The program is written in C and Quintus Prolog.

**composition of substitutions,** *n.* the combining of substitutions appearing in NATURAL DEDUCTION statements into a single expression.

**computational linguistics,** *n.* the use of computers in the study of language.

**computer–assisted instruction (CAI),** *n.* an application in computer-assisted education that explicitly attempts to provoke and control learning. In many cases, learning may take place while the student is involved in some activity like a situation or a game. The role of AI computer-based instructional applications is viewed as making possible a new kind of learning environment. The goal of CAI research is to build instructional programs that incorporate well-prepared course material in lessons that are most appropriate for each student. Early CAI programs were either electronic 'page turners', which simply printed prepared text, or drill-and-practice monitors, which printed problems and responded to the student's solutions using prestored answers and remedial comments. In the Intelligent CAI (ICAI) programs of the 1970s, course material was represented independently of teaching procedures, so that problems and remedial comments could be generated differently for each student.

**Computer–Based Consultant (CBC),** *n.* a computer system containing a body of specialized knowledge about a particular task DOMAIN and, in addition, that makes that knowledge conveniently available to users working in that domain.

**COMPUTER COACH,** *n.* an approach to computerized teaching. Development of the first computer coach was undertaken at Bolt Beranek and Newman, Inc. The computer coach was used for the children's board game 'How the West Was Won'. (See COACHING.)

**CONAD,** *n.* an expert system developed by Nixdorf

(Germany) for checking orders and configuring NCR computers. Twaice, Nixdorf's Mprolog-based tool, is the development software.

**concavity and gradients,** *n.* the relationship in the projection of 3-dimensional space between line labels and the GRADIENT SPACE. If two surfaces meet along a concave or convex edge, their gradients lie along a line in gradient space that is perpendicular to that edge in the image. For example, if two planes intersect at an edge that is imaged as vertical in the image plane, then the gradients of the two planes must lie on a horizontal line in gradient space.

**concept,** *n.* a descriptive SCHEMA for a class of things or a particular instance of the schema, with some of its general properties distinguished in order to characterize the specific subclass or element that instantiates the class description.

**concept formation,** see LEARNING.

**conceptual bug,** *n.* the term used in ICAI to account for a persistent procedure that a student follows that leads to incorrect responses.

**conceptual dependency (CD),** *n.* a theory of meaning representation developed by Shank and used extensively at Yale. The theory relies on deep 'conceptual' SEMANTIC PRIMITIVES and CASE FRAMES in order to provide strong decomposition of word and text meaning. In particular, it involves the construction of all semantic notions from a set of elementary concepts. Emphasis is placed on key primitive acts along with required properties of the fillers of their (obligatory) roles in order to drive primarily semantic expectation-based parsing. Shank developed CD as a representation for the meaning of phrases and sentences. The 'basic axiom' of CD theory is:

> For any two sentences that are identical in meaning, regardless of language, there should be only one representation of that meaning in CD.

Shank thus allies himself with the early machine translation concept of INTERLINGUA, or intermediate language. Another important idea of CD is that the CD representations are composed of a very small number of semantic primitive acts and primitive states (with associated ATTRIBUTE values).

**conceptualization,** *n.* combinations of detailed RULES providing for the ways that elements can be combined into RE-PRESENTATIONS of meaning. There are two basic kinds of combination. One involves an ACTOR (a picture producer – PP) doing a PRIMITIVE ACT; the other involves an OBJECT (again, a PP) and a description of its state (a picture aider – PA). Conceptualizations can be tied together by relations of instrumentality or causation, among others. The primitive elements occurring in conceptualizations are not words but CONCEPTS. The primitives reflect a level of thought underlying language rather than language itself. Consequently, representations of text in CONCEPTUAL DEPENDENCY are said to be language-free.

**CONCHE,** *n. acronym for* CONsistency CHEcker, an expert system tool used to affirm the ACCURACY of DOMAINrr knowledge and theory construction related to organic reaction mechanisms. From an INTERACTIVE DIALOGUE with a chemist, the program infers a set of RULES associated with the relative strengths of organic acids. CONCHE represents essential DOMAIN knowledge as MYCIN-like rules and additional domain knowledge encoded as facts in a SEMANTIC NET. BACK-CHAINING, together with MYCIN-like CERTAINTY FACTORS, comprise the program's control scheme. CONCHE's explanations appear in terms of rule-chaining, facts accessed, and unsatisfied or unsatisfiable conditions. Implemented in a combination of LISP and FUZZY, CONCHE was developed at the University of Leeds.

**concordance,** *n.* an index to a text that includes the CONTEXTS in which the words or phrases occur.

**condition,** *n.* the left-hand side of a PRODUCTION RULE. See ANTECEDENT. Compare ACTION CLAUSE, CONSEQUENT.

**conditional formation,** *n.* in DEDALUS, the TRANSFORMATION RULES that impose some condition P (e.g., l is nonempty, x is nonnegative) that must be satisfied for the RULE to be applied. Suppose that, in attempting to apply a particular rule, the system failed to prove or disprove the condition P, where P is expressed entirely in terms of the primitive constructs of the TARGET LANGUAGE; in such a case, the conditional formation rule is invoked. This rule allows the introduction of CASE ANALYSIS to consider separately the cases in which P is true and in which P is false. If the result is both a program segment $S_1$ that achieves the GOAL under the assumption that P is true and another program segment $S_2$ that achieves the goal under the assumption that P is false, the conditional-formation principle puts these two program segments together into a conditional expression *if P then $S_1$ else $S_2$*, which achieves the goal regardless of whether P is true or false. During the generation of $S_2$, .the system could discover that a conditional expression was unnecessary: The generation of $S_2$ may not have required the assumption that P was false. In such a case, the program constructed would be simply $S_2$.

**conditional plans,** *n.* PLANS used when the truth value of certain CONDITIONS cannot be evaluated until execution time.

**conditional rule application,** *n.* a RULE application that is restricted by a CONTROL STRATEGY. A control statement at the beginning of the program tests whether a certain condition exists or whether a fact that fits a certain pattern exists. If the conditions are met, the rule is applied; if not, backtracking results.

**conditional substitution,** *n.* a SUBSTITUTION that contains a conditional expression. In resolution within and/or graphs, conditional substitutions based on a complementary pair of unifiable LITERALS are used to avoid multiplying a formula out into clause form.

**confidence factor,** *n.* the measure of confidence a person has in a fact or relationship. In AI, the confidence factor contrasts with probability, which measures the likelihood that an event will occur.

**conflict resolution,** *n.* a phase of each cycle of the operation of a typical, large PRODUCTION SYSTEM. In practice, more than one RULE could fire in each cycle of the production system. The system is required, in this case, to chose one rule from among a set of rules called the conflict set. The conflict resolution phase of each cycle accomplishes basic cognitive traits such as action sequencing, attention focusing, interruptibility, and control of instability. The following describes several different approaches to conflict resolution. Each rule involves choosing:

(a) the first rule that matches the CONTEXT, where 'first' is defined in terms of some explicit linear order of the RULE BASE;

    (b) the highest priority rule, where 'priority' is defined by the programmer according to the demands and characteristics of the task (as in DENDRAL);

    (c) the most specific rule, that is, the rule with the most detailed condition part that matches the current context;

    (d) the rule that refers to the element most recently added to the context;

    (e) a new rule, that is, a rule-binding INSTANTIATION that has not occurred previously;

    (f) a rule arbitrarily;

    (g) not to choose – exploring all the applicable rules in parallel (as in MYCIN).

Different systems use different combinations of these simple conflict-resolution methods. Some methods can become complicated SCHEDULING ALGORITHMS.

**conflicting subgoals,** *n.* a situation that occurs when sub-problems interact. This occurs commonly in problems involving the expenditure of scarce resources.

**CONGEN,** *n.* an expert system that uses a variety of graph-theoretic ALGORITHMS to help structural chemists establish an exhaustive set of possible structures for an unknown compound. Chemists supply CONGEN with spectrographic and chemical data along with a set of required and forbidden CONSTRAINTS on the possible interconnections among the atoms in the compound. This input enables CONGEN to determine all possible configurations of the atoms in molecular structures that satisfy the specified constraints. CONGEN then generates a presentation of structural drawings that describe the list of possible structures.

    CONGEN was developed as part of the DENDRAL project and serves as Heuristic DENDRAL's hypothesis generator. Implemented in INTERLISP, CONGEN was developed at Stanford University.

**conjunction,** *n.* in logic, a single formula that is composed of two or more formulas connected by 'and'. Each component formula is called a conjunct. If each conjunct is a well-formed formula, then the conjunction is a well-formed formula.

**conjunctive normal form,** *n.* a formula that is written as the CONJUNCTION of disjunctions of LITERALS is in conjunctive normal form. Any formula can be transformed into this form.

**conjunctive subgoal,** *n.* a subgoal in BACK-CHAINING, where CONJUNCTIONS must be specially handled. The GOAL (SHOW: r') will chain through (if(and p q) r) to generate the subgoal (SHOW:(and p' q')). This conjunctive subgoal is handled by finding variable bindings that are answers to both (SHOW: p') and (SHOW: q'). In practice, this is done by generating answers to one conjunct, and throwing away those that don't work on the other conjunct.

**connection graph,** *n.* a CONTROL structure for backward, RULE-BASED DEDUCTION SYSTEMS. Before solving any specific problems with the rules, a rule connection graph can be constructed by writing down each rule in the set in AND/OR GRAPH form and then drawing MATCH ARCS between LITERALS in RULE ANTECEDENTS and in matching RULE CONSEQUENTS. When an actual problem is posed, its AND/OR GOAL literal NODES and FACT nodes can be connected to all matching literals in rule consequents and rule antecedents, respectively. The resulting expanded connection graph can then be searched to find CANDIDATE SOLUTION GRAPHS.

**Connection Machine,** *n.* a special ARCHITECTURE for the purpose of concurrently manipulating knowledge stored in SEMANTIC NETWORKS. It avoids the problems of manipulating semantic networks on a sequential machine by giving each NODE and link in the network its own simple processor. Not intended for use as a general-purpose parallel computer, the connection machine is meant to be very fast at a few simple operations important for ARTIFICIAL INTELLIGENCE applications such as searching and deduction from SEMANTIC INHERITANCE networks.

**connectionism,** *n.* a paradigm in AI that models systems through the use of so-called NEURAL NETWORKS.

**connective,** *n.* a term such as 'and' or 'or' that is used to make complex formulas from ATOMIC FORMULAS.

**connector,** *n.* a hyperarc that connects the parent NODE of an AND/OR GRAPH to a set of SUCCESSOR or descendant nodes. In the special case where all of the connectors are 1-connectors, the GRAPH is an ordinary one.

**CONNIVER,** *n.* a high-level AI language developed by Sussman and McDermott in response to the shortcomings of PLANNER. CONNIVER provides various control PRIMITIVES allowing programmers to specify more flexible control regimes. In particular, the more important contributions of CONNIVER are the context and corouteing of primitives. Supporting all the PLANNER data structures, CONNIVER also provides users with context tags and POSSIBILITY LISTS. The CONSEQUENT and ANTECEDENT THEOREMS of PLANNER become the if-needed, if-added, and if-removed of CON-NIVER. All solutions to a given goal may be collected and stored on a possibility list. Corouteing facilities permit the suspension and activation of processes, enabling programmers to specify other than a DEPTH-FIRST SEARCH of the SEARCH SPACE. The data base in CONNIVER is organized into CON-TEXTS whereby the assertions and methods (theorems) are true in a certain context. A context may be created from other existing contexts and use the 'tag' or name associated with each context. The context mechanisms permit flexibility in the order in which subgoals are solved. Work on one subgoal can be suspended while another is solved, with attention returning to the original (whose state has been saved) at a later date.

**CONPHYDE,** *n. acronym for* CONsultant for PHYsical property DEcisions, an expert system that helps chemical engineers select physical property estimation methods. The program handles the selection of vapour–liquid equilibrium coefficients for setting up process simulation. It takes as input information about required accuracy and the expected concentrations, temperatures, and pressure ranges. A combined RULE-BASED and SEMANTIC NETWORK formalism, similar to PROSPECTOR, is used for KNOWLEDGE REPRESENTATION. INFERENCES are based on the use of CERTAINTY FACTORS and Bayesian decision theory for propagating probabilities associated with the data. Implemented in KAS, and using the KAS explanation facility, CONPHYDE was developed at Carnegie–Mellon University.

**cons,** *n.* a LISP function for building lists. The function cons (for construct) creates a new list whose first element (its CAR) is the first argument to cons, and whose subsequent members (its CDR) are the second argument.

**consequent,** *n.* the right-hand side of an implication formula constructed by connecting two formulas with a right-directed arrow. The left-hand side is the ANTECEDENT.

**consequent theorem,** *n.* a type of theorem in MICRO-PLANNER. A consequent theorem is called when its pattern matches a subgoal to be solved.

**conservative threshold,** *n.* a method in region segmentation that involves delaying classification of PIXELS with FEATURE values near the threshold or boundary of the discriminant surface. In a second pass, the pixels are classified according to the labels of their neighbours.

**cons cell,** see CELL.

**CONSIGHT,** *n.* an expert system developed by General Motors. It is an industrial MACHINE VISION object-recognition system using special lighting to produce silhouette-like images.

**consistency,** *n.* **1.** that quality of a DEDUCTION system whereby all deductions are correct, therefore all conclusions necessarily follow from the premises. Most THEOREM PROVING systems have this property, but PROCEDURAL SYSTEMS often do not. An example is DEFAULT REASONING. Default reasoning can introduce inconsistency in the presence of incomplete knowledge. For instance, if we use the fact that Ace is a bird in order to conclude that he can fly, and later discover that Ace is an ostrich, we will have inconsistency. As with completeness, consistency is not always desirable because much of our reasoning is done by revising our beliefs in the presence of new information. Most of our knowledge is not absolute; it often consists of caveats and exceptions.

**2.** in VISION STUDIES, a condition forced by the rule that each line in the picture must be assigned one and only one label (i.e., $+$, $-$, $>$) along its entire length. If not, the adjoining planes would have different orientations in different parts of the scene.

**consistency assumption,** *n.* a condition of a general STATE SPACE graph. The general idea of the assumption is that a form of the triangle inequality holds throughout the SEARCH SPACE. Specifically, the assumption is that for any NODES m and n, the estimated distance $h^\star(m)$ from m to a GOAL should always be less than or equal to the actual distance from m to n plus the estimated remaining distance, $h^\star(n)$, from n to a goal. For an $h^\star$ not satisfying the consistency assumption on a general state-space graph, it has been shown that $A^\star$ is not optimal with respect to the number of EXPANSIONS.

**consistency of substitutions,** *n.* that quality of substitution in unification in which the terms and variables can be applied consistently. In particular after applying more than one rule to an AND/OR graph, it contains more than one MATCH ARC. In computing the sets of clauses represented by an AND/OR graph having several match arcs, one counts only those solution graphs terminating in LITERAL NODES having match arc substitutions that are consistent. The clause represented by a consistent solution graph can be obtained by the substitution called unifying composition to the disjunction of literals on its TERMINAL NODES. Suppose there is a set of substitutions $\{s_1, s_2, \ldots, s_n\}$. Each $s_1$ is a set of pairs. $s_1 = \{t_{i1}/v_{i1}, \ldots, t_{im(i)}/v_{im(i)}\}$ where t is a term and v is a variable. From $(s_1, \ldots, s_n)$ define the two expressions: $U_1 = (v_{1i}, \ldots, v_{1m(1)}, \ldots, v_{nm(n)})$ and $U_2 = (t_{1i}, \ldots, t_{1m(1)}, \ldots, t_{nm(n)})$. The substitutions $(s_1, \ldots, s_n)$ are consistent if $U_1$ and $U_2$ are unifiable.

**constancy in visual perception,** *n.* the psychological phenomenon whereby perceptions of size, shape, brightness, and colour are computed at an early stage in the visual process. This phenomenon corroborates the appropriateness of INTRINSIC IMAGES in IMAGE UNDERSTANDING.

**constraining knowledge,** *n.* the limiting of KNOWLEDGE to what can be expected in a DOMAIN. It is a central idea in all successful SPEECH UNDERSTANDING systems, for example.

**constraint,** *n.* a factor that determines the values of a type. A VALUE in that subset satisfies the constraint.

**constraint structured planning,** *n.* a system for solving problems by means of a DEPTH-FIRST SEARCH ALGORITHM, finding locations for successive OBJECTS and backing up when it cannot proceed without violating some CONSTRAINT. The search is aided by a constraint graph that represents, by restrictions on the amount of area left, the effects of constraints between pairs of objects. Thus, by attacking the most restrictive constraint first, the search is relatively efficient.

**constrictor relation,** *n.* a manifestation of a disease in INTERNIST-II that uses the same knowledge base as INTERNIST-I/CADUCEUS. These manifestations do not identify a particular disease but, rather, a general area of infirmity. For example, jaundice alerts clinicians to the presence of liver disease. The observation does not discriminate among liver diseases, but it does delimit this disease areas. Formally, a disease area constrained by a constrictor manifestation is a subtree of the disease TREE, in this case, the subtree of liver diseases.

**constructive bug,** *n.* in ICAI, a method for making a bug constructive by establishing for the student that there is something less-than-optimal in his approach. Additionally, it supplies enough information so that the student can use what he or she already knows in order to identify and characterize the bug and avoid this failing in the future.

**consultation paradigm,** *n.* a PARADIGM that describes generic types of PROBLEM-SOLVING scenarios. Individual system-building TOOLS are typically good for one or a few consultation paradigms, but inadequate for others. Most commercial tools are designed to promote rapid development of expert systems that can deal with the DIAGNOSTIC or PRESCRIPTIVE PARADIGM.

**content addressing,** *n.* a form of PATTERN MATCHING that allows data to be retrieved by meaning or form rather than address. In contrast to most computer languages, where a datum needs to be accessed by its name (e.g., the name of a VARIABLE), the content addressing approach eliminates the need for arbitrary names of things, and instead specifies the form (or meaning) of the item of data in order to access it. A pattern such as ((FATHER-OF ?X) ?Y) is used as a kind of sketch of the datum being sought in the DATA BASE and 'matches' against stored items like ((FATHER-OF MARY) (FLIES KITES)). Thus, there is no need to remember the name or address of the stored information.

**context,** *n.* **1.** a buffer-like data structure used in PRODUCTION SYSTEMS. The context, which is also called the data or short-term memory buffer, is the focus of attention of the PRODUCTION RULES. The context data structure may be a simple list, a very large array, or, more typically, a medium-sized buffer with some internal structure of its own. The left-hand side of each production in the RULE BASE represents a condition that must be present in the context data structure before the production can fire. The actions of the production rules can change the context, in order that other rules will have their condition parts satisfied.

**2.** a distinct DATA BASE, which when combined with others is used to replace a global data base. Contexts have been found especially useful in hypothetical reasoning systems. The contexts are arranged in a TREE because each context represents a distinct STATE OF THE WORLD (or set of assumptions about its state): As the WORLD changes, a context naturally gives rise to 'descendant' contexts, which differ slightly from each other and from their common parent. Conceptually, each context is a full data base in its own right. In reality, most of the information in a given context will be the same as in the (parent) context just above it, so that, to save space, only the differences are actually stored. The root of the tree is actually a full data base.

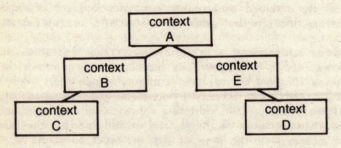

**Context (sense 2)**

**context–free grammar,** *n*. a collection of PHRASE-STRUCTURE RULES that does not include a statement of the context in which they can be applied. Each such rule names a constituent type and specifies a possible expansion thereof. The standard notation is:

$$LHS \rightarrow RHS_1 \ldots RHS_n$$

where LHS, the left-hand side, names the constituent, and $RHS_1$ through $RHS_n$ names the expansion, the right-hand side. Because the expansion is unconditional – that is, the ENVIRONMENT of the constituent to be expanded is irrelevant – the above rules are context-free rules. A context-free GRAMMAR is a collection of such rules as those described here when they are combined with an initial symbol (usually S). Within the syntax of the grammar, NON-TERMINALS are those constituents that are expanded – that is, those constituents appearing in the left-hand side. The terminals are those appearing only on the right-hand side. For interpreting such a grammar as specifying a language, there exist two standard approaches: the RE-WRITING interpretation and the well-formedness interpretation. The rewriting interpretation says that a grammar generates the set of strings of terminals that can be produced by the following non-deterministic method:

(a) Write down the initial symbol;

(b) Choose a non-terminal SYMBOL in the string, and a rule from the grammar that expands it. Replace one instance of the non-terminal with the expansion given in the rule;

(c) If no non-terminals remain in the string, the process is complete. Otherwise, go back to step b.

The well-formedness interpretation actually generates TREES, not strings. It admits to the language all singly rooted trees whose root is the initial symbol and for each of whose non-leaf nodes there is a rule in the grammar such that LHS is the NODE label and RHS$_n$ are the labels of its descendants in order. (See TYPE 2 GRAMMAR.)

**context mechanism,** *n.* the subdividing of a KNOWLEDGE BASE into contexts suitable to attaching a subproblem. For example, in robot planning the robot can simulate alternative sequences of actions, creating contexts to represent the different STATES OF THE WORLD that result. If the consequences of an action are undesirable, the robot planner can delete the context and try something else.

**context-sensitive grammar,** see TYPE 1 GRAMMAR.

**context tree** or **object tree,** *n.* a structured arrangement of the OBJECTS (contexts) or conceptual entities that make up the consultation DOMAIN. More than one context may exist. A static context tree is an arrangement of context types (e.g., a patient for whom cultures have been prepared). The context tree used in EMYCIN is the central component of the consultant program.

**context-parameter-value triplets,** *n.* a KNOWLEDGE RE-PRESENTATION method for representing factual knowledge. A CONTEXT designates an actual or conceptual entity in the DOMAIN of the consultant (e.g., a patient, an aircraft, or an oil

71

well). Parameters, also called ATTRIBUTES, designate properties associated with each context (e.g., age and sex of a patient or location of an oil well). VALUES can be attached to each parameter; for example, the value '50' could be attached to the 'age' parameter. EMYCIN uses context–parameter–value triplets. See OBJECT-ATTRIBUTE-VALUE TRIPLETS.

**contour line,** *n.* a line formed at the boundary between the OBJECTS in a picture and the outer background.

**contradictory information,** *n.* information that is contrary or exceptional. A common dilemma is how to qualify generalizations sufficiently to be accurate, while at the same time maintaining the simplicity of the PREDICATE CALCULUS. On the one hand, many general descriptive or synthetic statements about the world are incorrect unless they are qualified, and contradictory deductions may result. On the other hand, FORMALISM becomes impossible if these qualifications must be included explicitly. One solution is to qualify general statements only after a specific case occurs that would contradict the statement.

**contrapositive,** *n.* that form of an implication that results by exchanging the CONSEQUENT with the ANTECEDENT. For example, to prove that Fernand is not a horse, it is sufficient to prove that he is not an animal.

**contrast,** *n.* the ratio between the maximum and minimum luminance values of a display.

**control,** *n.* any explicit or implicit PROCEDURE that determines the order of events of a PROBLEM-SOLVING activity. Control refers to the temporal organization of subprocesses. Control of a KNOWLEDGE SYSTEM is the method used by the INFERENCE ENGINE to regulate the order in which reasoning occurs. BACK-CHAINING, FORWARD CHAINING, and BLACKBOARD agendas are all examples of control methods.

**control knowledge,** *n.* the knowledge about a problem that is represented by the CONTROL strategy and used to coordinate the PROBLEM-SOLVING process.

**control point,** *n.* a point that can be found in an image and whose precise location in the ideal image is already known.

**control strategy,** *n.* **1.** a method for choosing subsequent actions from among alternative choices of actions available to a given PROBLEM-SOLVING activity. BACK-CHAINING is an

example of a control strategy used in PRODUCTION SYSTEMS.
**2.** a flexible CONTROL strategy under which component DATA BASES are processed not in a predetermined order, but in an order that is determined during processing (for decomposable systems).

**Conversational LISP,** see CLISP.

**CONVERSE,** *n.* an early system for NATURAL LANGUAGE UNDERSTANDING that used limited logic for representing a sentence.

**co-occurrence matrix,** *n.* in second-order, or dipole statistics, the factor that summarizes the probability of the INTENSITY VALUES of a pair of values. These statistics are computed for pairs of PIXELS in different positional relations. For instance, let $\delta = (r, \theta)$ denote a VECTOR in the image that represents a displacement by r in the orientation of $\theta$. $P_\delta(I_1, I_2)$ denotes a probability that a pair of pixels displaced by $\delta$ has intensities $I_1$ and $I_2$: The first pixel has intensity $I_1$ and the second, displaced by $\delta$ from the first, has intensity $I_2$. If intensity takes one of n possible values, a co-occurrence matrix is an $n \times n$ matrix and records all the $P_\delta(I_1, I_2), 1 \leqslant I_1, I_2 \leqslant n$, for one $\delta$.

**Cooker Advisor,** *n.* an expert system developed at Texas Instruments for internal use at Campbell Soup. It troubleshoots electrostatic soup 'cookers.' PERSONAL CONSULTANT is the development software.

**COOP,** *n.* a computer system designed to respond to mistaken presumptions about the state of the DATA BASe. Based on the user's query, if COOP inferred that the state of the data base violated the user's presumptions, COOP would formulate a corrective, indirect response that was more informative than the formally correct response.

**cooperating knowledge source,** *n.* a specialized module used in expert systems. Sets of these modules operate independently to analyse the data and communicate via a central, structured DATA BASE called a BLACKBOARD.

**cooperative response,** *n.* a response to a DATA BASE theory that may not answer the question literally but attempts to return the most useful answer. For example, in a situation where the user asks 'Which students failed COM 1315 last spring?' but the course is offered only in the fall, a simple, direct, and literal response of 'none' is misleading, although correct. A more accurate response would be to cooperatively inform the user that the course was not offered in the spring. The cooperative response aims to remedy the inadequacy of the direct, literal response in situations where the literal response to a user's natural language query may not be what he or she wants and could serve to mislead the USER.

**coroutining,** *n.* an AI CONTROL structure used to relax the strict control hierarchy found in most languages (including LISP), in which every procedure runs for a while, then returns control to the procedure that called it, and disappears. Coroutines are procedures that can pass control to any other coroutine and, furthermore, can suspend themselves and continue later. To speak of procedures or coroutines suspending or disappearing is inaccurate: A PROCEDURE is a piece of code. To draw the distinction, an INSTANTIATION of a procedure, a copy of the code that is actually running, can be called a process. For a process to suspend, its current state must be saved (the current values of its variables and the point at which to resume execution). Initially, there is only one process, and it can create new processes. A process can be in one of three states once it is created: running, suspended, or terminated. If control is transferred to the process when it is created, it is running; otherwise, it is suspended, or terminated. A running process can resume or activate some other process (pass control to the other process, causing itself to suspend). While a process is suspended, its state is preserved but nothing happens. A running process can also terminate as it passes control to another process. Coroutines are such processes.

**correspondence problem,** *n.* the task in conventional stereo vision and motion parallax of finding the features of an image that occur in both images of the stereo pair.

**Corrosion Expert,** *n.* an expert system developed at Texas Instruments for internal use at Westinghouse Electric Company. It assists the design of steam generators by recommending alloys to avoid corrosion. PERSONAL CONSULTANT is the development software.

**cost (of a solution tree),** *n.* **1.** the sum of all arc costs in the TREE. This is the SUM COST.
**2.** the sum arc costs along the most expensive path from the

root to a terminal NODE. This is called the max cost. For example, if every arc in the solution tree has cost 1, then the sum cost is the number of arcs in the tree and the max cost is the depth of the deepest node.

**Counter–Agent,** *n.* a deep case in CASE GRAMMAR which indicates the force or resistance against which the action is carried out.

**CPM,** *n.* in MACSYMA, a fast but limited inference ALGORITHM that supplements the DATA BASE retrieval routines. CPM performs taxonomic deductions, property inheritances, set intersections, and other simple inferences. For example, given the facts that x is an integer, integers are rational, and the real numbers are partitioned into rationals and irrationals, CPM automatically deduces that x is not an irrational. Given the fact that a rational can be written as an integral numerator over an integral denominator, CPM automatically deduces that x can be so written. The algorithm was developed to enhance the retrieval capabilities of a high–level data base system organized as a SEMANTIC NETWORK. CPM is an elaboration of work on constraint expressions, but it has been carefully restricted so that it can be implemented on parallel hardware. The CPM algorithm is a highly compiled form of domain-independent (see DOMAIN INDEPENDENCE) constraint propagation, in which constraints, represented by labels on the NODES of the network, propagate across links to other nodes according to the laws of LOGIC.

**crack,** *n.* in vision studies, a flat edge that is also the bounding edge of an object.

**credit–assignment problem,** *n.* the assignment of credit to RULES that are relevant to new information. The relevance of new rules must be clear. Blame for failures is often assigned rather than credit for successes.

**Crew Control Mock–up Expert System,** *n.* an expert system developed at Lockheed for internal use at NASA. It advises on either space station reconfiguring or simulation for anticipated problems. ART is the development software.

**CRIB,** *n.* an expert system that applies hardware and software fault diagnostic expertise to help computer engineers and system maintainers locate computer hardware and software faults. The program takes as input a description of the engineer's observations, which the engineer supplies in simple, English-like terms. The program then matches the engineer's input against a DATA BASE containing known faults. It progressively matches larger and larger groups of symptoms with the incoming descriptions in order to arrive at a subunit that is either reparable or replaceable. When a subunit is reached and a fault is not corrected, the program automatically backtracks to the last decision point and tries to find another match. The program's diagnostic expertise is contained as a collection of action–symptom pairs (called symptom patterns) in which the action is designed to elicit the symptom from the machine. A simple hierarchy of subunits in a SEMANTIC NETWORK is used to model the machine under diagnosis. Implemented in CORAL 66, CRIB was developed as a combined effort by International Computers Limited (ICL), the Research and Advanced Development Centre (RADC), and Brunel University.

**critical node,** *n.* in ABSTRIPS: **1.** the ROOT NODE and all first successors (see SUCCESSOR NODE) of type 1 NODES.
**2.** all further successors (except the first) of type 1 nodes and all successors of type 3 nodes.
**3.** the first successors of type 2 nodes.

**criticality value,** *n.* in ABSTRIPS, a number attached to LITERALS to indicate their relative importance. The preconditions for an OPERATOR are stated as a list of predications, or literals, concerning the WORLD MODEL to which the operator is to be applied. The HIERARCHY of PROBLEM SPACES is then defined in terms of levels of criticality: In the space of criticality n, all operator preconditions with criticality less than n are ignored.

**CRITICS,** *n.* a set of PROCEDURES in NOAH that are sensitive to those effects of actions that would jeopardize success of a PLAN. These procedures are used to detect and correct interactions, eliminate redundant operations, and so forth.

**CRITTER,** *n.* an expert system that uses knowledge of circuit diagrams and circuit analysis techniques to help circuit design engineers analyse the performance capacity of VLSI circuit-designs. The program assesses the precision, timing, robustness, and speed of a VLSI circuit design. It builds a comprehensive model of the circuit's performance from circuit schematics and I/O specifications it accepts from the engineer.

Then it summarizes this information and presents it to the engineer along with a feasibility analysis of the circuit design and diagnostic and repair information. The program represents its knowledge of circuit diagrams as FRAMES and other knowledge in the form of algebraic formulas and PREDICATE CALCULUS. Implemented in INTERLISP, CRITTER was developed at Rutgers University.

**cross–correlation,** *n.* a technique for matching the TEMPLATE to the scene by moving the template across the figure while looking for one or more points of maximum coincidence.

**CRYSALIS,** *n.* an expert system that uses knowledge of protein composition and X-ray crystallography to infer the three-dimensional structure of a protein from an electron density map (EDM). To do so, it applies HEURISTICS to generate and test hypotheses about plausible protein structures. In order to infer the atomic structure, CRYSALIS interprets both X-ray diffraction data composed of position and intensity of diffracted waves. Independent knowledge sources contained in a BLACKBOARD ARCHITECTURE build and test a multi-level hypothesis structure. Implemented in LISP, CRYSALIS was developed at Stanford University.

**CSF Advisor,** *n.* an expert system developed at IBM for commercial use. It guides development of cost estimates for moving DPS equipment. E.S. Environment/VM is the development software.

**CSRL,** *abbrev. for* Conceptual Structures Representation Language, a KNOWLEDGE ENGINEERING LANGUAGE for developing FRAME-based REPRESENTATION. It represents concepts in a diagnostic HIERARCHY as a collection of specialists. It also handles an establish-refine approach to diagnosis, which is implemented within CSRL through message-passing among CONCEPTS. Included in CSRL is a SYNTAX checker, commands for invoking any concept with any message, and a simple TRACE FACILITY. Implemented in ELISP, CSRL uses a version of FRL, and operates on a DEC 20/60 computer system. CSRL was developed at Ohio State University.

**cumulative frequency distribution (CFD),** *n.* the sum of histogram VALUES up to each intensity level.

**CV Filter,** *n.* an expert system developed by Helix Expert Systems London, England for internal use. It screens resumes of job applicants. Helix Expert Edge is the development software.

# D

**DAA,** *abbrev. · for* Design Automation Assistant, an expert system that uses hardware allocation ALGORITHMS collected from expert designers along with knowledge of the CMU/DA allocator to help VLSI designers. The program performs a hardware allocation from an algorithmic description of a VLSI system. It takes as input a data flow description of a VLSI system in order to produce a list of technology-independent registers, operators, data paths, and control signals. The program is a FORWARD CHAINING RULE-BASED SYSTEM. Implemented in OPS5, DAA was developed at Carnegie-Mellon University.

**DART,** *n.* an expert system developed for IBM's internal use. It diagnoses computer faults. EMYCIN is the development software.

**DART,** *n. acronym for* Diagnostic Assistance Reference Tool, an expert system that uses information about the structure and behaviour of a newly created computer hardware device design to diagnose potential faults in the device. The program applies a device-independent inference procedure similar to a type of RESOLUTION THEOREM PROVING. The inference procedure works to generate a proof related to the cause of the device's malfunction. DART has been used for simple computer circuits and the teleprocessing facility of the IBM 4331. Implemented in MRS, DART was developed at Stanford University.

**DART,** *n. acronym for* Duplex Army Radio/radar Targeting aid, an expert system that Command, Control, and Communications (C3) countermeasures analysts can use to help process intelligence information. It advises the analyst about the identity of critical enemy C3 network NODES and assists in processing messages related to battle situations. Implemented in PASCAL and C, DART runs on VAX 11/780 computers. It was developed by Par Technology Corporation.

**data base,** *n.* the set of facts, assertions, and conclusions, integrated with the conditional statements of a RULE-BASED SYSTEM, that describes both the current TASK-DOMAIN situation and the GOAL. A variety of different kinds of data structures can make up the data base, including ARRAYS, LISTS, sets of PREDICATE CALCULUS expressions, PROPERTY LIST structures and SEMANTIC NETWORKS. In theorem proving, for example, the current task-domain situation consists of ASSERTIONS that represent AXIOMS, lemmas, and theorems already proved; the goal is an assertion representing the theorem to be proved. In information-retrieval applications, the current situation consists of a set of facts, and the goal is the query to be answered. In robot problem solving, a current situation is a WORLD MODEL consisting of statements describing the physical surroundings of the robot, and the goal is a description that is to be made true by a sequence of robot actions.

**data base management system (DBMS),** *n.* a set of computer programs that essentially consists of (a) an organized collection of data about some subject; and (b) a data-manipulation language for querying and altering the data. A DBMS may also include the following: a data base SCHEMA, which describes the organization of the data; CONSTRAINTS, for ensuring the integrity of the data base; views, for presenting individual users with a 'customized' version of the DATA BASE; provisions for concurrency (simultaneous access by several users); backup, which is recovery of data in the event of a system crash; and security, which serves to confine the access of various users to the parts of the data base that they may access and to the operations that they may perform.

**data-directed inference,** see FORWARD CHAINING.

**data-driven,** see FORWARD REASONING.

**data-processing system, synthesis of,** *n.* the process in AUTOMATIC PROGRAMMING by which the modelling, understanding, and writing of a data-processing PROGRAM is AUTOMATED.

**data manipulation language,** *n.* in accessing the DATA BASE, the dominant aspect of the INTERFACE that allows the user to operate on the information stored in it.

**Data Protection Act Advisor,** *n.* an expert system developed at Helix for commercial use. It classifies sensitive data. Helix Expert Edge is the development software.

**data reduction,** *n.* the process of refining the original information down to the essentials for performance. ROTE LEARNING can be viewed as the lowest level of a hierarchy of data reductions. The process of rote learning generally involves attempting to save the input/output details of some calculation and so bypass a future need for the intermediate computation process. Thus, if a calculation task is valuable and stable enough to be remembered, it is reduced to an access task.

**dead position,** *n.* see QUIESCENT POSITION.

**debugging,** *n.* the process of locating and correcting any errors within a computer routine or within the computer's hardware.

**decision table,** *n.* a method of encoding PRODUCTION RULES in order to make their execution more efficient. Assume the following set of production rules:

R1: if A and B, then D
R2: if B and (not C), then (not E)
R3: if A and B and (not C), then F

In evaluating these rules (see EVALUATION (VS DEDUCTION)), A and C are evaluated twice and B is evaluated three times. A decision table encoding these three rules appears as:

|   | R1 | R2 | R3 |
|---|----|----|----|
| A | +  |    | +  |
| B | +  | +  | +  |
| C |    | −  | −  |
| D | +  |    |    |
| E |    | −  |    |
| F |    |    | +  |

**Decision table**

A column of the decision table corresponds to a RULE. A condition is evaluated only once, and the result is used in each applicable column, thereby saving processing time.

**decision theory,** *n.* that body of knowledge that deals with choosing the best course of action. It is based on the assignment of probabilities and payoffs to all the possible outcomes of each decision.

**declarative knowledge,** *n.* the representation of FACTS and ASSERTIONS. The knowledge can be stored and retrieved but not immediately executed. The knowledge is encoded in passive data structures that must be interpreted by other procedures (PROCEDURAL KNOWLEDGE).

**DEDALUS,** *n.* an expert system that transforms program descriptions in order to aid automatic program generation. (See AUTOMATIC PROGRAMMING.)

**deduction, natural,** see NATURAL DEDUCTION.

**deduction system, rule–based,** *n.* a system in which KNOWLEDGE is represented as a set of rules that can be applied by the user to deduce conclusions.

**deductive inference,** see AUTOMATIC DEDUCTION; INFERENCE.

**deep knowledge,** *n.* KNOWLEDGE that contrasts with SURFACE KNOWLEDGE. Deep knowledge includes knowledge of basic theories, first principles, AXIOMS, and facts about a DOMAIN.

**deep structure,** *n.* a level in a GENERATIVE GRAMMAR. In the standard theory of TRANSFORMATIONAL GRAMMAR, sentence generation begins from a CONTEXT-FREE GRAMMAR generating a sentence structure and is followed by a selection of words for inserting into this structure from the lexicon. The context-free grammar and lexicon are said to form the base of the grammar; their output is called a deep structure.

**default,** *n.* a VALUE that is used when no other value is specified. Often, computer programs have prespecified values that the programs will use unless the programs are given alternative values. KNOWLEDGE SYSTEMS often store values that are used in lieu of facts. For example, a medical program may assume that a patient has been exposed to some common organism unless the user asserts that such exposure can be ruled out.

**default reasoning,** *n.* a form of extended–logical INFERENCE. The various forms of default reasoning extend beyond those inferences found in classical logical systems. One form of default, as implemented in PLANNER, is the THNOT PRIMITIVE. For example, the expression:

(THNOT OSTRICH (X) ASSUME FLIES (X))

refers to all birds, X, and means that unless it can be shown that X is an ostrich, assume that it can fly.

**degree of a tree (symbolic branching factor),** *n.* the number of successors (see SUCCESSOR NODES) of nontip NODES in a TREE.

**delete list,** *n.* a corresponding list of formulas to be deleted from a model upon application of an OPERATOR.

**delimited language,** *n.* a subclass of CONTEXT-free language.

**DELTA,** *n. acronym for* Diesel–Electric Locomotive Trouble-shooting Aid, an expert system that applies diagnostic strategies for locomotive maintenance to assist maintenance personnel to identify and correct defects in diesel electric locomotives. The program directs users through entire repair procedures. It uses computer-aided drawings to display parts and subparts, videodisk movies to present repair sequences, and it supplies specific repair instructions to correct detected problems. DELTA is a RULE-BASED SYSTEM using FORWARD and BACK-CHAINING and CERTAINTY FACTORS to handle uncertain rule premises. The program was prototyped in LISP and later implemented in FORTH to enable installation on microprocessor-based machines. It was developed by General Electric at their research and development centre in Schenectady, New York, for commercial use.

**demon,** *n.* a procedure that is activated for the purpose of accessing or changing VALUES in a DATA BASE. It is a type of suspended process that is 'waiting' for a certain kind of event to occur, such as a certain kind of update operation on a data base. The demon activates when the special event occurs, performs the job, and either terminates or suspends while awaiting another event. Demons are typically used to make INFERENCES as new information comes into the data base, to perform bookkeeping tasks of some kind, or to recognize important occurrences.

**DENDRAL,** *n. acronym for* DENDRitic ALgorithm, an expert system that uses a special ALGORITHM to infer the molecular structure of unknown compounds from mass spectral and nuclear magnetic response data. The algorithm systematically enumerates all possible molecular structures. To do so, it uses chemical expertise to reduce the list of possibilities into a manageable size. DENDRAL represents its knowledge as procedural code for the molecular structure generator and as RULES for the data-driven component and evaluator. The KNOWLEDGE about the fragmentation process in a mass spectrometer is represented in the form of PRODUCTION RULES. Each rule specifies a bond fragmentation in a particular CONTEXT in a molecule. These rules are used by DENDRAL during its test phase in order to predict mass-spectral data points, given a certain molecular structure. Implemented in INTERLISP, DENDRAL was developed at Stanford University.

**dependencies and assumptions,** *n.* a technique for recording the INFERENCE STEPS taken by a REASONING program using DEPENDENCY records to link conclusions with reasons behind them.

**dependency,** *n.* a relation occurring between the ANTECEDENTS and corresponding CONSEQUENCE that is produced when an INFERENTIAL RULE is applied. Dependencies provide a record of the manner in which decisions are derived from prior data and decisions.

**dependency grammar,** *n.* a CONTEXT-FREE GRAMMAR with word-dependency information attached to each production. That is, the right-hand side of each RULE in the GRAMMAR has a 'distinguished symbol'; the 'head' of the phrase associated with that rule is the head of the phrase associated with the distinguished symbol. All other words that are part of the phrase associated with the production are said to depend on this head. For instance, given the following simple dependency grammar and the sentence, 'The thin women in France eat vegetables' the parser could produce an ordinary phrase-structure derivation tree and also the dependency tree shown opposite.

**dependency-directed backtracking,** *n.* a programming technique that permits a system to remove the effects of incorrect assumptions during its search for a solution to a problem. As the system infers new information, it keeps DEPENDENCY records of all its deductions and assumptions, showing how they were derived. When the system finds that an assumption was incorrect, it backtracks through the chains of inferences, removing conclusions based on the faulty assumption.

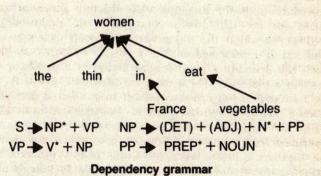

$$S \rightarrow NP^* + VP \qquad NP \rightarrow (DET) + (ADJ) + N^* + PP$$
$$VP \rightarrow V^* + NP \qquad PP \rightarrow PREP^* + NOUN$$

**Dependency grammar**

**depth,** *n.* a measure of the height of a TREE in terms of the number of levels of NODES present in the tree.

**depth bound,** *n.* a limit on the depth of NODES. To prevent consideration of paths that are too long, a maximum is often placed on the depth of nodes to be expanded, and any node at that depth is treated as if it has no successors. However, even when a depth bound is used, the SOLUTION path found is not necessarily the shortest one.

**depth map,** *n.* an indicator of depth in an IMAGE PROCESSING system. For example, in order to determine the accuracy of a TIME-OF-FLIGHT system, there are two important parameters to operate on: the beam width, W, and the smallest measurable unit of time, δt. The size of RESOLUTION elements in the dimension perpendicular to the sensor in a depth map depends on W, the beam width. The size of the resolution element in the depth dimension is determined by δt and V.

**depth–first search,** *n.* in contrast to a BREADTH-FIRST SEARCH, a search strategy within a hierarchy of RULES or OBJECTS in which one rule or object on the highest level is examined and then rules or objects immediately below that one are examined. Expanding the most recently generated, or deepest, NODE first, the system searches down a single branch of the hierarchical tree until the branch ends. Formally, the depth of a node in a TREE is defined as follows:

(a) The depth of the start node is 0.

(b) The depth of any other node is one more than the depth of its predecessor.

The search follows a single path through the STATE SPACE downward from the start node, beginning by expanding the deepest node first. If, and only if, the search reaches a state that has no successors does the search strategy consider an alternate path. In the case of alternate paths, the path is systematically redirected from those previously tried, changing only the last n steps while keeping n as small as possible. In order to prevent consideration of paths that are too long, a maximum is often placed on the depth of nodes to be expanded, and any node at that depth is treated as if it had no successors. A maximum depth (DEPTH BOUND) is used in problem spaces in which the state-space tree may be of infinite depth, or at least may be deeper than some known upper bound on the length of an acceptable SOLUTION SPACE. When implementing a depth-first search, it should be remembered that even if a depth bound is used, the solution path found is not necessarily the shortest path. The following algorithm describes depth-first search with a depth bound:

(a) Put the start node on a list, OPEN, of unexpanded nodes. If it is a goal node, it is a solution.
(b) If OPEN is empty, no solution exists.
(c) Move the first node, n, on OPEN to a list, CLOSED, of expanded nodes.
(d) If the depth of node n is equal to the maximum depth, go back to (b).
(e) Expand node n. If it has no successors, go back to (b).
(f) Place all successors of node n at the beginning of OPEN.
(g) If any of the successors of node n is a goal node, a solution has been found. Otherwise, again go to (b).

**derivation tree,** *n.* a data structure that depicts the relations between words in the sentence (e.g., 'this adjective modifies that noun, the object of a prepositional phrase ...') and is used to represent the syntactic structure of the sentence.

**design notebook,** *n.* in the PROGRAMMER'S APPRENTICE, the design notebook holds the sum total of what the Apprentice knows about the program being worked on. This information triggers additional activity by the modules.

**design space,** *n.* the middle layer at which the expert system

MOLGEN plans. At this level, MOLGEN makes decisions about how its plan is to develop. The operators of the design space dictate steps taken in the design of a plan (e.g., proposing a goal or refining an operator). The objects in this space include GOALS and CONSTRAINTS. MOLGEN reasons about plans with the objects and operators in the design space, just as it reasons about molecular genetics with the objects and operators in the planning space.

**detachment,** *n.* an operation in THEOREM PROVING where, to show X, you find an AXIOM or theorem of the form A ⊃ X and transform the problem to the problem of showing A.

**DETEKTR,** *n. acronym for* Development Environment for TEKtronix TRoubleshooters, an expert system-building tool that DOMAIN EXPERTS can use to develop expert troubleshooting systems. It features a diagram manager, a communications manager, a rule processor, and a rule acquisition subsystem built upon GLIB. Experts interact with the program via direct manipulation of OBJECTS represented on the screen. The program handles user display requirements such as displaying multiple diagrams relating to the task at hand, managing the pointing relations between them, waveform pictures, English rule text, and question-answering dialogues. Implemented in SMALLTALK-80, DETEKTR runs on the Tektronix 4404 Artificial Intelligence System. It was developed by Tektronix as a research system.

**DFT,** *abbrev. for* Design For Testability system, an expert system that applies a logical approach to checking for RULE violations in VLSI designs, and then transforms the design in order to eliminate the errors. It uses a technique called the level sensitive scan design method to help VLSI designers locate, analyse, and correct any DFT-rule violations. The program also extracts control and observation information for use in automatic test pattern generation. The program's knowledge of a digital design is represented within a LOGIC-oriented framework consisting of a set of LOGIC ASSERTIONS describing the VLSI NODE interconnects and the functions of the nodes. Implemented in PROLOG, DFT was developed at Syracuse University.

**DIA 8100,** *n.* an expert system developed by Teknowledge for Traveler's Insurance Co.'s internal use. It diagnoses routine failures of data processing equipment. M.1 is the development software.

**Diagnoser,** *n.* an expert system developed at Ross Laboratories for internal use. It diagnoses problems in manufacturing equipment. EXSYS is the development software.

**DIAGNOSER,** *n.* an expert system that uses knowledge of cardiac physiology, anatomy, and the pathophysiology of the causal structures underlying congenital heart disease to help physicians identify a congenital anomaly known as total pulmonary venus connection. The program takes as input auscultation and X-ray data, and hypothesizes about possible diseases in evidence using prototypes that fit its observations. RULES embedded in FRAMES provide the representation scheme for its diagnostic reasoning knowledge and its disease knowledge is represented as frames. DIAGNOSER was originally developed as an aid to ARTIFICIAL INTELLIGENCE researchers developing and testing predictions about the nature of errors in diagnostic reasoning. Implemented in LISP 1.4, DIAGNOSER was developed at the University of Minnesota.

**diagnostic/prescriptive consultation paradigm,** *n.* a CONSULTATION PARADIGM used for problems requiring users to identify symptoms or characteristics of a situation in order to determine an appropriate solution from among available alternative solutions. Most expert systems and tools are designed to handle this paradigm.

**Diagnostics 1,** *n.* an expert system developed by Expert Ware Inc. for commercial use. It assists DSM-111 psychiatric diagnoses. EXSYS is the development software.

**diagram, reasoning from,** *n.* a method of reasoning in the GEOMETRY THEOREM PROVER that relies heavily on a diagram to guide the proof. The system uses PROBLEM REDUCTION TECHNIQUES using the diagram for input to a set of PRUNING heuristics.

**dialectical argumentation,** *n.* a form of argumentation that uses DEPENDENCIES in explicitly guiding program actions through the process of decision-making.

**dialogue management,** *n.* the process of managing the NATURAL LANGUAGE interaction between a user and the system. (See also MIXED-INITIATIVE DIALOGUE.)

**DIALYSIS THERAPY ADVISOR,** *n.* an expert system

that applies the reasoning of medical experts specifying initial haemodialysis prescriptions in order to help physicians select an initial dialysis regimen for a patient beginning dialysis treatment. The program takes as input the patient's sex, height, weight, urine volume, and urea nitrogen concentration to generate a list of appropriate therapies. The system uses FORWARD and BACK-CHAINING to access RULES and incorporates equation solving, explanation handling, DATA BASE retrieval routines, metarules for planning, and a communication facility for user interaction. Implemented in FRANZ LISP, DIALYSIS THERAPY ADVISOR was developed at Vanderbilt University.

**difference measures,** *n*. a measure of the lack of similarity in pairs of inputs and outputs. For example, in AUTOMATIC PROGRAMMING, a classification process selects the general structure (SCHEMA) of the target program, and an INSTANTIATION process completes the details of the target program. Every schema defines a subclass of programs in the problem DOMAIN and every set of example pairs defines a family of programs in the domain. Thus, the classification process must associate this set of example pairs with one of the subclasses of programs in the domain. In order to accomplish this task, a set of characteristics is associated with each schema (subclass), which, if present in the set of example pairs, guarantees that the set specifies a program of this type. Usually, this task is accomplished by: (a) providing a set of difference measures that are applied to the inputs and outputs of an example pair, as well as to different example pairs in the input collection (if it consists of more than one), and (b) providing a set of HEURISTICS for each program schema that determines a fit measure of the example set that accompanies it. The task of classifying the example set is then reduced to choosing the schema with the highest value for fit.

**differential diagnosis,** *n*. in PIP, a technique that indicates mutually exclusive disorders, the patient may have one of them, and not the disorder represented by the current FRAME.

**differential modelling,** *n*. in ICAI, a technique that compares what the student is doing with what an expert would do in his or her place. The differences that result suggest hypotheses about what the student does not know or has not yet mastered.

**DIGITALIS ADVISOR,** *n.* an expert system that uses knowledge of patient histories to base recommendations for appropriate digitalis therapy for patients with congestive heart failure or conduction disturbances of the heart. Queries physicians about the patient's age, cardiac rhythm, and serum potassium level, enable DIGITALIS ADVISOR to generate a set of recommendations for initial therapy. From an additional set of questions to the physician, the program then analyses the patient's reaction to the initial dose and recommends a new dosage regimen. A hierarchy of concepts represented in a SEMANTIC NETWORK supplies the program's digitalis therapy expertise. An interpreter executes plans to produce relationships in the KNOWLEDGE BASE such as checking for digitalis sensitivity due to advanced age. The program's explanation facility produces explanations directly from the executed code. Implemented in OWL 1, DIGITALIS ADVISOR was developed at MIT. It differs from most other medical AI systems in that this system concentrates primarily on the problem of continuing patient management and integrates both quantitative and qualitative models.

**digitization,** *n.* the process of converting an analog signal to a digital one. For example, computer vision systems work with digitized signals rather than continuous signals direct from a TV camera. An analog-to-digital (A-D) converter is used to digitize the continuous-intensity signal, which is sampled at each PIXEL position. The number of bits required to encode the analog intensity depends on the dynamic range and the S/N ratio of the input device (typically 6 to 8 bits for most applications). For standard TV signals, 200 to 500 samples (pixels) are taken from a scan line in approximately 60 $\mu$s. Thus, sampling and A-D conversion happens every 0.12 to 0.3 $\mu$s, and data throughput is between 3 Mbyte/s and 7.5 Mbyte/s. When fast-access computer memory was expensive, many methods were devised to reduce this throughput. Today, it is common to have a buffer memory for one or more FRAMES, and the video signal is digitized in real time.

**Dipmeter Advisor,** *n.* an expert system that uses knowledge about dipmeter patterns and geology to recognize features in dipmeter data and relate them to underground geological structure. In order to infer subsurface geological structure, the program interprets dipmeter logs along with the measurements of the conductivity of rock in and around a borehole as it relates to its depth below the surface. Users interact with a menu-driven graphical interface that incorporates smooth scrolling of the log data. The program's KNOWLEDGE REPRESENTATION SCHEME is rule-based (see RULE-BASED SYSTEMS) and controlled by FORWARD CHAINING. Implemented in INTERLISP-D, DIPMETER ADVISOR runs on Xerox 1100 series workstations. It was developed by Schlumberger-Doll Research.

**direct modelling,** *n.* a method of constructing a distortion model. If there are a satisfactory number of control points, or landmarks, in an image, the distortion model can be constructed from them. A control point is a point that can be found in the distorted image and whose precise location in the ideal image is known.

**direct representation** or **analogical representation,** *n.* a KNOWLEDGE REPRESENTATION method which more naturally represents the KNOWLEDGE required to solve problems. It is useful in problem DOMAINS requiring interpreting visual scenes such as with maps, models, diagrams, and sheet music that can represent knowledge about certain aspects of the world in especially natural ways. An example of direct representation is a visual scene from a robot's camera that is encoded as an ARRAY. The array represents a grid over the scene, and the VALUES of the elements of the array represent the average brightness over the corresponding area of the scene. Representing the scene in this direct manner can be useful for such tasks as finding the boundaries of the objects in the scene. Direct representation is central to many AI tasks but seems at first quite different from the usual PROPOSITIONAL REPRESENTATION schemes like LOGIC and SEMANTIC NETWORKS. For example, a street map is a direct representation of a city in the sense that the distance between two points on the map must correspond to the distance between the places they represent in the city. It is a form of connection between the representation and the situation of what is more of a homomorphism (structural similarity) rather than a denotation.

**direction of reasoning,** see BACK-CHAINING; FORWARD CHAINING.

**directness of inference,** *n.* the extent to which the path of an INFERENCE is straightforward; the use of DOMAIN-specific HEURISTICS to avoid irrelevant or unnatural lines of reasoning.

**directness of reasoning,** *n.* the control of the reasoning process in order to guide or control the direction of reasoning. One form of control is to indicate the direction in which an implication can be used. For example, to encode the idea that to prove that something flies you might want to show that it is a bird, from which the desired conclusion follows, one might write:

$$\text{(IF-NEEDED FLIES (X)}$$
$$\text{TRY-SHOWING BIRD (X))}$$

Thus, if we are trying to prove that Ace can fly, this HEURISTIC tells us to try first to prove that he is a bird.

**DIRECTOR,** *n.* an ACTOR-based animation system.

**discourse procedure,** *n.* in ICAI, procedures that formalize how the program should behave in general terms, not in terms of the data or outcome of a particular case. A discourse procedure is a sequence of actions to be followed in a dialogue under conditions determined by the complexity of the material, the student's understanding of the material, and tutoring goals for the session. Each option available to the student generally has a discourse procedure associated with it.

**discovery in AM,** *n.* the process of learning in the system called AM. The AM PRODUCTION system modelled the process of learning in mathematics in terms of an HEURISTIC search. AM started with a minimal knowledge of mathematical concepts and used heuristics, represented as PRODUCTION RULES, to expand its KNOWLEDGE about these concepts and to discover new ones. In the course of its operation, AM discovered a large number of important mathematical CONCEPTS, such as prime numbers and the arithmetic functions, and also two mathematical concepts that had not been discovered before.

**discovery learning,** *n.* in ICAI, a method of instruction that assumes that the student constructs an understanding of a situation or a task based on prior knowledge. According to this theory, the notion of misconception, or BUG, plays a central role in the construction process. Ideally, a bug in the student's knowledge will cause an erroneous or less-than-adequate behaviour, which the student will notice. If the student has enough information to determine what caused the error and can correct it, the bug is referred to as constructive. The role of a tutor in an informal environment is to give the student extra information in situations that would otherwise be confusing. The student can then determine what caused the error and can convert nonconstructive bugs into constructive bugs.

**discrimination,** *n.* a process of learning that involves distinguishing INSTANCES from noninstances. The process involves refining an overgeneralization of a concept in order to exclude any noninstances that were once mistakenly classified as instances of the concept. The term also refers to a particular learning procedure that uses feedback information about erroneous classifications in order to refine an overgeneralization of a concept.

**discrimination net** or **discrimination tree,** *n.* a mechanism for allocating an input data item to its class by applying successive tests for different individual PREDICATES: The terminal NODES of the net represent the results to be returned for the various possible sequences of predicates. A discrimination net (D-net) is thus a nest of IF … THEN … ELSE tests all applicable to one data item, or more formally, a binary, directed, acyclic graph with unary predicates at non-terminal nodes. An example of the use of a discrimination net of this basic kind is in NATURAL LANGUAGE generation in choosing an output word for an input meaning representation. The basic mechanism can be extended by, for instance, using n-ary rather than branch selection functions, by the use of VARIABLES in the data item description and net patterns, and by use of sophisticated means of indexing. With such extensions, a net can be used, for example, to implement a PLANNER-style DATA BASE optimized for retrieving individual ASSERTIONS. Discrimination nets have an obvious attraction when the set of classes involved is high; but clearly a prerequisite for their effective application is being able to identify clear test sequences for data items.

**discussion agenda,** *n.* in SCHOLAR, an AGENDA keeps track of topics that are being discussed. Timing considerations and relevance (IMPORTANCE TAGS) affect the generation and PRUNING of topics on this agenda. Continuity between questions is weak, however, since SCHOLAR does not plan a series of questions to make a point. SCHOLAR is capable of diagnosing a student's misunderstanding by following up one question with a related question, thus leading the discussion.

**disease tree,** *n.* in INTERNIST, a method of organizing knowledge of diseases. A disease tree, otherwise known as a TAXONOMY, uses the 'form-of' relation (for example, in the case of hepatocellular disease, this disease is a form of liver disease). The top-level classification in the disease tree is by organs: heart disease, lung disease, liver disease, etc. A disease NODE's offspring are refinements of that disease, TERMINAL NODES being individual diseases. A nonterminal node and its subtree are referred to as a disease area, while a terminal node is referred to as a disease entity. The disease hierarchy is predetermined and fixed in the system. The disease tree used by INTERNIST appears below:

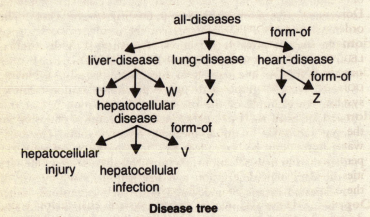

**Disease tree**

**Dispatcher,** *n.* an expert system developed by Digital Equipment Corporation for internal use. It selects, transports, and delivers parts for assembly while maintaining inventory records. VAX OPS5 is the development software.

**distributed processing,** *n.* a data processing task that performs the calculations necessary in a distributed computer network. The simultaneous performance of operations in several interconnected processors of a distributed computer network improves the efficiency of the data processing task.

**distributional analysis,** *n.* a set of HEURISTICS based on the idea of the distribution of substrings in the language. In CONTEXT-FREE LANGUAGES, certain classes of strings, such as noun phrases and prepositional phrases, tend to appear in the same contexts in different sentences. This suggests that we might discover interesting classes of strings by looking at their surroundings in the set of sample sentences.

**divide–and–conquer,** see PROBLEM REDUCTION

**domain,** *n.* **1.** a topical area of KNOWLEDGE. Examples of very large domains include engineering, medicine, or management science.
**2.** in mathematics, the set of VALUES that the argument to a function may assume. Existing KNOWLEDGE SYSTEMS provide competent advice only within very narrowly defined domains.

**domain expert,** *n.* an expert in a specific field of endeavour or knowledge whose expertise informs the EXPERT SYSTEM. Domain experts work closely with KNOWLEDGE ENGINEERS in order to build KNOWLEDGE-BASED SYSTEMS.

**domain independence,** *n.* the separation of DOMAIN KNOWLEDGE from the reasoning component of a system.

**domain knowledge,** *n.* specific knowledge about a problem DOMAIN, for example, knowledge about geology in an expert system, which is used to find mineral deposits.

**domain model,** *n.* the declarative part of SAFE that specifies the types of OBJECTS manipulated by the process, the different ways they might relate to each other, the actions that may be performed on various object types, and other global regularities of the problem DOMAIN. The procedural portion specifies the controlled application of objects.

**Doppler Diagnosis,** *n.* an expert system that helps train doctors to use non-invasive echo effect equipment. BASIC is the development software.

**DPL,** *abbrev. for* Design Procedure Language, a KNOWLEDGE ENGINEERING LANGUAGE for creating FRAME-based representations of LSI designs. It features a uniform REPRESENTATION scheme placing both design and structure information in a single set of data structures. The uniform representation scheme can serve as a DATA BASE for answering questions about the connectivity of the device as well as serve to simulate the device's behaviour. An interactive graphics editor enables users to create LSI designs as DPL procedures. Implemented in ZETALISP, DPL runs on Symbolics 3600 Lisp Machines. It was developed at MIT.

**DRAGON,** *n.* an expert system developed by Systems Designers Software for ICL (British) internal use. It configures orders for ICL's Series 39 computers. Envisage is the development software.

**Dragon,** *n.* an early speech–understanding system developed at CMU.

**DRILLING ADVISOR,** *n.* an expert system that uses knowledge of geological formations at drill sites. It uses observations of relationships between the symptoms and suspected causes of problems related to a drilling mechanism sticking within the borehole during drilling in order to help oil-rig supervisors diagnose the most likely causes of the sticking. The program recommends a set of PROCEDURES to correct the problem and reduce the potential for a recurrence. It uses a RULE-based KNOWLEDGE REPRESENTATION scheme with BACK-CHAINING. Originally implemented in KS300 and re-implemented in S.1, DRILLING ADVISOR was developed by Teknowledge in cooperation with Société Nationale Elf Aquitane.

**Drug Interaction Advisor,** *n.* an expert system developed at Miami Veterans Administration Medical Center for internal use. It detects harmful drug interactions. EXSYS is the development software.

**DRUG INTERACTION CRITIC,** *n.* an expert system that uses knowledge of drug interaction characteristics in order to help physicians decide how to administer drugs in the presence of other drugs. The program specifies both the adverse and beneficial interactions of the drugs, explains why the interactions occur, answers questions about the interactions, and suggests corrective actions for adverse effects. It also features a NATURAL LANGUAGE interface and a spelling checker, which is useful when users type the names of drugs incorrectly. Drug types are arranged as a hierarchy of FRAMES in a KNOWLEDGE BASE that includes information about specific drugs, such as a drug's affinities, storage sites, and interaction characteristics. Knowledge about the mechanism of drug interaction is represented in frames according to one of the four mechanism types: chemicophysical, pharmacodynamic, pharmacokinetic, and physiologic. Implemented in PROLOG, DRUG INTERACTION was developed at Virginia Polytechnic Institute & State University.

**DSCAS,** *abbrev. for* Differing Site Condition Analysis System, an expert system that uses a model of the decision process lawyers use when analysing differing site condition (DSC) claims in order to supply contracting officers at sites with the legal expertise to handle claims. DSC claims provide a contractually granted remedy for additional expenses incurred by a contractor when physical conditions at a site differ from those indicated in the original contract. In cases where DSCAS determines a reason for not including the additional expenses, it terminates its analysis and issues an explanation for its decision to reject the additional expenses. The program is a RULE-BASED SYSTEM with FORWARD CHAINING. Implemented in ROSIE, DSCAS was developed at the University of Colorado.

**dual semantics,** *n.* the idea of viewing a computer program from either of two equally valid perspectives: PROCEDURAL SEMANTICS, referring to what happens when the program is run, and declarative semantics, referring to the knowledge the program contains.

**DUCK,** *n.* a KNOWLEDGE ENGINEERING language for LOGIC-BASED REPRESENTATION. It features logic programming, RULE-BASED SYSTEMS, NON-MONOTONIC REASONING, deductive search, and a notation based on first-order PREDICATE CALCULUS where the conditions and actions of rules are logical predicates. It achieves non-monotonic reasoning via DEPENDENCY-DIRECTED BACKTRACKING that uses a TRUTH MAINTENANCE system and data pools, and supports FORWARD and BACK-CHAINING control schemes. Implemented in NISP, a portable dialect of LISP, DUCK operates on DEC VAX's running UNIX or VMS, the Symbolics 3600, and Apollo workstations. Smart Systems Technology developed DUCK for commercial use.

**DWIM,** *abbrev. for* Do What I Mean; in INTERLISP, a facility that attempts to figure out what the programmer really meant to say when he or she typed in an uninterpretable command; for instance, DWIM corrects spelling errors.

**Dyke Maintenance,** *n.* an expert system developed by Systems Designers Software for Rykwaterstaat Adviesdienst internal use. It advises on repairs and maintenance of dykes. Sage is the development software.

**dynamic allocation,** *n.* that property of a system that allows for the space to be used by a data object to be not fixed ahead of time but rather allowed to grow and shrink as needed (an essential attribute for list processing).

**dynamic knowledge base,** *n.* that portion of a PRODUCTION SYSTEM's memory that is allowed to change. An expert system constantly checks RULES and seeks VALUES. All values that are established must be kept immediately available until all the rules have been examined. The working memory of an expert system consists of all the ATTRIBUTE-VALUE relationships that are established during the consultation process. Working memory, which contains the DATA BASE of the system, changes as rules are executed. (See WORKING MEMORY.)

**dynamic ordering,** *n.* a procedure for reordering moves in game playing. Since accurate move–ordering is important to maximizing alpha-beta cutoffs, it might be worthwhile to go back, reorder the moves, and start again with a different estimated best move. If dynamic ordering is carried to its limit, so that reordering is considered every time a NODE is expanded, instead of only under more limited conditions, the search PROCEDURE in effect changes from DEPTH-FIRST SEARCH to BEST-FIRST SEARCH.

**dynamic process,** *n.* a process that is not represented (see RE-PRESENTATION) as a static state. For example, CASNET performs medical diagnosis of glaucoma not as a static state but as a dynamic process, modelled as a network of causally linked pathophysiological states. The system diagnoses a patient by determining the pattern of pathophysiological causal pathways present in the patient and identifying this pattern with a disease category.

**dynamic programming,** *n.* a TEMPLATE matching technique that allows the template to be 'stretched' in a linear fashion to find a best fit with the input pattern. Dynamic programming, a general purpose technique with many applications, has been used in SPEECH RECOGNITION for the purpose of recognizing words from a limited vocabulary within spoken utterances.

**dynamic range,** *n.* the ratio between the brightest and the dimmest light levels in IMAGE PROCESSING.

**dynamic scoping,** *n.* **1.** the process in a program by which VARIABLES can be referred. Accomplished dynamically, any PROCEDURE can call any other, and variable VALUES are passed down the CONTROL chain rather than being determined by the static block structure. Say a variable is declared or otherwise allocated during the execution of procedure A, it can then be accessed from within any procedure B that A calls, or any procedure C that B calls, and so forth, regardless of where A, B, and C appear in the actual program text.
**2.** scoping in LISP depends only on the calling order of FUNCTIONS and not on when or where they were declared in the program text (static scoping). During the EVALUATION of a function F, a nonlocal variable x will have the value bound to it most recently in the calling hierarchy. In other words, if x was assigned a value by the function that called F, say G, that would be the one bound to it by the function that called G.

**dynamic weighting,** *n.* a generalization of the HPA EVALUATION FUNCTION which says: $f^{\star}(n) = g^{\star}(n) + w(n)h^{\star}(n)$. That is, the relative weight w to be attached to $g^{\star}$ and $h^{\star}$ is no longer constant; the FUNCTION $w(n)$, which may be greater than or equal to 1, is defined to vary with the depth of NODE n. Using a definition of w that weights $h^{\star}$ less heavily as the search goes deeper, and with the assumption that $h^{\star}$ is a lower bound on h, it can be shown that HPA will find a solution to the travelling-salesman problem whose cost is bounded by the ratio:

$$\frac{\text{cost of tour found}}{\text{cost of optimal solution}} < 1+e$$

where e is a constant in [0,1], which appears in the definition of w.

# E

**early processing,** see PREPROCESSING.

**ECESIS,** *n. acronym for* Environmental Control Expert System In Space, an expert system that automates the control of an ENVIRONMENTAL CONTROL/life support subsystem (EC/LSS) for use aboard a manned space station. During transitions from shadow to sun, the program decides how to shift the modes of the EC/LSS subsystems. While monitoring the EC/LSS, the program responds to events by selecting and executing the appropriate action for the EC/LSS. To provide a demonstration of the system when necessary, ECESIS supplies an EXPLANATION FACILITY. ECESIS incorporates a hybrid ARCHITECTURE of both RULE-based and SEMANTIC NET schemes. To handle uncertainty, the program applies the Bayesian scoring model developed for PROSPECTOR. Implemented in YAPS, ECESIS was developed at Boeing Aerospace Company.

**economy principle,** *n.* an organizing principle for HIERARCHIES where properties of NODES are not repeated at each node which they apply, but at the highest possible node above all the subsets to which the property applies. The properties of subsets are then inferred from the superordinate nodes at which they are stored.

**EDAAS,** *n.* an expert system that uses its knowledge of both the Toxic Substances Control Act (USA) and criteria for classifying information as confidential to help information specialists decide which information about the manufacturing and distribution of toxic chemicals must be released to the public and which information may be withheld for proprietary purposes. The program reaches decisions via a RULE-based KNOWLEDGE representation scheme which applies a linear programming ALGORITHM. Implemented in FORTRAN, EDAAS was developed by Booze, Allen & Hamilton for use by the Environmental Protection Agency (EPA).

**EDDS,** *n.* an expert system developed by the Environmental

Protection Agency for internal use. It advises clerical personnel about what information in DATA BASES can be disseminated upon request.

**edge detection,** *n.* a technique for locating places in images corresponding to informative scene events, such as the SHADOW or the obscuring boundary of an object. PROJECTION of such events produces steep gradients and discontinuities in image intensity, hence the basic methods of edge detection are: to differentiate the image and threshold the resulting gradient image; to differentiate the image twice and find the ZERO-CROSSINGS in the second derivative; and TEMPLATE matching. In terms of computation, the process normally involves convolution of a neighbourhood OPERATOR with the image at every point in the image. A large number of operators have been implemented, but because precisely specifying the GOAL of edge detection is so difficult, comparing operator performance becomes difficult. Recent theories of edge detection involve applying operators to the same image at different RESOLUTIONS in resolution cones in an attempt to provide a better description of the intensity changes present in the image.

**EDITSTRUC,** *n.* an interactive structure editor in the interface of CONGEN.

**EEG ANALYSIS SYSTEM,** *n.* an expert system that uses the knowledge of an electroencephalographer to analyse electroencephalograms (EEGs) recorded from renal patients. To accept a patient's EEG directly from the EEG machine as input, the program applies a fast Fourier transformation method. On the basis of the spectral features, the program classifies the EEG as either normal or abnormal. The program uses RULES with associated CERTAINTY FACTORS as its KNOWLEDGE BASE. It explains its results by displaying the outcomes of certain rules. In addition, the program supplies a rule-editing program written in C for system developers to use when they maintain and update the rules. Implemented in assembly language and C, the EEG ANALYSIS SYSTEM is embedded in a Motorola MC6801 single-chip microprocessor. It was developed at Vanderbilt University.

**eight (8) puzzle,** *n.* a square tray containing eight square tiles of equal size, numbered 1 to 8. The space for the ninth tile is vacant. The eight-puzzle is a well-known, straight-forward example of STATE-SPACE REPRESENTATION. A tile may be moved by sliding it vertically or horizontally into the empty square. The puzzle presents the problem of transforming some particuular tile configuration, say, that of the figure (a), into another tile configuration as in figure (b).

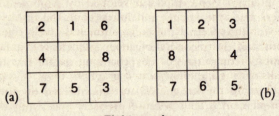

(a)                                                          (b)

**Eight puzzle**

A particular configuration of tiles constitutes a STATE. Each state can be represented in a 3x3 matrix, similar to the examples above. The OPERATORS, corresponding to possible moves, can be defined with separate operators for each of the tiles 1 to 8. A more concise definition is made possible by viewing the empty square as the object to be moved and stating the operators in terms of the movements of this square. In this formulation, only four operators are used:

UP          Move the blank up one square
DOWN        Move the blank down one square
LEFT        Move the blank left one square
RIGHT       Move the blank right one square

An operator may be inapplicable in certain states, as when it would move the blank outside the tray or tiles. (See FIFTEEN (15) PUZZLE).

**EL,** *n.* an expert system that uses knowledge of general principles of electronics and knowledge of circuit component characteristics to perform a steady-state analysis of resistor-diode-transistor circuits. The program takes as input a description of a circuit schematic. It then analyses the circuit to determine values of various circuit parameters such as voltage or current values at given points. The program is rule-based with FORWARD CHAINING and uses an indexed DATA BASE of facts and assertions. It supplies an explanation facility, which draws from the program's memory of its justifications for new assertions. Implemented in ARS, EL was developed at MIT.

**ELAS,** *n. acronym for* Expert Log-Analysis System, an expert system that supplies advice about how to control and interpret results from INLAN, a large-scale interactive program for well log analysis and display developed by Amoco. ELAS assists users by summarizing and interpreting the results of user-INLAN interaction. It also recommends well log analysis methods and warns users of inconsistencies or unfavourable directions of their analysis. By changing parameters or invoking tasks through a sophisticated graphical display, users direct both the mathematical analysis of INLAN and the interpretive analysis of ELAS. The program is rule-based. Implemented in EXPERT, ELAS was developed at Rutgers University in co-operation with Amoco Production Research.

**Eleusis,** *n.* a card game in which players attempt to discover a secret RULE developed by the dealer. The game is modelled in the learning system SPARC.

**elimination,** *n.* the process by which connectives such as → and QUANTIFIERS such as ∀ can be eliminated from a clause in LOGIC by a RULE or set of rules that substitute a different clausal form without that connective or quantifier. For example, MODUS PONENS is a form of → elimination.

**ELIZA,** *n.* a software product that permits a person to converse with the computer. It is a PATTERN-MATCHING NATURAL LANGUAGE program written at MIT. ELIZA assumes the role of a Rogerian or 'nondirective' therapist in its dialogue with the user. The computer interacts with the user by issuing typical English-like responses or questions. Although not strictly an artificial intelligence program, ELIZA is often cited as such.

**ellipsis,** *n.* the omission of DEEP STRUCTURE components in the surface realization of a sentence.

**embedding,** *n.* the process in NATURAL LANGUAGE where clauses, as constituents of a sentence, are generated from a NON-TERMINAL SYMBOL. For example, a relative clause is often generated by embedding it in a noun phrase via the rewrite rule NP → NP S.

**embedding algorithm,** *n.* an ALGORITHM in CONGEN that combines substructures found by partitioning into complete molecular structures.

**EMERGE,** *n.* an expert system that applies medical knowledge derived from medical outlines known as criteria maps to help physicians in emergency-room environments analyse chest pains. The program decides if an emergency-room patient should be admitted to the hospital. It also provides advice on treatment choices and indicates the severity of the condition. The criteria maps constitute a body of knowledge collected over a period of years from consultations with experts. The program represents this knowledge as RULES organized in a hierarchy while applying CERTAINTY FACTORS. An EXPLANATION FACILITY charts the logical paths taken by the rule searches. Implemented in PASCAL, EMERGE runs on mainframes, microcomputers, and minicomputers. It was developed at UCLA.

**EMYCIN,** *n. acronym for* Essential MYCIN, a skeletal KNOWLEDGE ENGINEERING language for RULE-based REPRESENTATION. EMYCIN was the first expert system building tool. After the developers of MYCIN (a PRODUCTION RULE system designed for medical consultations) completed that system, they decided that they could remove the specific medical knowledge from MYCIN, resulting in the Essential MYCIN shell. It features a restrictive BACK-CHAINING control scheme suitable for diagnosis and consultation-type problems, CERTAINTY handling, and automatic user querying facilities. It also includes a sophisticated interface for both acquiring new KNOWLEDGE and explaining the system's reasoning. In sum, EMYCIN is a domain-independent (see DOMAIN INDEPENDENCE) version of MYCIN. Problem-specific knowledge is represented as production rules where the ANTECEDENT is effectively a Boolean function or PREDICATES of ATTRIBUTE-OBJECT-VALUE TRIPLES and both the CONDITION and action have a certainty value associated with them. Implemented in INTERLISP, EMYCIN was originally designed to run on a DEC PDP-10 under TENEX or TOPS20. The program was developed at Stanford University.

**end-user,** *n.* the person who uses the finished expert system (or any other computer program). The person for whom the system was developed.

**enhancement,** *n.* the process of improving the input image, in later stages of IMAGE PROCESSING, by suppressing NOISE and emphasizing selected features.

**ensemble averaging,** *n.* a method in image processing used for reducing NOISE without loss of detail. The method involves obtaining multiple independent copies of the desired image. The image detail in each copy will then be identical, while the superimposed noise will vary randomly. Averaging corresponding PIXELS across the multiple copies cancels the noise without affecting the desired image, resulting in the effect of longer exposure time.

**environment,** *n.* **1.** in SOFTWARE engineering, the software and hardware available or necessary for the operation of a system.
**2.** in learning, the information from the surroundings used by a LEARNING ELEMENT for constructing a KNOWLEDGE BASE. (See also PROGRAMMING ENVIRONMENT.)

**environmental approach,** *n.* in CAI, the approach that allows the student more or less free-style use of the machine. In the case of LOGO, the student is involved in programming. It is conjectured that learning problem-solving methods takes place as a side effect of working with tools that are designed to suggest good problem-solving strategies to the student.

**envisioning,** *n.* a particular kind of qualitative reasoning. The theory of envisioning has two principal characteristics: It can be used to predict the qualitative behaviour of devices, and it is a theory of causality useful for producing causal explanations acceptable to humans. In producing a causal explanation for the behaviour of a physical system, envisioning serves to explain how disturbances from equilibrium propagate. Envisioning should not be confused with qualitative simulation, which constitutes envisioning only in its most degenerate form.

**EPES,** *n. acronym for* Emergency Procedures Expert System, an expert system that uses knowledge about aircraft features (e.g., canopy, pilot) and mission goals (e.g., maintain the current state of the aircraft) to help F-16 pilots respond to in-flight emergencies. EPES monitors the aircraft, helping to maintain constant airspeed, heading, and altitude. When emergencies arise that violate the constant values, the system warns the pilot and then takes corrective action, sending changes to a robot-pilot. The program's knowledge is represented in both RULE-based and SEMANTIC NETWORK form. The rules govern decisions the program makes about when to set net GOALS and are linked via a semantic net to all parts and goals that affect their activation. Implemented in ZETALISP, EPES was developed at Texas Instruments.

**epipolar line,** *n.* the line BC in the figure below. The image of the object in the right picture must lie somewhere along the projection of the ray OA onto the right plane, which is the epipolar line BC.

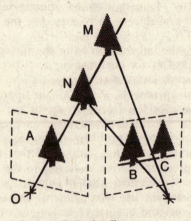

**Epipolar line**

**episode,** *n.* a sequence of event NODES connected by conjunctions.

**epistemological adequacy,** *n.* in KNOWLEDGE REPRESENTATION the adequacy of the structure to represent the basic KNOWLEDGE. For example, in a learning system a REPRESENTATION that is capable of expressing advice without losing any information.

**epistemology,** *n.* the study of the nature of KNOWLEDGE.

**error (in training instances),** *n.* mistakes in instances. If the descriptions of the instances are incorrect, for example, if a two of clubs is incorrectly observed to be a two of spades, the error is a measurement error. If, on the other hand, the classification of the hand (as being a flush) is incorrect, the error is a classification error. Two kinds of classification error can occur. The program can be told that a sample hand is a flush when in fact it is not (a false positive instance) or that it is not a flush when in fact it is (a false negative instance).

**ERS,** *n*. Embedded Rule-based System, a KNOWLEDGE ENGINEERING language for RULE-BASED REPRESENTATION. It features a PROSPECTOR-like SEMANTIC NETWORK that links rule components, automatic user querying, CERTAINTY handling routines including Bayesian and FUZZY LOGIC techniques, and the ability to invoke a set of application-specific PRIMITIVE FUNCTIONS for evaluating evidence NODES. The primitive functions can consult various DATA BASES for factual information. In addition, ERS graphically displays the results of analysis and explanations for its reasoning. Implemented in PASCAL, ERS runs on the IBM PC-XT and DEC VAX 11/780. It was developed by PAR Technology Corporation.

**ESPm,** *n*. an expert system developed at NCR for internal use. It analyses computer maintenance logs to identify future faults. S.1 is the development software.

**ETS,** *abbrev. for* Expertise Transfer System, a TOOL that DOMAIN EXPERTS can use to construct and analyse OPS5 KNOWLEDGE BASES. It serves as a system-building aid by first interviewing the expert and then helping the expert analyse an initial set of HEURISTICS and parameters for the problem. Applying elicitation techniques based on personal construct theory work in psychotherapy, the program helps the expert express the problem in terms of a rating grid. The program generates RULES with CERTAINTY FACTORS that experts can review and modify. Implemented in INTERLISP-D, ETS runs on Xerox 1100 series workstations and was developed by Boeing Computer Services.

**EURISKO,** *n*. a system that learns new HEURISTICS and new DOMAIN-specific definitions of CONCEPTS in a problem domain. The program can learn by discovery in a number of different problem domains, including VLSI design. In particular, EURISKO has undertaken the problem of inventing new kinds of three-dimensional microelectronic devices that can be fabricated using laser recrystallization techniques, and has also designed new and interesting microelectronic devices.

The program operates by generating a device configuration, computing its input/output behaviour, assessing its functionality, and then evaluating the device against other comparable devices. Implemented in INTERLISP to run on Xerox 1100 series workstations, EURISKO was developed at Stanford University. The program is more an AI program for learning by discovery than an expert system.

**EVAL,** *n.* a function in LISP that serves as an INTERPRETER for LISP and as a formal definition of the language.

**evaluation (versus deduction),** *n.* the calculation of a value. If a description of a problem situation is complete in terms of the OBJECTS, properties, and relations relevant to the problem, any question can be answered by evaluation–deduction is unnecessary. To illustrate, if we have a KNOWLEDGE BASE of personnel information for a company and we want to know whether there is any salesman who is older than a vice-president, we could express this question in FIRST-ORDER LOGIC as:

$$\text{SOME } (X, Y) \; ( \; (\text{TITLE}(X) = \text{SALESMAN}) \text{ AND}$$
$$(\text{TITLE}(Y) = \text{VICE-PRESIDENT}) \text{ AND}$$
$$(\text{AGE}(X) > (\text{AGE}(Y))).$$

If we have recorded in our knowledge base the job title and age of every employee, we can simply find the age of each salesman and compare it with the age of every vice president. No deduction is involved in this process. (See also VALIDATION.)

**evaluation function,** *n.* In SEARCH, the measure by which the promise of a NODE is estimated. It is a procedure used to determine the VALUE or worth of proposed intermediate steps during an exploration through a SEARCH SPACE.

**event,** *n.* an occurrence, usually contrasted with OBJECT.

**event–driven,** *n.* a characteristic of processing which uses EVENTS as inputs. See BACK-CHAINING.

**event list,** *n.* a LIST of current EVENTS that triggers the KNOWLEDGE SOURCES most likely to make headway. It is used in CRYSALIS, which uses an EVENT-DRIVEN CONTROL structure. Within this scheme, the state of the HYPOTHESIS space determines what to do next. The monitor continually refers to the event list.

**event queue,** *n.* a list of potential MATCHES to the phonetic input to HWIM.

**evolutionary development (of software),** *n.* the technique of iteratively designing, implementing, evaluating, and refining computer applications, especially characteristic of the process of building expert systems.

**EXAMINE,** *n.* a function in CONGEN to survey, classify, display, or discard structures. Often in the course of a structure-elucidation problem, a large number of candidate structures, perhaps a hundred or more, are generated, and additional CONSTRAINTS must be derived, either from further data analysis or from new experiments. The EXAMINE function is very useful to the chemist who is searching for features common to a large number of the structures or for features that are unique to certain structures. The insights gained from EXAMINE can be used in planning new experiments or in further data analysis. In pursuit of these objectives, the chemist can define functional groups and other structural features or can work with a predefined library of them. The EXAMINE function is then called, and it examines the list of candidate structures for the presence or absence of these features. While CONGEN is always able to discard or prune away structures not satisfying certain constraints, EXAMINE provides the interactive ability to develop Boolean combinations of constraints for PRUNING, substructure SEARCH, or subsequent classification.

**EXAMINER,** *n.* an expert system that uses HEURISTIC and medical knowledge to analyze a physician's diagnostic behaviour when diagnosing cases in internal medicine. The program presents a physician with a hypothetical case and requires the physician to determine the disease most likely to cause the symptoms of the case. It also allows the physician to indicate any other diseases or problems that could be present or result from the case. To perform its analysis of the physician's responses to the case, the program relies on two types of KNOWLEDGE: heuristic knowledge about how to relate diseases to their manifestations, and medical knowledge obtained from the INTERNIST DATA BASE. EXAMINER presents and evaluates the physician's diagnosis in a text commentary in which the physician's correct assumptions are acknowledged and incorrect assumptions are noted and explained. Procedures embodying the principles of internal medicine structure the program's knowledge. Implemented in LISP, EXAMINER was developed at the University of Pittsburgh.

**example–driven system,** see INDUCTION SYSTEM.

**EXCHECK,** *n*. an expert system that teaches university-level courses in LOGIC, set theory, and proof theory.

**exhaustive search,** *n*. a systematic PROBLEM-SOLVING technique used to find an acceptable solution involving a 'brute-force' attempt to try all possible solutions. A SEARCH is exhaustive if every possible path through a decision TREE or network is examined. For many problems, exhaustive search is a costly or impossible process. KNOWLEDGE SYSTEMS often search exhaustively through their KNOWLEDGE BASES.

**existential quantification,** *n*. the notion in PREDICATE CALCULUS, denoted by E, that states that the clause P(X) is true for at least one object.

**expanding procedure calls,** *n*. the substituting of the body of a PROCEDURE for each of the calls to it. The potential benefit arises from simplifications made possible by use of the local CONTEXT.

**expansion of a node,** *n*. the PROCEDURE for finding all the SUCCESSORS of a given NODE, that is, all the states that can be reached from the current state by a single OPERATOR application.

**expectation–based filtering,** *n*. a process that selects TRAINING INSTANCES that contradict the hypothesis in H. The hypotheses in H are used to filter out those instances that are expected to be true (i.e., those that are consistent with H), in order that the learning program can focus its attention on those instances in which its current hypotheses break down.

**expectation–driven processing,** *n*. a method of looking for things that are expected based on the CONTEXT one thinks one is in. FRAMES provide a structure, a framework, within which new data are interpreted in terms of CONCEPTS acquired through previous experience.

**expectation–driven reasoning,** *n*. a CONTROL PROCEDURE that uses current data and decisions in order to formulate hypotheses about EVENTS not yet observed but predictable from CONTEXT. The procedure also serves to confirm, disprove, or monitor expected events.

**experiencer,** *n.* a deep case in CASE GRAMMAR that indicates the entity that receives, accepts, experiences, or undergoes the effect of an action.

**experiential knowledge,** *n.* knowledge that results from actual experience. In contrast to DEEP KNOWLEDGE of formal principles or theories, experiential knowledge typically consists of specific facts and SURFACE KNOWLEDGE rules-of-thumb.

**experiment planning,** *n.* see INSTANCE SPACE.

**EXPERT,** *n.* a KNOWLEDGE ENGINEERING language for RULE-based REPRESENTATION that is used often for medical applications. It features a FORWARD CHAINING CONTROL scheme designed for diagnosis or classification-type problems, CERTAINTY handling routines, and efficient and transportable code. A sophisticated user interface provides facilities for explanation, acquisition, and consistency checking. Implemented in FORTRAN, EXPERT runs on both DEC and IBM computers. It was developed at Rutgers University.

**Expert (in PSI),** *n.* a module type of the PSI system. The system has eight experts: parser/interpreter, dialogue moderator, explainer, examples/trace inference, task domain, program-model builder, coding, efficiency.

**Expert Agriculture Information System,** *n.* an expert system developed for the National Agriculture Library USDA for commercial use. It helps library users find references. First Class is the development software.

**EXPERT NAVIGATOR,** *n.* an expert system that monitors, manages, and reconfigures navigation sensors aboard tactical aircraft. The program confirms the ability of navigation sensors such as radio aids, inertial navigation systems, and digital terrain aids to support the aircraft's primary mission. It also issues remedial advice when the primary mission is threatened. RULES operating within a BLACKBOARD ARCHITECTURE constitute the program's KNOWLEDGE. Implemented in LISP, EXPERT NAVIGATOR runs on the Symbolics 3600 workstation. It was developed at the Analytic Sciences Corporation.

**expert system,** *n.* a computer program with a KNOWLEDGE BASE of EXPERTISE capable of reasoning at the level of an expert in some given DOMAIN; a computer program that can perform at, or near, the level of a human expert. Evaluations of MYCIN judge its competence at or near that of highly specialized physicians. Configuration systems like XCON (RI) may well exceed human competence. The term is often used to refer to any computer system that was developed by means of a loose collection of techniques associated with AI research. In effect, any computer system developed by means of an expert system building tool qualifies as an expert system, even if the system was so narrowly constrained that it could never be said to rival a human expert. Some prefer to reserve the term 'expert system' to denote systems that truly rival human experts and use 'KNOWLEDGE SYSTEM' when speaking of small systems developed by means of AI techniques. As computer programs that use expert knowledge to attain high levels of performance in a narrow problem area, expert systems typically represent knowledge symbolically, examine and explain their reasoning processes, and address problem areas that require years of special education, training, and experience for humans to master. The user of an expert system typically interacts with the system in a consultation dialogue, just as he or she would interact with a human who possesses some type of expertise. For example, the user would explain the problem, perform tests suggested by the expert, and ask questions about proposed solutions. In sum, expert systems can be viewed as an instrument providing a medium for both human experts, who interact with the systems in a KNOWLEDGE ACQUISITION mode, and human users, who interact with the systems in a consultation mode.

**EXPERT-EASE,** *n.* a TOOL that DOMAIN EXPERTS can use to construct an expert system. The expert first defines the problem in terms of procedures that lead to particular results. The program then serves as a system-building aid by querying the expert for examples describing conditions that lead to each result in order to generate a decision TREE to represent the problem-solving procedure. Implemented in PASCAL, EXPERT-EASE runs on IBM PCs and XTs with 128k of memory. It was developed by Intelligent Terminals Ltd. of Great Britain for commercial use.

**expertise,** *n.* proficiency in a specialized DOMAIN. The skill and knowledge some people possess and use to achieve above average performance. Expertise typically involves combining large amounts of information with rules-of-thumb (HEURISTIC RULES that simplify and improve approaches to problem-solving), rare facts, METAKNOWLEDGE and METACOGNITION, and compiled forms of behaviour that yield substantial economy in skilled performance. An expert system should simulate expert performance proportional to that of a human expert with 5 to 10 years of training and experience in the DOMAIN.

**expertise module,** *n*. the 'expert' component of an ICAI system that is charged with the task of generating problems and evaluating the correctness of the student's solutions.

**expert–system–building tool,** *n*. the programming language and support package KNOWLEDGE ENGINEERS use to build an EXPERT SYSTEM.

**EXPERT-2,** *n*. a KNOWLEDGE ENGINEERING language for RULE-based REPRESENTATION. It features a BACK-CHAINING RULE interpreter and support for analytic subroutines permitting full access to its underlying FORTH system. The subroutines include routines for interfacing with users or specialized data processing. Implemented in FORTH, EXPERT-2 runs on the Apple II microcomputer. It was developed by Helion Inc. as an experimental system.

**explanation,** *n*. the process of describing how an expert reached conclusions or why an expert asked particular questions of a user. Explanations typically serve to justify decisions or choice of PROBLEM-SOLVING strategies. In KNOWLEDGE SYSTEMS, explanations help users to understand the actions of the system. Many systems permit users to ask 'Why,' 'How,' or 'Explain'. For each case, the system presents information intended to reveal any assumptions or inner reasoning it applied in its actions. The system presents the goals, laws, or HEURISTIC RULES that motivated a given action.

**explanation facility,** *n*. the part of an expert system that explains how solutions were reached. It serves to justify the steps used to reach the solutions.

**explicit versus implicit knowledge representation,** *n*. the controversy concerning whether or what part of a KNOWLEDGE scheme can be explicit and which can be computed. What knowledge can the programmer and the system manipulate, and what knowledge is built in? For example, an operating system has an explicit representation of its priority queues, but its full knowledge about deciding which of several users to serve first is typically hidden deep in a large body of code. The knowledge is there, because the system behaves in a knowledgeable way, but it is implicit in the system's program. A particular advantage of explicit representation schemes is that, because the facts are in a form allowing a global interpretation, the same fact can be used for more than one purpose.

**EXPRS,** *abbrev. for* EXpert PRolog System, a KNOWLEDGE ENGINEERING language for RULE-based REPRESENTATION. It features an English-like rule format, an ATTRIBUTE-OBJECT-VALUE TRIPLE KNOWLEDGE REPRESENTATION scheme, and a FORWARD and BACK-CHAINING INFERENCE mechanism. The English-like nature of the rules aids the adding of complex rules and enables EXPRS to generate automatically answers to questions about why and how a rule fired. EXPRS has an automatic bookkeeping system that supports the EXPLANATION FACILITY. PROLOG code can also be accessed directly using a rule clause form. Implemented in PROLOG, EXPRS runs on DEC-10 computers and was developed by the Lockheed Palo Alto Research Laboratory.

**extended discourse,** *n.* that part of TEXT GENERATION that deals with lengthy dialogues and such notions as SPEECH ACTS.

**extended grammar parser,** *n.* a parser that extends the concept of PHRASE-STRUCTURE RULES and derivations by adding mechanisms for more complex representations and manipulations of sentences. Methods such as AUGMENTED TRANSITION NETWORK grammars (ATNS) and charts provide additional resources for the parser to draw on beyond the simple phrase-structure approach. These mechanisms vary with respect to some linguistic theory; others are merely computationally expedient. (See PHRASE STRUCTURE GRAMMAR.)

**extended inference,** *n.* INFERENCE modes that are outside the provision of ordinary LOGIC. These include intuitionistic logic and recursive function theory.

**extensibility,** *n.* a feature of a programming language that allows for additional features to be added (e.g., QLISP, which is an extension of INTERLISP versus PLANNER and CONNIVER, which are distinct LANGUAGE SYSTEMS built on MACLISP).

# F

**facet,** *n.* a FRAME representation element that is filled with designated information about the particular situation. Facets denote the intrinsic features, such as name, definition, or creator. Facets may also represent derived attributes, such as VALUE, significance, or analogous objects. A facet is also an attribute associated with a NODE in a frame system. The node may stand for an object, concept, or EVENT. (See also SLOT.)

**fact,** *n.* a PROPOSITION or datum whose validity is accepted. In most KNOWLEDGE SYSTEMS, a fact consists of an attribute and a specific associated VALUE. (See DECLARATIVE KNOWLEDGE.)

**FAITH,** *n.* an expert system that uses knowledge of data contained in the telemetry stream to troubleshoot general spacecraft problems. The program monitors the telemetry stream, evaluating the data in an effort to determine the source of a problem. The telemetry stream is a transmission to earth that contains test measurements from a variety of a spacecraft's subsystems. FRAMES are used to represent declarative KNOWLEDGE and they are expanded into logical assertions when necessary. PRODUCTION RULES are used to represent PROCEDURAL KNOWLEDGE. PREDICATE LOGIC in combination with FORWARD and BACK-CHAINING are also used in the knowledge scheme. FAITH was developed at the Jet Propulsion Laboratory.

**FALCON,** *n.* an expert system that identifies probable causes of process disturbances in a chemical process plant by interpreting data consisting of numerical VALUES from gauges and the status of alarms and switches. The program interprets the data by using KNOWLEDGE of the effects induced by a fault in a given component and of how disturbances in the input of a component will lead to disturbances in the output. Knowledge is represented in two ways — as a set of RULES controlled by FORWARD CHAINING and as a causal model in network form. Implemented in LISP, FALCON was developed at the University of Delaware.

**fallacy,** *n.* an assertion that, no matter what assignment of VALUES is used, is always false. Formally:

$$\neg\,(x \vee y) \equiv \neg(\,\neg\,y \wedge \,\neg\,x)$$

describes a contradiction or fallacy. It states : 'To say X or Y is false, is the same as saying "X is false and Y is false" is false.'

**Fan Vibrator Advisor,** *n.* an expert system developed at Stone & Webster for internal use. It troubleshoots industrial fan problems. EXSYS is the development software.

**fan-out,** *n.* in logic circuitry, the number of parallel loads within a given logic family that can be driven from one output mode of a circuit.

**feature,** *n.* characters of a MACHINE VISION image, including edges, contours, silhouettes, transitions from black to white, or vice versa, PIXEL amplitudes, edge-point locations and textual descriptors, or more elaborate patterns such as boundaries and REGIONS.

**feedback,** *n.* the return of information to the user. The role of feedback in LEARNING SYSTEMS is to provide some routine for evaluating the hypotheses that have been proposed by the learning element. The role of the performance element is to provide such feedback.

**FG502-TASP,** *n.* an expert system that applies ad hoc RULES together with HEURISTICS compiled from experienced technicians to help technicians diagnose malfunctioning Tektronix FG502 FUNCTION generators. The program queries technicians for the guidelines of the diagnosis. It also provides technicians with a display of the parts layout on the relevant circuit board and depicts the appropriate waveform as it appears when measured at a given point on the board. It is an object-oriented system (see OBJECT-ORIENTED METHODS) implemented in SMALLTALK-80 at Tektronix.

**fifteen (15) puzzle,** *n.* a task like the EIGHT (8) PUZZLE but which uses 15 titles in a 4 × 4 array.

**fifth-generation computers,** *n.* a name for the next generation of computers. With fundamentally new designs, these computers will likely be larger and faster than the present available technology. Substantially increased computational power is expected to result from PARALLEL PROCESSING – that is, the ability of a computer to process several different programs simultaneously. Since expert systems tend to be very large and involve a large amount of processing, it is unlikely that expert systems will reach maturity until these more powerful machines are available.

**filtering,** *n*. excluding either the data or RULES from the MATCH process for the sake of efficiency.

**Financial Advisor,** *n*. an expert system developed by Palladian Software for commercial use. It helps managers analyse capital investment proposals. LISP is the development software.

**finite termination property,** *n*. that property of a REDUCER in THEOREM PROVING where there is no sequence of expressions $t_0, t_1, ..., t_n$, where $t_{i+1}$ is an immediate reduction of $t_i$.

**finite–state transition diagram (FSTD),** *n*. a theoretical device that consists of a set of states (NODES) with ARCS leading from one state to another. One state is designated the START state. The arcs of the FSTD are labelled with the terminals of the grammar (i.e., words of the language), indicating which words must be found in the input to allow the specified transition. A subset of the states is identified as FINAL; the device is said to accept a sequence of words if, starting from the state at the beginning of the sentence, it can reach a FINAL state at the end of the input. FSTDs can recognize only regular (type 3) languages. In order to recognize a language, a machine must be able to tell whether an arbitrary sentence is part of the language or not. FSTD's are only powerful enough to recognize regular languages (those languages whose REWRITE RULES are restricted to the form $Y \rightarrow aX$ or $Y \rightarrow a$). These are the simplest languages. In other words, building an FSTD that can dependably distinguish the sentences in even a context-free language is impossible. For example, the FSTD opposite has the start state S as the left-most node and the final state is labelled F. It will accept any sentence that begins with the definite article 'the,' ends with a noun, and has an arbitrary number of adjectives in between. Following through the net with the input phrase 'the handsome lad' begin in the S state and proceed along the arc labelled 'the' because that is the left-most word in the input string. This leaves us in the middle box, with 'handsome lad'

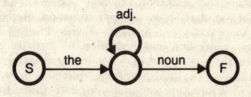

**Finite-state transition diagram**

left as the string to be parsed. After one loop around the adjective arc, we are again at the middle node, but this time with the string 'lad' remaining. Since this word is a noun, we proceed to the F node and arrive there with no words remaining to be processed. Thus, the parse is successful; in other words, our sample FSTD accepts this string.

**first–order logic,** *n.* a LOGIC that permits quantification over individuals but not over PREDICATES and FUNCTIONS. A statement that says, 'All predicates have only one argument,' cannot be expressed in a first order theory.

**FIT,** *n.* a program for LOGIC-BASED REPRESENTATION, which can be viewed as an INTEGRATION of some of PROLOG's relational features with functional LISP features. Consisting of a kernel and an interactive user interface, the principal characteristics of FIT include breadth–oriented, nonchronological parallelism, and the ability to define ALGORITHMS as FUNCTIONS or RELATIONS and then dynamically use the functions as relations or the relations as functions. FIT retains the nonsequenced meaning of logical conjunction by using simultaneous evaluation (AND parallelism). Implemented in a purely functional subset of UCI-LISP, FIT runs on DEC-10 computers, and was developed at the University of Hamburg.

**fixed ordering of successor nodes in search,** *n.* a scheme devised for ordering the successors of a NODE, so that the best successor of each node is chosen. Such fixed ordering of successors is an example that applies the STATIC EVALUATION FUNCTION to the successors. In general, it is desirable that the best successor of each node be the first one evaluated. In effect, the first move MAX considers should be its best move, and the first reply considered for MIN should be the move that is best for MIN and worst for MAX. Fixed ordering applies the static evaluation function, taking the results of this preliminary evaluation as an approximation of their expected BACKED-UP VALUES. A method of this kind will result in depth-first generation and evaluation of a partial game TREE, subject to the DEPTH BOUND or other criteria for terminating the SEARCH. The fixed-ordering method is probably the simplest idea for move ordering. For each move from a node, generate a new node for the resulting position, apply the static evaluation function to the position, and order the nodes according to this preliminary estimate. For greater efficiency, several programs have used a separate function for move ordering, which applies to the move itself instead of the position that results from it.

**fixed-increment perceptron algorithm,** *n.* an ALGORITHM in perception models that computes a weight ratio to minimize the CLASSIFICATION (ID3) errors. If $x_k$ is an instance of class 1 and $y = w_k x_k$ is less than 0, instead of greater than 0, an error has been made. The magnitude of this error is $e = 0 - w_k x_k$, that is, the difference between the desired VALUE for the output of the system ($y = 0$) and the value computed by the model ($y = w_k x_k$). This is usually written as the PERCEPTRON criterion,

$$J_p = -w_k x_k,$$

and the goal of learning is to minimize $J_p$. The fixed-increment algorithm updates $w_k$ whenever $J_p > 0$ according to

$$w_k + 1 = w_k + x_k.$$

**FLAVORS,** *n.* a programming language for OBJECT-ORIENTED REPRESENTATION within ZETALISP. FLAVORS augments the ZETALISP ENVIRONMENT, permitting ZETALISP to support OBJECTS (similar to the way STROBE provides object-oriented support for INTERLISP). The principal characteristics of FLAVORS include simple definition of abstract types, message passing, and GENERALIZATION HIERARCHIES. The language also allows PROPERTY LISTS to be associated with objects. Implemented in ZETALISP, FLAVORS runs on the

Symbolics 3600 series workstations, and was developed by Symbolics for commercial use.

**focus of attention,** see SELECTIVE ATTENTION.

**FOL,** *n.* a flexible proof checker for proofs stated in FIRST-ORDER LOGIC. A NATURAL DEDUCTION system performs deduction using introduction and ELIMINATION rules of INFERENCE.

**FOLIO,** *n.* an expert system that uses knowledge about classes of securities (dividend-oriented, lower-risk stocks, and commodity-sensitive, higher-risk stocks) and their properties (rate of return) to help portfolio managers establish client investment goals and select portfolios to best meet the goals. The program queries the user about the client's needs and recommends funds based on the most favourable percentage of each fund to meet the client's GOAL. The program uses a RULE-based KNOWLEDGE scheme controlled by FORWARD CHAINING to infer client's goals and applies linear programming to maximize the value between the goals and the portfolio. Implemented in MRS, FOLIO was developed at Stanford University.

**FOO,** *n.* a program that accepts advice about how to play the card game of hearts.

**FOREST,** *n.* an expert system that uses knowledge of the use of circuit diagrams, general electronic troubleshooting principles, and expert engineers' experience to isolate and diagnose faults in electronic equipment. The program supplements the fault detection capabilities of current automatic test equipment (ATE) diagnostic software. The program's KNOWLEDGE is represented using RULES with PROSPECTOR-like CERTAINTY factors combined with a MYCIN-like EXPLANATION facility. Implemented in PROLOG, FOREST was developed at the University of Pennsylvania in cooperation with RCA Corporation.

**forgetting,** *n.* the loss of information or its becoming inaccessible in a cognitive system.

**formal derivative,** *n.* the formal derivative of a set of strings:

$$D_s L = \{t | \text{the string } st \text{ is in the language L}\},$$

that is, all of the strings *t* that follow *s* in the given language L in sentences where *s* is at the beginning of the sentence.

Formal derivatives are employed in constructing regular GRAMMARS.

**formalism,** *n.* any transcription system that represents KNOWLEDGE in a way such that SYNTACTIC and SEMANTIC rules can be applied on some OBJECT in order to achieve an INTERPRETATION easily and correctly.

**formal language,** *n.* a (possibly infinite) set of strings of finite length formed from a finite vocabulary of SYMBOLS.

**formal reasoning,** *n.* a reasoning process that involves the syntactic manipulation of data structures in order to deduce new ones following prespecified rules of INFERENCE. Mathematical logic is the typical formal representation.

**formula,** *n.* a REPRESENTATION of the sense of a word in Wilks's MACHINE TRANSLATION system. It is composed of elements combined into a binarily bracketed list-data structure.

**forward chaining,** *n.* one of several CONTROL STRATEGIES that regulate the order in which INFERENCES are drawn. Forward chaining is a control procedure that produces new decisions recursively by first asserting the truth of all the CONSEQUENT propositions associated within an inferential RULE whose if-clauses (ANTECEDENT conditions) are true. Given the facts already established, additional rules that might be true can then be checked. The process is repeated until the program reaches a GOAL or runs out of new possibilities. For example, to prove X where X has the form $A \supset C$, find an AXIOM or theorem of the form $A \supset B$ and transform the problem of proving $B \supset C$.

**forward pruning** or **plausible-move generation,** *n.* a technique of limiting the number of moves to be considered. Forward pruning works by generating all LEGAL MOVES at a position, using a fixed-ordering scheme to sort them according to their apparent goodness, or PLAUSIBILITY, and then discarding all but the best few moves. In tapered forward pruning the number of moves to be retained is a function of the DEPTH at which they were generated. (See GOODNESS OF FIT, FIXED ORDERING OF SUCCESSOR MODES IN SEARCH.)

**forward reasoning,** *n.* applying OPERATORS to those structures in the DATA BASE that describe the task-DOMAIN situation in order to produce a modified situation. The objective of forward reasoning is to bring the situation, or problem

STATE, forward from its initial configuration to one satisfying a GOAL CONDITION. For example, an initial situation might be the placement of chessmen on the board at the beginning of the game; the desired goal, any board configuration that is a checkmate; and the OPERATORS, RULES for the legal moves in chess.

**frame (object or unit),** *n*. a data structure (or KNOWLEDGE REPRESENTATION method) for representing DECLARATIVE and procedural information in terms of predefined internal relations. Frames associate FEATURES with NODES representing concepts or objects, and are similar to the PROPERTY-LIST, SCHEMA, UNIT, and RECORD, as these terms are used in conventional programming. In the case of a frame that represents a cat, the frame could consist of KNOWLEDGE hooks, also called SLOTS. The slots contain facts typical of knowledge associated with cats, such as the BREED, OWNER, and NAME. The frame can include an attached procedure for identifying the cat's owner if the owner is unknown. The frame-like language KRL could produce a cat frame in the following form:

```
Generic CAT Frame
    Self    :    an ANIMAL; a PET
    Breed   :    Persian
    Owner   :    a PERSON
                 (If-Needed: find a PERSON with pet=myself)
    Name    :    a PROPER NAME (DEFAULT =Felix)
CAT-NEXT-DOOR Frame
    Self    :    a CAT
    Breed   :    tom
    Owner   :    Alice
    Name    :    Garfield
```

Frames may be arbitrarily complex, and have PROCEDURES (self-contained pieces of code) attached to the slots for the purpose of adding or removing VALUES from the slots. DEFAULT values for the slots are helpful when frames are exploited in the absence of full INSTANTIATION data. The character of frames suggests a hierarchical organization of sets of frames, but non-hierarchical filling of one frame slot by another is possible. Many regard frame structures as not implying temporal or causal relations between their slots. Thus, frame structures are often contrasted with SCRIPTS. However, consensus surrounding the use of frames is far from consistent; one person's frame is often another's script, and vice versa. The central problem encountered in systems using frames is frame selection and replacement. In addition, where CASE representations deal primarily with single sentences or acts, frames are applied to whole situations, complex objects, or series of events. In analysing a sentence, narrative, or dialogue, a frame-based LANGUAGE UNDERSTANDING system tries to match the input to the PROTOTYPES of objects and EVENTS in its DOMAIN that are stored in its DATA BASE.

**frame-based representation,** *n.* a form of KNOWLEDGE REPRESENTATION which relies on FRAMES as its major data structure.

**frame problem,** *n.* the inability of many REPRESENTATION FORMALISMS to model side effects, or sequences, of actions taken in the WORLD by modifying the DATA BASE that represents the STATE OF THE WORLD. The frame problem identified by McCarthy and Hayes has no relationship to frames as a representation formalism. As an example of a frame problem, suppose we are reasoning about a robot, with a key, moving from BEDROOM A to BEDROOM B to find and unlock a box. The initial situation, $S_0$, might be represented in the data base with assertions like:

   (a) IN (BEDROOM A, ROBOT, $S_0$)
   (b) IN (BEDROOM A, KEY, $S_0$)
   (c) IN (BEDROOM B, BOX, $S_0$)

After the robot has moved from BEDROOM A to BEDROOM B, the system must somehow know that assertions (a) and (b) are now false, while assertion (c) is still true. In a large system with many facts, keeping track of these changes can be an intractable task; especially in the case of keeping track of the side effects of actions, like moving the key to the box. Propagating those facts that have not changed is sometimes easier to achieve in a PROCEDURAL SYSTEM: the PROCEDURE that performs the actions can update the data base immediately.

**frame-based methods,** *n.* programming methods using

FRAME hierarchies for INHERITANCE and PROCEDURAL ATTACH-MENT.

**frame–oriented CAI,** *n.* a phrase coined to stress dependence on author-specified units of information. The term FRAME as it is used in this context predates the usage in AI research on KNOWLEDGE REPRESENTATION, and refers to a page or unit of text. (See CAI.)

**Fregean knowledge representation,** see PROPOSITIONAL KNOWLEDGE REPRESENTATION.

**frequency domain,** *n.* in IMAGE PROCESSING, the spatial frequencies in the image. Edges constitute high frequency, and homogeneous or blurred regions, low frequency.

**FRL,** *abbrev. for* Frame Representation Language, a KNOWLEDGE REPRESENTATION language that is based on FRAMES. For each 'frame,' there are a certain number of 'SLOTS,' with each slot consisting of a number of 'FACETS.' Each 'datum' (facet entry) can have a list of 'comments', where each comment consists of some label or keyword followed by a list of 'messages'. FRL's principal characteristics include support for multiple IN-HERITANCE, defaults, CONSTRAINTS such as requirements and preferences, abstraction, and indirection. FRL permits PROCEDURAL ATTACHMENT; three of the six standard facet names being 'if-added', 'if-removed', and 'if-needed'. FRL is implemented as an INTERPRETER written in LISP, and was developed at MIT.

**full–width searching,** *n.* the idea that all legal moves from a position must be examined, at least sufficiently to establish that they can be safely pruned by the ALPHA-BETA PRUNING method. (See PRUNING.)

**FUNARG,** *n.* a mechanism of LISP that permits FUNCTIONS to be used in CONTEXT-dependent ways when desired. FUNARG is a call to a LISP function together with an ENVIRONMENT, or context for the variables used by the function. For example, FUNARGs can be used to implement GENERATORS.

**function** or **operator,** *n.* a component of PREDICATE CALCULUS that takes a fixed number of arguments in a fashion similar to predicates. In contrast to the TRUE or FALSE values predicates return, functions return OBJECTS related to their arguments. The function Father of, for instance, when applied to the individual Stephen, would return the value

Raoul. Other examples of functions are absolute-value, plus, and left-arm-of. In addition, each of the arguments of a function can be a VARIABLE, a constant, or a function containing its own arguments. Further, combining functions occurs in many cases. An example of combining a function would be (father-of (father-of (Stephen))), which would return the value Luke, Stephen's paternal grandfather.

**Functional Description Compiler,** *n*. a compiler that uses a MEANS-ENDS ANALYSIS to transform a known (compiled) routine into a new (desired) routine. It is a precursor to later work in automatic modification and DEBUGGING of programs.

**functional grammar,** *n*. a declarative expression of the relation between SURFACE STRUCTURE and functional structure in a NATURAL LANGUAGE. Functional grammar is equally suitable for use in PARSING and generation. A directed acyclic graph of ATTRIBUTES and VALUES indicating the functional roles played by sentence constituents (e.g., subject, modifier) characterizes the functional structure. Functional grammar has been adopted by a number of language generation systems as the basis of their GRAMMAR.

**functional relationship,** *n*. a factor that usually specifies DOMAIN-specific KNOWLEDGE about events. A functional relationship has four components: (a) a set of ACTORS, each with a role in the process; (b) a set of factors that affect the process, all of which are ATTRIBUTES of the actors (e.g., water is an actor in the evaporation relationship and its temperature is a factor); (c) the result of the process, which is always a change in an attribute of one of the actors; and (d) the relation that holds between the actors and the result, or how an attribute gets changed. These functional relationships may be the result of models from other domains that are applied metaphorically to the domain under discussion.

**FUZZY,** *n*. a language designed to aid certain types of reasoning with fuzzy sets. The design of the FUZZY language was motivated by the theory of fuzzy sets, a generalization of Boolean set theory that allows for 'graded' set membership (rather than all-or-none). For instance, in the cases of many NATURAL LANGUAGE concepts, there exists no sharp boundary between situations for which the concept applies and situations for which it does not. Taking as an example, the concept 'tall', we may say that people over 6'2″ are tall and those below 5'4″ are not tall. However, there is no particular day at which a person's height switches from 'not tall' to 'tall'; rather, this is a gradual transition. In fuzzy set theory, the concept of 'tall' in this context is expressed by a 'membership function' representing the degree to which a person of a particular height can be considered to be tall. FUZZY has been used for various AI projects, including the AIMIDS/BELIEVER system at Rutgers University and HAM-RPM, a KNOWLEDGE-based conversationalist at University of Hamburg.

**fuzzy automata,** *n.* based on Zadeh's FUZZY set concept, fuzzy automata provide an alternate, but similar, approach to that used with STOCHASTIC AUTOMATA. Set-membership criteria are applied, rather than probabilistic CONSTRAINTS, in the selection of transitions and outputs. Fuzzy automata are also able to make higher-order transitions than stochastic automata and, consequently, they can usually learn faster.

**fuzzy logic** or **fuzzy set theory,** *n.* an approach to approximate reasoning where the rules of INFERENCE are approximate rather than exact; it is useful in manipulating information that is incomplete, imprecise, or unreliable. TRUTH VALUES and QUANTIFIERS are defined as possibility distributions that carry linguistic labels, such as true, very true, not very true, many, not many, few, and several. Fuzzy logic is an extension of conventional set theory, with the grade of membership for an element in a set taking a value anywhere in the range of [0,1], instead of 0 or 1 only. Developed as a means of avoiding the complexity in descriptions of subjective or ill-understood processes, fuzzy logic extends the simple Boolean operators and can express implication.

# G

**G set,** *n.* the set of general elements in a set of HYPOTHESES. The set H of plausible hypotheses can be represented by two subsets: the set of most general elements in H (called the G set) and the set of most specific elements in H (called the S set).

**GALEN,** *n.* an expert system that uses models of pediatric cardiology diseases to help physicians diagnose cases of congenital heart disease in children. The program identifies heart disease from data describing the patient's medical history, physical examinations, EKGs, and X-rays. It submits a set of possible diseases weighted according to the degree that the patient's data agrees with the VALUES the program expects for each disease. The program represents KNOWLEDGE in the form of RULES and FRAMES. The rules describe conditions for which a hypothesis can be considered, accepted, rejected, or modified. The frames represent information material to each disease. GALEN was developed at the University of Minnesota.

**game tree,** *n.* the representation by trees of strategies in game playing. A game-playing problem must be represented in a way that takes into account the opponent's possible moves as well as the player's own. Game-playing problems differ from most other problems due to the presence of adversary moves. A complete game tree is a representation of all possible plays of such a game. The ROOT NODE is the INITIAL STATE, in which it is the first player's turn to move. The successors to the initial state are the states the player can reach in one move. The next successors are the states resulting from the other player's possible replies, and so on. Terminal states are those representing a win, lose, or draw. Each path from the root node to a TERMINAL NODE gives a different complete play of the game. Other approaches to variations on PROBLEM REPRESENTATION include STATE SPACE and PROBLEM REDUCTION approaches. A noteworthy difference between a game tree and a state-space tree is that the game tree represents moves of two opposing players, say, A and B, whereas the ARCS of a state-space tree are all 'moves' of a single PROBLEM-SOLVING AGENT.

**game-tree search,** *n.* a technique used for traversing a GAME TREE. Among such techniques are the MINIMAX PROCEDURE, NEGMAX, and ALPHA/BETA PRUNING.

**GAMMA,** *n.* an expert system that uses knowledge about characteristic radiation energies and intensities emitted by different substances to help physicists determine the composition of unknown substances. It interprets the gamma-ray activation spectra produced when the substance is bombarded with neutrons. The program uses the GENERATE-AND-TEST PARADIGM to generate its knowledge. GAMMA was developed by Schlumberger-Doll Research.

**GA1,** *abbrev. for* Geneticist's Assistant 1, an expert system that uses a textbook model of the mechanism involved in enzyme digestion analysis of DNA structures, and knowledge of the nature of errors as they occur in laboratory test environments, to analyse DNA structure from restriction enzyme segmentation data. The program determines plausible DNA structures through an iterative process of generating and ruling out candidate structures. Following the GENERATE-AND-TEST PARADIGM used in DENDRAL, hypotheses are proposed via a generator based on a procedure for enumerating all possible solutions. The program supplies a user-adjustable contradiction tolerance level to compensate for small amounts of erroneous data. Implemented in INTERLISP, GA1 was developed at Stanford University.

**garbage collection,** *n.* a technique for recycling computer memory cells no longer in use.

**GCA,** *abbrev. for* Graduate Course Advisor, an expert system that uses KNOWLEDGE of sequences of courses taken by computer science students, and knowledge of departmental and university regulations, to help graduate students of computer science plan their curricula. Based on a student's academic history and interests, the program acts as a faculty advisor by suggesting a schedule of courses to meet a student's requirements. Knowledge is represented as RULES with associated CERTAINTY factors. The program's knowledge is structured into four interacting subsystems governed by a MANAGER PRO-GRAM. The subsystems determine the following four categories of advice: the number of courses the student should take, the courses the student is qualified to take, the most favourable selection of courses, the most favourable schedule for the student. Implemented in PROLOG, GCA was developed at Duke University.

**General Problem Solver (GPS),** *n.* one of the earliest AI programs. It was developed by Newell, Shaw, and Simon beginning in 1957. The research had a dual intention: It was aimed at devising machines to solve problems requiring intelligence and at developing a theory of how human beings solve such problems. GPS was the successor of the earlier LOGIC THEORIST program.

The name 'General Problem Solver' derives from the fact that GPS was the first PROBLEM SOLVING program to separate its general problem-solving methods from KNOWLEDGE specific to the type of task at hand. In effect, the problem-solving part of the system gave no information about the kind of task being worked on; task-dependent knowledge was collected in data structures forming a task ENVIRONMENT. Among the data structures were OBJECTS and OPERATORS for transforming the objects. A task was normally given to GPS as an initial object and a desired object, into which the initial object was to be transformed. GPS objects and operators were similar to the states and operators of a STATE SPACE problem RE-PRESENTATION. However, the general problem-solving technique introduced by GPS does not fit neatly into either the state-space or the problem-reduction representation formalisms. It differs from a standard state-space SEARCH in the way it decides what path to try next. This technique is a major theoretical contribution to the program, and is called MEANS-ENDS ANALYSIS. Means-ends analysis assumes that the differences between a current object and a desired object can be defined and classified into types and that the OPERATORS can be classified according to the kinds of differences they might reduce. At each stage, GPS selects a single relevant operator to try to apply to the current object. The search for a successful operator sequence proceeds as a DEPTH-FIRST SEARCH as long as the chosen operators are applicable and the path shows promise. Backup is possible if the current path becomes unpromising (e.g., if eliminating one difference has introduced a new one that is harder to eliminate).

**General Space Planner,** *n.* a system that arranges things in a space (e.g., furniture in a room) subject to given CONSTRAINTS that must be satisfied (e.g., room for walkways and no overlapping). The system uses a DIRECT REPRESENTATION, called a VARIABLE DOMAIN ARRAY. Since the structure of the representation reflects the structure of the space, with respect to the properties of size, shape, and position, the system can be described as analogical for those properties. The system solves problems by means of a DEPTH-FIRST SEARCH ALGORITHM, finding locations for successive objects and backing up when it cannot proceed without violating some constraint. The search is aided by a constraint graph that represents, by restrictions on the amount of area left, the effects of constraints between pairs of objects. Thus, by attacking the most restrictive constraint first, the search is relatively efficient. This method has been called CONSTRAINT STRUCTURED PLANNING.

**General Syntactic Processor (GSP),** *n.* a system for PARSING and generating strings in NATURAL LANGUAGE. GSP can directly emulate several other syntactic processors, including Wood's ATN grammar, Kay's MIND parser, and Friedman's TEXT GENERATION system. GSP represents an effort both to synthesize the formal characteristics of different parsing methods and to construct a unifying framework within which to compare them. In this respect, GSP is a meta-system. It is not in itself an approach to language processing, but rather it is a system in which various approaches can be described. GSP gains much of its power through the use of a single, basic data structure – the chart – to represent both the grammar and the input sentence. A chart can be described as a modified TREE, which, in turn, is usually defined as a set of NODES that can be partitioned into a root and a set of disjoint subtrees.

**generality versus power,** *n.* an issue of AI systems design in which a trade-off emerges between general methods for problem-solving and the power achieved from very specific DOMAIN KNOWLEDGE.

**generalization,** *n.* a natural reasoning process for humans that is difficult to implement in a computer program. The human capability to perform generalizations and abstractions may be fundamental to human learning processes, yet generalization has not become a useful technique in AI as yet. For an example of generalization, suppose one knows that sparrows have wings, that eagles have wings, and that pigeons have wings, eventually one will believe that all birds have wings.

**generalization method,** *n.* a way by which a RULE, for example, might satisfy more instances. Among generalization methods are adding options, climbing a concept TREE, curve-fitting, disjunction, dropping CONDITIONS, and partial matching.

**generalization principle in DEDALUS,** *n.* the result of PROCEDURE-FORMATION RULES for AUTOMATIC PROGRAMMING in the DEDALUS system. Suppose, in deriving a program, that we obtain two subgoals:

Goal A: compute $R(a(x))$
Goal B: compute $R(b(x))$,

neither of which is an INSTANCE of the other, but both of which are instances of the more general expression:

compute $R(y)$.

In such a case, an extended PROCEDURE FORMATION RULE proposes the introduction of the new procedure, whose output specification is:

$$g(y) \leftarrow \text{compute } R(y).$$

GOALS A and B can then be achieved by PROCEDURE calls to $g(a(x))$ and $g(b(x))$, respectively.

**generalized bug,** *n.* in HACKER, a DEMON that both inspects new plans to see if they contain an instance of the BUG and provides an appropriate bug fix.

**generalized cylinder,** *n.* a method for three-dimensional shape description. Generalized cylinders or cones make up a class of OBJECTS obtained by extending the definition of a cylinder. An ordinary cylinder constitutes the volume swept out by a circular disc moving perpendicular to a straight line segment that passes through its centre, the axis or spine of the cylinder. A generalized cylinder is then obtained by extending the definition to include things like:

(a) a curved spine.

(b) the radius of the disc varying as a function of the position along the spine.

(c) the cross section being some planar figure other than a circle.

(d) the cross section held at a non-perpendicular angle to the spine.

**generalized AND/OR graph,** *n.* an AND/OR GRAPH that differs in particular from an ordinary AND/OR graph in that reduction OPERATORS are permitted to take two more NODES as input.

**generalized subroutine,** *n.* in HACKER, a subroutine similar to a STRIPS macro operator. The generalized subroutine provides a sequence of actions for achieving a general GOAL.

**general-purpose knowledge engineering language,** *n.* a computer language that is designed both for building expert systems and for incorporating features enabling the use of the language for applications to different problem areas and types.

**general-to-specific ordering,** *n.* the ordering of RULES that cover the most general case first. SYNTACTIC rules of GENERALIZATION can be used to generate partial ordering. In general, any RULE SPACE can be partially ordered according to the general-to-specific ordering.

**generate-and-test,** *n.* a PROBLEM-SOLVING technique that uses a GENERATOR to produce possible solutions and an evaluator to test whether solutions are acceptable.

**generative CAI,** *n.* an early form of CAI that stressed the ability to generate problems from a large DATA BASE, which represented the subject taught.

**generative grammar,** *n.* a formal GRAMMAR of a language expressed as a set of RULES. The rules generate all the sentences of the language and disallow any sentences not possible in the language. The rules are a set of REWRITE RULES of finite length and are capable of: (a) accounting for the infinite number of possible sentences in the language, and (b) assigning to each a structural description that captures the underlying KNOWLEDGE of the language held by an idealized native user. It can be used for classifying or PARSING sentences in a language.

**generative semantics,** *n.* a model of GENERATIVE GRAMMAR, where syntax and semantics cannot be sharply separated and, consequently, a distinct level of syntactic DEEP STRUCTURE does not exist. (Contrast INTERPRETIVE SEMANTICS.)

**generator,** *n.* a PROCEDURE introduced in IPL for computing a series of VALUES. The generator produces one value each time it is called and is then suspended, so that it starts from where it left off the next time it is called. An important idea, a generator appeared later in CONNIVER and similar languages. The generator is a common specialization of the coroutine. Generators are used when a potentially large set of results may be produced by a FUNCTION, such as a function that looks for matches in a DATA BASE, but only one subset of the results is needed at a time. A generator is a coroutine that runs until it produces one item and then suspends itself. When a process needs another piece of information, it resumes the generator. A generator always returns control to the routine that activated it. This continues until there are no more items to produce, and the generator terminates.

**generic example for program specification,** *n.* the use of examples of a general sort. This is useful in avoiding problems inherent in partial specifications. For instance, the generic example:

$$REVERSE[(x_1x_2x_3 \ ... \ x_n)]=(x_n \ ... \ x_3x_2x_1)$$

describes a list-reversal FUNCTION. Here, the $x_1x_2x_3 \ ... \ x_n$ are VARIABLES and the list $(x_1x_2x_3 \ ... \ x_n)$ corresponds to any list of arbitrary length – a generic list. This specification is still partial but is more complete than any specification of this function given by nongeneric examples of input/output pairs.

**generic trace,** *n.* a TOOL used in PROGRAM SPECIFICATION in AUTOMATIC PROGRAMMING where a generic statement is used of the sequence of changes of the data-structure and control-flow decisions that can cause the change during execution.

**Genesis,** *n.* an expert system developed by Intelligenics for commercial use. It assists in recombinant DNA research. UNITS is the development software.

**GEN-X,** *abbrev. for* GENeric-eXpert system, a KNOWLEDGE ENGINEERING language for RULE-based REPRESENTATION, which also supports FRAME-BASED and DECISION TABLE approaches to representation. It features a knowledge manager that supplies an interactive text and graphics editor for creating KNOWLEDGE BASES, INTERPRETERS for the various representations underlying consultation sessions, and CODE GENERATORS to translate both the knowledge base and the appropriate interpreters into programs written in C, ADA, PASCAL, and FORTRAN. Implemented in C, GEN-X runs on IBM PCs and various minicomputers. It was developed at General Electric's Research and Development Center.

**geography tutor,** *n.* one of a class of intelligent CAI systems for teaching geography. The first such system was SCHOLAR.

**geometrical correction,** *n.* an IMAGE-ENHANCEMENT technique. The most common distortion to be corrected is the perspective projection that depends on the position and orientation of the IMAGING DEVICE relative to the object. Another distortion is the aberration in an optical sensor or an electronic scanning device. Geometrical distortion is defined by a set of transforming equations from ideal coordinates $(x,y)$ to distorted coordinates $(x',y')$:

$$x'=h_1(x,y)$$
$$y'=h_2(x,y).$$

The ideal image $f(x,y)$ becomes the distorted image $g(x',y')$. The problem is to sample the distorted image at a coordinate $(x',y')$, but recover the values at the coordinate $(x,y)$ in the ideal image. The geometrical correction to recover $f(x,y)$ from $g(x',y')$ is accomplished by first constructing a distortion model $(h_1,h_2)$ and then placing the PIXEL value $g(x',y')$ in the correct position $(x,y)$ to give the ideal image $f(x,y)$. This latter process is called RESAMPLING. There are cases in which resampling is not necessary so that it is possible to do image processing with the original image and the distortion model, avoiding the need to resample.

**Geometry Theorem Prover,** *n.* a program written in 1959 at the IBM Research Center in New York to solve problems taken from high school textbooks and final examinations in plane geometry. The program was written in extended FORTRAN, the FORTRAN List Processing Language, and implemented on an IBM 704 computer. The formal system within which the geometry program worked contained AXIOMS on parallel lines, congruence, and equality of segments and angles. This set of axioms, which was not meant to be either complete or nonredundant, was along the lines of an elementary textbook. The axioms played the role of PROBLEM-REDUCTION OPERATORS. The operators for establishing congruence split the problem into three subproblems, each to be solved separately by showing equality for one pair of elements. The geometry machine was the first program that was able to handle CONJUNCTIVE SUBGOALS. The program worked backward from the theorem to be proved, recording its progress in what amounted to an AND/OR tree.

**GEOX,** *n.* an expert system developed by NASA for identifying minerals from the hyperspectral–image data from satellites. The program is implemented in LISP.

**GETREE,** *n.* a TOOL that helps KNOWLEDGE ENGINEERS manage KNOWLEDGE BASES organized as a network that forms an AND/OR GRAPH representation of RULES. It acts as a system-building aid using the AND/OR graph to document the rules. The system answers how, how not, why, and why not questions about conclusions and facts, for displaying execution traces of FORWARD or BACK-CHAINING inferences, for modifying INFERENCE strategies, and for teaching the rules to a user. GETREE supplies an interactive graphical interface using the VT100 alphanumeric terminal with graphics character set and spoken output via a speech synthesizer. The program runs on DEC VAX computers under the VMS operating system. It was developed by General Electric Company.

**Glaucoma Consultation System,** see CASNET.

**GLIB,** *n. acronym for* General Language for Instrument Behavior, a KNOWLEDGE ENGINEERING language for RULE-BASED REPRESENTATION used by KNOWLEDGE ENGINEERS to acquire troubleshooting rules for electronic instruments. It supplies a vocabulary and syntax to express rules and specifications, and to express observations about the behavior of analog devices. It also features menu–based rule acquisition via expectation tables that provide the alternative choices for each word in the rule as it is being constructed. Implemented in SMALLTALK-80, GLIB runs on the Tektronix 4404 Artificial Intelligence System and was developed by Tektronix, Inc.

**goal,** *n.* **1.** a deep case in CASE GRAMMAR that indicates the place to which something moves. The process of understanding plan-based stories involves determining the ACTOR'S GOAL, establishing the subgoals that will lead to the main goal, and matching the actor's actions with the plan boxes associated with the subgoals.

**2.** in GPS, the goal is an encoding of the current situation (an OBJECT or list of objects), the desired situation, and a history of the attempts so far to change the current situation into the desired one. Three main types of goals are provided:

(a) Transform object A into object B.

(b) Reduce a difference between object A and object B by modifying object A.

(c) Apply OPERATOR Q to object A.

Associated with the goal types are methods, or PROCEDURES, for achieving the goals. These methods can be understood as PROBLEM/REDUCTION operators that give rise to either AND NODES, in the case of transforming an object or applying an operator, or to OR nodes, in the case of a difference reduction goal.

**goal-directed reasoning,** see BACKWARD REASONING.

**goal-directed theorem proving,** see NATURAL DEDUCTION.

**goal reduction,** see PROBLEM REDUCTION.

**goal regression,** *n.* a technique for constructing a plan by solving one CONJUNCTIVE SUBGOAL at a time. The purpose of the technique is to check each solution, ensuring that no solution will interfere with the other subgoals already achieved. If an interference occurs within the sequence of subgoal accomplishments, the offending subgoal is moved to an earlier noninterfering point in the sequence.

**goal state,** *n.* the end NODE in a GRAPH. A solution to a STATE SPACE problem is a finite sequence of applications of OPERATORS that changes an initial state into a goal state. A state-space problem is then the triple (S,O,G), where the complete specification of a state-space problem has three components. One is a set O of operators or operator schemata. In addition, one must define a set S of one or more initial states and find a PREDICATE defining a set G of goal states.

**Gold's theorems,** *n.* a set of THEOREMS that show that the formal problem of learning a CONTEXT-FREE GRAMMAR from positive instances alone is impossible.

**GOLUX,** *n.* a system for logical processing that formalizes control of processing together with REPRESENTATION of the KNOWLEDGE.

**goodness of fit,** *n.* the closeness between specific INSTANCES and the prototypical (see PROTOTYPE) data resident in a FRAME. For example, the general knowledge in PIP is knowledge about diseases, the patient situation (findings, results of the physical examination, and reported symptoms), and the relationships among these entities. This medical knowledge is organized in a FRAME system. The SLOTS in the frame are grouped into categories. The typical findings are those that are expected in a patient having this disorder. However, when a patient with the disorder does not exhibit all of the typical findings, the matching ALGORITHM can catch the lack of 'goodness of fit' between the findings and a frame.

**GPS,** see GENERAL PROBLEM SOLVER.

**GPSI,** *abbrev. for* General Purpose System for Inferencing, a tool KNOWLEDGE ENGINEERS can use to construct RULE-BASED SYSTEMS. It serves as a system-building aid, supplying the user with an integrated set of TOOLS including: a monitor for supervising how differing units in the system interact, a KNOWLEDGE ACQUISITION unit, an INFERENCE ENGINE, a rule compiler, and a user interface. The knowledge acquisition unit enables users to construct RULES with an editor that handles both text and graphics editing. In addition, the knowledge acquisition unit handles bookkeeping and answers user queries about the system's rules. Also provided are routines for CERTAINTY handling and automatic user querying. GPSI can apply the inference engine to the compiled rules in order to execute the expert system. It was developed at the University of Illinois.

**graceful degradation,** *n.* the slow deterioration of system performance. In a DISTRIBUTED PROCESSING implementation, where different knowledge sources are running as processes on different machines, a modular system can be less sensitive to transient failures of processors and communication links and can recover parts or let them be decommissioned slowly.

**gradient descent,** see HILL CLIMBING.

**gradient space,** *n.* a two-dimensional space used to represent surface orientation in terms of its vertical and horizontal components. Thus the plane surface $-Z = P.X + Q.Y + C$

is represented by the point (P,Q) in gradient space. The steepness of the surface is the square root of $P^2+Q^2$ and the direction of the slope is $\tan^{-1}(Q/P)$. Such a representation does not make explicit spatial location or extent of surface lines in the gradient space; in the case of planar surface discontinuity edges these will be perpendicular to the edge in the image space, with order along the line determined by the convexity/concavity.

**gradual refinement,** *n.* a transformation process that reduces a high-level specification to an IMPLEMENTATION fully within the TARGET LANGUAGE. Each application of a RULE is said to produce a partial implementation, or refinement, of the program, and the TRANSFORMATIONAL RULES are called refinement rules.

**grain size,** *n.* the degree of detail of a REPRESENTATION scheme used or required by a system. Questions concerning the scope and grain size of a representation scheme can help determine how suitable a given FORMALISM is for solving a particular problem. Such questions include: What portion of the external world can be represented in a system? In what detail are OBJECTS and EVENTS represented? And how much of this detail is actually needed by the reasoning mechanisms? These questions are often difficult to answer. The answers depend on the particular application intended. For instance, a KNOWLEDGE REPRESENTATION based on logic might be an extremely fine-grain representation in a mathematical reasoning program, but might result in a coarse simplification for a vision program. Exactly how much detail is needed depends on the performance desired. In general, uniformity of detail across the OBJECTS and EVENTS is desirable for a given reasoning task.

**grammar,** *n.* a scheme for specifying sentences allowed in a language. A grammar describes the SYNTACTIC RULES for combining words into well-formed phrases and clauses.

**grammarless parser,** *n.* a parser that is based on special procedures, often centred on individual words rather than on SYNTACTIC elements. The procedures use SEMANTICS-based techniques to build up structures relevant to meaning. The structures bear little resemblance to the normal structures that result from syntactic PARSING.

**grammatical inference,** *n.* the inferring of a GRAMMAR that describes a language, given several examples of strings of that language.

**granularity,** *n.* the level of detail in a chunk of information, e.g., a RULE or FRAME.

**graph,** *n.* a representation scheme consisting of NODES and links. For example, the states in a STATE-SPACE REPRESENTATION are represented by a graph rather than by a TREE since there may be different paths from the root to any given NODE. Trees are an important special case because they are commonly used in implementing CONTROL STRATEGIES. In a state-space representation, a tree might be used to represent the set of problem states produced by OPERATOR applications. In such a representation, the ROOT NODE of the tree represents the initial problem situation or state. Each of the new states that can be produced from the initial state by the application of just one operator is represented by a SUCCESSOR NODE of the root node. Subsequent operator applications produce successors of these nodes, and so on. Each operator application is represented by a directed ARC of the tree.

**graph deformation condition,** *n.* a HEURISTIC that states that branches in the HAM representation of a sentence are not allowed to cross. This heuristic rules out certain parses that would result in an ill-formed HAM structure.

**graph grammar,** *n.* a kind of CONTEXT-FREE GRAMMAR that constructs a GRAPH of TERMINAL NODES instead of a string of TERMINAL SYMBOLS. REWRITE RULES in the grammar describe how a nonterminal NODE can be replaced by a subgraph. In syntactic PATTERN RECOGNITION problems, it is often important to represent the two- or three-dimensional structure of 'sentences' in the language. Traditional context-free grammars, however, generate only one-dimensional strings. Graph grammars can represent more than one.

**graph traverser,** *n.* an early heuristic ALGORITHM whose object is to minimize SEARCH effort instead of solution cost. The EVALUATION FUNCTION used is of the form $f^\star = h^\star$, and the object is to minimize total search effort in finding solutions to the EIGHT (8) PUZZLE and other problems.

**graphics,** *n.* drawn images created using computer technology, which are usually displayed on a terminal or plotter.

**grey scale,** *n.* the number of discrete levels of light that a sensor can represent.

**grey-level correction,** *n.* the adjustment of the intensity of light falling on a sensor. In order to compensate for the non-uniformity of sensitivity of sensors in the sensor plane, the grey level sensed by each PIXEL is corrected according to the sensitivity at its location. The sensitivity of pixels can be calibrated by illuminating the sensor plane with a source of uniform brightness.

**grey-scale picture,** *n.* a digitized image in which the brightness of the PIXELS can have more than two values, typically 128 or 256. These images require greater storage space and more sophisticated image processing than is possible in binary images but generally improve visual sensing.

**grey-scale transformation,** *n.* a process typically undertaken to modify the grey level (intensity) of PIXELS in an image in order to stretch the contrast in the image (the range between the darkest and lightest points in the image).

**ground restriction,** *n.* a requirement in THEOREM PROVING that a clause A should have no VARIABLES. An intuitive justification for the ground restriction is that, since A is an assertion made by the HYPOTHESIS about specific OBJECTS (the ground terms) in the WORLD, immediate consequences (B(0)) should be explored.

**ground space,** *n.* a level of REPRESENTATION for a problem set. Using distinct levels of PROBLEM REPRESENTATION, a simplified version of a problem occurs in a higher-level PROBLEM SPACE or ABSTRACTION SPACE. The details of the problem are removed. The detailed version of the problem now occupies the GROUND SPACE. A HIERARCHY of problem spaces is thus obtained via a slight extension, providing for several levels of detail instead of just two. In general, each SPACE in the hierarchy serves both as an abstraction space for the more detailed space just below it and as a ground space with respect to the less detailed space just above.

**GSP,** see GENERAL SYNTACTIC PROCESSOR.

**GUESS/1,** *n. acronym for* General pUrpose Expert Systems Shell, a KNOWLEDGE ENGINEERING language for RULE-based representation, which also supports relational tables, hierarchical TREES, SEMANTIC NETWORKS, and FRAMES. CONTROL KNOW-

LEDGE is encoded in frames and RULES,, which allow both BACK- and FORWARD CHAINING. Frames can trigger rules and rules can invoke frames. Multiple KNOWLEDGE SOURCES communicate via a BLACKBOARD mechanism. A multilevel security mechanism allows each table, tree, network, or frame to be labelled to control access on the basis of a user's security clearance. The SUPPORT ENVIRONMENT includes an explanation facility and a NATURAL LANGUAGE and menu facility. Implemented in PROLOG, GUESS/1 runs under the VMS operating system on a DEC VAX 11/780, and was developed at the computer science department of Virginia Polytechnic Institute and State University.

**GUIDON,** *n.* an expert system that instructs students in how to select antimicrobial therapy for hospital patients with bacterial infections. The program first chooses a case and solves it, then presents the case to the student to solve, and finally analyses the responses and queries the student enters during the problem session. The program then evaluates the student's performance according to how the student's diagnosis procedure compares with the procedure the program used to diagnose the case. GUIDON uses the MYCIN expert system to solve the cases. The students in turn learn the RULES and PROCEDURES contained in MYCIN. Rules and META-RULES are used to encode GUIDON's knowledge. Implemented in INTERLISP, GUIDON was developed at Stanford University.

**GUS,** *n.* one of the first expert systems to use FRAMES. Designed as a prototype of an automated airline reservation assistant, the system demonstrates how various aspects of dialogue understanding – such as handling MIXED-INITIATIVE DIALOGUES, indirect answers, and ANAPHORIC REFERENCES – can be aided by the ability to make expectations and DEFAULTS available with frames. The system was also used to explore PROCEDURAL ATTACHMENT issues.

# H

**HACKER,** *n.* a system that detects and generalizes new differences (BUGS) and defines appropriate OPERATORS in order to resolve them (patches). The emphasis on generalizing from experience, on trying old techniques in new situations, the acceptance of the fact that users have an incomplete understanding of the desired program, and the GOAL-purpose annotation technique are all steps in the development of AUTOMATIC PROGRAMMING and learning systems. HACKER uses many significant AI techniques and language features, which include: learning through practice how to write and debug programs (see DEBUGGING); modular, pattern-invoked expert PROCEDURES (chunks of PROCEDURAL KNOWLEDGE); and hypothetical WORLD MODELS for subgoal analysis.

**HAM-RPM,** *n.* a KNOWLEDGE-based conversationalist that reasons with FUZZY information. It was developed at the University of Hamburg.

**HANNIBAL,** *n.* an expert system that uses data about location and signal characteristics of detected communications from communications intelligence to perform situation assessments. The program interprets data from sensors that monitor radio communications. The data enables HANNIBAL to identify enemy organizational units and their order of battle. The program's KNOWLEDGE is represented in a BLACKBOARD ARCHITECTURE using multiple specialists or KNOWLEDGE SOURCES. Implemented in AGE, HANNIBAL was developed by ESL.

**HARPY,** *n.* a SPEECH UNDERSTANDING system developed at Carnegie-Mellon University after extensive evaluation of two earlier systems, HEARSAY-1 and DRAGON. HARPY's integration of diverse forms of KNOWLEDGE into a single NETWORK REPRESENTATION is its principal contribution. The most important characteristic of the program is its use of a single, precompiled, network knowledge structure. The network contains knowledge at all levels: acoustic, phonemic, lexical,

143

syntactic, and semantic. It stores acoustic representations of every possible pronunciation of the words in all of the sentences that HARPY recognizes. The alternative sentences are represented as paths through the network, and each NODE in the network is a TEMPLATE of ALLOPHONES. The paths through the network can be thought of as 'sentence templates', much like the word 'templates' in ISOLATED WORD RECOGNITION.

**HASP,** see SIAP.

**HAWKEYE,** *n.* an integrated interactive system for cartography or surveillance. It combines aerial photographs and generic descriptions of objects and situations with the topographical and cultural information found in traditional maps. The user queries the DATA BASE and invokes IMAGE-PROCESSING tasks through a LIFER NATURAL LANGUAGE interface. Unique to this interface is the ability to input a combination of natural language and nontextual forms.

**HCPRVR,** *abbrev. for* HORN CLAUSE theorem PRoVeR, a LOGIC-based programming language and INTERPRETER that allows the use of LISP functions in place of PREDICATE names. The programs consist of an ordered list of AXIOMS where each axiom is either an ATOMIC FORMULA or an implication. Atomic formulas are arbitrary LISP expressions starting with a LISP ATOM that is referred to as its predicate name. Instead of requiring the HCPRVR interpreter to prove the formula, HCPRVR programs permit just the FUNCTION call. The interpreter is a Horn clause-based THEOREM PROVER. Implemented in LISP, HCPRVR was originally designed to run on DEC PDP-10 computer systems. It was developed at the University of Texas at Austin.

**HDDSS,** *abbrev. for* Hodgkin's Disease Decision Support System, an expert system which uses knowledge of both radiotherapy and patient data to help physicians determine and select appropriate treatment for patients with Hodgkin's disease. The program applies Bayesian estimation techniques to produce a priori probabilities of the extent of tumour spread. The results are used to select a diagnostic procedure or treatment. BAYES'S THEOREM is then applied to revise the probabilities. The process serves to produce a set of diagnostic plans beginning with the most favourable plan followed by alternative plans. The radiotherapy KNOWLEDGE is represented as a TAXONOMY and a relational DATA BASE contains the patient data. Implemented in MACLISP, HDDSS was developed at MIT.

**HEADMED,** *n.* an expert system that uses knowledge about the differential diagnosis of the major affective disorders, schizophrenia, and the general category of organic brain disorders, to provide advice to physicians on matters of clinical pyschopharmacology. The program diagnoses a range of psychiatric disorders and recommends drug treatment using approximately 120 clinical parameters to perform its diagnosis and treatment recommendations. The KNOWLEDGE BASE also includes the Minnesota Multiphasic Personality Inventory (MMPI) along with structural knowledge of neurosis, behaviour disorders, and substance abuse. HEADMED was designed for use as a tutorial and consulting aid. Implemented in EMYCIN, including EMYCIN's CERTAINTY FACTORS, explanation utility, KNOWLEDGE ACQUISITION, and other support facilities, HEADMED was developed at the University of California.

**HEARSAY,** *n.* a SPEECH UNDERSTANDING system developed as part of the ARPA-funded speech understanding research project. The system was one of the most influential of all AI programs over the years. The importance of HEARSAY lies not in how well the system understands speech, but in the way that it is constructed. Its design is based on the idea of independent KNOWLEDGE SOURCES cooperatively solving a problem by posting hypotheses on a global BLACKBOARD data structure. As a modular ARCHITECTURE – modular because the knowledge sources do not address each other directly – the design proved to allow significant flexibility as the system evolved and different combinations of knowledge sources and CONTROL STRATEGIES were tried.

**HEARSAY-I,** *n.* the first implementation of the HEARSAY system was based on the idea of cooperating, independent KNOWLEDGE SOURCES. The three knowledge sources in HEARSAY-I represented knowledge about the following:
(a) Acoustics and phonetics (the features in the speech signal that are evidence for each type of syllable), including ways the signal may change because of different speakers

145

and noise in the environment.
(b) The syntax of legal utterances.
(c) The semantics of the DOMAIN.
The domain was VOICE CHESS, which pits the computer against a person.

**HEARSAY-II,** *n*. the ARCHITECTURE of Hearsay-II is based on the view that the inherently errorful nature of processing connected speech can be handled only through the effective and efficient cooperation of multiple, diverse sources of KNOWLEDGE. In addition, the experimental approach needed for system development requires the ability to add and replace sources of knowledge and to explore different CONTROL STRATEGIES. The chief focus of the design of the system was the development of a framework for experimenting with the REPRESENTATION of and cooperation among these diverse sources of knowledge.

**HEARSAY-II architecture,** *n*. the organization of a PROBLEM-SOLVING system in terms of several cooperating, independent specialists. The specialists represent diverse areas of KNOWLEDGE that exchange partial results via a BLACKBOARD and collectively assemble an overall solution incrementally and opportunistically (see OPPORTUNISTIC PROBLEM-SOLVING).

**HEARSAY-III,** *n*. a domain-independent programming facility, which evolved from work on SPEECH UNDERSTANDING, for developing prototype expert systems. It uses a central BLACKBOARD to store and coordinate information about the DOMAIN and state of computation. Most of the domain-specific KNOWLEDGE is organized in complex PRODUCTION RULES called KNOWLEDGE SOURCES (KS). A general-purpose CONTROL structure supports interaction among numerous and diverse sources of knowledge and competing subproblems. HEARSAY-III supports the design of systems requiring asynchronous processing of information and the design of control structures for handling multiple GOALS. Implemented in LISP, HEARSAY-III was developed by Information Sciences Institute. See DOMAIN-INDEPENDENCE.

**HEART IMAGE INTERPRETER,** *n*. an expert system that uses knowledge about the structural properties of the heart and left ventricle, the motational phases of a heart cycle, and rules for relating medical evidence to diagnosis, to help physicians perform a diagnostic interpretation of the motational behaviour of the heart. The program analyses two-dimensional intensity distribution images of the heart produced by injecting radionuclide substance Technetium 99-m into the patient's vein. The program then analyses and interprets a sequence of 12 to 64 images produced from a scintillation camera. A SEMANTIC NETWORK containing FRAMES and associated RULES, which uses CERTAINTY FACTORS, is used to encode the program's knowledge of IMAGE PROCESSING and medical diagnosis. Implemented in RATFOR, a dialect of FORTRAN, HEART IMAGE INTERPRETER was developed at the University of Erlangen.

**HEME,** *n.* an expert system that helps physicians diagnose haematological diseases. The program contains KNOWLEDGE about estimates of the frequency of occurrence of a given disease, the probability that a patient with a disease has a given disease, the probability that a patient with the disease has a given finding, and the probability that a patient without the disease has a given finding. These conditional probabilities represent the judgments of experienced haematology clinicians and include measures of how confident the clinicians are about their original probability estimates. The program uses patient findings entered by a physician and a version of BAYES'S THEOREM to compute the probability that a patient has each of the diseases currently registered in the system. It was developed at Cornell University.

**Herbicide Advisor,** *n.* an expert system developed by Shell for internal use. It assists in identifying new herbicides based on structural properties of chemicals.

**Herbicide Selector,** *n.* an expert system developed by Systems Designers Software for British Gas in selecting herbicides for use in pipelines. Envisage is the development software.

**heuristic,** *n.* a rule-of-thumb or other device that simplifies, reduces, or limits SEARCH in large PROBLEM SPACES; in particular, searches for solutions in DOMAINS that are difficult and poorly understood. Unlike ALGORITHMS, heuristics do not guarantee correct solutions. The most frequently used dictionary definition for heuristic as an adjective is 'serving to discover'. As a noun, the term refers to an obscure branch of philosophy, specifically the study of the methods and rules of discovery and invention. In defining heuristic as a term used to describe AI techniques, some writers made a distinction between methods for discovering solutions and methods for producing them algorithmically. A heuristic (heuristic rule, heuristic method) is, basically, a rule of thumb, strategy, trick, simplification, or any other kind of device that drastically limits search for solutions in large problem spaces. Heuristics do not guarantee optimal solutions; in fact, they do not guarantee any solution at all. The best that can be said for a useful heuristic is that it offers solutions that are good enough most of the time. A problem arises even with this definition, because it lacks a historical dimension. A device originally introduced as a heuristic may later be shown to guarantee an optimal solution after all. When this happens, the label 'heuristic' may or may not be dropped. It has not been dropped, for example, with respect to the A* ALGORITHM. ALPHA/BETA PRUNING, on the other hand, is no longer called a heuristic. It should be noted that the above definitions refer to heuristic RULES, methods, and programs, but they do not use the term 'HEURISTIC SEARCH'.

**Heuristic Compiler,** *n.* a system that regards the task of writing a program as a PROBLEM-SOLVING process that applies HEURISTIC techniques, like those of GPS. The work recognized the value of both a state language, to describe PROBLEM STATES and GOALS, and a process language, to represent the solver's actions.

**Heuristic Dendral,** *n.* an expert system, developed at Stanford University, that establishes the structure of a molecule. It takes as input both the atomic formula of the molecule (e.g., $H_2O$ for water) and its mass spectrogram. The program works by finding the relatively small set of possible molecular structures of known constituent atoms that could account for the given spectroscopic analysis of an unknown molecule.

**Heuristic Path algorithm,** *n.* a generalization of the GRAPH TRAVERSER algorithm, A* ALGORITHM, and others. It gives an ordered STATE-SPACE SEARCH with an EVALUATION FUNCTION:

$$f* = (1-w)g* + wh*$$

where w is a constant in [0, 1] giving the relative importance to be attached to g and h. Choosing w=1 gives the Graph Traverser algorithm, w=0 gives BREADTH-FIRST SEARCH, and w=.5 is equivalent to the A$\star$ function f$\star$=g$\star$+h$\star$.

**heuristic problem-solving,** see PROBLEM SOLVING; EXPERT SYSTEM.

**Heuristic Programming Project,** *n.* the research group at Stanford University that principally pioneered the field of KNOWLEDGE ENGINEERING. It produced a large collection of expert systems.

**heuristic rule,** *n.* a procedural tip or incomplete method for performing some task. RULES written to capture the HEURISTICS an expert uses to solve a problem. One of the problems is converting an expert's heuristic KNOWLEDGE, especially if the expert's original heuristics may not have taken the form of IF-THEN RULES. The power of a KNOWLEDGE SYSTEM reflects the heuristic rules in the KNOWLEDGE BASE.

**heuristic search,** *n.* a search scheme that includes information about the DOMAIN. Heuristic search is distinguished from a PROBLEM-SOLVING method called GENERATE-AND-TEST. The difference between the two methods is that the latter simply generates elements of the SEARCH SPACE (i.e., STATES) and tests each in turn until it finds one satisfying the GOAL CONDITION; whereas in heuristic search the order of generation can depend both on information gained in previous tests and on characteristics of the goal.

The distinction between heuristic search and blind search is also important. Blind search corresponds approximately to the systematic generation and testing of search-space elements, but blind search operates within a FORMALISM that leave room for additional information about the specific problem DOMAIN to be introduced, rather than excluding it by definition. If such information, going beyond that needed merely to formulate a class of search problems, is used, it can restrict search drastically. This search is then called heuristic rather than blind.

**Hi Class,** *n.* an expert system developed by Hughes Aircraft for internal use. It assists in solving circuit board assembly problems and provides on-line instruction. The program is implemented in C.

**hierarchical planning,** *n.* a technique that generates a hierarchical plan via successive generation of its component levels from top to bottom. A variant of the technique uses criticalities assigned to OPERATOR preconditions. In general, however, DOMAIN-specific plan elaboration rules are required. Top-down plan elaboration is closely related to automatic top-down programming techniques See PLAN.

**hierarchical search,** *n.* an attempt to reduce the problem of combinatorial explosion. A COMBINATORIAL EXPLOSION looms for all problem solvers that attempt to use HEURISTIC SEARCH in a sufficiently complex problem DOMAIN. The idea behind hierarchical search is to use an approach to problem-solving that can recognize the most significant features of a problem, develop an outline of a solution in terms of those features, and deal with the less important details of the problem only after the outline has proved adequate.

**hierarchy,** *n.* an ordered network of CONCEPTS or OBJECTS in which some are subordinate to others. Hierarchies normally imply INHERITANCE; and therefore objects or concepts higher in the organization include the objects or concepts that are beneath them. Typically, hierarchies characterize biological and social taxonomies and corporate organizational charts. Tangled hierarchies occur when more than one higher-level entity inherits characteristics from a single lower-level entity.

**high-emphasis frequency filtering,** *n.* the use of a transfer function to emphasize areas of high frequency in an image. In point of fact, any linear OPERATOR in the SPATIAL DOMAIN (such as the discrete version of the LAPLACIAN) can be converted into an equivalent transfer function in the frequency domain. Just as a linear operator can be designed to emphasize abrupt changes in intensity, so a transfer function can be designed to emphasize areas of high frequency (i.e., areas with abrupt changes in intensity). Both approaches yield the same result: edges and other high-frequency components of an image are sharpened.

**high-level language,** *n.* a programming language with features including the statement of PROCEDURES and RECURSION. High-level languages incorporate more complex constructs than the simpler languages. Computer languages lie on a spectrum ranging from machine instructions through intermediate languages like FORTRAN and COBOL to high-level languages like ADA and PASCAL.

**hill climbing,** *n.* a method for finding an extreme point in a curve. Hill climbing requires taking repeated steps through the multidimensional space to the minimum. The simplest idea is called steepest descent. On each iteration, we find the direction in which f is decreasing fastest (this direction is called the gradient vector of f). Next, a BINARY SEARCH or some other one-dimensional method to find the minimum along that vector is applied. This is called the 'line search' phase. The gradient from the point found by the line search is computed, and the process then repeated.

**homogeneous coordinate,** *n.* a REPRESENTATION used for expressing PROJECTION as a linear transformation.

**horizon effect,** *n.* the effect in a game-playing environment where, whenever SEARCH is terminated prior to the end of the game, and a STATIC EVALUATION FUNCTION is applied, the program exists in terms of the output of the static evaluation function, and anything that is not detectable at evaluation time does not exist as far as the program is concerned. Two kinds of error can result: the negative horizon effect and the positive horizon effect. In the negative horizon effect, the program manipulates the timing of moves to force certain positions to appear at the search horizon. This can cause the program to conclude that it has avoided some undesirable effect when in fact the effect has only been delayed to a point beyond the horizon. In the positive horizon effect, an error that involves reaching for a desirable consequence results. Either the program wrongly concludes that the consequence is achievable or it fails to realize that the same consequence could also be achieved later in the game in a more effective form. This last problem can be met by finding ways to represent and use more KNOWLEDGE than traditional programs have included. However, in most cases of the errors coming from the horizon effect, the reason is that the typical descriptions of QUIESCENCE are highly oversimplified.

**Horn clause,** *n.* in LOGIC programming, an expression connected by 'or' with at most one positive PROPOSITION. It is a formula of first order PREDICATE CALCULUS of the form:

$$A_1 \ \& \ A_2 \ \& ... \& \ A_n \ or \ A_1 \ \& \ A_2 \ \& ... \& \ A_n$$

where each of the $A_i$ are ATOMIC FORMULAE, i.e., of the form $R(C_1 \ldots ,C_n)$, where R is a RELATION, each $C_j$ is a term, and $n \geqslant 0$.

Horn clauses form the basis for the logic programming language PROLOG; each predicate in a PROLOG program has a Horn clause definition. The above formulae would be written respectively as PROLOG programs in the following manner:

A :- A1,A2, ... ,An. and ?- A1,A2, ... ,An.

Logic programming is made more efficient by restricting the type of logical assertions to Horn clauses in much the same way that PRODUCTION SYSTEMS insist on having KNOWLEDGE stated in terms of IF-THEN RULES.

**Hotline Helper,** *n.* an expert system developed at Texas Instruments for internal use. It helps hotline workers give advice to callers with hardware malfunctions. PERSONAL CONSULTANT is the development software.

**Hough transform,** *n.* a method for detecting, in images, lines and other shapes distinguishable by analytic functions. The Hough transform technique has been extended to handle the correlation of two-dimensional and three-dimensional shapes having no analytic description. It is possible to use a CLUSTERING method in order to detect multiple straight lines from a set of edge points. To do so, represent a line in the x-y picture plane by:

$$x \cos \theta + y \sin \theta = p.$$

The figure opposite provides a graphical interpretation of this equation. Assuming a parameter space made of $(p,\theta)$, the previous equation is then a transformation from $(x,y)$ to $(p,\theta)$ with the following properties:

(a) A line in the x-y space is transformed to a point $(p,\theta)$ in the p-$\theta$ SPACE and vice versa.

(b) A point $(x,y)$ is transformed to a sinusoidal curve in the p-$\theta$ space, and vice versa. The $(p,\theta)$ on this sinusoidal curve mean all the lines that pass the point $(x,y)$.

**How The West Was Won,** *n.* a computer-simulated board game designed on the PLATO computer-based education system at the University of Illinois. The original program was nontutorial. Its purpose was to give elementary school

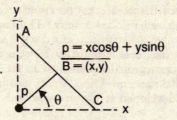

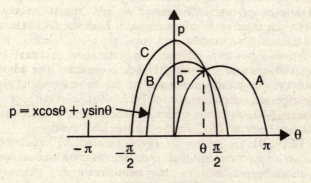

**Hough transform**

students drill and practice in arithmetic. The game resembles the popular 'Snakes and Ladders' board game. At each turn, a player receives three numbers (from spinners) with which the player constructs an arithmetic expression using the operations of addition, subtraction, multiplication, and division. The numeric value of the completed expression is the number of spaces the player can move. The object of the game is to get to the end first.

**HP4760AI Electrocardiograph,** *n.* an expert system developed by Hewlett-Packard/McMinnville Division for commercial use. It aids physicians in interpreting electrocardiograph readings. The program was written in LISP.

**HPRL,** *abbrev. for* Heuristic Programming and Representation Language, a KNOWLEDGE ENGINEERING language for FRAME-BASED REPRESENTATION that is an extension of FRL. Integrating a FRAME representation scheme with a RULE-based representa-

153

tion, an essential set of LISP functions execute rules governed by a frame-based rule interpreter. The language supports FORWARD and BACK-CHAINING CONTROL schemes along with META-RULES that enable users to construct arbitrarily complex REASONING strategies. Implemented in PSL, a portable dialect of LISP, HPRL runs on DEC VAX and HP-9836 computers. HPRL was developed at Hewlett-Packard.

**HSRL,** *n.* a KNOWLEDGE ENGINEERING language that provides LOGIC programming capabilities. Embedded in SRL, HSRL effectively combines FRAME-BASED and LOGIC-based representations. Logic programs are expressed as SRL FRAMES. ATOMIC FORMULAE can refer to information from both the SRL KNOWLEDGE BASE and the AXIOMS in a logic-program schema. The SUPPORT ENVIRONMENT includes an interactive facility for creating, editing, and executing HSRL programs. The HSRL INTERPRETER is a modified version of the HCPRVR logic program interpreter. Implemented in FRANZ LISP, HSRL is an extension to SRL and runs under UNIX. It was developed at the Robotics Institute of Carnegie-Mellon University.

**HT-ATTENDING,** *abbrev. for* HyperTension-ATTENDING system, an expert system that uses KNOWLEDGE about anti-hypertension agents used in outpatient treatment, treatment modalities, and conditions affecting hypertension management, to critique a physician's pharmacologic management of essential hypertension. The program extends the process that ATTENDING uses to the DOMAIN of hypertension. The program takes as input conventional patient information (age, medical problems, etc.) along with a description of the patient's present antihypertensive regimen and the proposed change to the regimen. The program then uses the patient information to generate a critique of the change proposed by the physician. The program presents the critique in the form of several paragraphs of English text. A FRAME-BASED KNOWLEDGE SCHEME implemented in *LISP,* HT-ATTENDING was developed at Yale University.

**Hueckel operator,** *n.* a TOOL used in EDGE DETECTION in IMAGE PROCESSING. PATTERN MATCHING for edge detection assumes a model of an edge. Its location in the image is determined to be where its intensity profile best matches the model. Given a circular region D about the origin of an x-y coordinate system, Hueckel's ideal edge is the step function:

$$f(x, y, c, s, p, b, d) = \begin{cases} b & \text{if } cx + sy \leq p; \\ b+d & \text{otherwise.} \end{cases}$$

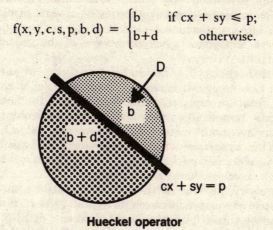

**Hueckel operator**

The ideal edge is a function of the VARIABLES listed: the background intensity b, the intensity difference d across the edge, and the parameters for the edge orientation and location c,s, and p.

**Huffman's $\theta(\theta')$-point test,** *n.* the necessary and sufficient condition for a cut set of lines (equivalently, a set of regions separated by those lines) to be realizable by plane surfaces.

**Human Associative Memory,** see HAM.

**human engineering,** *n.* the task of designing human–machine interfaces in order to permit humans to use the machine's functions. Human engineering is especially important in the design of computer systems that have a component that adapts to the user.

**human information processing,** *n.* a perspective on how humans think, which is influenced by how computers work. Human information processing is an approach to psychology that begins by focusing on the information that a person uses to reach some conclusion and then asking how one could design a computer program that would begin with that same information and reach the same conclusion. This perspective is widespread in cognitive psychology and has influenced the design of both computer languages and programs.

**Human Problem Solving,** *n.* a classic book on information processing psychology by Allen Newell and Herbert Simon (1972). It summarizes and synthesizes their years of pioneering research into computational models of human cognition. The 'Historical Addendum' gives their view of the origins of the discipline.

**humiliation theory,** *n.* the underlying theory of paranoia in Colby's PARRY system. Paranoid behaviour arises, according to Colby, from attempts to avoid humiliation. In the PARRY simulation, humiliation arises, and is strongly avoided, during an interview with a doctor. A paranoid individual (and PARRY) is hypersensitive to any comment that can be interpreted as reflecting on his or her own inadequacy. Any such comment increases shame and humiliation.

**HWIM,** *abbrev. for* Hear What I Mean, a SPEECH UNDERSTANDING system developed between 1974 and 1976 at Bolt, Baranek, and Newman. HWIM was the successor to BBN's earlier SPEECHLIS speech understanding system and to BBN's work on NATURAL LANGUAGE UNDERSTANDING. The BBN speech understanding system evolved within a general framework for viewing perceptual processes. Central to this framework is an entity called a theory. A theory represents a particular hypothesis about some or all of the sensory stimuli that are present. Perception is viewed as the process of forming a believable, coherent theory that can account for all of the stimuli. In such a framework, the process of developing a theory is achieved by successive refinement and extension of partial theories until the best complete theory is found. In the setting of speech understanding, a typical theory is a set of compatible word hypotheses, with possible gaps between words, and partial SYNTACTIC and SEMANTIC interpretations. HWIM was used to answer questions in the role of a travel budget manager, using a DATA BASE of facts about trips and expenses.

**hybrid control strategy,** *n.* a method of CONTROL containing more than one approach. For example, a strategy explored in the HWIM system is a hybrid one between ISLAND DRIVING and the left–to–right strategy. So the problem of not being able to understand any of the first words in the sentence is overcome by trying to understand any of the first three or four words. Then the expansion of this word is in one direction at a time:

first back to the beginning of the sentence, and then to the end. This process dramatically reduces the number of extension HYPOTHESES that must be considered at one time.

**HYDRO,** *n.* an expert system that helps a hydrologist use HSPF, a computer program that simulates the physical processes by which precipitation is distributed throughout a watershed. The program assists in describing watershed characteristics to HSPF in the form of numerical parameters. HYDRO estimates these parameters, using KNOWLEDGE about soil type, land use, vegetation, geology, and their affect on the specific parameter in question. Patterned after PROSPECT, HYDRO uses a combination RULE-based and SEMANTIC NETWORK formalism to encode its knowledge and bases its INFERENCES on the use of CERTAINTY FACTORS and the propagation of probabilities associated with the data. Implemented in INTERLISP, HYDRO was developed by SRI International.

**hypothesis,** *n.* in PIP, an INSTANTIATION of a disorder FRAME. Hypotheses occur in three categories: confirmed, active, and semi-active. Confirmed hypotheses have ratings (computed by the scoring process) that are higher than a preset threshold. Active hypotheses are those with at least one confirmed TRIGGER finding, and they contend for the focus of attention. Semi-active hypotheses are the immediate neighbours of the active hypotheses in the frame system. They correspond to hypotheses that are not strong enough to be investigated, yet still occur to the physician as an outside possibility.

**hypothetical worlds,** *n.* structuring knowledge in a KNOWLEDGE-BASED SYSTEM in a way that defines the contexts (hypothetical worlds) in which facts and RULES apply.

# I

**I & W,** *abbrev. for* Indications & Warning, an expert system that uses KNOWLEDGE about common indicators of troop activity to help intelligence analysts predict where and when an armed conflict will occur next. The program analyses incoming intelligence reports about troop activity such as troop location and troop movement. A BLACKBOARD ARCHITECTURE is used to structure the program's knowledge, which is represented in the form of both FRAMES and FORWARD CHAINING RULES. Implemented in INTERLISP-D, I&W runs on the Xerox 1100 series workstations. It was developed through a joint effort by ESL and Stanford University.

**ICAI,** *n. acronym for* Intelligent Computer-Assisted Instruction, instructional software that makes use of ARTIFICIAL INTELLIGENCE techniques in order to analyse the student's errors and then make appropriate changes in the instruction. Most instructional software currently available can modify the presentation only by computing the number of student errors and directing the student to supplementary exercises or tutorials. AI techniques allow the system to develop a model of the individual student's understanding of the subject and then correct or enlarge that understanding systematically. ICAI systems normally involve dialogues between the student and the system in which the system uses the student's mistakes to diagnose the student's misunderstandings.

**iconic representation,** *n.* the representation of the intrinsic characteristics of a scene as images. The various intrinsic VALUES are computed for each individual PIXEL, representing the intrinsic characteristics of the surface that is imaged in that pixel. In this REPRESENTATION, there is an image for reflectance values, one for orientations, one for distance, and one for incident illumination. These are all in registration with the original image.

**ICOT,** *abbrev. for* Institute for New Generation Computer Technology. Composed of many of Japan's leading corporate and educational technology researchers. ICOT was formed by MITI to lead the Fifth Generation Project.

**IDEA,** *n.* an expert system developed at Pacific Bell for internal use. It troubleshoots telephone switching equipment. Exsys is the development software.

**ideational function,** *n.* in SYSTEMIC GRAMMAR, the function that serves for the expression of content. It relates to the speaker's experience of the world.

**IDT,** *n.* an expert system that uses knowledge about PDP 11/03 computers to help PDP 11/03 technicians locate the field replaceable units the technicians must replace to fix faults. The program selects and executes diagnostic tests and interprets the result. It is a RULE-BASED PROGRAM that uses FORWARD CHAINING. Implemented in FRANZ LISP and OPS5, IDT was developed by Digital Equipment Corporation.

**ID3,** *n.* a version of the CLS learning ALGORITHM that uses a feature–vector REPRESENTATION to describe training instances. The features must each have only a small number of possible discrete VALUES. Concepts are represented as decision TREES. For instance, if the features of shape (circle, square, and triangle) and colour (red, blue) are used to represent the training instances, then the concept of a red circle (of any size) could be represented as the tree shown below.

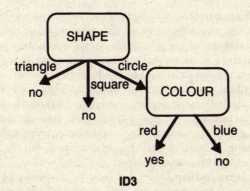

ID3

**if-then rule,** *n.* a statement of a relationship among a set of facts. The relationships may be definitional (e.g., If male and married, then husband) or HEURISTIC (e.g. If going to beach, then take bathing suit).

**ILOG,** *n.* an expert system developed by Digital Equipment Corporation for internal use. It assists manufacturing scheduling.

**IMACS,** *n. acronym for* Intelligent Management Assistant for Computer System manufacturing, an expert system that supplies a detailed plan for managers in a computer systems manufacturing environment to follow while constructing a given system. The program takes a customer's order as input and generates a rough plan, which it uses to estimate the resource requirements for the order. When the computer system is actually ready to be built, IMACS generates the detailed plan and uses it to monitor the computer system's implementation. The program assists managers with paperwork management, capacity management, inventory management, and other tasks related to managing the manufacturing process. Organized as a set of cooperating subsystems, it is a RULE-BASED PROGRAM and uses FORWARD CHAINING. IMACS is implemented in OPS5, and was developed by Digital Equipment Corporation.

**image domain,** *n.* in VISION STUDIES, a systematic approach to polyhedral SCENE ANALYSIS, which involves the projection of SCENE DOMAIN properties onto the two-dimensional picture plane.

**image enhancement,** *n.* ENHANCEMENT of the quality of an image. Noise filtering, contrast sharpening, edge enhancement, etc. are examples of image enhancement operations.

**image feature,** *n.* an aspect of an image used to infer scenes. Image features include length and angles in an image, intensity, colour, and texture. Junction, line, and region are characteristics of image features (compare SCENE FEATURE).

**image processing,** *n.* the analysis of two-dimensional representations of an OBJECT by a computer program. It is an application of digital signal processing and can be used, for example, in IMAGE ENHANCEMENT.

**image understanding,** *n.* the ability of a system to recognize visual images. Somewhat synonymous with computer vision and SCENE ANALYSIS, image understanding applies geometric modelling and the techniques of KNOWLEDGE REPRESENTATION and cognitive processing to develop scene interpretations from image data. Dealing extensively with three-dimensional objects, image understanding usually operates not on an image but on a symbolic representation of it.

**Image Understanding Program,** *n*. a program sponsored by ARPA beginning in 1975 to investigate application of a priori knowledge to facilitate an understanding of the relationships among objects in a scene.

**imaging device,** *n*. a device that has the ability to access distinct elements of a scene separately.

**imaging geometry,** *n*. the geometric representation of an image in space. For example, in the figure below the viewer is at the origin, the z-axis is taken as the optical axis of the viewer, and the picture plane is at z=0 and is parallel to the x-y plane.

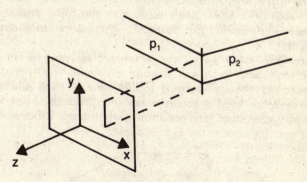

**Imaging geometry**

**IMP,** *n*. an expert system developed at Texas Instruments, which troubleshoots epitaxial reactor machinery. PERSONAL CONSULTANT is the development software.

**implementation** or **implementation environment,** *n*. the ENVIRONMENT in which an expert system operates, including the hardware, the operating system, the programming language, and the interfaces with other systems or peripherals. Most expert systems require very specific environments.

**implicational molecule,** *n*. a set of clauses related by psychological implication. For example:

[A likes B, A helps B].

Implicational molecules are used in modelling BELIEF SYSTEMS.

**implicit knowledge,** *n.* that KNOWLEDGE that can be derived procedurally and not explicitly stored in a static structure.

**IMPORT,** *n.* a measure of the importance of a PROPERTY in INTERNIST. In INTERNIST, various properties are associated with each manifestation of a disease. The most important properties are TYPE and IMPORT. The IMPORT of a manifestation is a measure of how easily it can be ignored in a diagnosis. The manifestation 'Shellfish ingestion' can be easily ignored, but a liver biopsy that shows caseating granulomas must be explained.

**importance tag,** *n.* in SCHOLAR, a VALUE used to measure the relevance of a NODE with respect to the topic under discussion. The lower the number, the more important the property.

**impossible object,** *n.* the resultant analysis of an image whereby such an object cannot exist. In VISION STUDIES a picture may be well-formed locally; that is, each junction has one or more valid SCENE-DOMAIN interpretations. But when a globally consistent interpretation is attempted, it becomes clear that one does not exist. For example:

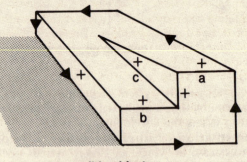

**Impossible objects**

**IMPULSE,** *n.* an editing resource for KNOWLEDGE ENGINEERS using the STROBE KNOWLEDGE ENGINEERING language. It acts as a system-building aid in the form of a display-oriented KNOW-LEDGE BASE editor. Engineers use the editor in order to edit at four levels: a top-level knowledge base manager, a knowledge base editor, an object/SLOT editor, and a FACET editor. At each level, IMPULSE supplies a window accompanied by a command menu for working at that level. TREE and GRAPH HIERARCHIES can be graphically displayed. Users can select objects for editing from menus and from NODES graphically displayed in trees. Implemented in INTERLISP-D, IMPULSE runs on Xerox 1100 series workstations. The program was developed by Schlumberger-Doll Research.

**IN-ATE,** *n.* an expert system that helps troubleshoot a Tektronix Model 465 oscilloscope by analysing symptoms and producing a decision TREE of test points to be checked by the technician. The program applies two types of RULE: those supplied by an expert diagnostician, and those generated automatically from an internal model of the oscilloscope, which is a block diagram of the unit augmented with component failure rates. KNOWLEDGE is represented as rules incorporating probabilistic measures of BELIEF about circuit malfunctions. As the rules are applied, the beliefs are updated through a procedure similar to minimaxing. Implemented in FRANZ LISP, IN-ATE was developed at the Naval Research Laboratory.

**IN-ATE/KE,** *abbrev.* *for* INtelligent-Automated Test Equipment/Knowledge Engineering, a system-building aid for constructing fault diagnosis expert systems. KNOWLEDGE is represented as a high-level block diagram of the unit under test and includes information about component/test point connectivity. IN-ATE/KE supports a PROSPECTOR-like, rule-based SEMANTIC NETWORK and a DATA BASE containing component failure rates, accessible test points, test and setup costs, and component replacement costs. Semantic CONSTRAINTS on testing order are specified through RULE preconditions. IN-ATE/KE generates an expert system in the IN-ATE framework and produces a testability report that includes a binary fault diagnosis decision TREE. IN-ATE/KE was developed at Automated Reasoning Corporation.

**incomplete knowledge,** *n.* a measure of the size of the KNOWLEDGE BASE in SCHOLAR. To look for all OBJECTS in the system that satisfy some condition, a distinction is made about whether the resulting set of these objects is closed (explicitly contains all such objects) or open (contains some and need not contain all such objects). In SCHOLAR's net, sets are tagged by the courseware author as either open or closed, thus giving an explicit indication of the incompleteness of the system's knowledge.

**incremental compiler,** *n.* in POP-2, a compiler that allows an interactive style of programming similar to that of LISP. The programmer can type in any statement and have it executed immediately, or he or she can define functions and edit them.

**incremental query formulation,** *n.* the construction of a query to a data base used in the RENDEZVOUS system. Instead of specifying the query in full, complex detail, the user receives help from the system in constructing the query.

**incremental simulation,** *n.* a technique employed at the beginning of the HWIM project for the purpose of exploring the process of SPEECH UNDERSTANDING. Individuals simulated in stages the not-yet-developed components of the system, and their interactions were analysed. These were then incorporated into the next stage of development. This technique has found wide acceptance in KNOWLEDGE-BASED SYSTEM development.

**indeterminacy,** *n.* a feature of KNOWLEDGE REPRESENTATION FORMALISMS in which a particular fact or EVENT can be encoded. For instance the fact that parrots have wings can be represented in either of the SEMANTIC NETWORKS below:

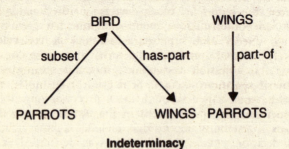

**Indeterminacy**

The first is interpreted as 'All parrots are birds, and all birds have wings'. The second states directly that 'Wings are a part of all parrots'. Although this inherent indeterminacy could be used to advantage by allowing redundant storage of information with an eye to future relevance, instead it often gives rise to confusion and expense. The system does not know exactly what structures to look for when it is time to retrieve a given fact.

**individualization of instruction,** *n.* a style of CAI often dubbed ad-hoc, FRAME-oriented (AFO) CAI for the purpose of stressing its dependence on author-specified units. The term FRAME as it is used in this context predates the more typical usage in AI research on KNOWLEDGE REPRESENTATION and refers instead to a page or unit of text. In CAI, the courseware author attempts to anticipate every wrong response, pre-specifying branches to appropriate remedial material based on his or her ideas about what the underlying misconceptions might be that would cause each wrong response. The first step toward individualization of instruction was branching on the basis of response. The design of ad-hoc frames was originally based on Skinnerian stimulus-response principles.

**INDUCE,** *n.* a program intended to be applied in structural-learning situations (situations in which each training instance has some internal structure). It addresses the problem of learning a single CONCEPT from positive training instances only.

**induction** or **inductive inference,** *n.* an 'educated guess' about a user's query based on program specifications that only partially describe the program's behaviour. Such specifications are often the examples of input/output pairs and program TRACES, in both regular and generic form. For each of these kinds of specification, the corresponding AUTOMATIC PROGRAMMING system must determine the general RULES on the basis of a specification containing only a few examples (or in the generic specifications, a limited class of examples) of program behaviour.

**induction axiom,** *n.* in AUTOMATIC PROGRAMMING a SCHEMA such as:

$$[P(h(NIL),NIL) \wedge Ax. [ATOM(x)$$
$$\wedge P(h(cdr(x)), cdr(x)) \supset P(h(x),x)]]$$
$$\supset Az.[P(h(z),z)],$$

165

where P is any predicate and h is any FUNCTION. This predicate and function must be determined. To require the user to supply this induction AXIOM for each program to be synthesized defeats the purpose of automating the synthesis, since it might be easier to specify the entire program some other way. Having the system generate induction axioms randomly until one of them works is also not feasible. Automatic programming systems with this approach most often attempt to determine P and h by means of various HEURISTICS used to limit SEARCH.

**induction of programs,** see AUTOMATIC PROGRAMMING.

**induction system,** *n*. a KNOWLEDGE SYSTEM having a KNOW-LEDGE BASE that consists of examples. From the examples, an ALGORITHM builds a decision TREE and the system proceeds to deliver advice. Induction systems do not support the development of HIERARCHIES of RULES.

**induction template,** *n*. a skeletal induction form that includes the variable substitutions needed in the BOYER-MOORE THEOREM PROVER. If, in the course of rewrites, a theorem has still not been reduced to T, the Boyer-Moore Theorem Prover automatically formulates a valid induction argument in order to try to prove the theorem. Inductions are formulated by using information collected at the time the FUNCTION is defined and at the time the actual induction is needed. When a function is defined, the system must prove that the function terminates before allowing the definition. Termination is proved by finding a well-founded function that decreases when applied to a subset of the arguments used in all recursive calls. The system exhaustively searches through all lexicographic orders of all well-founded functions applied to all subsets and permutations of a function's arguments. These are all collected in the set of induction templates that are associated with the newly defined function. These templates include the form of the induction to be performed and all of the variable substitutions that will need to be made.

**industrial vision system,** see ROBOTIC VISION.

**inexact knowledge,** see UNCERTAINTY.

**inexact reasoning,** *n*. reasoning involving CONFIDENCE FACTORS that are attached to the conclusion part of each production in PRODUCTION SYSTEMS, for example, to help determine the relative strengths of alternatives.

**inference,** *n.* **1.** the process of reaching a conclusion from an initial set of propositions, the truths of which are known or assumed.

**2.** a process of deriving new facts from known facts by IN-DUCTION, deduction, or ABDUCTION. The RULES that govern this process are called the rules of inference. The rule of IN-STANTIATION, for example, allows us to make statements about a particular individual in a group, given facts about that group as a whole. A rule, such as 'If the sky is blue, then the time is day', when combined with a rule of inference (e.g., MODUS PONENS) and a known fact, such as 'The sky is blue', results in a new fact: The time is day. A complex series of inferences can be organized to proceeds from ANTECEDENT propositions that are given to whatever consequent propositions are justified. The FORWARD CHAINING process called data inference, accomplishes this type of inference. When a complex series of inferences proceeds from a specification of the desired consequence and tries to prove antecedents that will justify concluding the CONSEQUENT, the process of BACK-CHAINING accomplishes the inference. Back-chaining achieves a model-directed or goal-directed inference.

**inference, data-directed,** *n.* an INFERENCE that is driven by EVENTS rather than by GOALS. An inference that is made when a fact is added to the DATA BASE, rather than when a request for information is made. (See FORWARD CHAINING.)

**inference, goal-directed,** *n.* an INFERENCE that is driven by GOALS rather than data. An inference that is made when a request for information is made, rather than when a fact is added to the data base. (See BACK-CHAINING.)

**inference, model-directed,** see EXPECTATION-DRIVEN REASONING.

**inference chain,** *n.* the sequence of steps or RULE applications used by a RULE-BASED SYSTEM to reach a conclusion.

**inference engine,** *n.* also known as the control structure or RULE interpreter, the section of an expert system that controls the system's operation; that part of a KNOWLEDGE SYSTEM or expert system that makes INFERENCES based on information in the DATA BASE. The inference engine selects rules to use, accesses those rules, and determines when a solution has been found. It is the part of a KNOWLEDGE-BASED SYSTEM or expert system that contains the general problem-solving KNOWLEDGE, and processes the DOMAIN KNOWLEDGE (located in the KNOWLEDGE BASE) in order to reach new conclusions. In sum, an inference engine is a software framework or shell structure that is applied to the information in a knowledge base for the purposes of making relationships and decisions about the information; it contains subsystems that control how knowledge is acquired and how the user interacts with the system. Using standard OBJECT rules inherent in the inference engine, the program is designed to make logical assumptions, cross-references, and inferences about the knowledge programmed into an expert system. Inference engines vary. A given inference engine is characterized by the inference and CONTROL strategies it uses. The inference engine of MYCIN, for example, uses MODUS PONENS and BACK-CHAINING.

**inference method,** *n.* the technique or strategy used by the INFERENCE ENGINE to access and apply the DOMAIN KNOWLEDGE; that is, to make INFERENCES based on the information in the DATA BASE (e.g., FORWARD and BACK-CHAINING).

**inference net,** *n.* all possible INFERENCE CHAINS that can be generated from the RULES in a RULE-BASED SYSTEM.

**inference rule,** *n.* a RULE of logic that allows new sentences to be deduced from previously given sentences. An inference rule asserts the fact that a given new sentence is true if the original sentences were true. MODUS PONENS (the rule of universal INSTANTIATION) is the best-known inference rule.

**informant presentation,** *n.* a language learning situation in which if a learning program can pose questions to an informant (e.g., ask a person whether or not a given string was grammatical), the 'true' language can be learned.

**information processing psychology,** *n.* also called cognitive science, that branch of psychology that tries to account for human problem-solving capabilities.

**informedness,** *n.* a characteristic by which two ALGORITHMS can be compared. Two otherwise similar algorithms, say, $A_1$ and $A_2$, can be compared with respect to their choices of the $h\star$ function, say, $h_1\star$ and $h_2\star$. Algorithm $A_1$ is said to be more informed than $A_2$ if, whenever a NODE n (other than a

GOAL node) is evaluated,

$$h_1{}^\star(n) > h_2{}^\star(n).$$

**infrared image,** *n.* an image captured on film sensitive to infrared light. It is commonly used in analysis of ground coverage from aerial or satellite images; for example, vegetation reflects green and infrared radiation and is therefore relatively easy to detect with such film.

**inheritance,** *n.* a process in which the assumption is that one particular individual in a group has characteristics that are similar to other individuals in that group.

**inheritance hierarchy,** *n.* a structure in a SEMANTIC NETWORK (associative framework) or FRAME system that permits items lower in the net (subordinate items) to inherit properties from items higher up in the net.

**initial state,** *n.* the beginning STATE(s) in a STATE-SPACE SEARCH. A solution to a STATE-SPACE problem is a finite sequence of applications of OPERATORS that changes an initial state into a GOAL STATE. A state-space problem is then the triple (S,O,G), where the complete specification of a state-space problem has three components. One is a set O of OPERATORS or OPERATOR SCHEMATA. One defines a set S of one or more INITIAL STATES and a predicate defining a set G of goal states.

**instance,** *n.* also called TOKENS, unique names made up for each individual in a set in order to guarantee that there is only one assigned individual per name.

**instance selection,** see INSTANCE SPACE.

**instance space,** *n.* the space of possible TRAINING INSTANCES.

**instantiation,** *n.* a PATTERN or FORMULA in which the VARIABLES have been replaced by constants. The association of a particular individual with the characteristics of some class, or the assignment of particular VALUES to the parameters of a PROCEDURE. An instantiation can be represented as an ordered pair. The first member identifies the RULE that has been satisfied, and the second member is a list of working memory elements that match the condition elements of the rule. In a PRODUCTION SYSTEM, an instantiation is the result of successfully matching a rule against the contents of data memory.

**instructional software,** *n.* software that assists in the learning or performance of some task. Instructional software includes not only software used strictly for educational purposes but also that used for job training or job aid. Small expert systems that assist in the performance of some task are a type of instructional software.

**instructional strategy,** see TUTORING STRATEGY.

**instrument,** *n.* a deep case in the CASE GRAMMAR that indicates the stimulus or immediate physical cause of an EVENT.

**integration,** *n.* a software design concept allowing users to move easily between application programs or to incorporate data from one program to another; for example, moving data displayed in a graphics program into a text document.

**integration problem,** *n.* the problem of integrating (see INTEGRATION) a new RULE into an existing set of rules.

**Intelligent Building Management,** *n.* an expert system developed for Johnson Controls' commercial use. It performs intelligent building management. PICON is the development software.

**Intelligent Computer-Assisted Instruction (ICAI),** *n.* an area of research in ARTIFICIAL INTELLIGENCE with the goal of creating training programs that can analyse a student's learning pattern and appropriately modify the teaching techniques used in the training. An ICAI program consists of PROBLEM-SOLVING expertise, a student model, and a TUTORING MODULE.

**Intelligent Peripheral Troubleshooter,** *n.* an expert system developed by Hewlett Packard for internal use. It troubleshoots computer peripheral equipment.

**Intelligent Software Configurator,** *n.* an expert system developed at Honeywell for internal use. It helps configure software for DPS 6 computers. The program is implemented in both LISP and LOOPS.

**intensional operator,** *n.* an OPERATOR that produces sentences whose TRUTH VALUES depend fully on the meanings, not just the truth values, of their arguments.

**interacting subgoals,** see SUBGOAL.

**interactive dialogue,** see MIXED-INITIATIVE DIALOGUE.

**interactive knowledge acquisition,** see KNOWLEDGE ACQUISITION.

**Interactive LISP,** see INTERLISP.

**interactive program specification,** *n.* a programming methodology that interacts with the user to obtain missing information, to verify HYPOTHESES, or to point out inconsistencies in the specification.

**interactive transfer of expertise,** *n.* one of two processes for handcrafting KNOWLEDGE BASES that were used in DENDRAL. The DOMAIN-specific RULES that constitute DENDRAL's knowledge about mass spectrometry were derived from consultation with experts in that field. The process of interactive transfer of expertise is designed to reduce the time-consuming consultation process.

**interdependent subproblem,** *n.* a subproblem in a SEARCH TREE for which the start cannot be reduced to a conjunction of subproblems and/or all subproblems cannot be solved independently, so that the solution to one subproblem has an effect on the solution to any other. Two kinds of examples of these are: (a) problems requiring consistent binding of VARIABLES and (b) problems involving the expenditure of scarce resources.

**interest operator,** *n.* a technique for finding unambiguous matches in the regions of pictures having high information content, or high variance. Unambiguous matches are more likely to be found in such regions. The interest OPERATOR first computes the sum of the squares of the differences between each PIXEL in a window and the pixel's neighbours in each of four directions (horizontal, vertical, and two diagonals). This computation results in four sums, and the interest measure for each pixel is the minimum of the sums. Interesting points are those for which the interest measure attains a local maximum. Thus, interesting points have a high variance in all directions and are therefore likely to find an unambiguous match in the other image. An interest operator tends to select corners, for example.

**interestingness,** *n.* the quality of a RULE or problem that can augment the program's model by specifying class-specific KNOWLEDGE to the program. This capability provides a way of forming new RULES in the context of additional intuitions or biases. A KNOWLEDGE ENGINEER can thus see the most interesting rules (as defined by the augmentations) before the other rules. For example, one might be interested in rules that mention at least one nitrogen atom before one looks at the generally less interesting rules that mention only carbon and hydrogen substructures.

**interface,** *n.* a shared boundary between two devices, two or more programs, or a system and a human operator. It is the structure that governs how a system interacts with the outside world. KNOWLEDGE SYSTEMS typically have interfaces that determine how the system acquires knowledge (the KNOWLEDGE ACQUISITION interface) and how it interacts with the user (the user interface). It may also have interfaces that allow it to interact with other systems or peripheral devices.

**interference matching,** *n.* a technique used in learning to discover concepts expressed in an existentially quantified (see EXISTENTIAL QUANTIFICATION.) conjunctive statement in PREDICATE CALCULUS. Another method is the maximal unifying GENERALIZATION METHOD. Both methods can be viewed as implementations of an update-procedure with respect to slightly different REPRESENTATION languages in that they learn from positive TRAINING INSTANCES only. The interference matching ALGORITHM starts out as a BREADTH-FIRST SEARCH of all possible matchings. The search proceeds by growing common subexpressions until a space limit is reached. A HEURISTIC utility function then prunes unpromising matches, and the growing process continues in a more DEPTH-FIRST manner. The utility of a partial match is equal to the number of predicates matched less the number of variables matched. If the space limit is approximately the same as the largest common subexpression, the algorithm becomes truly depthfirst, since only one subexpression fits within the space limit. The interference matching algorithm thus tends to find one good common subexpression rather than finding all maximal common subexpressions.

**interlingua,** *n.* a universal language that is used in some machine translation systems. Translating between languages A and B involves going from language A to the intermediate language (interlingua) and then to the language B equivalent.

**INTERLISP,** *n.* a programming language for PROCEDURE-ORIENTED REPRESENTATION. As a dialect of LISP, INTERLISP has all the standard LISP features plus an elaborate SUPPORT

ENVIRONMENT including sophisticated DEBUGGING facilities with tracing and conditional breakpoints, a LISP-oriented editor, and a DWIM (Do What I Mean) facility that immediately corrects many kinds of errors. It also includes CLISP (Conversational LISP), a set of surface syntax constructs that are translated into ordinary LISP. It has various abbreviations, a record package, a PATTERN MATCHING compiler, algebraic notation, in addition to other features. CLISP is actually implemented through the error-catching mechanism of INTERLISP: Any input that cannot be recognized as LISP is analysed to see if it is valid CLISP before the system indicates that an error has been made. The name INTERLISP stands for 'Interactive LISP.' INTERLISP is a 'residential' system in that the facilities reside in a core and can be called without the user leaving LISP. The INTERLISP ENVIRONMENT permits users to modify aspects of the system that are normally fixed, such as interrupt characters and GARBAGE COLLECTION allocation. It functions as a general-purpose programming environment suited for a broad spectrum of development requirements and programming styles using the natural, functional style of LISP. In addition, INTERLISP supports a style of programming called structured growth or incremental development. Data representation methods used in INTERLISP help make it easier to write LISP programs that examine and change other LISP programs. FUNCTIONS in INTERLISP are easy to extend, making INTERLISP especially appropriate for users who need to modify the language. Because user-defined functions may be referenced exactly like INTERLISP primitive functions, the programming process can essentially be viewed as extending the language. Developed by Xerox Corporation as a commercial system, INTERLISP runs on a variety of Xerox machines.

**INTERLISP-D,** *n.* a dialect of LISP, designed for high resolution, bit-mapped display. The PROGRAMMING ENVIRONMENT includes an in-core editor for structures, TOOLS for automatic error-correction, syntax extension and structure declaration and access, and extensive usage of display-oriented tools and facilities.

**intermediate OR node,** *n.* a NODE in a SEARCH TREE that dominates a subproblem connected by an OR.

**internal line,** *n.* a line resulting from the intersection of two surfaces of the same object.

**Internal Problem Description,** *n.* a network in NLPQ, where the system uses the information it obtains from an English dialogue to build and complete a partial description of a desired simulation.

**INTERNIST-I/CADUCEUS,** *n.* an expert system that uses knowledge of disease profiles to assist physicians making multiple and complex diagnoses in general internal medicine. The program takes as input a patient's history, symptoms, and laboratory test results. With over 500 diseases described in terms of 3500 manifestations of disease contained in the program's knowledge base, INTERNIST-I/CADUCEUS is one of the largest medical expert systems. The program accesses a network-representation of findings and diseases based on the CONSTRAINTS of the disease taxonomy and causality relations. Implemented in LISP, the first version of the system was called INTERNIST-I; the second version, CADUCEUS. The program was developed at the University of Pittsburgh.

**interpersonal function,** *n.* in a SYSTEMIC GRAMMAR, a function that relates to the purpose of the utterance. (See also IDEATIONAL FUNCTION and TEXTUAL FUNCTION.)

**INTERPLAN,** *n.* a nonhierarchical planner developed at Edinburgh. It uses a declarative representation called a TICK LIST in order to allow PROTECTION VIOLATIONS to be detected.

**interpret,** *n.* In scene interpretation, a routine that proceeds as follows:

(a) Segmentation. The picture is partitioned into pieces corresponding to individual forms. Some of the lines in the original picture may not appear in any of these pieces.

(b) Completion. Add lines to complete, or to partially complete, some of the forms. One of the form descriptions is complete.

(c) Recognition. Each form is identified as an instance of a MODEL and is located in three-dimensional space. This constitutes an INTERPRETATION of the scene. Although this step does not require that the forms in the picture be complete, it is more likely to succeed if there are no missing lines.

(d) Prediction. To check that the interpretation of the scene is consistent with the original picture, the three-dimensional locations and identities of the MODELS are used to generate a predicted line drawing.

(e) Verification. The prediction and the original picture are compared to see how closely they align. If the two are approximately the same, the scene interpretation is assumed to be correct. Otherwise, part of the scene is re-analysed to produce a more consistent interpretation.

**interpretation,** *n*. **1.** the transformation of a NATURAL LANGUAGE statement or form into a formal REPRESENTATION. **2.** the inferencing from training examples in a learning ENVIRONMENT.

**interpreter,** *n*. that portion of a PRODUCTION SYSTEM that controls its activity. By analysing the programming code, the interpreter has the task of deciding which production to fire next. More specifically, in an expert system, the interpreter is the part of the INFERENCE ENGINE that determines how to apply known facts.

**interpretive semantics,** *n*. a model of GENERATIVE GRAMMAR where both the DEEP STRUCTURE of a sentence and its subsequent transformations are input to the SEMANTIC COMPONENT. In contrast with GENERATIVE SEMANTICS, interpretive semantics keeps the SYNTACTIC COMPONENT an autonomous system.

**intersection search,** *n*. a search strategy in which a common NODE is used. In SCHOLAR, answering questions of the form 'Can X be a part of Y?' (e.g., 'Is Buenos Aires in Argentina?') is done by an intersection search: the superpart (SUPERP) ARCS of both NODES for X and Y are traced until an intersection is found (i.e., a common superconcept node is found). If there is no intersection, the answer is 'No.' If there is an intersection node Q, SCHOLAR answers in the following manner:

If $Q = Y$, then 'Yes';
If $Q = X$, then 'No, Y is an X.'

**intonation,** *n*. the prosodic quality of an utterance that relies on pitch differences.

**intrinsic images,** *n*. a set of retinotopic maps, each of which makes explicit the VALUE of a certain PROPERTY that is intrinsic to the surfaces in the scene. Intrinsic images all have the same viewer-centred coordinate system but carry information about different surface properties, such as surface orientation, depth, reflectance, colour, texture and optic flow field in the scene. Computation of intrinsic images is non-trivial since many of the images are undetermined when considered independently, but global consistency CONSTRAINTS can be cooperatively exploited (e.g., surface boundary information carried by the reflectance image can be used to constrain the computation of the surface orientation from shading information). Intrinsic images are important at the stage in computing a REPRESENTATION that is intermediate between the lowest levels of image processing, where descriptions are essentially two-dimensional pictorial or iconic descriptions (see ICONIC REPRESENTATION) of the scene, and the higher levels of processing, which describe the shapes of objects in terms of an OBJECT-CENTRED viewer-independent COORDINATE SYSTEM. Intrinsic images are the first representations of explicit information concerning the three-dimensional structure of a scene.

**introduction rule,** *n.* a RULE in a NATURAL DEDUCTION system that introduces, for example, a QUANTIFIER, which is then eliminated by an ELIMINATION rule.

**intrusion,** *n.* in a recall task, the appearance of a list from members of another list.

**I/O,** *abbrev. for* input/output devices. The communication between a program or system and its user.

**IPL,** *n.* an early LIST PROCESSING programming language, created by Newell, Shaw, and Simon for their early AI work on problem-solving methods. IPL's design was guided by ideas from psychology, especially the intuitive notion of association. Symbols, as opposed to numbers, were the primary elements of the language. To form associations of these symbols, list processing was introduced, which allowed programs to build data structures of unpredictable shape and size. When PARSING a sentence, choosing a chess move, or planning robot actions, one cannot know ahead of time the form of the data structures that will represent the meaning of the sentence, the play of the game, or the plan of action. The unconstrained form of data structures is an important characteristic of list processing languages.

**IRIS,** *n.* an expert system that uses knowledge of medical diagnosis to help physicians diagnose and treat diseases. In order to choose a diagnosis and treatment, the program takes as input a patient's history and symptoms. A SEMANTIC NETWORK is used to define relationships among symptoms, diseases, and treatments. DECISION TABLES associated with the NODES of the network control the INFERENCE process. For help in choosing a diagnosis, the program generates MYCIN–like CERTAINTY FACTORS through the semantic network. IRIS is more of an ENVIRONMENT to help physicians explore medical decisions rather than a conventional expert system. It was developed at Rutgers University.

**IR-NLI,** *abbrev. for* Information Retrieval–Natural Language Interface, an expert system that acts as a front-end providing nontechnical users with a NATURAL LANGUAGE INTERFACE to the information retrieval services offered by on-line DATA BASES. As a front-end to several available data bases, IR-NLI decides which will be the most appropriate for answering the user's requests. IR-NLI combines the EXPERTISE of a professional intermediary for on-line SEARCHING with the capability for understanding natural language and carrying out a dialogue with the user. KNOWLEDGE is encoded as RULES that operate on two KNOWLEDGE BASES. One contains DOMAIN-specific knowledge and the other vocabulary knowledge. The domain-specific knowledge base uses a SEMANTIC NETWORK REPRESENTATION technique to define the data base concepts and indicate how the concepts are related. The vocabulary knowledge base uses FRAMES to define the LEXICON of the application DOMAIN. Implemented in FRANZ LISP, IR-NLI was developed at the University of Udine, Udine, Italy.

**ISA,** *n.* **1.** the principal relation, denoting taxonomy, in many knowledge-based systems.
**2.** an expert system developed for Digital Equipment Corporation's manufacturing scheduling.

**ISIS,** *n. acronym for* Intelligent Scheduling and Information System, an expert system that uses knowledge of the organizing principles, physical constraints, and causal constraints governing scheduling decisions surrounding factory job shop schedules in order to construct the schedules. The program selects a sequence of operations needed to complete the order, assigns necessary resources to each operation, and establishes a timeframe in which to complete the job. During the term of the job, the program acts as an intelligent assistant helping plant schedulers adhere to the constraints of due dates, cost control, physical limitations of machines, and the ordering of operations as they must occur throughout the job. The program uses a FRAME-based KNOWLEDGE scheme together with RULES for resolving events where CONSTRAINTS conflict. Implemented in SRL, ISIS was developed at Carnegie-Mellon University and tested at the Westinghouse Electric Corporation turbine component plant.

**island driving,** *n.* a method for deciding how words and constituents will be either combined (BOTTOM-UP) or expanded (TOP-DOWN) in the context of either a top-down or bottom-up technique. The method in both cases, using island driving, involves proceeding systematically in one direction (normally left to right) or to start anywhere and systematically look at neighbouring chunks of increasing size. In the HEARSAY and the SRI/SDC SPEECH SYSTEMS, a MIDDLE-OUT SEARCH STRATEGY was used: find whatever words can be immediately identified, then expand out to either side of all of them. This strategy is called island driving because it establishes islands in the rest of the sentence. One problem with the strategy is that the number of hypothesized extensions of islands can be very large, and this COMBINATORIAL PROBLEM is compounded by having many islands, especially if the islands are not really reliable HYPOTHESES and will soon be abandoned.

**iso–intensity contours,** *n.* lines in a contour map with the same intensity. The figure opposite shows the REFLECTANCE MAP for a lambertian surface, drawn as a series of iso–intensity contours for the case $p_s = 0.7$, $q_s = 0.3$, and $p = 1$. The surface orientations on a single contour generate the same image intensity. Those to the left of the straight lines $p_s p + q_s q + 1 = 0$ correspond to the orientations that face away from the illumination and, thus, do not give rise to any brightness. The function $R(p,q)$ is called a reflectance map.

**isolated word recognition,** *n.* the recognition of individual words in a speech system. Isolated-word recognition systems compare the incoming SPEECH SIGNAL with an internal REPRESENTATION of the acoustical pattern of each word in a

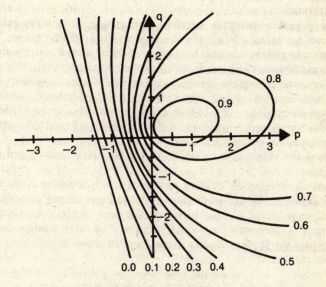

**Iso-intensity contours**

relatively small vocabulary, and then, using some distance metric, select the best MATCH. The technique gives rise to several characteristics of the speech signal, which must be overcome. One problem is that the microphone and background noise introduce interference into the recording of a spoken utterance. Another problem is that a given speaker does not pronounce a particular word identically every time he or she speaks. Even if the program is tuned to one speaker, the matching process between the acoustical pattern of the vocabulary words (the TEMPLATES) and the actual utterance is inherently inexact. If the system must recognize words spoken by more than one speaker, the matching task becomes much more difficult.

**ISPEC,** *n. acronym for* Information SPECification, a KNOW-LEDGE structure in IRIS used to store patient-specific knowledge gathered during consultation. It is a FRAME making an ASSERTION about the patient.

**ISS Three,** *n.* an expert system developed by International

Systems Services Corporation for commercial use. It manages computer capacity.

**issues and examples tutoring strategy,** *n*. a strategy that provides a framework for meeting the two CONSTRAINTS that ICAI comments should be both relevant to the situation and memorable to the student. Issues are CONCEPTS used in the diagnostic process to identify, at any particular moment, what is relevant. Examples provide concrete INSTANCES of these abstract concepts. Providing both the description of a generic Issue (a concept used to select a strategy) and a concrete example of its use, increases the chance that the student will integrate this piece of tutorial commentary into his knowledge.

**item,** *n*. a category of data type in SAIL's associative-DATA BASE mechanism. Items were the major feature of the earlier LEAP language, which was incorporated into SAIL. An item is either a PRIMITIVE identifier (ATOM) or a triple of items. Triples are formed by the association of three items:

$$\text{Attribute} \otimes \text{Object} \equiv \text{Value}.$$

**iterative deepening,** *n*. a variation of a fixed-depth SEARCH used in CHESS 4.5. Iterative search involves a complete search and investigating all legal moves (subject to ALPHA/BETA PRUNING) done to depth 2, returning a move. The search is then redone to depth 3, again to depth 4, and so on until a preset limit is exceeded. Despite its weaknesses, many programs involving GAME TREE SEARCH still use a fixed-depth search, extended for checks and capture sequences.

**iterative endpoint fit,** *n*. an ALGORITHM for generating a multiple-line description from a given set of points. The algorithm begins by choosing from the set two extreme points, A and B, and approximates the entire set by the line joining these two endpoints. If the fit is good, the procedure stops; otherwise, it chooses the point farthest from the fitted line, C, and replaces the one-line description AB by a two-line description, AC, CB. The process is repeated on each of these segments until sufficiently good MATCHES are achieved for all segments. Unfortunately, this simple algorithm can be strongly influenced by a single noisy input. It is essential that it operate in a virtually noise-free environment, provided by an earlier smoothing process.

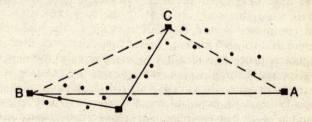

**Iterative endpoint fit**

# J

**job aids (performance aids),** *n.* devices that help individuals perform tasks. Well-constructed job aids allow the performer to avoid memorization. They therefore allow individuals to perform jobs more quickly and more accurately than they would if they had been trained in any conventional manner. Moreover, since performers memorize frequently-used responses while using job aids, these aids serve as structured on-the-job training. Whenever they are appropriate, job aids are the current medium of choice among instructional designers. Small KNOWLEDGE SYSTEMS are ideal job aids for a wide variety of tasks and will rapidly replace most of the checklists, procedures manuals, and other common job aids currently in use. (See also PERFORMANCE AIDS.)

**JUDITH,** *n.* an expert system that uses KNOWLEDGE of premises and of constructing premises in order to help lawyers reason about civil law cases. The program begins the process of accounting for all relevant premises the lawyer should consider in a case by first interviewing the lawyer to establish the factual and legal premises of the cause of the action. Based on the interview data, the program presents additional premises for the lawyer to consider, and also specifies the relationships between sets of given premises. The program is particularly useful as an AI ENVIRONMENT to explore legal reasoning rather than as a traditional expert system. Implemented in FORTRAN, JUDITH was developed at the Universities of Heidelberg and Darmstadt.

**judgemental knowledge,** *n.* KNOWLEDGE that is more intuitive or uncertain than that of a body of accepted facts.

**junction type,** *n.* a connection in IMAGE PROCESSING. In VISION studies, the junction types include the Huffman-Clowes junctions (L, ARROW, FORK, T) plus four-line and some five-line junctions.

**juncture rule,** *n.* in PHONETICS, a RULE that accounts for contextual effects between words.

**justification,** *n.* one of the two fundamental data structures involved in DEPENDENCY records. The other is NODES. Nodes label DATA BASE entries, INFERENCE RULES, procedures, and so forth, for use in justifications. Justifications represent INFERENCE steps from combinations of nodes to another node (more properly, from the referents of combinations of nodes to the referent of another node).

# K

**KANDOR,** *n.* a KNOWLEDGE ENGINEERING language for FRAME-based representation designed to conceal its internal structure from the user. The user INTERFACE consists of FRAMES, SLOTS, restrictions, and slot fillers. KANDOR's expressive power is limited in order to provide computational flexibility and easy use. Implemented in LISP, it was developed at the Fairchild Laboratory for Artificial Intelligence Research.

**KARNAK,** *n.* an expert system developed for Digital Equipment Corp. in circuit board wave soldering diagnostics.

**KAS,** *n. acronym for* Knowledge Acquisition System, the KNOWLEDGE ENGINEERING language PROSPECTOR with its knowledge of geology removed. It is used for RULE-based REPRESENTATION. To encode knowledge, this language uses a partitioned SEMANTIC NETWORK and INFERENCE RULES with associated CERTAINTY FACTORS. FORWARD CHAINING and BACK-CHAINING provide the basis for inferences and the generation of probabilities through the semantic network. The language features explanation and KNOWLEDGE ACQUISITION facilities, and also accommodates synonym recognition, answer revision, summarization, and tracing. Implemented in INTERLISP, KAS was developed at SRI International.

**KBS,** *abbrev. for* Knowledge-Based Simulation system, a KNOWLEDGE ENGINEERING language for OBJECT-ORIENTED and FRAME-based representation. It is particularly useful in object-oriented modelling for purposes of simulation. The SUPPORT ENVIRONMENT contains interactive MODEL construction and modification tools that are supported by generic SCHEMATA from model libraries of objects and RELATIONS. It also contains model consistency and completeness checking facilities. Implemented in SRL, KBS runs under the VAX FRANZ LISP system, and was developed at the Robotics Institute of Carnegie–Mellon University.

**KE,** *n. acronym for* KNOWLEDGE ENGINEER.

**KEE,** *n. acronym for* Knowledge Engineering Environment, a

KNOWLEDGE ENGINEERING language for FRAME-based RE-
PRESENTATION, which also supports RULE-based, procedure-
oriented (see PROCEDURE-ORIENTED METHODS), and OBJECT-
oriented representation. It features multiple KNOWLEDGE BASES
for use in modular system design, and applies FORWARD
CHAINING and BACK-CHAINING to its rule INTERPRETER. The
USER INTERFACE includes a graphics-oriented debugger and an
explanation facility that graphically displays INFERENCE CHAINS.
Implemented in INTERLISP, KEE runs on Xerox 1100 and
Symbolics 3600 computers. It was developed by Intellicorp.

**KES,** *n. acronym for* Knowledge Engineering System, a KNOW-
LEDGE ENGINEERING language for RULE-based and FRAME-based
REPRESENTATION. It features a statistical pattern classification
subsystem based on the BAYES'S THEOREM, BACK- and FOR-
WARD CHAINING control scheme, and certainty handling. The
USER INTERFACE includes an explanation facility capable of
illustrating the program's reasoning and KNOWLEDGE ACQUISI-
TION strategy. Implemented in FRANZ LISP, KES runs on a
variety of computers. KES was developed by Software
Architecture and Engineering, Inc.

**killer heuristic,** *n.* an approach to move ordering where, if a
move has served as a REFUTATION MOVE in some previously
examined position that is similar to the current one, it is also
likely to be a refutation (showing that the move is bad) in the
current position.

**kinetic depth effect,** *n.* the ability of humans to perceive
correctly three-dimensional structures from a two-dimensional
movie. Three-dimensional structures can be derived from
movement while in theory, there is no unique structure consistent with a given motion in two-dimensional space.

**KITCHENWORLD,** *n.* an implementation of MEMOD
whose DOMAIN is recipes.

**KLAUS,** *n.* an INTERFACE system between the user's need and
the resources of the computer system. KLAUS's goal is to assist users in the management of information that occurs in various forms. Ideally, the user of a DBMS should be able to
interact with the system in terms of the enterprise being
modelled. The system should not confine the user's questions
to concepts and terminology inherently covered by the DATA
BASE. The user should be able to ask questions about the data

base (e.g. about the kinds of information stored in the given data base). These are some of the goals of the KLAUS system.

**KL-ONE,** *n.* a KNOWLEDGE ENGINEERING language for FRAME-based representation. It features subsumption and other relations for use in SEMANTIC NETWORKS, automatic INHERITANCE, and an automatic classifier. The USER INTERFACE includes display tools and an interactive KNOWLEDGE BASE editor. Implemented in INTERLISP-D, KL-ONE runs on Xerox 1100 and DEC VAX computers. It was developed by Bolt, Baranek, and Newman.

**KMS,** *abbrev. for* Knowledge Management System, a KNOWLEDGE ENGINEERING language for FRAME-based and RULE-based representation that incorporates various subsystems. Each subsystem contains its own KNOWLEDGE REPRESENTATION and INFERENCE METHODS. KMS features include rule-based deduction, statistical pattern classification using BAYES'S THEOREM, linear discriminant and other scoring functions, and frame-based INFERENCE generation. Implemented in LISP, KMS runs on the Univac 1100/40. It was developed at the University of Maryland.

**KNEECAP,** *n.* an expert system that uses KNOWLEDGE about orbiter vehicles, launch and landing sites, astronauts' skill qualifications, current payloads, shuttle activities, and crew roles, to help plan crew activity on board the space shuttle. The program checks for inconsistencies in a schedule as the user plans an entire flight mission. Using a REPRESENTATION method similar to FRL, the program's knowledge is encoded as FRAMES. The program is implemented in INTERLISP within a frame network. It was developed by the MITRE Corporation.

**KNOBS,** *n. acronym for* KNOwledge Based System, an expert system that helps a controller at a tactical air command and control centre perform mission planning. The program uses KNOWLEDGE about targets, resources, and planned missions in order to check the consistency of plan components, to rank possible plans, and to help generate new plans. Knowledge in KNOBS is in the form of FRAMES and BACK-CHAINING RULES. The program also uses a NATURAL LANGUAGE subsystem for data base queries and updates. In the KNOBS literature, early articles refer to KNOBS as the expert system for mission planning. Later articles use the term KNOBS to mean the KNOBS ARCHITECTURE rather than a specific expert system. Implemented in FRL and ZETALISP, KNOBS was developed by the MITRE Corporation.

**knowledge,** *n.* the information a computer must possess in order to behave intelligently. This includes FACTS, BELIEFS, and HEURISTIC RULES. Thus knowledge is an integrated collection of facts and relationships that, when exercised, produces competent performance. The variety of situations in which a person or computer program can obtain successful results provides a basis for judging the quantity and quality of knowledge either might possess.

**knowledge acquisition,** *n.* the process of extracting, structuring, and organizing KNOWLEDGE from some source, usually from a human expert, for use in a program. Locating, collecting, and refining the knowledge often requires interviews with experts, research in a library, or introspection. The person undertaking the knowledge acquisition must convert the acquired knowledge into a form that enables a computer program to use it.

**knowledge base,** *n.* a collection of KNOWLEDGE represented in the form of RULES, PROCEDURES, schemes, or working memory elements. Any highly structured and interconnected DATA BASE; the repository of knowledge in a computer system. ARTIFICIAL INTELLIGENCE systems using a knowledge base are called KNOWLEDGE-BASED SYSTEMS. The knowledge base consists of FACTS and HEURISTICS about a DOMAIN. Within a knowledge-based system, a knowledge base contains structured, codified knowledge and heuristics for use in problem-solving. In an expert system, the knowledge base generally contains a model of the problem domain, and a level of general-purpose knowledge.

**knowledge-based system,** *n.* a program in which the DOMAIN KNOWLEDGE is explicit and separate from the program's other knowledge. A computer program that applies specialized knowledge to the solution of problems. An expert system is an example of a knowledge-based system used for the purpose of capturing the expertise of human DOMAIN EXPERTS.

**knowledge compiler,** *n.* in HARPY, the program that actually builds the network. The task of the knowledge compiler is to generate allophonic representations (see ALLOPHONE) of all possible sentences, given HARPY's SYNTAX and LEXICON.

**knowledge engineer,** *n.* a person who designs and builds (implements) an expert system. Knowledge engineers interview DOMAIN experts in order to obtain raw KNOWLEDGE. The knowledge obtained from domain experts is then formulated into RULES and programs in a fashion the computer can handle. In sum, a knowledge engineer is a person whose speciality is assessing problems, acquiring knowledge, and building KNOWLEDGE SYSTEMS. In general, knowledge engineers possess training in cognitive science, computer science, and ARTIFICIAL INTELLIGENCE. A titled knowledge engineer generally has had experience in the actual development of one or more expert systems.

**knowledge engineering,** *n.* the discipline concerned with the task of building EXPERT SYSTEMS. The process of building expert systems involves the use of TOOLS and methods that support the development of an expert system.

**knowledge needed for learning,** *n.* that knowledge that is presupposed as necessary for learning. This includes single concepts, large amounts of DOMAIN KNOWLEDGE, knowledge of analogies, and examples.

**knowledge, opacity of,** *n.* the hiding of knowledge from the user. For example, a major portion of the DENDRAL expertise resides in a procedure that is conceptually opaque to the typical user. The PROBLEM-SOLVING expertise of the system is in a form that is not at all similar to the expertise that a human expert would apply to obtain the solution. In the case of DENDRAL programs, the GENERATOR of chemical-structure candidates employs a procedure for exhaustively producing possible structures based on various graph-theoretic notions that organic chemists who use the system are unlikely to know or care about. The generator was developed because the method used by chemists to find solutions for these problems is, in fact, incomplete, while the method used by the DENDRAL program has been mathematically proven to be complete.

**knowledge representation,** *n.* the process of structuring KNOWLEDGE about a problem in a manner that makes the problem easier to solve; a scheme for incorporating knowledge about the world into AI programs. Enabling such programs to demonstrate intelligent behaviour, knowledge representation schemes consist of special data structures. Programs applying knowledge representation techniques implement routines to manipulate the data a given knowledge representation contains in order for the programs to make intelligent INFERENCES. SEMANTIC NETWORKS, OBJECT-ATTRIBUTE-VALUE TRIPLETS, PRODUCTION RULES, FRAMES, and logical expressions are all ways to represent knowledge.

**knowledge representation language,** *n.* a programming language used to construct and operate on the formal knowledge structures of AI. These languages include FRL, KRL, KL-ONE, and UNITS.

**knowledge source,** *n.* a collection of RULES, PROCEDURES, and/or data used for the purpose of solving problems of a very specific type. Larger than a rule but smaller than an expert system, a knowledge source is generally a body of DOMAIN KNOWLEDGE relevant to a specific problem. Thus a knowledge source is a codification applied to an expert system. In BLACKBOARD ARCHITECTURES, each process that has access to the shared memory is considered a knowledge source. The knowledge sources in HEARSAY systems separate the different types of knowledge into coherent modules. For example, there might be a prosody (see PROSODICS) knowledge source that examines the speech signal for intonation and stress patterns and makes hypotheses about syllable, word, and phrase boundaries. The knowledge sources are viewed as independent modules of expertise that cooperate in analysing the speech signal.

**knowledge system,** *n.* a computer program that uses KNOWLEDGE and INFERENCE PROCEDURES to solve difficult problems. In contrast to expert systems, knowledge systems are often designed to solve small, difficult problems rather than large problems that require true human expertise. In view of the knowledge necessary to permit a computer to perform at the level of a knowledge system, combined with the inference procedures that the system uses, a knowledge system can be thought of as a model of the expertise of skilled practitioners. In many cases, small knowledge systems are useful due to their ease of use rather than their ability to capture knowledge that would be difficult to represent in a conventional program.

**KRL,** *abbrev. for* Knowledge Representation Language, a KNOWLEDGE ENGINEERING language for FRAME-based representation, which also supports PROCEDURAL REPRESENTATION methods. Its principal characteristics include PROCEDURAL ATTACHMENT, such as associating procedures with the SLOTS in a FRAME, INHERITANCE of procedural as well as declarative properties of an OBJECT, and multiple perspectives, such as permitting descriptors corresponding to different viewpoints to be attached to a single object. Implemented in INTERLISP, KRL was developed by the Xerox Palo Alto Research Center.

**KRT,** *n.* a system-building aid that helps members of a large engineering development effort record, communicate, and integrate their designs with other members of the team. Using the KRT system, team members can describe what a particular engineering system (e.g., guidance analysis, navigation) does, how it functions, how it is organized, and how its parts are related. This includes a data flow diagram to provide a system overview, process specifications to show how input data are transformed into output data, and a data dictionary that provides a hierarchical description of data. Implemented in ZETALISP and FLAVORS for the Symbolics 3600, KRT was developed by McDonnell Douglas.

**KRYPTON,** *n.* a KNOWLEDGE ENGINEERING language for FRAME-based and LOGIC-based representation. It features a component for applying terms to both frame definitions and networks of frames, and a component for applying ASSERTIONS that uses a nonclausal CONNECTION GRAPH RESOLUTION theorem prover (see THEOREM PROVING). The assertion component is used for maintaining a DATA BASE of logical assertions about items defined using frames. KRYPTON is implemented in INTERLISP-D.

# L

**LADDER,** *n. acronym for* Language Access to Distributed Data with Error Recovery, a system that is meant to provide real-time NATURAL LANGUAGE access to a very large DATA BASE spread over many smaller data bases in computers scattered throughout the United States.

**language, formal,** see FORMAL LANGUAGE.

**language definition system,** *n.* a system for the complete specification of the portion of the English language to be accepted by a system. The LEXICON is divided along semantic boundaries into categories. The language definition contains RULES for combining these words and phrases into larger phrases. Associated with each phrase-rule are PROCEDURES for calculating attributes of member words such as mood, number, meaning representation, and acoustic form, and a procedure for evaluating the acceptability of the phrase hypothesis in context. These rules also specify which attributes can be assigned to the new phrase. For example, they determine the focus of the phrase or relate the semantics of a particular word to the whole phrase. PROSODIC information in voice systems is also included, such as the expected change in pitch at the end of an interrogative utterance.

**language understanding,** see NATURAL LANGUAGE UNDERSTANDING.

**language-tool spectrum,** *n.* a continuum that encompasses the full range of software products, from specialized programs (TOOLS) that perform only specific tasks to general purpose languages that are used in many different applications.

**Laplacian,** *n.* the lowest (second) order circularity symmetric differential OPERATOR. It computes the non-directional second derivative of a two-dimensional function (e.g., an image) when convolved with a two-dimensional function.

**Laplacian image,** *n.* an image of the second derivative of the original image.

**large hybrid system-building tools,** *n.* a class of KNOW-

LEDGE ENGINEERING TOOLS that emphasizes flexibility. These tools aid the building of large KNOWLEDGE BASES. Normally, the tools consist of a hybrid collection of different INFERENCE and CONTROL STRATEGIES and incorporate FRAMES and OBJECT–oriented programming.

**large narrow system-building tools,** *n.* a class of KNOWLEDGE ENGINEERING TOOLS that sacrifices flexibility in order to aid efficient development of more narrowly defined expert systems. Presently, most large, narrow tools emphasize PRODUCTION RULES.

**LAS,** *abbrev. for* Language Acquisition System, a program that attempts to learn a CONTEXT-FREE GRAMMAR of English from training INSTANCES that include a representation of the meaning of each sentence. The HUMAN ASSOCIATIVE MEMORY (HAM) network notation used in the system serves to represent these meanings.

**laser pointer,** *n.* a device used in the SRI Consultant system. A television camera and a laser range-finder provide the visual component for the system. The laser range-finder can also work as a visual pointer, so that the system can respond to requests such as 'Show me the toggle switch' by illuminating it with the laser beam.

**LDS,** *n.* an expert system that uses both formal legal doctrine and informal principles and strategies of attorneys and claims adjusters to assist legal experts in settling product liability cases.

The program takes as input a description of a product liability case and proceeds to calculate defendant liability, case value, and an equitable settlement amount. It calculates the value of a case by analysing the effect of five parameters. Loss is the special and general damages resulting from the injury. Liability is the probability of establishing the defendant's liability. Responsibility is the proportion of blame assigned to the plaintiff for the injury. Characteristics are the subjective considerations, such as attorneys' skill and litigants' appearance, and context includes considerations based on strategy, timing, and type of claim. The program is RULE-based. Implemented in ROSIE, LDS was developed by the Rand Corporation.

**LEAP,** *n.* an associated retrieval system incorporated into SAIL.

LEAP permits rapid lookup of multiply indexed facts in a small DATA BASE.

**learning,** *n.* the process of improving performance by acquiring new KNOWLEDGE or greater control in a specific DOMAIN. Any change in a system that alters its long-term performance. Learning in PRODUCTION SYSTEMS is effected by the automatic addition, deletion, or modification of rules.

**learning, object of,** *n.* a classification for classes of approach implemented in LEARNING SYSTEMS. They include learning single concepts, learning multiple concepts, and learning to perform multiple tasks.

**learning by analogy,** *n.* a form of learning where the information provided by the ENVIRONMENT is relevant only to an analogous performance task and, thus, the learning system must discover the analogy and hypothesize (see HYPOTHESIS) analogous rules for its present performance task.

**learning by being told,** *n.* a form of learning in which the information provided by the ENVIRONMENT is too abstract or general and, thus, the learning element must hypothesize the missing details.

**learning element,** *n.* a module of a learning system that uses information supplied by the ENVIRONMENT to make improvements in an explicit KNOWLEDGE BASE.

**learning from examples,** *n.* a form of learning where the information provided by the ENVIRONMENT is too specific and detailed and, thus, the LEARNING ELEMENT must hypothesize (see HYPOTHESIS) more general RULES.

**learning method,** see OPERATIONALIZATION.

**learning problem,** *n.* a member of a class of problems of interest in a MACHINE LEARNING environment. These problems include credit assignment, errors in training instances, disjunctive concepts, integrating new knowledge and new terms, and the interpretation of TRAINING INSTANCES.

**learning situation,** *n.* the approach to the learning task taken by a system. Typical approaches are by ROTE LEARNING, LEARNING BY BEING TOLD, LEARNING BY ANALOGY, LEARNING FROM EXAMPLES, and by advice taking (see ADVICE TAKER).

**learning system,** *n.* an AI system or component that acquires KNOWLEDGE, as in the model overleaf.

**least recently used (LRU) algorithm,** *n.* a replacement

# LEAST-MEAN-SQUARE (LMS) ALGORITHM

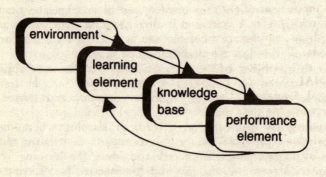

**Learning system**

ALGORITHM that is one of the most common SELECTIVE FORGETTING techniques. Each ITEM stored in memory is tagged with the time when it was last retrieved. Every time an item is retrieved, time of last use is updated. When a new item is to be memorized, the least recently used item is forgotten and replaced by the new one. Variations in this scheme take into consideration the amount of storage required for the item, the cost of recomputing the item, and so on.

**least–mean–square (LMS) algorithm,** *n.* an ALGORITHM that improves the FIXED-INCREMENT PERCEPTRON ALGORITHM by choosing how far in the direction of the gradient to go at each step. The LMS algorithm updates the weight vector w according to:

$$w_{k+1} = w_k + Pc_k x_k$$

where P is a positive value and $c_k$ is the magnitude of the error, that is, $-w_k x_k$. This algorithm tends to minimize the mean-squared error:

$$J_s = \sum_k (w_k x_k)^2$$

even when the classes are not linearly separable.

**LEGAL ANALYSIS SYSTEM,** *n.* an expert system that

uses references to judicial decisions and secondary legal authority to help lawyers perform simple legal analysis about the intentional torts of assault and battery. The program takes as input a set of FACTS entered by the user and relates the facts to relevant legal doctrine. It then presents conclusions along with an explanation of the LOGIC it used to reach its conclusions. The program's KNOWLEDGE is represented in the form of a SEMANTIC NETWORK. Implemented in PSL, LEGAL ANALYSIS SYSTEM was developed at MIT.

**Legal Expert,** *n.* an expert system developed at More For Less Hawaii for internal use. It supplies legal advice on estate planning and investment. GURU is the development software.

**legal-move generator,** *n.* the set of TRANSITION OPERATORS in the STATE SPACE of a game-playing program.

**length-first search,** *n.* a SEARCH in which a complete plan for reaching the GOAL is formed at each NODE before moving on to any lower-level node. This type of search is efficient because it can direct the development of the SEARCH TREE in fruitful directions.

**LES,** *n. acronym for* **1.** Lockheed Expert System, a KNOWLEDGE ENGINEERING language for RULE-based representation, which also permits FRAME-based representation. It features FORWARD and BACK-CHAINING control schemes, an agenda of relevant GOALS and subgoals manipulated by DEMONS, and NATURAL LANGUAGE explanation facilities. A CASE GRAMMAR frame format is used to support rules. Implemented in PL/1, LES was developed by the Lockheed Palo Alto Research Laboratory. **2.** Liquid oxygen Expert System, an expert system that uses KNOWLEDGE about the liquid oxygen (LOX) loading process for the space shuttle orbiter in order to monitor the process. The program takes as input a sequence of time-tagged measurements from the launch processing system (LPS), a real-time process controller used to control liquid oxygen loading. To determine if the LPS is receiving valid sensor data, the program monitors measurements such as temperature, pressure, flow rate, and valve position. In the event LES detects an anomaly, it notifies monitoring personnel and executes troubleshooting ALGORITHMS. When LES cannot ascertain the problem, it supplies a list of components likely to cause problems and includes instructions for performing tests to isolate the faulty component. The program uses FRAMES to encode knowledge about the LOX loading system, including information about components, measurement values, and relations between components. The KNOWLEDGE REPRESENTATION METHOD is similar to that of the FRL language. Implemented in ZETALISP within a framework taken from the KNOBS expert system, LES was developed by the Mitre Corporation in cooperation with the Kennedy Space Center.

**Letter of Credit Advisor,** *n.* an expert system developed for Bank of America (UK). It assists in processing foreign letters of credit. EXPERT Edge is the development SOFTWARE.

**LEX,** *n.* a system that learns to solve simple symbolic INTEGRATION PROBLEMS from experience. LEX is provided with an initial KNOWLEDGE BASE of roughly 50 integration and simplification OPERATORS. The goal of LEX is to discover HEURISTICS for when to apply these operators.

**lexicon,** *n.* the word list in a NATURAL LANGUAGE processing system. Entries are sometimes tagged with phonetic, SYNTACTIC, SEMANTIC, and pragmatic information.

**LHASA,** *n. acronym for* Logic and Heuristics Applied to Synthetic Analysis, the earliest of programs in computer-aided organic synthesis. LHASA was written at Harvard University.

**LIBRA,** *n.* the EFFICIENCY-ANALYSIS expert of the PSI system. It was developed in conjunction with the PSI project at Stanford University.

**LIFER,** *n.* a system developed at SRI for creating English language INTERFACES to integrate with other SOFTWARE systems, such as DATA BASE query systems. The program was designed to elicit DOMAIN- and task-referring expressions appropriate to a given application software system, and to extract from these the SYNTAX and SEMANTICS of a GRAMMAR for an appropriately specialized NATURAL LANGUAGE interface system. The designers of LIFER intended it to be a contribution to human engineering for system-building, and they instilled the program with sufficient power, robustness and flexibility for convenient interface building and use by persons without technical linguistic expertise. In sum, LIFER is designed to serve as an off-the-shelf utility for building natural language user interfaces for applications in any domain. LIFER's two major components, the language specification functions and the parser, essentially allowed interface bootstrapping from a quite small base. The successor to LIFER is TEAM.

**light spot,** *n.* a point of light used in stereo vision to replace one of the cameras. It is a method in active illumination that helps avoid the problem of finding corresponding points in two images.

**light stripe,** *n.* a ribbon of light used in stereo vision to replace one of the cameras.

**limited inference algorithm,** *n.* a fast but limited INFERENCE ALGORITHM in MACSYMA, which performs taxonomic deductions, property inheritances, set intersections, and other simple inferences.

**limited-logic system,** *n.* early KNOWLEDGE-BASED SYSTEMS with limited LOGIC RULES. Information in the DATA BASE is stored in some formal notation, and mechanisms are provided for translating input sentences into this internal but simple form (SEMANTIC ANALYSIS). Examples of limited-logic systems include SIR, TLC, DEACON, and CONVERSE.

**line,** *n.* a feature of an image that helps determine boundaries, contours, and internal structure.

**line completion,** *n.* the process in machine vision that simplifies the recognition of OBJECTS by the completion of lines. Such methods include:

(a) If, as in Figure A below, a face F is incomplete because

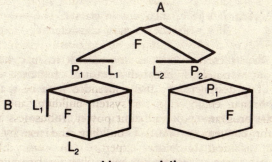

**Line completion**

of two dangling collinear lines, replace the two lines ($L_1$ and $L_2$) by a single line.

(b) If a face F is incomplete because of two dangling lines that can be extended to form a corner as in Figure B above, complete the face by extending the lines.

(c) If, as in Figure C above, there is a pair of L-type junctions with parallel sides at points $P_1$ and $P_2$, add a line between these two points and split the face F into two faces.

**line finding,** *n*. the task of segmenting continuous contours into lines, one of the basic problems in VISION. First, an edge detector produces as output a set of edge elements – for example, the set of points where the gradient of the picture function exceeds a certain threshold (see EDGE DETECTION). The task is then to group elements that form some continuous contour and segment these into lines and curves.

**line junction,** see JUNCTION TYPE.

**lineal feature,** *n*. that feature of an image that deals with edges (rather than areas).

**linear–discriminant function,** *n*. a FUNCTION used in such applications as connectionist networks and systems using binary classification, where the classifier must indicate in which of the two pattern classes the input pattern, x, belongs. This is typically accomplished by taking the output, y, of a linear functional and comparing it to a threshold, b (see THRESHOLDING):

If $y > b$, then x is in class 1.
If $y < b$, then x is in class 2.

Usually, the INSTANCE SPACE is normalized, so that the threshold b is zero. This linear-discriminant function can be thought of as a hyperplane that splits the instance space into two REGIONS.

**linear systems theory,** *n*. a field in MACHINE LEARNING dealing with ADAPTIVE SYSTEMS. The focus is on PATTERN RECOGNITION and control theory.

**linear–input–form strategy,** *n*. a resolution strategy that involves choosing RESOLVENTS so that one resolvent is always from the base set, the set of original clauses. It is more efficient than the SET-OF-SUPPORT STRATEGY, but is not complete, that is, there are cases in which it will not find a contradiction when one exists. Nonetheless, the strategy is often used because of its simplicity and efficiency.

**linearity assumption,** *n.* an assumption in HACKER, which, whenever the PLANNER is faced with the problem of achieving a pair of CONJUNCTIVE SUBGOALS, assumes that they can be achieved independently. As a result of this linearity assumption, the plan developed by the planner is naive and may not work.

**linearly separable,** *n.* the characteristic of TRAINING INSTANCES in the LEARNING PROBLEM of finding a weight vector. This can be viewed as the problem of finding a hyperplane that separates training instances of class 1 from training instances in class 2. When it is possible to find such a hyperplane, the training instances are said to be linearly separable.

**linguistics, computational,** see COMPUTATIONAL LINGUISTICS.

**link type,** *n.* a kind of connector used to tie NODES in a SEMANTIC NETWORK. These are used to build associations.

**LISP,** *n.* a programming language designed specifically to manipulate symbols rather than numeric data. Data elements in LISP are lists of symbols that can represent any object, including LISP's own processing functions. As a programming language for PROCEDURE-ORIENTED REPRESENTATION, programs written in LISP consist primarily of collections of independent procedures called FUNCTIONS. The language contains a small set of primitive functions and enables users to construct higher-level functions tailored to the needs of an application. LISP is popular among U.S. programmers due to its ease of programmability and the amount of control and flexibility it permits. It has mechanisms for manipulating symbols in the form of LIST STRUCTURES. List structures provide useful elements with which to represent complex concepts. Automatic memory management and the uniform treatment of code and data enable a LISP program to modify its own code. Although LISP was introduced by John McCarthy in the early 1960s, the language has continually developed and remains the most widely used language in ARTIFICIAL INTELLIGENCE. The PROLOG language is the primary competitor of LISP. LISP has also been used advantageously for systems programming. As the principal programming language in AI, LISP provides an elegant, recursive, untyped, and applicative framework for symbolic computing. Actually a family of variants, LISP is available in many dialects including INTERLISP, MACLISP, FRANZLISP, COMMON LISP, and ZETALISP, among others.

**list,** *n.* an ordered set of OBJECTS.

**list processing,** *n.* the representation of data as linked LIST STRUCTURES in the machine and as multilevelled lists on paper.

**list structure,** *n.* a collection of ITEMS enclosed by parentheses. Each item can be either a symbol or another list.

**literal,** *n.* an OBJECT in a program whose value does not change.

**LITHO,** *abbrev. for* LITHOlog, an expert system that uses log data obtained from oil-well logs along with knowledge about a region's geological environment to help geologists interpret the data. The program uses the log data and geological knowledge to specify the constitution of a rock encountered in a well. It specifies the porosity, permeability, composition, texture, and type of layering of the rock. Oil-well logs include data covering curves reflecting measurements of rock density, resistivity, sound transmission, and radioactivity. In order to cite features directly from the log data, LITHO uses a separate PATTERN RECOGNITION program. The program is RULE-based and uses BACK-CHAINING. Implemented in EMYCIN, LITHO was developed by Schlumberger.

**local averaging,** *n.* a simple method for removing NOISE in an image. This can be accomplished by replacing the GREY-SCALE intensity of every point by an average of the image intensity within some window around the point. In general, the average may be weighted, with lower weights assigned to points farther from the centre of the window. This processing can be accomplished by a linear operator similar to that used in sharpening. The weighting will remove noise but at the expense of blurring the image. Reducing the size of the window will result in less blurring, but it is less effective for removing noise. An alternative is to change a PIXEL only if its value differs from the average by more than a given threshold (see THRESHOLDING). This is less likely to blur desired detail but still effectively removes salt-and-pepper noise. This is called local averaging and is especially efficient for BINARY

IMAGES, since a binary pixel has only two VALUES (light and dark). A pixel's value can be made consistent with that of the immediate neighbourhood simply by complementing it or by leaving it unchanged.

**logic,** *n*. a process for describing the form (SYNTAX) of statements and for determining the truth of a statement. A logic manipulates the syntax of formulas considering two related properties of a statement. The first consideration concerns the relations and implications one can formalize – the AXIOMS of a system. The second consideration concerns the deductive structure of a formula – the rules of INFERENCE governing legitimate inferences if certain axioms are taken to be true. Logic was one of the first REPRESENTATION schemes used in AI. The expressive power of a logic-based representational system results from building larger expressions from smaller ones. Beginning with a simple notion such as truth or falsehood, and then including additional notions like CONJUNCTION and PREDICATION, a more expressive logic develops in which more subtle ideas can be represented.

**logical averaging,** *n*. in IMAGE PROCESSING, an averaging where binary input and output values are defined as a logical function of the binary PIXELS in the neighbourhood.

**logic programming,** *n*. a family of higher-level languages and an associated programming style based on writing programs as sets of ASSERTIONS. These assertions are viewed as having declarative meaning as descriptive statements about entities and RELATIONS. In addition, the assertions derive a procedural meaning by virtue of being executable by an INTERPRETER. Hence, executing a logic program is much like performing a deduction on a set of FACTS.

**LOGIC THEORIST,** *n*. a program written in 1956 by Newell, Shaw and Simon of the Rand Corporation and the Carnegie Institute of Technology. It was one of the first programs in which HEURISTICS were used in theorem proving in PROPOSITIONAL CALCULUS. The heuristics were used primarily to limit the SEARCH SPACE by facilitating an apt problem formulation, but were also applied in the choice of OPERATORS.

**logical decision criteria,** *n*. in PIP, RULES that permit the confirmation or rejection of a HYPOTHESIS on the basis of a small number of key findings.

**logic-based methods,** *n*. programming methods which use PREDICATE CALCULUS to structure the program and guide execution.

**LOGO,** *n*. a packaged system that consists of a programming language and ENVIRONMENT. The programming environment includes a graphical module that outputs either to the screen or a 'turtle.' The graphics are based on TURTLE GEOMETRY emphasizing movement relative to the current position of the 'turtle' rather than Cartesian geometry. LOGO also embodies an educational philosophy that seeks to promote creative learning via the exploration of an environment.

**long-term memory,** *n*. the segment of memory that contains all the information not currently being processed. In humans, the part of memory that contains all the information that is not currently being processed but that can be recalled at will.

**look ahead power,** *n*. a method for improving the performance of a GAME-TREE SEARCH further into the future and thus better approximating a full search of the tree. This process is referred to as 'improving the look-ahead power' of the program.

**LOOPS,** *n*. *acronym for* LISP Object-Oriented Programming System, a KNOWLEDGE ENGINEERING language for OBJECT-oriented REPRESENTATION, which also permits RULE-based, access-oriented, and PROCEDURE-ORIENTED representation. It enables users to integrate its four programming schemes in a manner that allows the PARADIGMS to be used together when building a system. For example, RULES and RULESETS are considered LOOPS objects, and PROCEDURES can be LISP FUNCTIONS or rulesets. The program provides display-oriented DEBUGGING tools such as break pages and editors. Implemented in INTERLISP-D, LOOPS runs on Xerox 1100 series workstations. LOOPS was developed at the Xerox Palo Alto Research Center.

**low emphasis filtering,** *n*. a form of filtering for NOISE removal. A simple low-pass filter will remove high-frequency noise, smoothing the image, but also blurring high-frequency components of the image signal, such as those corresponding to edges and junctions. This is acceptable in some systems, especially if much of the noise energy is above the highest desired frequency. If not, it may still be possible to improve the image by filtering a selected band of frequencies, allowing the high-frequency edge detail to remain. Bandpass filtering is especially useful if the noise energy is concentrated at a particular frequency (e.g., if it is periodic). Restoration techniques can be used to obtain the optimal filter when the characteristics of the FREQUENCY DOMAIN, such as the spectrum of the noise, are known.

**LRS,** *abbrev. for* Legal Research System, an expert system that helps lawyers retrieve information about court decisions and legislation in the DOMAIN of negotiable instruments law, an area of commercial law dealing with checks and promissory notes. LRS contains subject descriptors that link each data item to the subject area concepts that the item covers. A SEMANTIC NETWORK containing more than 200 legal concepts, built up from six PRIMITIVE CONCEPTS (party, legal instrument, liability, legal action, account, and amount of money), forms the basis for this KNOWLEDGE. The knowledge in LRS enables the program to make INFERENCES about the meanings of queries and to extend user queries to include terms that are implied but not mentioned by the user. LRS was developed at the University of Michigan.

**LUNAR,** *n.* a NATURAL LANGUAGE information retrieval system that helps geologists access, compare, and evaluate chemical-analysis data on moon rock and soil composition obtained from the Apollo-11 mission. The program translates a question that a user enters in English into an expression in a formal QUERY LANGUAGE. The translation is performed via an AUGMENTED TRANSITION NETWORK (ATN) parser coupled with a rule-driven SEMANTIC INTERPRETATION PROCEDURE, which guides the analysis of the question. The query that results from this analysis is then applied to the DATA BASE in order to produce the answer to the request. The query language is a GENERALIZATION of the PREDICATE CALCULUS. The central feature of the query language is a QUANTIFIER FUNCTION capable of expressing, in a simple manner, the restrictions placed on the data base-retrieval request by the user. This quantifier function is used in combination with special enumeration functions for classes of data base OBJECTS, freeing the quantifier function from explicit dependence on the structure of the data base.

# M

**M.1,** *n.* a KNOWLEDGE ENGINEERING language for RULE-based representation. It is a microcomputer version of S1, written in PROLOG. It features BACK-CHAINING and an English-like language SYNTAX. The SUPPORT ENVIRONMENT contains graphics-oriented interactive DEBUGGING tools for tracing system operation, facilities for explaining the system's reasoning process, and mechanisms for automatically querying the user when the DATA BASE lacks the required information. M.1 was developed by Teknowledge.

**machine-aided heuristic programming,** *n.* a methodology in which a computer is instructed to perform a new task in much the same manner as a person is taught. The program FOO (First Operational Operationalizer) is a result of this work. FOO investigates principles, problems, and methods involved in converting high-level advice into effective, executable PROCEDURES.

**machine language,** *n.* a low-level language used to communicate PRIMITIVE instructions to the computer. A language written in a series of bits that are understandable to the computer and can therefore instruct the computer. A low-level computer language as compared with a somewhat higher assembly language or a still higher COMPILER language.

**machine learning,** *n.* a research effort with the goal of creating computer programs capable of learning from experience. Such programs would remove a major barrier to the development of very large expert systems.

**machine translation,** *n.* an area of AI research aimed at using computers to translate text from one language to another. Translation programs often use a combination of NATURAL LANGUAGE understanding and generation.

**machine vision,** *n.* the process of understanding of a scene by an electronic device (in contrast to human or animal vision).

**MACLISP,** *n.* a major dialect of LISP, which is distinguished by the use of both a linked text-editor for structure editing, and a powerful COMPILER requiring some type declarations in the SOURCE. MACLISP is commonly used for systems programming. It was developed at MIT.

**macro operator (MACROPS, triangle table),** *n.* **1.** a combined sequence of OPERATORS that becomes a macro operator. The macro operator has the effect of the sequence of operators. The list of preconditions of a macro operator contains all preconditions of the first operator of the sequence, plus those of later operators in so far as they have not been satisfied by previous operators in the sequence. Macro operators can be represented like basic operators and be added to the set of existing operators. This is a form of learning that will SEARCH in new problems.
**2.** a sequence of PRIMITIVE OPERATORS that is discovered by a program and added to its initial set of operators for possible application to other problems. STRIPS is an example of a program that discovers and remembers macro operators.

**MACSYMA,** *n.* a large system that applies mathematical EXPERTISE to perform symbolic manipulation of algebraic expressions and to handle problems involving limit calculations, symbolic integration, solution of equations, canonical simplification, and PATTERN MATCHING. An extremely large program, MACSYMA can perform at least 600 distinct mathematical operations. In addition to the above list, the operations include Taylor series expansions, matrix operations, vector algebra, and order analysis, among others. Sophisticated pattern matching routines select from individual KNOWLEDGE SOURCES comprising the program's mathematical knowledge. When a problem has no algebraic solution, MACSYMA can resort to numerical approximation. The program is widely used by engineers since it achieves reliable and efficient performance on the mathematical problems within its scope. Also, MACSYMA includes an extensive numerical subroutine library (IMSL) and plotting package. The implementation of MACSYMA is based on the belief that the way to produce a high-performance program for general mathematics is to build in a large amount of knowledge. This approach to system construction is an example of knowledge-based programming. The primary goal of research on algebraic manipulation has been to invent and analyse new mathematical ALGORITHMS and to extend previously known numerical algorithms to symbolic manipulation. While most of the algorithms incorporated into MACSYMA were known to mathematicians prior to its construction, a substantial number came about as a result of this research. The current system consists of about 230 000 words of compiled LISP code and an equal amount of code written in the MACSYMA programming language. MACSYMA was developed at MIT.

**maintenance of an expert system,** *n*. the changing of RULES or data in expert systems. Most expert systems in use are constantly improved upon by the addition of new rules. In most applications, the user group establishes a regular routine to capture and incorporate new KNOWLEDGE into the system. Unlike conventional computer software that is only infrequently updated, expert systems by their nature are very easy to modify. One person should be made responsible for entering new rules whenever data or PROCEDURES change or whenever questions rise that the current system can not answer.

**manageability of production systems,** *n*. the ability to amend the RULE BASE or the INTERPRETER of PRODUCTION SYSTEMS. This quality is one of the strongest attractions of production systems as a KNOWLEDGE REPRESENTATION scheme. Manageability results from an ability to change the productions, particularly by adding conditions, switching the order of the productions in the rule base around, adding new productions, and so forth.

**man–machine interaction,** see USER INTERFACE.

**MARGIE,** *n*. *acronym for* Meaning Analysis, Response Generation, and Inference on English, an early experimental LANGUAGE UNDERSTANDING and paraphrase-generating system developed at the Stanford AI Laboratory. A principal purpose was to show that language can be understood without directing attention to details of syntax. Programmed in LISP 1.6, the MARGIE system was divided into three components. The first was a conceptual analyser, which took English sentences and converted them into an internal CONCEPTUAL DEPENDENCY (CD) representation. The conversion was achieved via a system of 'requests,' which are similar to DEMONS or productions. In essence, a request is a piece of code that looks for some surface linguistic construct and then takes a specific action if the construct is found. The request consists of both a test condition, to be searched for in the input, and an action, to be executed if the test is successful. The test can be as specific as a particular word or as general as an entire conceptualization. The action might contain information about what to look for next in the input, what to do with the input just found, and how to organize the representation. The flexibility of this formalism allows the system to function without depending heavily on syntax, although it is otherwise quite similar to the tests and actions that make ATNs a powerful PARSING mechanism. The middle phase of the system was an INFERENCE ENGINE designed to accept a proposition stated in conceptual dependency and to deduce a large number of facts from the proposition in the current context of the system's memory. The rationale behind this component was the assumption that humans understand far more from a sentence than is actually stated. 16 types of INFERENCES were identified, including cause, effect, specification, and function. The inference KNOWLEDGE was represented in memory in the form of a modified SEMANTIC NETWORK. Inferences were organized into 'molecules', for the purpose of applying them. An example of this process might be:

John loved Mary

from which the system might infer:

John was pleased with Mary
Mary might kiss John
Mary might be happy

This inference module performs relatively unrestricted forward inferencing, producing large numbers of inferences for any given input. The last part of the system was a text generation module. In a two-part process, the TEXT-GENERATION module took an internal conceptual dependency representation and converted it into English-like output. A DISCRIMINATION NET was used to distinguish between different word-senses. This permitted the system to use English-specific contextual criteria for selecting words, especially verbs to name conceptual patterns. An ATN was then used to linearize the conceptual dependency representation into a surface-like structure.

**Marr's theory of vision,** *n.* a theory of vision that emphasizes the importance of choosing appropriate RE-PRESENTATIONS for different levels of the vision process. The underlying assumption is that it is important to understand vision at two levels. The first level specifies what is being computed and why, a COMPETENCE theory. The second level specifies particular ALGORITHMS to execute the computation, a performance theory.

**MARS,** *n. acronym for* Multiple Abstraction Rulebased System, a KNOWLEDGE ENGINEERING language for RULE-based RE-PRESENTATION of hierarchical, discrete, EVENT-DRIVEN simulators. It features a hierarchical specification of the structure and behaviour of a design, FORWARD and BACK-CHAINING control schemes, and symbolic simulation. A COMPILER is included to compile general, rule-based specifications into special PROCEDURES for simulation. A mixed mode simulator permits simulation of different parts of a design at different levels of abstraction. The program also includes an explanation facility. Implemented in MRS, MARS was developed at Stanford University.

**masterscope,** *n.* in INTERLISP, a cross-referencing facility for creating a model of a user's program for use in helping to manage a large system.

**masterscript,** *n.* a higher-order structure in a system called the Cold War Ideologue, which spelled out several general contingencies for the fate of the free world. Part of the script says that the communists want to dominate the world and will do so unless the free world exercises its power, in which case the free world will prevail. Generic EVENTS are considered instances of very general masterscript events.

**match,** *n.* in a PRODUCTION SYSTEM a process that compares a set of patterns from the left-hand sides of RULES against the data in data memory in order to find all possible ways in which the rules can be satisfied with consistent bindings such as INSTANTIATIONS.

**Matchware,** *n.* an expert system developed at Matchware Computer Services for commercial use. It assists accountants in selecting appropriate software.

**Material Handling,** *n.* an expert system developed for EXXON (LMI) for commercial use. It assists materials handling and scheduling of discrete manufacturing areas. PICON is the development software.

**MATHLAB 68,** *n*. an expert system that assists mathematicians, scientists, and engineers with the symbolic algebraic manipulation encountered in analysis problems. The program performs differentiation, polynomial factorization, indefinite integration, and direct and inverse Laplace transforms, and solves linear differential equations with constant symbolic coefficients. The program's expertise is contained in individual modules, each with a particular functional speciality. Users' data are classified into three categories: expressions, equations, and FUNCTIONS. RULES for the algebraic manipulation of the data vary with the categories. Implemented in LISP, MATHLAB 68 formed the cornerstone for the development of MACSYMA. MATHLAB 68 was developed at MIT.

**max cost,** *n*. see COST (OF A SOLUTION TREE).

**MBUILD,** *n*. a PRIMITIVE ACT in CONCEPTUAL DEPENDENCY that signifies the construction of new information from old. Imagining, inferring, and deciding include MBUILDs.

**MDX,** *n*. an expert system that diagnoses the existence and cause of the liver syndrome known as cholestasis. The program bases its diagnosis on patient history, signs, symptoms, and clinical data. MDX functions as a community of cooperating expert diagnosticians, each with different specialities. These experts call upon one another to resolve problems requiring special knowledge and expertise. Communication occurs via a BLACKBOARD mechanism. MDX's expertise consists of diagnostic HEURISTICS and a hierarchical (see HIERARCHY), deep MODEL of the conceptual structure of cholestasis. The program's KNOWLEDGE is represented as RULES and FRAMES organized around the cholestasis model. PATREC and RADEX are members of the community of expert systems called upon by MDX. Implemented in LISP, MDX was developed at Ohio State University.

**means-end analysis,** *n*. a PROBLEM-SOLVING technique that differs from standard STATE-SPACE SEARCH in that it does not select an OPERATOR on the basis of immediate availability, but rather it determines the difference between the current task-domain situation and the current GOAL and then selects the operator that will most significantly reduce that difference. If the operator is not immediately applicable subgoals are set up to modify the current PROBLEM STATE so that the operator may be applied.

**MECHO,** *n.* an expert system that solves problems in mechanics, such as pulley systems, moment-of-inertia, and distance-rate-time problems. Given a problem in the form of English text, MECHO builds a KNOWLEDGE BASE of FACTS, INFERENCES, and DEFAULT values derived from the problem statement. It uses a means-end search strategy base similar to that used by GPS (General Problem Solver) to produce sets of simultaneous equations and inequalities. It passes them to an algebra module, which solves them and produces a final answer. MECHO is a RULE-based system. Implemented in PROLOG, MECHO was developed at the University of Edinburgh.

**MECS-AI,** *abbrev. for* MEdical Consultation System by means of Artificial Intelligence, an expert system that uses KNOWLEDGE about cardiovascular and thyroid disease diagnosis obtained from DOMAIN experts to help physicians diagnose and plan treatment for cardiovascular and thyroid diseases. The program was originally developed for cardiovascular diseases, but was revised into a more general medical consultation tool and applied to thyroid diseases. It is a RULE-based system using BACK-CHAINING. Additionally, the program contains a KNOWLEDGE BASE editor to enable further defining and modification of the system's expertise. MECS-AI exists in two versions, one is implemented in INTERLISP, the other in EPICS-LISP. The program was developed at the University of Tokyo Hospital.

**Med Ex,** *n.* an expert system developed by Perceptronics for commercial use. It provides an intelligent INTERFACE to medical information for the layman.

**MEDICO,** *n.* an expert system that uses general clinical knowledge to advise opthalmologists managing chorioretinal disease treatment. The program's KNOWLEDGE BASE consists of a large DATA BASE of FACTS about previous patients and events. The program is RULE-based and uses FORWARD CHAINING. It handles CERTAINTY by associating the rules with likelihood estimates provided by DOMAIN EXPERTS. A KNOWLEDGE ACQUISITION and maintenance module (KAMM) supports interactive rule acquisition from domain experts. To examine, update, and re-organize the rules in the knowledge base, the program makes use of a second module, RAIN (Relational Algebraic INterpreter). Implemented in the C, MEDICO was developed at the University of Illinois.

**MED-1,** *abbrev. for* Meta-level Diagnostics System, an expert system that uses physicians' findings such as heart beat frequency and blood pressure to help physicians diagnose the disease or diseases associated with a patient's chest pain. The program first involves a process of FORWARD CHAINING through RULES that accumulate evidence suggesting disease hypotheses. It then subjects the most significant diagnosis to further evaluation using BACK-CHAINING through MYCIN-like rules. The result either confirms the hypothesis or suggests alternatives. Using a modified version of MYCIN's CERTAINTY FACTOR scheme, MED-1 transforms the score of a disease diagnosis into one of seven probability classes from 'excluded' to 'confirmed'. It also supplies KNOWLEDGE ACQUISITION and explanation facilities. Implemented in INTERLISP, MED-1 was developed at the University of Kaiserslautern.

**MELD,** *n. acronym for* MEta-Level Diagnosis, a KNOWLEDGE ENGINEERING language for RULE-BASED REPRESENTATION, which also supports FRAME-BASED REPRESENTATION. It features separation of object-level and meta-level HEURISTIC and causal RULES. The meta-level rules contain all the knowledge required to select and apply the object-level (task-specific) rules. It uses the OPS5 CONFLICT RESOLUTION strategy to select meta-level rules. The language also supports FORWARD and BACK-CHAINING, CERTAINTY handling, and complex CONTROL schemes. Implemented in OPS5, MELD was developed by the Westinghouse Research and Development Center.

**memo function,** *n.* a FUNCTION that allows abstraction from the details of how a function is computed. Memo functions are provided by one of the POP-2 libraries. The memo function is based on dynamic lists that allow the programmer to abstract away from the details of how a list is produced, whether it is computed once or is extended when needed. The name 'memo function' comes from the notion that a function, if it is called several times with the same argument, would do better to 'make a memo of it', i.e. remember the answer, and store it in a lookup table.

**mental models,** *n.* the symbolic network and pattern of relationships that experts use when they attempt to understand a problem. Often, mental models take the form of simplified analogies or metaphors that experts use when they first examine a problem. Occasionally, the models can be converted into PRODUCTION RULES. These models are the object of considerable research in cognitive psychology.

**MES,** *abbrev. for* Maintenance Expert System, an expert system that uses KNOWLEDGE taken from aircraft maintenance manuals and aircraft technician DOMAIN EXPERTS to help aircraft technicians diagnose aircraft problems. The purpose of the program is to compensate for the shortage of technically qualified aircraft maintenance personnel by supplying less qualified personnel with a tool to accurately isolate aircraft problems. The program's knowledge taken from maintenance manuals includes component weight and dimension, ground operations, and troubleshooting and repair procedures. The program is RULE-based using FORWARD CHAINING. Implemented in LISP, MES runs on the Apple II+ microcomputer. MES was developed at the Air Force Institute of Technology.

**mesa effect,** *n.* the effect that occurs when once a game program has found a winning position, all moves look good, and the program tends to wander aimlessly.

**MESSAGE TRACE ANALYZER,** *n.* an expert system that uses general DEBUGGING HEURISTICS and facts about the specific system being debugged to help debug real-time systems such as large telecommunication switching machines containing hundreds of processors. The program examines interprocess message traces both to identify illegal message sequences and to isolate a fault in the process. To do so, the program takes account of the sender ID, the receiver process ID, the message type, and the stamp fields of messages in the trace. The program is RULE-based and uses both FORWARD and BACK-CHAINING. Also included in the program is an interactive explanation facility to explain the program's reasoning. Implemented in PROLOG, MESSAGE TRACE ANALYZER was developed at the University of Waterloo.

**meta-,** *prefix denoting* that a term is being used to refer to itself. For example, a meta-rule is a RULE about other rules.

**metacognition,** *n.* the process or capability of thinking about thought processes.

**META-DENDRAL,** *n.* an expert system that helps chemists determine the dependence of mass spectrometric fragmentation on substructural features. It accomplishes this by discovering fragmentation RULES for given classes of molecules. The system derives these rules from TRAINING INSTANCES consisting of sets of molecules with known three-dimensional structures and mass spectra. The program first generates a set of highly specific rules, which account for a single fragmentation process in a particular molecule. Then the program uses the training examples to generalize these rules. Lastly, the program reexamines the rules in order to remove redundant or incorrect rules. Implemented in INTERLISP, METADENDRAL was developed at Stanford University.

**metaknowledge,** *n.* the knowledge that we have about our knowledge. The knowledge we have about the limits or reliability of our understanding of a subject and the knowledge that we have about the strengths and weaknesses of human cognition are both examples of metaknowledge.

**meta-level reasoning,** *n.* reasoning that involves knowledge about the origin, limits or importance of knowledge. According to research in the fields of psychology and AI, meta-level reasoning plays an important role in human cognition, and efforts have been made to incorporate this kind of knowledge into AI systems.

**Metals Analyst,** *n.* an expert system developed at General Electric Corporation for commercial use. It identifies commercially used metals and alloys. Exsys is the development software.

**meta-planning,** *n.* planning at a high level. Plans can be constructed in one layer, decisions about the design of the plan made in a higher layer, and strategies that dictate the design decisions made at a still higher level.

**meta-rule,** *n.* **1.** a RULE that helps to direct the use of object-level rules in the KNOWLEDGE BASE and to provide a mechanism for encoding PROBLEM-SOLVING strategies. An approach that adds ordering rules that indicate explicitly which regular rules should be applied before others.

**2.** any statement that increases the expressive power of a grammatical formalism. In the context of linguistics, a grammar with meta-rules added to it provides two ways of including rules: explicitly, by adding individual rules, or implicitly, by adding meta-rules. A meta-rule says that if there is a rule of some form in the grammar, then take the grammar as also containing another rule of a like form.

**method of analogies,** *n*. a method of improving the efficiency of a SEARCH by eliminating in advance lines of reasoning that are known to be unfruitful based on analogies to lines that have already been refuted in similar searches. If it is possible to determine the conditions under which a line of reasoning is guaranteed to be refuted, then that line can be eliminated when it is applicable in those conditions.

**MI,** *n*. *abbrev*. *for* Myocardial Infarction system, an expert system that analyses enzyme activity to help physicians diagnose myocardial infarction. It applies KNOWLEDGE about how to work with the time-dependent nature of the medical findings, including techniques for automatically updating, revising, and interpreting a patient's record. The program checks for elevated levels of certain enzymes in the blood over a period of several days in order to diagnose heart damage. MI is a RULE-based system using FORWARD CHAINING. Implemented in a version of EXPERT modified to represent and manipulate time-dependent rules and data, MI was developed at Rutgers University.

**Micro,** *n*. an expert system developed at Helena Laboratories at Rutgers University for commercial use. It analyses blood serum protein readings on instrument printouts. EXPERT is the development software.

**Micro Genie,** *n*. an expert system developed by Sci Soft Inc. It performs DNA and RNA analysis. PASCAL is the development SOFTWARE.

**middle-out search strategy,** see ISLAND DRIVING.

**mid-run explanation,** *n*. an explanation that a system gives during processing at the request of the USER. The explanation may concern what the program has accomplished, what it will do next, etc. The ability to give such explanations is characteristic of expert systems, not conventional systems.

**MIND,** *n*. a context-free, BOTTOM-UP PARSER developed by Kay.

**minimal cost,** *n*. that sum of all ARCS in a SOLUTION GRAPH that is smallest for a given solution. If there is more than one solution, the minimal cost solution is the one with the smallest DEPTH.

**minimax procedure,** *n*. a technique for searching GAME TREES.

**MITI,** *n*. Japan's Ministry of International Trade and Industry, the organization that has initiated the Fifth Generation Project in order to be a world leader in new artificial intelligence technologies. See FIFTH GENERATION COMPUTERS.

**mixed-initiative dialogue,** *n*. an INTERFACE in which both the system and the user can initiate conversation by asking questions. The dialogue includes strategies involving decisions about how often to question the user and methods for the presentation of new material and, possibly, review. For example, a coaching program, by design, is nonintrusive and only rarely lectures. On the other hand, a Socratic tutor (see SOCRATIC STYLE OF TUTORING) questions repetitively, requiring the student to pursue certain lines of reasoning. RULES select alternative dialogue formats on the basis of economy, DOMAIN LOGIC, and user GOALS. Arranged into PROCEDURES, these rules cope with various recurrent situations in the dialogue, for example, introducing a new topic, examining a user's understanding after he or she asks a question that indicates unexpected EXPERTISE, relating an INFERENCE to one just discussed, discussing the next plan of attack after the user completes a task, and wrapping up the discussion of a topic.

**MIXER,** *n*. an expert system that aids programmers in writing microprograms for Texas Instruments' TI990 chip. It uses KNOWLEDGE about TI990 microprogramming taken from manuals and from an analysis of the microcodes in the TI990 control ROM. It uses this knowledge to determine which microoperations are best suited to implement the microprogram. The microprogramming knowledge includes how to map written descriptions into sets of intermediate operations, how to allocate appropriate registers to variables, and how to expand intermediate operations into sets of microoperations. The program takes as input a microprogram description and then generates optimized microcodes for the TI990. Knowledge representation in the program is in the form of RULES and data used with inferencing controlled UNIFICATION and dynamic backtracking. Implemented in PROLOG, MIXER was developed at Tokyo University.

**mnemonic,** *n.* any technique assisting or designed to assist memory. A term used to describe the process of assigning numbers and letters in a combination that is mnemonic or memory-aiding to the eye or ear. Whenever the ability to memorize code designations becomes advantageous, mnemonic symbols are used almost exclusively for coding.

**mode method,** *n.* a technique that is suitable for analysing pictures with a single feature, such as black-and-white images. The usual technique for deciding when to split a region is to form a histogram of the PIXEL VALUES within the region (a graph that indicates, for each pixel value, how many pixels have that value). Under the assumption that each surface or OBJECT will contain many pixels of similar value, peaks in the histogram will indicate surfaces. If a region consists of a single surface or object, its histogram will therefore consist of a single peak; if the histogram contains several peaks, the region may contain several surfaces and is a candidate for splitting. If a histogram is made, it can be used to decide how to split a region. A valley in the histogram between two peaks corresponds to a pixel value that does not occur, or occurs only infrequently. The pixel value at the valley can be used as a threshold, and the region can be split into two collections of pixels: those whose value is above the threshold and those whose value is below the threshold (see THRESHOLDING). Groups of contiguous pixels from either collection become new regions, each of which is examined by the same technique to see if it should be split further.

**model,** *n.* a formal REPRESENTATION of an OBJECT, process, or CONCEPT.

**model building,** *n.* an approach that matches data from a particular situation against MODELS that describe a moderately large number of disjoint classes of situations. For example, in PROSPECTOR'S DOMAIN, the models are formal descriptions of the most important types of ore deposits, and the data are primarily surface geological observations. The available data are assumed to be uncertain and incomplete, so that the conclusion is expressed as a probability or a degree of match. In addition, the program alerts the user to different possible interpretations of the data and identifies additional observations that would be most valuable for reaching a more definite conclusion. A typical consultation session with PROSPECTOR begins with the user giving the system the information about the most significant features of the prospect: the major rock types, minerals, and alteration products. The program matches these observations against its models and, when the user has finished volunteering information, proceeds to ask the user for additional information that will then help confirm the best matching model.

**model in vision systems,** *n.* a prototypical design against which an IMAGE-PROCESSING system can compare its analysis. Some are used to verify results, others are used to control what to see where. Most use a TOP-DOWN approach. Recent MODEL-based systems make a clear distinction between observable image features, object-class models, and the specific object model.

**model of cognition,** *n.* computer MODEL of human thinking.

**model-driven schema instantiation,** *n.* an INSTANTIATION method used in learning that uses a set of RULE schemes to provide general CONSTRAINTS on the form of plausible rules. The method attempts to instantiate these schemes from the current set of TRAINING INSTANCES. The instantiated schema that best fits the training instances is considered the most plausible rule.

**MODIS,** *n. acronym for* Machine-Oriented Diagnostic Interactive System, an expert system that uses DOMAIN KNOWLEDGE of surgeons and therapeutic experts to help physicians diagnose various forms of arterial hypertension. The program takes as input patient information, including symptoms and laboratory test results. It then hypothesizes groups of illnesses based on the patient data. When several possibilities exist, the program selects the more probable group of illnesses according to medical expertise. An explanation facility presents its rationale for asking questions, formulating diagnoses, and examining hypotheses. A SEMANTIC NETWORK containing FRAMES whose SLOTS contain RULES as well as data is used to represent the program's knowledge. Implemented in LISP, MODIS was developed in Tbilisi, Georgia, USSR.

**modularity,** *n.* the ability to add, modify, or delete individual data structures more or less independently of the remainder of the DATA BASE.

**modus ponens,** *n.* an INFERENCE RULE that states that if one knows two sentences of the form X and X → Y are true, then one can infer that the sentence Y is true. More formally, the modus ponens rule can be expressed as:

$$(X \wedge (X \rightarrow Y)) \rightarrow Y.$$

Modus ponens is the best known inference rule. An example of the rule is if one knows the sentence 'Mary is a mother' is true one also knows 'If Mary is a mother, then Mary is a female' is true.

**moiré pattern,** *n.* a pattern produced when multiple stripes that are out of alignment with the TV scan lines are projected onto the scene. Each contour is a locus of the same depth. The moiré method is useful for detecting fluctuations in surface depths. However, the moiré pattern alone does not provide information about the absolute depth of a contour.

**MOLGEN,** *n.* an expert system that uses KNOWLEDGE about genetics to aid geneticists planning gene-cloning experiments. Knowledge about the user's GOAL enables the program to create an abstract plan and then to refine the plan to a set of specific laboratory steps. The experiments consist of splicing a gene coding for a desired protein product into bacteria that will manufacture the protein. The KNOWLEDGE REPRESENTATION scheme is OBJECT-oriented and FRAME-based. Implemented in LISP and UNITS, MOLGEN was developed at Stanford University as a means for testing approaches for reasoning about design.

**monotonic reasoning,** *n.* a REASONING system based on the assumption that once a fact is determined it cannot be altered during the course of the reasoning process. MYCIN is an example of a monotonic system. Once the user has answered a question, the system assumes that the answer will remain the same throughout the session. Given the brief duration of most MYCIN sessions, this is a reasonable assumption.

**monotonicity,** *n.* a principle that states that if a conclusion can be derived from a certain collection of facts, the same conclusion remains derivable if more facts are added.

**mood,** *n.* that part of GRAMMAR that expresses categories such as statement, question, command, and exclamation.

**MORE,** *n.* a KNOWLEDGE ENGINEERING tool that infers diagnostic RULES from interviews it conducts with DOMAIN EXPERTS. It acts as a system-building aid by compiling symptoms and findings domain experts introduce to the program as input. The program queries the domain expert for additional information based on the initial data the expert introduces. MORE then proceeds to develop a model of the DOMAIN in order to infer diagnostic rules. In addition, the program examines the rules for flaws as they accumulate and identifies inconsistencies in the way the expert assigns CERTAINTY factors to the RULES. The program then supplies advice suggesting types of KNOWLEDGE that would permit more powerful diagnostic rules to be generated. MORE was developed at Carnegie-Mellon University.

**More,** *n.* an expert system developed by Persoft Inc. for commercial use. It identifies potential buyers from mailing lists. The program is implemented in COBOL.

**morphemics,** *n.* RULES describing how morphemes (units of meaning) are combined to form words (formation of plurals, conjugations of verbs, etc.).

**Mortgage Advisor,** *n.* an expert system developed by Systems Designers Software for Nederlandische Medderstandsbank. It rates new mortgage applications. Sage is the development software.

**motion parallax,** *n.* the result achieved when a single camera takes images from arbitrary positions and orientations, for example, as an aerial camera takes images from two points in a flight. By contrast, in conventional stereo, as in human vision, two images are taken by laterally displaced sensing devices – eyes or cameras.

**MRS,** *abbrev. for* Meta-level Representation System, a KNOWLEDGE ENGINEERING language for RULE-based and LOGIC-based representation. It features a flexible control scheme permitting FORWARD and BACK-CHAINING, resolution theorem proving, and representing meta-level KNOWLEDGE – knowledge about the MRS system itself. Users can write statements about MRS subroutines in the same manner as statements about geology and medicine. MRS also supplies interactive graphics tools. Implemented in INTERLISP, MRS was developed at Stanford University.

**MTRANS,** *n*. a PRIMITIVE ACT in CONCEPTUAL DEPENDENCY MODELS that signifies the transfer of mental information between people or within a person. 'Telling' is an MTRANS between people; 'seeing' is an MTRANS within a person.

**MUD,** *n*. an expert system that uses KNOWLEDGE taken from DOMAIN experts about drilling fluids and diagnosing drilling problems in order to help engineers maintain optimal drilling fluid properties. The program diagnoses the causes of problems with drilling fluid, checking for contaminants, high temperatures or pressures, and inadequate use of chemical additives. It then suggests treatments to regulate the problem. The program is RULE-based and uses MYCIN-like CERTAINTY FACTORS. It also supplies explanations in support of its recommendations for treatments in a given instance. Implemented in OPS5, MUD was developed at Carnegie-Mellon University in cooperation with N.L. Baroid Co.

**multiple lines of reasoning,** *n*. a problem-solving technique in which a limited number of possibly independent approaches to solving the problem are developed in parallel.

**multiple representation,** *n*. in CAI, representing KNOWLEDGE in more than one way. It is useful for answering student questions and for evaluating partial solutions to a problem. For example, a SEMANTIC NETWORK of facts about an electronic circuit and PROCEDURES simulating the functional behaviour of the circuit would comprise a multiple representation.

**multiple sources of knowledge,** see KNOWLEDGE SOURCE.

**multiple-step task,** *n*. a task in which several RULES must be chained together into a sequence.

**multiprocessing,** *n*. a computer environment where many processes can run at once and freely pass messages back and forth.

**multivalued attribute,** *n*. an ATTRIBUTE that can have more than one VALUE. For example, if a system seeks values for the attribute restaurant, and if the restaurant is multivalued, then two or more restaurants may be identified.

**MUMPS,** *n*. a procedure-oriented programming language. Like

LISP, MUMPS is an interpreted, typeless language that supports ATOMIC and composite VARIABLES. In contrast to LISP, MUMPS supports multidimensional ARRAYS as multiway TREES with descendants ordered by the VALUES of the array indexes. The implicit ordering of data inserted into the tree structures provides automatic sorting by insertion key. MUMPS supports RECURSION and provides a set of FUNCTIONS for tree traversal. It has no provision for parametrized PROCEDURES or local ENVIRONMENTS; thus all variables are global in scope. Originally developed for use in medical computing, MUMPS is available for a wide variety of computer systems, and an ANSI standard definition of the language exists.

**mutilated chessboard problem,** *n*. a problem that asks: If two diagonally opposite corner squares are removed from a standard 8 by 8 square chessboard, can 31 rectangular dominoes, each the size of exactly two squares, be so placed as to cover precisely the remaining board? In response, if states are defined as configurations of dominoes on the mutilated board, and an operator has the effect of placing a domino, the search space for this problem is very large. If, however, one observes that every domino placed must cover both a red square and a black one and that the squares removed are both of one colour, the answer is immediate.

**MYCIN,** *n*. an expert system that uses KNOWLEDGE about the procedures experienced physicians follow when treating infectious diseases in order to help physicians select appropriate antimicrobial therapy for hospital patients with bacteremia, meningitis, and cystitis infections. The program first diagnoses the cause of the infection based on knowledge that shows a connection between infecting organisms and a patient's history, symptoms, and laboratory tests. It concludes by recommending drug treatment specifying the type and dosage. The program is RULE-based and is distinguished by its use of a BACK-CHAINING CONTROL structure and inexact reasoning, involving CONFIDENCE FACTORS that are attached to the conclusion part of each production to help determine the relative strengths of alternative diagnoses. It also supplies an EXPLANATION FACILITY. Implemented in LISP, MYCIN was developed at Stanford University.

# N

**named plan,** *n.* in PAM, a set of actions and subgoals for accomplishing a main GOAL. It is not very different from a SCRIPT, although the emphasis in named plans is on goals and the means to accomplish them.

**natural deduction,** *n.* a system of LOGIC in which two rules of INFERENCE apply for each CONNECTIVE; one that introduces the connective into given expressions, and one that eliminates the connective from the same expressions. Thus, MODUS PONENS is called the '→' elimination rule. Considering X and X → Y as two entries in a DATA BASE, the modus ponens rule replaces them with the single statement Y, thereby eliminating one occurrence of the connective '→'. Natural deduction proofs are TREES, the leaves of which represent the assumptions, and the root representing the conclusion that has been deduced from those assumptions. It is valid to assume temporarily certain formulae in natural deduction, and then, using particular cases of the deduction rules, 'discharge' these assumptions later in the proof. As a sound and complete system of logic, natural deduction is said to reflect the way in which humans reason.

**natural interpretation,** *n.* the interpretation of line drawings using CONSTRAINTS other than those that concern realizability.

**natural language,** *n.* a person's native tongue. Natural language systems attempt to enable computers to process language as people actually use it. Natural language systems uncomplicate the interaction between computer and user by allowing people to communicate with a computer without learning specialized programming languages. A segment of AI is devoted to using commands in the natural language of the user. Particularly appropriate ENVIRONMENTS for natural language systems include those where many nontechnical users or users who do not spend much time working with computers must operate a system. Such environments include DATA BASE inquiry systems and COMPUTER-ASSISTED INSTRUC-

TION systems. Most natural language systems are presently implemented in English. The systems handle user queries and responses in a conversational style instead of with computer-like commands or jargon. A machine truly capable of natural language can understand and resolve grammatical idiosyncracies and ambiguities. The result of the implementation of a natural language system is known as a natural language INTERFACE. Currently, systems can be built that will accept typed input in narrowly defined DOMAINS such as data base inquiries. In addition, the user interfaces of several expert systems incorporate some primitive form of natural language in order to aid the rapid development of new KNOWLEDGE BASES.

**natural language understanding,** *n.* the process by which a computer analyses NATURAL LANGUAGE input and creates a REPRESENTATION of the meaning of that input.

**NAVEX,** *n. acronym for* NAVigation EXpert, an expert system that monitors radar station data that estimate the velocity and position of a space shuttle, look for errors, and warn the mission control centre console operators when errors are detected or predicted. When it detects errors, the program recommends actions to take, such as excluding data from a particular radar station or restarting the analysis of the current data. The program is RULE-based and FRAME-oriented and runs in real time, making recommendations based on actual radar data. Implemented in ART, NAVEX was developed by Inference Corporation in cooperation with NASA at the Johnson Space Center.

**NDS,** *n.* an expert system that uses knowledge about the COMNET communications network, including the network's topology and composition, and knowledge of expert diagnostic strategies, to discover the location of multiple faults in the nationwide communications network. The program gathers evidence for the existence of faults within a given set of components based on the results of diagnostic tests it proposes to the user. The components the program examines include telecommunication processors, modems, telephone circuits, and computer terminals. The program is RULE-based. Implemented in ARBY, NDS was developed by Smart Systems Technology in cooperation with Shell Development Company.

**near-miss training instance,** *n.* an instance that just barely fails to be an example of a CONCEPT in question.

**negative evidence,** *n.* evidence that can be used to predict the non-occurrence of certain data.

**negmax,** *n.* a technique for searching game trees (see GAME TREE SEARCH) that is equivalent to MINIMAX PROCEDURE.

**NEOMYCIN,** *n.* an expert system that incorporates expertise derived from MYCIN to help physicians diagnose and treat patients with meningitis and similar diseases. MYCIN expertise is represented in NEOMYCIN in the form of RULES organized by disease hierarchy and controlled by FORWARD CHAINING META-RULES embodying the diagnostic procedure. The contrast between NEOMYCIN and MYCIN results from the way NEOMYCIN separates KNOWLEDGE REPRESENTATION of the diagnostic procedure from the disease knowledge. An EXPLANATION FACILITY supplies explanations of NEOMYCIN's diagnostic strategy, including those strategies drawn from a causal model of the DOMAIN. GUIDON2 uses the NEOMYCIN KNOWLEDGE BASE and diagnostic meta-rules as its source of teaching materials. Implemented in INTERLISP-D, NEOMYCIN was developed at Stanford University.

**NETL,** *n.* a KNOWLEDGE ENGINEERING language for FRAME-based representation of SEMANTIC NETWORKS. It features the ability to create and manipulate virtual copies of arbitrarily large and complex portions of the semantic network. These copies inherit the entire structure of the descriptions that are copied, including all parts, subparts, and internal relationships. Implemented in MACLISP, NETL was developed at MIT.

**Network Diagnostician,** *n.* an expert system developed by Systems Designers Software for Standard Telephone and Cables. It troubleshoots telephone switching equipment. Envisage is the development software.

**network representation,** see SEMANTIC NETWORK.

**neural network,** *n.* a form of KNOWLEDGE REPRESENTATION scheme where information is stored implicitly in the distribution of weights in a matrix rather than explicitly as in PRODUCTION RULES or FRAMES. The neural network MODEL (a form of CONNECTIONISM) is based on a simplified computer model of the human neuron. These neurons are organized into networks similar to those in the brain. They are highly simplified but have shown great success in LEARNING, abstracting and generalizing. In this model single neurons, each of which represents one piece of information, are combined to form networks which look like the following:

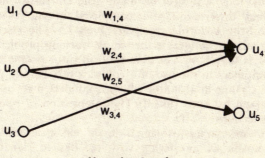

**Neural network**

In this figure $u_i$ represents a CELL; and $w_{i,j}$ the weight attached to the ARC from one cell to its successor.

**NEUREX,** *n.* an expert system that uses results of a neurological examination of unconscious patients to help physicians diagnose patients with diseases of the nervous system. The program locates the nervous system damage and then classifies the patient according to the damage locale - for example, a subtentorial lesion, nonfocal. The program is RULE-based using both FORWARD CHAINING and BACK-CHAINING and MYCIN-like CERTAINTY factors. An INFERENCE hierarchy, where successively higher levels in the HIERARCHY represent greater levels of abstraction of the information about the patient, operates in the form of rules containing neurological localization expertise. Implemented in Wisconsin LISP, NEUREX was developed at the University of Maryland.

**new-term problem,** *n.* the problem that arises when the SEARCH does not have a well-defined GOAL. In many learning situations, where there is no such guarantee, the learning program must confront the possibility that its REPRESENTATION of the RULE SPACE is inadequate and should be expanded. This is done by adding new terms.

**NIL,** *n.* a dialect of LISP, developed at MIT, that is a superset of COMMON LISP. It contains most of the special MACLISP extensions, such as defstruc, and a version of the FLAVORS system that allows OBJECT-oriented programming. It runs on VAXs under VMS.

**NLPQ,** *abbrev. for* Natural Language Programming for Queuing simulations, a project begun at Yale University in 1967 for a doctoral dissertation and completed at the Naval Postgraduate School during the years 1968–72. The research concerns simulation programs for simple queuing problems.

**NLS-SCHOLAR,** *n.* a system used to tutor people unfamiliar with computers in the use of a complex text-editing program.

**node,** *n.* a point in a GRAPH which is connected to other points in the graph by ARCS (links). The intersection of two or more interconnections.

**noise,** *n.* an extraneous signal in an electrical circuit or an image capable of interfering with the desired signal. In general, any disturbance that tends to interfere with the normal operation of a device or system.

**non-algorithmic,** *adj.* (of a problem-solving approach) not following a step-by-step procedure.

**NP complete,** *abbrev. for* Nondeterministic Polynominal-time complete.

**non-linear planning (NONLIN),** *n.* planners capable of maintaining an emerging plan as a partially-ordered network of ACTIONS, of which the first system was NOAH. Unnecessary ordering (linearization) of the actions is avoided. An ordering is imposed only in the event of conflicts between parallel branches of the plan (e.g., the inability to determine the answer to a query). Included in NONLIN is a complete treatment of the handling of alternatives and all legal linearizations after an interaction between SUBGOALS is detected. Another system, DEVISER, features the ability to use the same technique in the presence of time constraints on particular actions. Most non-linear planners use HIERARCHICAL PLANNING techniques as well.

**non-monotonic reasoning,** *n.* a technique that uses multiple lines of reasoning and allows facts or conclusions to be retracted on the basis of new information. This technique is valuable in applications in which there are multiple changes in VALUES in short periods of time. Non-monotonic reasoning involves adopting assumptions that may need to be abandoned in the light of new information. This reasoning is called non-monotonic because it stands in contrast with the monotonicity of deductive logic, in which the addition of new AXIOMS to a set of axioms can never decrease the set of THEOREMS or FACTS. Quite often in the case of deductive logic, the new axioms give rise to new theorems so that the set of theorems grows monotonically with the set of axioms. In non-monotonic logics, the set of theorems may lose members as well as gain members when new axioms are added. Non-monotonicity is a common feature of ordinary reasoning. For instance, if we are told Tweety is a bird, we assume (s)he can fly, but we negate this fact when we are told (s)he is a penguin. (See also DEFAULT REASONING, TRUTH MAINTENANCE.)

**nonresolution theorem proving,** see NATURAL DEDUCTION.

**nonsense syllable,** *n.* a syllable typically comprised of three letters, beginning and ending with a consonant, and supposed to be meaningless for most subjects (e.g., XUM, JUR, FAZ). Used in testing speech understanding systems.

**nonterminal symbols,** *n.* a SYNTACTIC CATEGORY, such as <SENTENCE> and <NOUN PHRASE>, which gets re-written in a GENERATIVE GRAMMAR. These syntactic categories are referred to as nonterminal symbols, or VARIABLES. Notationally, the nonterminals of a grammar are often indicated by enclosing the category names in angle brackets, as shown above.

**nontutorial CAI,** *n.* a form of learning by doing rather than by being taught. There is little room for a teacher role in learning by doing. The task provides its own feedback. The basic question in improving learning efficiency therefore becomes: What are good things for students to 'do'? Any activity is in some sense educational, but which activities provide the most value? And what are the right tools to give students?

**NPPC,** *abbrev. for* Nuclear Power Plant Consultant, an expert system that uses a model of the primary coolant system in a nuclear power plant to help plant operators determine the cause of an abnormal event such as greater than normal containment temperature. The model of the coolant system includes pumps, reactor, steam generator, and the emergency core cooling system. In conjunction with the model, the program applies diagnostic RULES to determine the cause of an event and also to suggest procedures for correcting the problem. A commonsense ALGORITHM network that accesses appropriate diagnostic rules is used to implement the model. NPPC was developed at the Georgia Institute of Technology.

**NTC,** *n.* an expert system developed for Digital Equipment Corporation for trouble-shooting the network system called DEC-net.

**NUDGE,** *n.* a FRAME-based system used to understand incomplete and possibly inconsistent management-scheduling requests and to provide a complete specification for a conventional scheduling ALGORITHM. Implemented in FRL language, the system also uses a FRAME-based SEMANTICS to resolve anaphoric requests.

# O

**object,** *n.* **1.** a deep case in CASE GRAMMAR that indicates the entity that moves or changes or whose position or existence is in consideration.

**2.** a physical or conceptual entity that is associated with a group of ATTRIBUTES. An object is described as 'static' if the group of attributes apply to a general class of objects; it is 'dynamic' if the attributes apply only to one instance of that class. The term 'object' is synonymous with CONTEXT in MYCIN or FRAME in OBJECT-oriented programming.

**object–attribute–value triplets (O–A–V triplets),** *n.* a method of representing factual KNOWLEDGE in which the OBJECT is an actual or conceptual entity, the ATTRIBUTES are properties of that object, and the VALUES describe the properties of a specific instance of that object. (In EMYCIN, the REPRESENTATION method is referred to as CONTEXT-PARAMETER-VALUE TRIPLETS.)

**object–centred,** *adj.* (of a model) having its own reference frame, independent of its position or orientation in the scene. For example, a model of a chair must express the essential features of the shape of a chair. The concept is used in VISION STUDIES and is contrasted with camera-centred.

**object–oriented,** *adj.* any program or programming language whose basic data types are items called OBJECTS.

**object–oriented methods,** *n.* programming methods based on the use of items called OBJECTS. The objects communicate with each other via messages in the form of global broadcasts.

**obligatory transformation,** *n.* a grammatical rule called a transformation, which must be applied if structural conditions on a TREE hold. (See also OPTIMAL TRANSFORMATION.)

**OCEAN,** *n.* an expert system developed by Teknowledge for NCR for internal use. It checks orders and configures NCR computers. S.1 is the development software.

**OCEAN SURVEILLANCE,** *n.* an expert system that uses KNOWLEDGE of deployment histories of particular vessel types, ongoing US/allied naval activities and movement in the area of interest, and the surveillance ship's own activities and movement to help naval personnel aboard a surveillance ship determine a remotely sensed vessel's destination and mission. The program uses a vessel's correlated tracks, history, location, and status to determine its likely destination, arrival time, and probable mission. The program is RULE-based using FORWARD CHAINING and CERTAINTY factors. It includes a simple EXPLANATION FACILITY. Implemented in OPS5 and FRANZ LISP, OCEAN SURVEILLANCE was developed at Science Applications, Inc.

**OCSS,** *n.* an expert system that assists chemists in synthesizing complex organic molecules. The program analyses target molecules devised by the chemist by recognizing functional groups, chains, rings and redundancy, or symmetry in the molecular skeleton, applying chemical transformations to them, and evaluating the resulting structure for correctness, uniqueness, and simplicity. Implemented on a DEC-PDP-1, OCSS was developed at Harvard University.

**OCULAR HERPES MODEL,** *n.* an expert system that uses a patient's clinical history and knowledge of disease categories to help physicians diagnose and treat ocular herpes complex. The program relates a patient's clinical history and laboratory findings with disease categories to diagnose and recommend treatment. It selects therapy based on drug effectiveness and a patient's resistance or allergic reaction to a drug. The program is RULE-based using FORWARD CHAINING. Implemented in EXPERT, OCULAR HERPES MODEL was developed at Rutgers University.

**Oleophilic Advisor,** *n.* an expert system developed by Teknowledge for Rockwell's internal use. It assists the lithography R&D group in choosing new materials. M.1 is the development software.

**OMF Advisor,** *n.* an expert system developed at IBM for internal use. It provides a query management facility that guides project service representatives through a problem-solving session with a client. E.S. Environment/VM is the development software.

**ONCOCIN,** *n.* an expert system that uses knowledge about 34 Hodgkin's disease and lymphoma protocols in order to assist physicians in treating and managing cancer patients undergoing chemotherapy. In order to select therapy, the program relates information about the patient's diagnosis, previous treatments, and laboratory tests to knowledge about PROTOCOLS, which are past experiments aimed at measuring the therapeutic benefits and toxic side effects of alternative cancer treatments. The program is RULE-based using both FORWARD and BACK-CHAINING. Implemented in INTERLISP, ONCOCIN was developed at Stanford University.

**opacity,** *n.* that property of matter such that each point in an image has a unique DEPTH associated with it and, thus, each image has at most one MATCH in some other image.

**open world,** *n.* the assumption made in the design of a system that the set of OBJECTS to be represented is incomplete.

**operating system,** *n.* a program that manages a computer's hardware and software components. The operating system determines when to run programs and also controls peripheral equipment. It is the computer software that instructs the computer on how to use programs, how to handle input and output, and how to use peripheral devices. In effect, the given operating system a computer uses performs the 'housekeeping' and communication chores of the more specialized systems within the computer. Conventional computers generally have standard operating systems, which any software designed to run on the computer makes use of. For example, the IBM personal computer makes use of a version of MS-DOS. In cases where an expert system and the operating system are in the same language, an ARTIFICIAL INTELLIGENCE language is used to write both the expert system and the operating system. LISP workstations, such as the Xerox 1100 series and the Symbolics machines, are computers that use a LISP operating system in order to improve their efficiency and flexibility when they run expert systems in LISP.

**operationalization,** *n.* a process of transformation involving a system that is given vague, general purpose KNOWLEDGE or advice. The system must transform this high-level knowledge into a form that can be readily used by the performance element of a LEARNING SYSTEM. The system must understand and interpret the high-level knowledge and relate it to what it already knows. Operationalization is an active process that can involve activities such as deducing the consequences of what the system has been told, making assumptions, filling in the details, and deciding when to ask for more advice. A taxonomy of operationalization methods is given below.

(a) Methods for evaluating an expression.

    (i) Procedures that always produce a result (assuming their inputs are available):

        Pigeonhole principle.

        Historical reasoning.

        HEURISTIC SEARCH.

    (ii) Procedures that sometimes produce a result:

        Check for a necessary or sufficient CONDITION.

        Make some simplifying assumption that restricts the scope of applicability.

    (iii) Procedures that produce an approximate result:

        Apply some formula for probability that randomly chosen subsets overlap.

        Characterize a quantity as an increasing or decreasing function of some VARIABLE.

        Use an untested simplifying assumption.

        Predict others' choices pessimistically.

(b) Methods for achieving a GOAL.

    (i) Sound methods — execution of plan, when feasible, will achieve goal.

        To empty a set, remove one element at a time.

        Find a sufficient condition and achieve it.

        Restrict a choice to satisfy the goal.

        Modify a plan for one goal to achieve an additional goal.

        To achieve some future goal, satisfy it now and then avoid violating it.

    (ii) HEURISTIC methods — execution of plan may not always achieve goal.

        Simplify the goal by arbitrarily choosing a value for one of its variables.

        Find a necessary condition and achieve it.

        Order a choice set with respect to goal.

**operator,** *n.* a RULE that transforms or simplifies a problem description so that it can be solved. If the problem cannot be solved immediately, the operator changes it into a set of subproblems that can be solved immediately or further transformed. Several operators can be applied to the same problem, or a single operator can be applied in different ways; in either of these cases, it suffices to find a solution to one of the subcases. Generally, operators are represented as three lists: a list of PRECONDITIONS, a list of FACTS that will no longer be true after application of the operator, and a list of facts that will involve VARIABLES that must be bound for any particular INSTANCE of the action. The difficulty encountered in fully capturing the effects of actions in non-trivial planning DOMAINS using such operators is an aspect of the FRAME PROBLEM. (See also FUNCTION.)

**operator schemata,** *n.* a set of OPERATORS that contains VARIABLES that can be INSTANTIATED in more than one way. Such a set of operators will yield more than one state, and so the term operator schemata is more accurate.

**opportunistic problem–solving,** *n.* a form of PROBLEM-SOLVING where the system's behaviour is guided primarily by what has been recently discovered, rather than by the requirement to satisfy SUBGOALS.

**opportunistic search,** *n.* a SEARCH method used by systems that do not have a fixed (GOAL-driven or data–driven) directional approach to solving a problem. Instead, a current focus for the search is identified on the basis of the most constrained way forward (see CONSTRAINT). The opportunistic approach can be visualized by a comparison of the current goals with the initial WORLD MODEL state, by consideration of the number of likely outcomes of making a selection, by the degree to which goals are INSTANTIATED, etc. Any PROBLEM-SOLVING component may summarize its requirements for the solution as constraints on possible solutions or restrictions on the VALUES of VARIABLES representing OBJECTS being manipulated. Thus, it can suspend its operations until further information becomes available. With many such systems, a BLACKBOARD operates through which the various components can communicate via constraint information. The scheduling of the various tasks associated with arriving at a solution may also be handled through the blackboard.

**opportunistic tutoring,** *n.* a tutoring method that takes the initiative to present new material to the student. This requires that the tutor have presentation methods that opportunistically adapt material to the needs of the dialogue. In particular, the tutor has to be sensitive to how a tutorial dialogue fits together, including what kinds of interruptions and probing are reasonable and expected in this kind of discourse. GUIDON demonstrates such sensitivity to these concerns when it corrects the student before quizzing him or her about missing hypotheses, asks questions about recently mentioned data to see if he or she understands how to use them, quizzes about rules that are related to one that has just been discussed, follows up on previous hints, and comments on the status of a subproblem after an INFERENCE has been discussed.

**OPS5,** *n.* a PRODUCTION SYSTEM language that, along with other ARTIFICIAL INTELLIGENCE applications, has been used for building expert systems. It features a design that supports generality in both data representation and control structures, a powerful PATTERN-MATCHING capability, and an efficient FORWARD CHAINING INTERPRETER for matching rules against the data. KNOWLEDGE is represented using the IF-THEN RULES in the production memory. Processing is usually data-driven and control takes the form of a RECOGNIZE-ACT CYCLE during which elements in a global DATA BASE called the working memory are matched, modified, deleted or added to. Elements consist of data represented in attribute-value pairs or vectors. Also included are DEBUGGING and editing packages, as well as a mechanism for help in determining why a rule did not fire when the programmer thought it should. OPS5 has been used for the R1 and XCON expert systems, each of which is used to configure VAX minicomputers, and is one of the most widely used KNOWLEDGE ENGINEERING languages. Three OPS5 interpreters have been written in Bliss-10, MACLISP, and FRANZ LISP. Although the INTERFACE with the host language and the front-end of OPS5 is unimpressive, even in the LISP versions, OPS5 has a powerful and versatile pattern-matching capability. Other languages derived from OPS5 include OPS10, OPS83, and YAPS. Developed at Carnegie-Mellon University as part of the OPS family of languages for AI and cognitive psychology applications, OPS5 is available as a commercial system.

**OPS83,** *n.* a COMPILER-based PRODUCTION SYSTEMS language. It

OPTIMALITY

retains the RULE-based PARADIGM of the OPS5 family but is en-
hanced by the integration of the FORWARD CHAINING, rule-
based programming paradigm and the procedural paradigm.
This enhancement permits PASCAL-like functions and
procedures to be used, augmented with the OPS5 constructs
of working memory elements and rules. OPS83 also provides
facilities for user-defined data types and permits the user to
define conflict resolution procedures, control regimes, and tracing routines. Developed at Carnegie-Mellon University as a
research system, OPS83 runs on a variety of computers.

**optimal solution,** *n.* a solution arrived at via a MINIMAL COST
(see COST (OF A SOLUTION TREE)). If the entire SEARCH SPACE
had been explored, then an optimal solution TREE could be
constructed and its cost measured as follows. Let c(n,m) be
the cost of the ARC from NODE n to a SUCCESSOR NODE m.
Define a FUNCTION h(n):

  (a) If n is a terminal node (a primitive problem), then
     h(n)=0.
  (b) If n has OR successors, then h(n) is the minimum, over
     all its successors m, of c(n,m)+h(m).
  (c) If n has AND successors and sum costs are used, then
     h(n) is the summation, over all successors m, of
     c(nm)+h(m).
  (d) If n has AND successors and max costs are used, then
     h(n) is the maximum, over all successors m, of
     c(n,m)+h(n).
  (e) If n is a nonterminal node with no successors, then h(n)
     is infinite.

According to this definition, h(n) is finite if and only if the
problem represented by node n is solvable. For each solvable
node n, h(n) gives the cost of an optimal solution tree for the
problem represented by node n. If s is the start node, then
h(s) is the cost of an optimal solution to the initial problem.

**optimality,** *n.* a measure for comparing the scope of two
ALGORITHMS. Two otherwise similar algorithms $A_1$ and $A_2$,
can be compared with respect to their choices of the h* function, say, $h_1$* and $h_2$*. Algorithm $A_1$ is said to be more informed than $A_2$ if, whenever a NODE n (other than a GOAL
node) is evaluated,

$$h_1{}^\star(n) > h_2{}^\star(n).$$

On this basis an optimality result for A$^\star$ can be stated: If A and A$^\star$ are admissible algorithms such that A$^\star$ is more informed than A, then A$^\star$ never expands a node that is not also expanded by A.

**optimal transformation,** *n.* a grammatical transformation that may be applied to produce a new structure. (See also OBLIGATORY TRANSFORMATION; TRANSFORMATIONAL GRAMMAR).

**ordered search,** *n.* a HEURISTIC SEARCH that always selects the most promising NODE as the next node to expand. DEPTH-FIRST, BREADTH-FIRST and UNIFORM-COST SEARCHES are all types of STATE-SPACE SEARCHES. The search is usually global, but can be local, as in depth-first searches. To determine whether or not to expand a node, an EVALUATION FUNCTION is first applied to the node to estimate, for example, the distance between it and the GOAL node, or whether that node has certain predetermined features.

**origami world,** *n.* a model of the world composed of planar surfaces, rather than solids. In this world, line drawings can be labelled by a technique much like the Huffman-Clowes-Waltz method, but the origami world allows more objects than are allowed by TRIHEDRAL WORLDS. The origami world provides insight to the issue of multiple interpretations and QUANTITATIVE SHAPE RECOVERY of NATURAL INTERPRETATIONS.

**orthographic projection,** *n.* in imaging, a point (x,y,z) in three-dimensional space is projected to a point (x,y) in the image rather than being foreshortened.

**overlapping concept descriptions,** *n.* in multiple concept learning, the overlapping of left-hand sides of diagnosis rules.

**overlay model,** *n.* a MODEL used in ICAI where a student model is formed by comparing the student's behaviour to that of the computer-based expert in the same environment. The modelling component marks each skill according to whether evidence indicates that the student knows the material or not. The student's understanding is represented completely in terms of the EXPERTISE component of the program.

**OWL,** *n.* a KNOWLEDGE ENGINEERING language for FRAME-based representation. It features a SEMANTIC NETWORK framework supporting a conceptual TAXONOMY with CONCEPT specialization and a flexible INHERITANCE routine. A single, large, unified KNOWLEDGE BASE augmented by a small set of embedded LISP and MACHINE LANGUAGE programs, and their associated data structures, serves to maintain the program's KNOWLEDGE. Implemented in LISP, OWL was developed at MIT.

# P

**PAGE1,** *n*. an expert system developed by Honeywell for internal use. It troubleshoots the non-impact Page Printing System. The program is implemented in LISP and LOOPS.

**PALLADIO,** *n*. an expert system that provides an interactive ENVIRONMENT for circuit designers to use when designing and testing VLSI circuits. The program has been used to design a variety of nMOS circuits. Features of the program include interactive graphics editors that manipulate high-level electronic components, a RULE editor that helps users modify the behavioural specifications of circuit components, a simulator that uses the structural and behavioural specification of a circuit to simulate the circuit, and TOOLS for refining and creating design specifications at different levels of abstraction. Implemented in LOOPS, PALLADIO provides for OBJECT-oriented, RULE-based, and LOGIC-based representation. It was developed at Stanford University. The program is named after the Italian architect, Andrea Palladio (1508–1580).

**PAM,** *n*. *acronym for* Plan Applier Mechanism, a program that understands stories by determining the GOALS that are to be achieved in the story, and by attempting to match the actions of the story with the methods that it knows will achieve the goals.

**pan,** *vb*. to rotate in the horizontal plane.

**paradigm,** *n*. the form of an approach to a problem. Consultation paradigms in particular describe generic types of PROBLEM-SOLVING scenarios. Particular system building TOOLS are typically good for one or a few consultation paradigms and not for others. Most commercial tools, for example, are designed to facilitate rapid development of expert systems that can deal with the diagnostic/prescriptive paradigm.

**Paradox,** *n*. an expert system developed by Ansa Software for commercial use. It assists in management of relational DATA BASES.

**parallel processing,** *n*. an ARCHITECTURE for computers that enables them to run several programs simultaneously. Parallel processing involves several central processors installed in the computer and simultaneously processing information instead of the sequential processing used in the conventional, von Neumann type of computer architecture. In sum, parallel processing is the operation of a computer in which two or more programs are executed concurrently. As an aid to ARTIFICIAL INTELLIGENCE applications where cross-referencing, indexing, and list processing are required, parallel processing enhances time and memory economies.

**parallel search,** *n.* a SEARCH for paths in memory from all of the input TERMINAL NODES in parallel. For example, after matching the terminal nodes of a probe to NODES in the memory structure, the system searches from each of the nodes in parallel to determine whether the paths that connect them are identical in memory and in the probe. However, if a node has more than one path emanating from it, they are searched sequentially. Consequently, the time required to establish that a node falls on a path is proportional to the number of ASSOCIATIONS it has – that is, the number of paths it belongs to.

**parallel-line heuristic,** *n.* a HEURISTIC that states that if two lines are parallel in a picture, they depict parallel lines in the scene. Under ORTHOGRAPHIC PROJECTION, this is not always the case. The converse, however, is always true: parallel lines in the scene will be depicted as parallel lines in the image. Consider the constraint that this heuristic places on the gradients of two planes if a pair of their boundary lines is parallel in the picture (as shown in the illustration overleaf): Their gradients should be on a gradient-space line that is perpendicular to the parallel boundary lines in the image. In fact, if a pair of boundary lines is really parallel in the three-dimensional space, one can translate one of the planes toward the other, without changing its orientation, and make the two planes intersect along those boundary lines. Therefore, the gradients of the two planes have the same relationship that holds for surfaces connected by a convex or concave line.

**parameter learning,** *n.* a mode of learning whereby a fixed functional form is assumed for the unknown system. The functional form has a vector of parameters w, that must be determined from the TRAINING INSTANCES. There is little or no

# PARAPHRASE

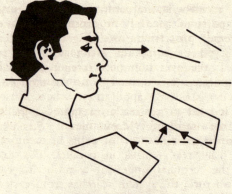

**Parallel-line heuristic**

probabilistic interpretation for the unknown parameters, unlike in statistical methods, and consequently, probability theory provides no guidance for estimating unknown parameters from the data. Instead, some form of criterion, usually the squared error averaged over all training instances, is minimized. Thus, the RULE SPACE is a space of possible vectors, and it is searched by HILL CLIMBING (also called gradient descent) in order to find that point that minimizes the error between the model and the unknown system.

**paraphrase,** *n.* a REPRESENTATION of the denotative meaning of a sentence in another sentential form.

**paraplate,** *n.* a PATTERN that spans two TEMPLATES in PREFER-ENCE SEMANTICS. Paraplates are used to resolve prepositional or case ambiguities. For example, the fragments 'he ran the mile' and 'in five minutes,' would be tied together by a para-plate for the TIMELOCATION case; had the second fragment been 'in a paper bag,' a CONTAINMENT case paraplate would be matched instead.

**PARRY,** *n.* a system that simulates the role of beliefs and affects in cognition. It is a model of the paranoid mode, a pattern of behaviour motivated by paranoid beliefs and intentions.

**parse tree,** *n.* a TREE-like structure that depicts the derivation of a sentence.

**PARSIFAL,** *n*. a NATURAL LANGUAGE processing system.

**parsing,** *n*. identifying the components of language statements as various parts of speech. The process of 'delinearization' of linguistic input, that is, the use of grammatical rules such as syntax and other sources of KNOWLEDGE to determine the functions of words in an input sentence in order to create a more complicated data structure, for example, a DERIVATION TREE.

Parsing is used to get at the meaning of the sentence. For example, the sentence 'Mary taught Stephen' could be matched to the pattern:

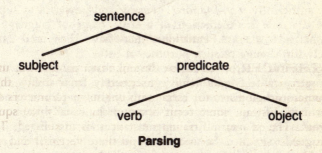

**Parsing**

The set of SYNTACTIC patterns used in a parser is determined by the grammar of the input language. In theory, by applying a comprehensive grammar, a parser can decide what is and what is not a grammatical sentence and can build up a data structure corresponding to the syntactic structure of any grammatical sentence it finds.

**partial function,** *n*. in PROBLEM REPRESENTATION, OPERATORS on the STATE SPACE. Each operator serves as a partial function, if it applies to a given state at all, and returns exactly one new state as its result.

**partial program specification,** *n*. in AUTOMATIC PROGRAM-MING, specification of a program allowing for partial or fragmentary descriptions of the desired program. Not all of the required information is present in the specification, or, when it is present, it may not be explicit.

**partial solution,** *n*. the solution to a subproblem in ICAI.

**partially developed node,** *n.* a NODE to which some but not all applicable OPERATORS have been applied. Also called a partially expanded node.

**partitioned semantic net,** *n.* a method for enhancing the organizational and expressive power of SEMANTIC NETWORKS via the grouping of NODES and links. Nodes and links may figure in one or more 'spaces', which may themselves be bundled into higher-level 'vistas', which can be exploited autonomously and structured hierarchically (See HIERARCHY). Serving as a central motivation for partitioning is the effective encoding of logical statements involving CONNECTIVES and QUANTIFIERS. However, the partitioning mechanisms involved are sufficiently well-founded, general, and powerful to support the dynamic representation of a wide range of language and WORLD KNOWLEDGE. Partitioned nets have been used extensively for a range of such purposes at SRI.

**PATHFINDER,** *n.* an expert system that uses KNOWLEDGE of lymph node pathology obtained from experienced haematopathologists to help pathologists interpret findings occurring from microscopic examinations of lymph node tissue. The program first queries a pathologist in a manner designed to reduce the uncertainty in the differential diagnosis. In doing so, the program can supply an explanation to justify the most recent question it posed. As criteria to make decisions, the program relies on a set of disease profiles that contain files normally associated with each disease. FRAMES are used to encode the program's knowledge. PATHFINDER was developed at Stanford University.

**pathway,** *n.* a series of links in a CASNET network. They usually connect causes.

**PATREC,** *n. acronym for* PATient RECords system, an expert system that uses a conceptual MODEL of medical data and a patient model to manage a DATA BASE of patient records. The program provides diagnostic physicians and the MDX expert system with sophisticated access to the records. Handling data in the context of diagnosing patient data for the syndrome cholestasis, the conceptual model includes data such as the significance of a particular lab test and its expected values, while the patient model includes data such as individual patient histories and clinical episodes. The program accepts as input data from the user and stores the data appropriately. A query language handles a user's questions. The program also supplies advice about diagnosis in the form of summary reports. KNOWLEDGE in the program is represented as FRAMES with attached RULES to perform bookkeeping functions, data input, and automatic temporal inferencing. Implemented in LISP, PATREC was developed at Ohio State University.

**pattern,** *n.* a structural sketch of an ITEM with some pieces left undefined.

**pattern matching,** *n.* the process by which a specific received data structure is established as an instance of a given general pattern; performed, in particular, to establish whether input data items can provide VALUES for PATTERN VARIABLES. According to the conditions on the individual pattern variables, and on their joint satisfaction, the matching can be made more or less fuzzy (see FUZZY SET THEORY). Pattern matching is important to AI because pattern matching illustrates the fact that complex general concepts exhibit considerable variation in particular manifestations, and the fact that individual elements of these participate in relationships with one another.

**pattern recognition,** *n.* identification of visual images by classification into categories. Usually acknowledged as a part of ARTIFICIAL INTELLIGENCE, pattern recognition usually uses statistical methods and TEMPLATE comparisons.

**pattern variable,** *n.* a VARIABLE embedded in a PATTERN. A pattern is a structure with variables embedded in it, and it matches another structure if it can be made identical to that structure by replacing its variables with some VALUES. Occurrences of the same variable must be replaced by the same value. For example, (A ?X C ← X) will match (A B C B) but not (A B C D), because once the variable ?X has been bound to B in the match, it cannot then be bound to D. The following are common pattern-variable types which are expressed in terms of matching patterns in lists:

   (a) An open variable (?X) matches to any element of a list, and binds X to that element.

   (b) A closed variable (←X) that has already been bound, as in the example above, and matches only the value already bound to X.

(c) A restricted variable may have arbitrary restrictions placed on it. These restrictions are procedurally attached to the variable in some way. For example, as a predicate that must be TRUE in order for the variable to match.

(d) Segment variables match to a sublist of any length, rather than to an element. Open and closed segment variables are denoted ??X and ← ← X and so on, ignoring the varying notations of the different AI programming languages.

**pattern-directed retrieval,** *n*. **1.** the process of retrieving a datum from a DATA BASE on the basis of syntactic form. Retrieval is accomplished by comparing a pattern (or TEMPLATE) of the required datum with the data in the data base. The data that 'match' with the pattern are then retrieved. A successful match may bind the unspecified parts (VARIABLES) of either or both of the pattern and 'target' datum.
**2.** in the case of PROCEDURE invocation, a pattern is associated with each procedure. Calls to a procedure are made when the current situation or GOAL matches the associated pattern of the procedure. This allows for a more flexible control flow since procedures are not called by name but by content. This form of retrieval/invocation is central to the PLANNER-type languages. Two-way PATTERN MATCHING (or unification) is the basis of the RESOLUTION principle on which PROLOG is based.

**PDS,** *abbrev. for* Portable Diagnostic System, an expert system that diagnoses malfunctions in machine processes by interpreting information from sensors attached to the process. The program uses diagnostic methods that relate sensor readings to component malfunctions. It uses a FORWARD CHAINING, RULE-based representation scheme implemented in SRL, which is a FRAME-based KNOWLEDGE ENGINEERING language. The result is an INFERENCE NET representation paradigm similar to that found in PROSPECTOR. The system was developed at Carnegie-Mellon University in cooperation with Westinghouse Electric Corporation.

**PEACE,** *n*. an expert system that assists engineers in the design of electronic circuits. The program is a CAD tool that performs analysis and synthesis of passive and digital circuits by applying knowledge about circuit design. This knowledge includes the functional description of basic circuit components, connection rules for forming more complex circuits and networks, functional and topological circuit transformations, strategies for analysis and synthesis, and HEURISTICS for anticipating failures. PEACE can synthesize passive circuits from their functional descriptions and digital circuits from the mathematical expression of their transfer functions. The program is logic-oriented. Implemented in PROLOG, PEACE was developed at the University of Manchester, UK.

**Peanut/Pest,** *n.* an expert system developed for the U.S. Department of Agriculture (Georgia). It recommends irrigation and pest control for peanut farmers. Exsys is the development software.

**PEC,** *n. acronym for* Primary Eye Care system, an expert system that uses KNOWLEDGE obtained from the World Health Organization guide to primary eye care in order to help primary health care workers diagnose and treat common and potentially blinding eye disorders. The program queries users first with a set of yes/no questions such as 'Is the eye red?' and continues with subsequent questions about the patient. On the basis of the queried information, the program first produces a summary of the case, and then presents its diagnostic conclusions and management recommendations. The program is RULE-based using FORWARD CHAINING. Initially, PEC was implemented in EXPERT, but was later converted to BASIC for use on microcomputers. It was developed at Rutgers University.

**PECOS,** *n.* an expert system that transforms program descriptions to aid automatic program generation.

**perceptron,** *n.* a parallel decision-making mechanism that superficially resembles the sort of processing possibly characteristic of the neurons in the brain. A PATTERN RECOGNITION device with a threshold, the perceptron fires if the linear combination of the weighted inputs is greater than some threshold value. It is possible for a perceptron to learn; for example, if the weights associated with the inputs that were active in the case of a false alarm are decreased, and the weights associated with the inputs that were active in the case of the miss are increased, then it is intuitively plausible that recognition performance will improve. There is a THEOREM that says a perceptron will learn to recognize a class correctly over a finite number of errors. Analysis of the mathematical properties of perceptrons reveals profound limitations to their competence. These limitations are due largely to the difficulties inherent in making global decisions on the basis of only local evidence. Thus, a perceptron can not discern whether a figure is connected or not, or whether there is one, and only one, instance of a PATTERN present. Nevertheless, an increased resurgence of interest in perceptrons is occurring around the development of connectionist schemes.

**perceptron algorithm,** *n.* an ALGORITHM for finding the desired weight vector in a PERCEPTRON model. (See also FIXED-INCREMENT PERCEPTRON ALGORITHM).

**perceptual primitive,** *n.* a PRIMITIVE concerning centre of area, contact finding, and similarity testing used in the WHISPER system.

**performance aids,** see JOB AIDS.

**performance element,** *n.* a module of a LEARNING SYSTEM that uses the KNOWLEDGE BASE to perform its task.

**performance evaluation of speech systems,** *n.* a measure of the quality of voice recognition by a machine system. Among the measures used have been number of different words across DOMAINS.

**performance grammar,** see SEMANTIC GRAMMAR.

**Performance Mentor,** *n.* an expert system developed by AI Mentor Inc. to provide guidance to managers involved in shaping the performance of subordinates. Exsys is the development software.

**performance standard,** *n.* a set of examples against which actual instances are compared. A frequently used technique for feedback in learning is to have the environment, often a teacher, provide an external performance standard. The system evaluates the performance element's store of hypotheses by observing how well the performance element is doing relative to the performance standard. In systems that learn a single CONCEPT classification from TRAINING INSTANCES, the performance standard is the correct classification of each training instance, that is, determining whether or not it is an instance of the concept to be learned. In many systems, a reliable teacher reclassifies the training instances. In the META-

DENDRAL system, the performance standard is the actual mass spectrum produced when a molecule of known structure is placed in the mass spectrometer.

**performance trace,** *n.* a TRACE of all actions that the PERFORMANCE ELEMENT considered, as well as those it actually performed. This allows a learning element to determine all of the RULES that might have been applicable at each step of the PROBLEM-SOLVING process. Such information makes it easier to solve the problem of integrating new rules into the KNOWLEDGE BASE.

**Permaid,** *n.* an expert system developed at Honeywell for troubleshooting large disc drives. The program was implemented in LOOPS on the Xerox 1109.

**PERSONAL CONSULTANT,** *n.* a KNOWLEDGE ENGINEERING language for RULE-based representation, which also permits FRAME-based representation. It features BACK- and FORWARD CHAINING, CERTAINTY handling routines, class HIERARCHIES with INHERITANCE, and the ability to access user-defined LISP functions. The USER INTERFACE provides windows using colour graphics and an explanation facility, a KNOWLEDGE BASE editor, a TRACING FACILITY, and a regression testing facility. Written in IQLISP (a dialect of LISP), PERSONAL CONSULTANT runs on the TI Professional computer, the TI Explorer computer, and other MS-DOS compatible microcomputers. The program was developed by Texas Instruments Inc.

**perspective projection,** *n.* a graphics display simulating depth and distance by representing parallel lines merging at a vanishing point.

**perspective transform,** *n.* a transform of an image in a central projection model with homogeneous coordinates by using a linear matrix operation.

**PHLIQA1,** *n.* a NATURAL LANGUAGE UNDERSTANDING system.

**phoneme,** *n.* an abstract representation that captures the common characteristics of a class of ALLOPHONES. For example, the phoneme /t/ is known to have at least four allophones in English, corresponding to four different ways in which it occurs: Two of the allophones of /t/ are the 'hard' t at the beginning of the word 'top' and the 'flat' t in the middle of the word 'rattle'.

**phonemics,** *n.* RULES describing variations in pronunciation that appear when sounds are combined together in sentences.

**phonetics,** *n.* REPRESENTATIONS of the physical characteristics of the sounds in the words in a vocabulary.

**phonological component,** *n.* that component of a TRANSFORMATIONAL GRAMMAR that assigns a PHONETIC interpretation to a SURFACE STRUCTURE.

**Photolithography Advisor,** *n.* an expert system developed by Hewlett-Packard that troubleshoots photolithographic problems in chip fabrication. HP-RL (a Hewlett-Packard proprietary tool) is the development software.

**photometric stereo,** *n.* a technique for recovering shape information from REFLECTANCE MAPS. Given an image and a reflectance map for one light source, the intensity at a particular image location constrains (see CONSTRAINT) the surface orientation to lie on a contour in the reflectance map. If three images are taken with different light source positions, the surface orientation must lie on a known contour in each of the three associated reflectance maps, hence the intersection of these contours specifies the surface orientation.

**phrase marker,** *n.* a TREE STRUCTURE generated by the phrase structure rules of a TRANSFORMATIONAL GRAMMAR.

**phrase structure grammar,** *n.* a type of grammar utilizing rewriting rules. CONTEXT-FREE and CONTEXT-SENSITIVE GRAMMARS are examples of phrase-structure grammars.

**PICON,** *n. acronym for* Process Intelligent CONtrol system, a TOOL for KNOWLEDGE ENGINEERS to use for developing process control expert systems. It acts as a system-building aid supplying a graphics-oriented INTERFACE for KNOWLEDGE ACQUISITION from DOMAIN EXPERTS. The interface helps to transfer structural information, process descriptions, and HEURISTICS from the DOMAIN EXPERT to the KNOWLEDGE BASE. The program permits OBJECT-oriented, FRAME-based, and RULE-based knowledge representation and combines both FORWARD and BACK-CHAINING for control. In addition, the program updates the EXPERTISE it contains and provides users with an explanation facility. Implemented in ZETALISP and C, PICON runs on LMI's Lambda/Plus workstations.

**Picture Aider,** *n.* a modifier of nominal concepts in CONCEPTUAL DEPENDENCY models.

**picture domain,** *n.* the DOMAIN of two-dimensional pictures as opposed to three-dimensional scenes.

**picture grammar,** *n.* a set of syntactic methods of SCENE ANALYSIS. It assumes a PARSER of OBJECTS and relationships in a scene, and a set of SEMANTIC PRIMITIVES, such as edges or PRIMITIVE bodies. These are the meaningful units from which INTERPRETATIONS of a scene are constructed. SYNTACTIC methods of scene analysis constitute a language theory of VISION. Patterns are regarded as sentences in a language defined by formal grammar. Thus, the process of recognizing a pattern or scene is analogous to the process of parsing an English sentence.

**picture interpretation,** see IMAGE UNDERSTANDING.

**PIE,** *n. acronym for* Personal Information Environment, a system-building aid that extends the capabilities of SMALLTALK-76 by aiding the representation and manipulation of designs. SMALLTALK-76 is an OBJECT-oriented programming language. PIE's principle feature is the use of multiple perspectives. This mechanism provides a means for specifying independent specialized behaviours for an object. The SUPPORT ENVIRONMENT consists of all of the features and support facilities of SMALLTALK. PIE was developed at the Xerox Palo Alto Research Center.

**Pine,** *n.* an expert system developed at IBM for helping to diagnose and fix problems with data bases. It is implemented in E. S. Evironment/VM.

**PIP,** *n. acronym for* Present Illness Program, an expert system that assists physicians by taking the history of the present illness of a patient with oedema. The program interweaves the processes of information gathering and diagnosis, alternating between asking questions to gain new information and in- tegrating this new information into a developing picture of the patient. KNOWLEDGE contained in PIP includes prototypical findings such as signs, symptoms, laboratory data, the time course of the given illness, and rules for judging how closely a given patient matches a hypothesized (see HYPOTHESIS) disease or state. PIP's questions are controlled by a set of diagnostic hypotheses suggested by the patient's complaints. The ability of the hypotheses to account for the findings of the case is averaged with the measure of fit to arrive at a final certainty measure for ranking hypotheses. The program is FRAME-based. Implemented in CONNIVER, PIP was developed at MIT.

**Pipeline Advisor,** *n.* an expert system developed by System Designers Software for the British Hydronomic Research Association. It helps determine flow characteristics within pipes. Poplog is the development software.

**pixel,** *n.* the smallest picture element. An array of pixels defines an image.

**pixel templates,** *n.* a PATTERN of fixed elements. Low-level pixel TEMPLATES occur in four varieties:

(a) total templates, which are fixed against a background;
(b) partial templates, which are free of the background;
(c) piece templates, which match one feature of a figure;
(d) flexible templates, which are modified to match possible distortions in the scene.

Each of these categories provides more flexibility than the previous one, but at the expense of time and complexity during the matching process.

**plan,** *n.* **1.** one particular way of viewing a program, or part of a program in the PROGRAMMER'S APPRENTICE.
**2.** the means by which GOALS are accomplished. Understanding plan-based stories involves discerning the goals of the ACTOR and the methods by which the actor chooses to fulfill those goals. The distinction between SCRIPT-based and plan-based stories is that in a script-based story, parts or all of the story correspond to one or more scripts available to the story understander. In a plan-based story, the understander must discern the goals of the main actor and the actions that accomplish these goals.

**plane of observations,** *n.* in the network of CASNET, plane of observations is a set of NODES representing evidence gathered from a patient, such as signs, symptoms, and laboratory tests. During a consultation with the program, some or all of these nodes will be instantiated (see INSTANTIATION). Nodes in this plane are linked to nodes in the pathophysiological plane. The links have associated confidences that are scaled between 1 and 5, reflecting the degree to which the particular test, symptom, or sign supports the associated state.

**PLANES,** *n.* a NATURAL LANGUAGE system focusing on DATA BASE access.

**plan–generate–test,** *n.* the tripartite division of HEURISTIC DENDRAL. Planning in this context refers to redefining the problem in terms that reduce the effort of the problem solver – for example, the problem of finding all possible combinations of a set of ATOMS is redefined to the problem of finding all such combinations consistent with CONSTRAINTS derived from mass spectrometry. Within the plan's constraints, the DENDRAL ALGORITHM generates only those structures that do not include forbidden subparts or exclude mandatory subparts. The test part of the program ranks the resulting list of candidate structures by simulating their behaviour in a mass spectrometer. The structures resulting in simulated spectra closest to the empirical one are ranked highest.

**PLANNER,** *n.* an INTERPRETER written in MACLISP that accesses some of the MACLISP programming support facilities. A noteworthy programming-support mechanism PLANNER offers programmers is the TRACE-as-you-go facility. Tracing involves going back through the steps of a computation, usually from some error break. In PLANNER, by saying (THTRACE <OBJECT>), the programmer can request a trace of a particular FUNCTION, a GOAL, all goals, or various other OBJECTS. Then, as the program runs, the system prints out information every time this object is activated. Because PLANNER's control structure results in an extensive TREE of goals and actions, it traces the whole tree as the tree develops, rather than backtracking from one particular NODE, in which case only one branch of the tree would be revealed.

**planner,** *n.* that module of an intelligent system which develops PROCEDURES for approaching a problem. This can be done through successive automatic DEBUGGING. The program called HACKER, for example, uses an initial situation and a GOAL and compares them to already known PLANS. Hence, a LEARNING ELEMENT must be included.

**planning,** *n.* **1.** in CONCEPTUAL DEPENDENCY models, a set of action-state sequences where each state enables a subsequent action until a final GOAL STATE is obtained. The structure of plans reflects that a set of sequential or parallel actions is usually required to achieve a goal.

**2.** in logic programs, the searching (see SEARCH) through a space of world models to find one in which a given condition is satisfied. In STRIPS, for example, it is performed with MEANS-END ANALYSIS.

**planning space,** *n.* the lowest layer for CONTROL of PLANNING in MOLGEN. The planning space contains a HIERARCHY of operations and OBJECTS typical to a gene-splicing experiment. At the lowest level of this layer are bacteria, drugs, and laboratory operations.

**planning system,** *n.* a computer program that incorporates a great deal of code for PLANNING. These include STRIPS, ABSTRIPS, HACKER, MOLGEN, and NOAH.

**Planpower,** *n.* an expert system developed at Applied Expert Systems for First Financial Planner Services. It assists financial planners. The program is implemented in LISP.

**Plant Safety Advisor,** *n.* an expert system developed at Stone & Webster Engineering that advises managers on appropriate safety procedures. MAIDService is the development software.

**PLANT/cd,** *n.* an expert system that uses knowledge about a particular field of corn in order to predict the damage caused to the corn by black cutworm. The program uses data associated with conditions such as moth trap counts, field wetness, larval age spectrum, soil condition, and corn variety in order to predict the damage the black cutworm will cause. A RULE-based program using BACK-CHAINING, it also uses a set of black cutworm simulation programs to produce the predictions. Implemented in ADVISE, PLANT/cd was developed at the University of Illinois.

**PLANT/ds,** *n.* an expert system that uses knowledge about disease symptoms and plant environment to provide advice about diagnosing soybean diseases. The program selects from approximately 15 diseases to arrive at a diagnosis. It bases its decisions on data that include the month of occurrence, the temperature, plant height, and condition of leaves, stems, and seeds. The program is RULE-based using two types of rule format: rules representing the program's diagnostic EXPERTISE, and rules obtained from AQ11, an automated inductive inference program. Implemented in ADVISE, PLANT/ds was developed at the University of Illinois.

**plausible move generation,** see FORWARD PRUNING.

**PLUME,** *n.* a TOOL for adapting NATURAL LANGUAGE INTER-
FACES to expert systems. Based on the DYPAR-II natural
language INTERPRETER developed at Carnegie-Mellon University, PLUME enables users to extend DYPAR-II's LEX-
ICON, writing FRAMES, and grammatical RULES to handle the
words and phrases commonly used within a given DOMAIN
application. Additionally, PLUME handles ellipsis, ambiguous
input, and pronoun resolution. The program includes tools for
grammar rule and CASE FRAME editing, and tools for DEBUG-
GING and tracing. Implemented in COMMON LISP, PLUME runs
on the Carnegie Group Workstations, the DEC VAX/VMS
systems, and the Symbolics 3600 series workstations. The program was developed by the Carnegie Group Inc.

**ply,** *n.* the predetermined depth to which a SEARCH TREE is to
be generated.

**POLY,** *n.* a program interpreting line drawings as three-
dimensional scenes. Unlike the labelling schemes of Huffman,
Clowes, and Waltz, POLY accomplishes the task by reasoning
about surface orientations based on the properties of the
GRADIENT SPACE.

**polynomial evaluation function,** *n.* a STATIC EVALUATION
FUNCTION investigated for the Checkers Player program. It is
a polynomial of the form:

$$value = \sum_i w_i f_{ig}$$

where $f_i$ are board features and $W_i$ are real-valued weights
(coefficients). For most experiments, a polynomial with 16
features is employed. The program faces two tasks in attempting to learn such a polynomial evaluation function. The first is
discovering which features to use in the function. The second
is to develop appropriate weights for combining the various
features in order to obtain a value for the board position.

**POMME,** *n. acronym for* Pest and Orchard ManageMent
Expert system, an expert system that uses DOMAIN KNOW-
LEDGE about pest control and weather-damage recovery
obtained from plant pathologists and entomologists. The program provides advice to farmers on how to improve apple

crops and better manage apple orchards. The KNOWLEDGE the program contains includes that of fungicides, insecticides, and freeze, frost, and drought damage. The program's knowledge is represented in the form of both RULES and FRAMES. Implemented in PROLOG, POMME runs on the VAX 11/780 computer. The program was developed at Virginia Polytechnic Institute and State University.

**POPLER,** *n.* a language based on PLANNER and embedded in POP-2, POPLER has an implementation of the spaghetti stack and makes the same distinction as QLISP between testing the DATA BASE and calling consequent PROCEDURES. Furthermore, POPLER distinguishes between those procedures that deduce the VALUE of an ASSERTION in a WORLD MODEL from those that achieve the assertion as a GOAL, producing a new world model from the old model.

**POP-2,** *n.* a programming language designed at Edinburgh University during the late 1960s. The AI researchers at the university developed the POP-2 language because good IMPLEMENTATIONS of LISP were not available on the machines they were using, and because they disagreed about the usefulness of some of the features of LISP and proposed that others could be improved. As a language intended for use in artificial intelligence research, POP-2 is conversational and provides extensive facilities for non-numerical as well as numerical applications. POP-2 is a common AI language in Great Britain, but it is not broadly used elsewhere. The features of POP-2 include a syntax allowing immediate execution and incremental compilation, and DYNAMIC SCOPING of identifiers. Not being an interpreted language, POP-2 has an incremental COMPILER allowing an interactive style of programming similar to that of LISP. It also includes a program module facility allowing data class definition with full run-time type checking. These classes can be defined by the program. A wide range of standard data structures, such as LISTS and ARRAYS, is provided. For its extended data, control, and PATTERN MATCHING, POP-2 relies on library packages. The library packages keep the core language small. The packages, however, cannot be integrated as tightly as the features in INTERLISP. It also has automatic GARBAGE COLLECTION. PRIMITIVES are provided for BACK-TRACKING, COROUTINING and non-local jumps. Functions are OBJECTS that can be manipulated by the program. They can be created by a program, assigned as VALUES to VARIABLES, and passed as arguments to, and returned as results from, other functions (or themselves). The 'closure' facility is particularly useful for function creation. As the internal structure of a function body is not accessible to the user, a significant amount of compilation can be done, providing good run-time speed without loss of flexibility. There are no separate INTERPRETER and compiler modes. The POP-2 editor does reside in core permanently. Some of the available packages include facilities for TRACING and DEBUGGING, timing of individual functions, automatic documentation of the various packages, and special routines for debugging stack errors. The POP-2 stack is explicitly manipulable by the program.

**positive evidence,** *n*. a majority of data points that are correctly explained by a general RULE (see also NEGATIVE EVIDENCE.)

**possibility list,** *n*. a data type in CONNIVER used during fetch operations on the DATA BASE.

**possible-world semantics,** *n*. a method for overcoming difficulties presented by INTENSIONAL OPERATORS in AUTOMATIC DEDUCTION by reformulating the statements in which they occur. Rather than talking about what statements a person believes, one refers instead to what states of affairs, or possible worlds, are compatible with what he or she believes.

**postprocessor,** *n*. a computer program that transforms cutter path coordinate data into a form that a specific system can interpret correctly.

**potential solution,** *n*. a path in a STATE-SPACE graph that may lead to a solution (see also SOLUTION GRAPH or TREE).

**Power Plant Management,** *n*. an expert system developed for Leeds and Northrup to provide power plant management. PICON is the development software.

**pragmatics,** *n*. RULES of conversation, such that in a dialogue, a speaker's response must be not only a meaningful sentence but also a reasonable reply to what was said to him or her. For instance, in the case of the question 'Can you tell me what time it is?' it is pragmatic knowledge that tells us the response to the question requires more than a simple 'Yes' or 'No'.

**pre-compiled network,** *n*. a principal ARCHITECTURE used in the ARPA SUR projects. The precompiled network represents all possible pronunciations of all possible sentences in one data structure. The other principal kind of system architecture explored in the ARPA SUR project is one in which the KNOWLEDGE about all of the sentences that are legal or meaningful in the task domain is precompiled into one decision-tree-like network. In this system architecture, NODES in the network are allophonic (see ALLOPHONE) TEMPLATES, representing the different sounds in the language, which must be matched against the voice signal. The links in the network are used to control the matching process in the following way. After a successful match at node N, only the nodes that are linked in the net to node N need be tried next – no other sounds are legal at that point.

**precondition,** *n.* a proposition that must be satisfied preceding the execution of a piece of code. If the precondition is satisfied and the code executed correctly, a postcondition will be true following execution of the code.

**predicate,** *n.* a statement about single individuals in relation to themselves or a statement about individuals in relation to other individuals. A predicate has a VALUE of either TRUE or FALSE when it is applied to a specific number of arguments. For example, when the predicate is-red, which takes one argument, is applied to the individual 'coke can,' the predicate returns the value true, and returns false when applied to the individual 'snow.' Is-red is known as a one-place predicate. Other examples of one-place predicates are less-than-zero, Greek, male, and made-of-paper. A one-place predicate can take only one argument. Beyond one-place predicates, the predicate is-greater-than is a two-place predicate from mathematics (e.g., is-greater-than (7,4)). Equals is an important two-place predicate. In geometry, a three-place predicate could be Pythagorean; it takes three line-segments as arguments and is TRUE whenever two are the sides of a right triangle with the third as its hypotenuse.

**predicate abstraction,** *n.* the construction of PREDICATES out of arbitrary complex formulas. If Alice is a woman is represented as WOMAN(ALICE), the predicate WOMAN can be retrieved when we ask the second-order question, 'What properties does ALICE have?' All the deduction system has to do is match X(ALICE) against WOMAN(ALICE) and return WOMAN as the value of the variable X. But from the assertion that ALICE is either a teacher or a banker, represented as:

TEACHER(ALICE) OR
BANKER(ALICE),

the system could not infer, without using predicate abstraction, that ALICE has the disjunctive property of being a teacher–or–banker.

**predicate calculus,** *n.* the RULES of the PROPOSITIONAL CALCULUS extended by PREDICATES, QUANTIFICATION, and the INFERENCE RULES for quantifiers. As an extension of the notions of the propositional calculus, predicate calculus preserves the meanings of the connectives (and, or, if-then, not), but changes the focus of the LOGIC. Where propositional calculus looks for the truth value of sentences, predicate calculus represents statements about specific OBJECTS and individuals. Examples of individuals are Fernand, this sheet of paper, the number 8, the queen of hearts, Mike, and that video tape. Simple true or false propositions do not adequately capture our knowledge of the world. The predicate calculus extends the adequacy of formal logic to enable expressions to speak about objects, to postulate relationships between objects, and to generalize the relationships over classes of objects.

**predicate function,** *n.* the first part of a clause in MYCIN. It is associated with a triple of ATTRIBUTE, OBJECT, and VALUE. MYCIN has 24 such domain-independent predicate functions, which act as conceptual PRIMITIVES for constructing RULES.

**prediction task,** *n.* the task of classifying a given example. In learning examples, the simplest performance task is this CLASSIFICATION or prediction task based on a single CONCEPT or RULE. This problem of learning single concepts from examples has received more study than any other problem in AI learning research.

**preference semantics,** *n.* an approach to the problem of word-sense AMBIGUITY, the primary problem encountered in the early attempts at MACHINE TRANSLATION. For example, to determine the sense of the word 'salt' in the sentence 'The old salt was damp' it is necessary to determine from the surrounding context whether salt refers to a chemical compound or a sailor. Preference semantics also addresses problems involving other kinds of ambiguity and extended word senses, as for the word 'drink' in 'My car drinks petrol.' The general idea of this approach is to use the KNOWLEDGE of possible word meanings to disambiguate other words. For example, part of the meaning of 'drink' is that drink prefers a fluid object, and that part of the meanings of 'wine' and 'petrol' is that they are fluids. Thus, if the best fit among possible word senses does not satisfy all preferences (in the case of 'drink', drink has a preference of an animate subject), then an extended word-sense can be accepted. Preference semantics recognizes that, in general, semantic CONSTRAINTS on word combinations cannot be absolute, as this would be incompatible with the creativity of language. For example, the semantic patterns embodied in CASE FRAMES, and expressed by SEMANTIC PRIMITIVES, indicate the mutual contextual preferences or words. For example, 'hit' – meaning STRIKE – prefers a HUMAN agent. A preference metric minimizes information in the interpretation selected. Thus word sense and sentence structure selection in text processing is then determined by maximum CONSTRAINT satisfaction, and does not depend on complete satisfaction. By analogy, where interpretation involves INFERENCE, the metric selects the interpretation depending on the shortest INFERENCE CHAIN.

**premise,** *n*. a first proposition on which subsequent reasoning rests.

**preprocessing,** *n*. the first step of visual data processing. The objectives of preprocessing are to reconstruct the ideal, high-fidelity image from the low-quality, distorted input image, and to improve or enhance the quality of the input image by suppressing NOISE and emphasizing selected features to aid later stages of image processing. All preprocessing techniques involve modifying an image in order to make the image correspond more with the ideal image. There are three major kinds of modification: geometrical correction, GREY SCALE modification, and sharpening and smoothing. Once a picture is obtained, preprocessing techniques suppress unwanted details, such as noise, and enhance aspects such as lines.

**prerequisite-clobbers-brother-goal,** *n*. a type of BUG solvable in HACKER, which arises from the LINEARITY ASSUMPTION.

There are often interactions between GOALS whereby achieving the prerequisites for one goal prevents the accomplishment of another, i.e., 'clobbers' the other.

**PRESS,** *n.* an expert system developed at Honeywell for DEBUGGING OPERATING SYSTEMS SOFTWARE. The program is implemented in OPS5 and MACLISP.

**primal sketch,** *n.* a REPRESENTATION making explicit the properties of intensity changes in retinal images. The Raw Primal Sketch makes explicit only very localized properties, such as size, position and orientation; the Full Primal Sketch, resulting from grouping elements of the Raw Primal Sketch, makes explicit more global properties such as alignment. The higher-level processes interact only with the primal sketch and its derivatives, not with the data from which the primal sketch is derived. The primal sketch is computed by dedicated processors, which are independent of higher-level processes.

**primitive,** *n.* **1.** an AXIOM in a KNOWLEDGE REPRESENTATION scheme.
**2.** a concept that is not defined but rather is taken as a given.
**3.** a program subroutine that automatically creates familiar and frequently used shapes, such as circles.

**primitive acts,** *n.* the minimal unit of meaning in CONCEPTUAL DEPENDENCY models of understanding. Conceptual dependency representations are made up of a very small number of SEMANTIC PRIMITIVES, including primitive acts and primitive states (with associated ATTRIBUTE VALUES). Examples of primitive acts are:

PTRANS The transfer of the physical location of an object. For one to 'go' is to PTRANS oneself. 'Putting' an object somewhere is to PTRANS it to that place.
PROPEL The application of physical force to an object.
ATRANS The transfer of an abstract relationship. To 'give' is to ATRANS the relationship of possession or ownership.
MTRANS The transfer of mental information between people or within a person. 'Telling' is an MTRANS between people; 'seeing' is an MTRANS within a person.
MBUILD The construction of new information from old. 'Imagining', 'inferring,' and 'deciding' are MBUILDs.

**primitive problem,** *n.* a problem whose solution is immediate.

**PRISM,** *n. acronym for* PRototype Inference SysteM, a KNOWLEDGE ENGINEERING language for RULE-based REPRESENTATION. It features both FORWARD and BACK-CHAINING, and CERTAINTY handling. Additionally, the program can organize the KNOWLEDGE BASE into hierarchical structures. At each level in the HIERARCHY of the knowledge base, the program dedicates an INFERENCE ENGINE and control strategy to operate independently for the level. Also included is an editor for creating and maintaining the knowledge base in the form of English-like rules. Implemented in PASCAL, PRISM runs on IBM System 370 computers under the VM/CMS operating system. The program was developed by the IBM Palo Alto Scientific Center.

**probabilistic reasoning,** *n.* the computation of matching scores and binding scores. In PIP, the system performs two types of reasoning, categorical and probabilistic. Decisions about the applicability of a HYPOTHESIS are determined using the logical decision criteria – (the IS-SUFFICIENT, MUST-HAVE, and MUST-NOT-HAVE rules) – that a physician applies. When these criteria are not sufficient, the probabilistic methods are used, such as the calculating of matching scores and binding scores.

**probabilistic relaxation algorithm,** *n.* a RELAXATION ALGORITHM that attaches CERTAINTIES to the labels and is applied in a parallel-iterative manner. A probabilistic, as opposed to a discrete, relaxation algorithm is useful in many low-level vision tasks in which the problem is to convert the intensity array into a vocabulary of low-level symbols, such as those representing lines or edges. Probabilistic relaxation can be used to draw out features and eliminate NOISE on the basis of consistency in neighbouring FEATURE detection responses. For example, if relaxation is used in line detection, the PROBABILITY that a PIXEL point P is a line point can depend on whether or not P extends a line that has already been detected with high probability.

**probability,** *n.* a method that can be used to predict the likelihood of a particular outcome. In most AI systems, CON-

FIDENCE FACTORS have generally been preferred over methods of determining probability.

**probability propagation,** *n.* the adjusting of PROBABILITIES at the NODES in an INFERENCE NET to account for the effect of new information about the probability at a particular node.

**problem area,** *n.* the area of intended application of an AI system, such as symbolic computation and querying.

**problem-oriented language,** *n.* a computer language designed for a particular class of problems, e.g., FORTRAN, designed for efficiently performing algebraic computations, and COBOL, with features for business record keeping. LISP is used for symbolic logic representation.

**problem reduction,** *n.* a PROBLEM-SOLVING approach in which OPERATORS are used to change a single problem into several subproblems. In particular it is a system that uses BACKWARD REASONING and whose operators transform the initial GOAL or problem into a conjunction of subgoals or subproblems, eventually reaching a set of subgoals whose solutions are immediate. If a number of operators can be applied to the initial goal, or if a single operator can be applied in a number of ways, then a solution arrived at by any one of the applications is sufficient.

**problem reformulation,** *n.* the conversion of a problem description into a form that allows efficient solution.

**problem representation,** *n.* the conceptualization of a problem in AI. REPRESENTATION schemes include STATE-SPACE REPRESENTATION, PROBLEM REDUCTION representation, GAME TREE, and THEOREM-PROVING REPRESENTATION.

**problem-solving,** *n.* a process in which one starts from an initial state and proceeds to SEARCH through a PROBLEM SPACE in order to identify the sequence of operations or actions that will lead to a desired GOAL. In order for problem-solving to result in a successful outcome, the initial state must be known, an acceptable outcome must be predetermined, and the elements and OPERATORS that define the problem space must be known. In the event the elements and operators are very large in number or if they are poorly defined, one will be faced with a huge or unbounded problem space and an exhaustive search can become impossible.

**problem-solving grammar,** *n.* in CAI, a REPRESENTATION of the EXPERTISE involved in writing computer programs. (See also GRAMMAR.)

**problem-solving method, weak or strong,** *n.* a HEURISTIC for control. A weak method is DOMAIN INDEPENDENT, while a strong method exploits DOMAIN KNOWLEDGE to achieve greater performance. The weakest methods are those that can be applied equally to any domain; the strongest are those that apply only to that domain.

**problem space,** *n.* a CONCEPT area that is defined by all the possible states that could be generated by the elements and OPERATORS of a particular DOMAIN. A graph in which the NODES represent all possible states of partial or complete solution of a problem and arcs represent operators that transform one state to another. Finding a solution to the problem under consideration is represented by the isomorphic problem of finding a path from the NODE representing initial state to a node representing a GOAL STATE. (See also SEARCH SPACE.)

**problem state,** *n.* the paths through a SEARCH SPACE that represent a complete or partial SOLUTION to the SEARCH problem.

**procedural attachment,** *n.* an executable procedure that is directly associated with one or more data structures in order to indicate when it should be used. Such procedures are often necessary in KNOWLEDGE REPRESENTATION. Attached procedures lie dormant until certain conditions are satisfied, at which point they are executed. In KRL, for example, two types of attached procedures are identified: servants and DEMONS. Servants are executed when a procedure is required to apply some operation to a data object or set of data objects; a selection mechanism may be required to select the correct procedure if more than one servant is available. Demons are invoked when something has been done or is about to be done (note that all demons whose conditions are met are activated).

**procedural knowledge,** *n.* KNOWLEDGE about the world that can be represented as one or more PROCEDURES. Implementing procedural knowledge involves writing small programs that know how to do specific things – programs that know how to proceed in a well-specified manner. In the case of a PARSER for a system that understands NATURAL LANGUAGE, knowledge about noun phrases would be procedural. Noun phrases can contain articles, adjectives, and nouns. This knowledge is represented in the program by calls (within the NP procedure) to routines that know how to process articles, nouns, and adjectives.

**procedural knowledge representation,** *n.* representing KNOWLEDGE about the world as PROCEDURES within the system. The meanings of words and sentences are expressed as programs in a computer language, and the execution of these programs corresponds to reasoning from the meanings.

**procedural net,** *n.* in NOAH, a REPRESENTATION for PLANS called the procedural net represents both procedural and DECLARATIVE KNOWLEDGE about PROBLEM-SOLVING. The procedural net contains several levels of representation of a plan, each level more detailed than the previous one. Each level consists of a partially ordered sequence of NODES that represents the GOALS at some level of abstraction. In order to avoid overconstraining the order in which goals are achieved, NOAH assumes they can be attained in parallel, until it has some reason to put one before or after another. Each node in the procedural net is attached to its more detailed expansion in the next level.

**procedural reasoning,** *n.* a type of reasoning that uses simulation to arrive at solutions to problems.

**procedural semantics,** *n.* an approach to NATURAL LANGUAGE processing in which statements are first converted systematically into a 'program' to be executed by the information retrieval component. Central to this approach is the idea of representing KNOWLEDGE about the world as PROCEDURES within the system. The meanings of words and sentences, expressed as programs in a computer language, and the execution of these programs, correspond to reasoning from meanings.

**procedural system,** *n.* a computer system which uses computable rather than static, DECLARATIVE KNOWLEDGE in its processing.

**procedural versus declarative,** *adj.* two complementary views of a computer program. Procedures tell a system what to do (e.g., multiply A times B and then add C). Declarations tell a system what to know (e.g., V=IR).

**procedural–declarative controversy,** see DECLARATIVE

# PROCEDURE

KNOWLEDGE, PROCEDURAL KNOWLEDGE REPRESENTATION.

**procedure,** *n.* an ordered set of program statements that can be repeatedly called from some other part(s) of a program.

**procedure formation,** *n.* a process used in achieving a GOAL. Given a TREE for a specification of the form:

$$f(x) \Diamond \text{compute } P(x) \text{ where } Q(x),$$

suppose the system encounters a subgoal:

$$\text{Goal B: compute } R(t).$$

This is an instance not of the output specification compute $P(x)$ but of some previously generated subgoal:

$$\text{Goal A: compute } R(x).$$

In this case the procedure-formation principle introduces a new procedure, $g(x)$, whose output specification is:

$$g(x) \Diamond \text{compute } R(x).$$

In this way, both goals A and B can be achieved by calls $g(x)$ and $g(t)$ to a single procedure. In the case where goal B has been derived from goal A, the call to $g(t)$ will be a recursive call; otherwise, both calls will be simple PROCEDURE calls.

**procedure–oriented,** *adj.* that characteristic of a programming language which uses a sequenced set of statements that is usually used more than once in a program. It has one or more input parameters yielding different results based on their varying input values.

**procedure–oriented methods,** *n.* programming methods using nested subroutines to organize and control program execution.

**process control,** see CONTROL STRATEGY.

**Process Optimization for Energy Savings,** *n.* an expert system developed for TEXACO (LMI) for aiding in process control. PICON is the development software.

**production rule,** *n.* a statement that takes the form, 'If this condition holds, then this action is appropriate'. For example, the rule:

Always add sugar to herbal teas.

can be encoded as the production rule:

IF the tea is herbal, THEN add sugar.

264

Termed the condition part or left-hand side, the IF part of a production states the condition that must be present in order for a given production to apply. In turn, the THEN part, called the action part or right-hand side of the production, specifies the appropriate action to take. During the execution of a RULE, a production whose condition part is satisfied fires, that is, the INTERPRETER executes the action part of the production. (See DECISION TABLE.)

**production system,** *n.* a KNOWLEDGE-BASED SYSTEM that represents KNOWLEDGE in the form of PRODUCTION RULES. A production system consists of three parts: (a) a rule base composed of a set of PRODUCTION RULES; (b) a special, buffer-like data structure called the CONTEXT; and (c) an INTERPRETER, which controls the system's activity. Developed by Newell and Simon in 1972 for their models of human cognition, production systems have become a staple of large AI programs. (See also DYNAMIC KNOWLEDGE BASE.)

**program model,** *n.* a definition of a program used in AUTOMATIC PROGRAMMING systems. For example, during the acquisition phase of the specification of a program, PSI has a model-building module that converts a PROGRAM NET describing the desired program into a complete, consistent description of the program.

**program net,** *n.* a network data structure in PSI that furnishes a loose description of the desired program.

**program schema,** *n.* a scheme that characterizes the entire class of programs for the DOMAIN. They are similar to skeletal programs and define the general structure of a program, omitting some details.

**program specification,** *n.* a specification of what a program is to do in AUTOMATIC PROGRAMMING. It can take the form of examples of desired input/output behaviour or statements in a NATURAL LANGUAGE such as English.

**program synthesis,** *n.* the derivation of a program to meet a given specification. The specification expresses conditions that the program must satisfy, but does not need to give an ALGORITHM or method. Typically, the program is derived such that its correctness with respect to the specification is guaranteed.

**program transformation,** *n.* a technique for developing programs. An initial specification is written, which is likely to be inefficient, and is then transformed to an efficient version using methods guaranteed to preserve the meaning of the program. Within the declarative languages, program transformations can be based on a small set of probably correct basic transformations, facilitating the development of semi-automatic transformation systems.

**program understanding,** *n.* an AUTOMATIC PROGRAMMING system's ability to talk about, analyse, modify, or write parts of a program.

**PROGRAMMAR,** *n.* a programming language embedded in LISP, developed in order to write SHRDLU's parser. The PROGRAMMAR language supplies primitive FUNCTIONS for use in building systematically described SYNTACTIC structures. The theory behind PROGRAMMAR is that the basic programming methods, such as PROCEDURES, iteration, and RECURSION, are also basic to the cognitive process. Implementing a grammar can therefore be achieved without additional programming implementations; special syntactic items (such as conjunctions) are handled via calls to special procedures. PROGRAMMAR operates basically in a TOP-DOWN, left-to-right fashion but uses neither a PARALLEL PROCESSING nor a backtracking strategy in dealing with multiple alternatives. It finds one PARSING rather directly, since decisions at choice points are guided by the semantic procedures. By functionally integrating its KNOWLEDGE of SYNTAX and SEMANTICS, SHRDLU can avoid exploring alternative choices in an ambiguous situation. If the choice does fail, PROGRAMMAR has PRIMITIVES for returning to the choice point with the reasons for the failure and informing the parser of the next best choice based on these reasons. This 'directed backup' is considerably different from PLANNER's AUTOMATIC BACKTRACKING in that the design philosophy of the parser is oriented toward making an original correct choice rather than establishing exhaustive backtracking.

**Programmer's Apprentice,** *n.* an expert system under development at MIT. The KNOWLEDGE BASE consists of program fragments called 'cliches'. Programmers make use of the cliches by way of a dialogue as if the expert system were, as the name suggests, a programmer's apprentice. The goal of this project is to implement a feasibility demonstration, integrating an analysis module, a synthesis module, a reasoning module, and a knowledge-based editor. See KNOWLEDGE-BASED SYSTEM.

**Programmer's Assistant,** *n.* In INTERLISP, a module that monitors and records a user's commands, retains a history of the computation, and permits selected commands to be undone, retried, or changed and retried. For instance, the user can ask the Assistant to repeat a command or undo the effect of one. In effect, the programmer's actions are watched by an attentive assistant who can tend to some of the repetitious tasks when the programmer wants to delegate them.

**programming environment,** *n.* the programming apparatus that includes the INTERFACE, the languages, the editors, and other programming TOOLS. A programming environment may be viewed as midway between a language and a tool: Languages allow users complete flexibility while a tool constrains the user in many ways. A programming environment, such as INTERLISP, provides a number of established routines that can speed development of certain types of program. The purpose of a programming environment is to help the programmer in all phases of program development, from initial writing of the code through modification, DEBUGGING, assembling of modules, and documentation (although not necessarily in that order). The principal limitation is the feasibility of a programming environment due to the difficulty of designing and implementing a programming environment; the process can produce as much work as implementing the language itself. The following list of programming-support features represents the important features of a good environment:

(a) An interactive language in which statements can be typed in as commands and are executed immediately. COMPILER-based languages are generally not interactive.

(b) A good editor that can deal with a program according to the structure of the program (not only as text composed of characters).

(c) Interactive debugging facilities that break, backtrack, and examine, and can change program VARIABLES.

(d) Input/output routines, the most common of which should be specially supported by standard system input/

output functions, so that the programmer is not burdened with such details.

**programming knowledge,** see REPRESENTATION OF PROGRAMMING KNOWLEDGE.

**PROJCON,** *n. acronym for* PROJect CONsultant, an expert system that uses DOMAIN KNOWLEDGE of project management experts to help a SOFTWARE development project manager diagnose problems occurring in a project. The program queries the project manager in order to build a model of the project at hand, and to highlight problems such as schedule overruns. Based on the evidence the program assembles, the program displays its diagnosis and supplies an explanation of its reasoning. The program is RULE-based and uses GOAL-directed, BACK-CHAINING. Implemented in EMYCIN, PROJCON was developed at Georgia Institute of Technology.

**projection,** *n.* the mapping of an object to a two-dimensional representation in vision systems. It involves the projecting of points on an object onto points on an image.

**PROLOG,** *n.* a programming language based on the idea of programming in logic. Designed to provide for practical programming and simplicity in programming, PROLOG programs may be viewed as logical clauses, and the INTERPRETER viewed as an efficient resolution theorem prover (see RESOLUTION THEOREM PROVING). Programs consist of RULES (INFERENCE relations) for proving relations among objects. The PROLOG interpreter attempts to find proofs of the truth of specified relations through BACK-CHAINING, using UNIFICATION and backtracking as needed. PROLOG provides as PRIMITIVES PATTERN-directed procedure invocation and non-determinism (backtracking). General recursive (TREE-like) data structures are accessed by PATTERN MATCHING rather than by explicit selector functions. Destructive operations are not applied to these data structures, yet structures may contain empty SLOTS (uninstantiated logical variables), which can be filled in later. Also, an assertional DATA BASE is used for relatively long-lived or permanent data. Many versions and implementations of PROLOG exist, a number of which embed PROLOG within a LISP ENVIRONMENT for additional flexibility. PROLOG has been adopted as the base language for the Japanese fifth-generation project, and as a result, the language has seen a significant rise in popularity. For almost every conceivable ARCHITECTURE, ranging from home micros to large-scale mainframes, PROLOG is used for both commercial and research implementations.

**pronunciation graph,** *n.* a NETWORK REPRESENTATION of phonetic KNOWLEDGE in HEARSAY.

**proof by contradiction,** *n.* a proof method that involves producing new clauses called RESOLVENTS from the union of the AXIOMS and the negated theorem. The resolvents are then added to the set of clauses from which they were derived, and new resolvents are derived. This process continues recursively until it produces a contradiction. RESOLUTION, a form of proof by contradiction, is guaranteed to produce a contradiction if the theorem follows the axioms.

**proof procedure,** *n.* a method used in automated reasoning. The two most widely used proof procedures are RESOLUTION and NATURAL DEDUCTION.

**proof summarization,** *n.* a technique used to analyse a proof by breaking it into parts (or subproofs) and isolating the mathematically important steps. It also permits a GOAL-oriented interpretation of the proof, in which the program keeps track of what is to be established at each point (that is, the current goal); which lines, terms and the like are relevant; and how the current line or part fits into the whole structure.

**proof theory,** *n.* a field of mathematics that deals with the reasoning involved in the proving of THEOREMS.

**PROPEL,** *n.* a PRIMITIVE ACT in CONCEPTUAL DEPENDENCY models that signifies the application of physical force to an object.

**property,** *n.* a characteristic of an object or entity.

**property inheritance,** *n.* the characteristic of SEMANTIC NETWORKS whereby properties of NODES connected by transitive links are inherited by adjacent nodes. For example, the semantic network segment illustrated on p.270 can be interpreted to mean that since sparrows are birds, and birds have wings, then sparrows have wings. In a semantic network, all that is necessary to deduce that sparrows have wings is to trace up the ISA HIERARCHY, assuming any facts asserted about higher NODES on the hierarchy can be considered assertions about the lower ones also, and to have done so without hav-

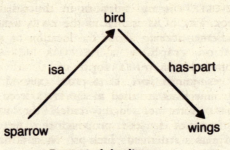

**Property inheritance**

ing to represent these assertions separately in the net. The lower nodes in the network inherit the properties explicated in the higher nodes. In AI terminology, this kind of reasoning is called property inheritance. The ISA link in particular is often referred to as a property inheritance link.

**property lists,** *n.* a construct for associating a list of name-value pairs with an OBJECT (such as a NODE of a SEMANTIC NETWORK). Each name represents a certain ATTRIBUTE of the object, and the corresponding VALUE of that attribute is assigned to the object. LISP-type languages provide a facility as a PRIMITIVE operation for the purpose of associating property lists with ATOMS.

**proposition,** *n.* a properly formed statement that has one of two possible TRUTH VALUES, TRUE or FALSE. Propositions are those statements we can call true or false. The sentence, 'Mary is Tim's mother', is an example of a typical proposition. Since propositions do not reduce into their constituent parts, one can assign the truth value TRUE to the proposition, 'Mary is Tim's mother', without regard for its meaning. The proposition states that Mary is Tim's female parent. The term 'Tim's mother' does not qualify as a proposition because one cannot assign a truth value to it.

**propositional calculus,** *n.* a system of formal LOGIC that provides a step-by-step INFERENCE system for determining whether a given proposition is true or false.

**propositional knowledge representation,** *n.* a representation form that, in contrast to direct representations, does not require a homomorphic correspondence between relations in the REPRESENTATION and relations in the situation. For instance, proximity of assertions in the DATA BASE of a LOGIC system indicates nothing about the location of objects in the world.

**propositional logic,** *n*. a form of LOGIC consisting of PROPOSITIONS joined by SENTENTIAL CONNECTIVES. When sentential connectives are used in the SYNTAX of propositions, the simplest form of logic, called the PROPOSITIONAL CALCULUS, applies to the proposition. The propositional calculus expresses statements such as, 'Mike is my friend' and 'If Joe has AIDS, then he will die.' The sentential connectives are intended to keep their natural interpretations, so that if X and Y are any two propositions:

$X \wedge Y$ is TRUE if X is TRUE *and* Y is TRUE; otherwise $X \wedge Y$ is FALSE.

$X \vee Y$ is TRUE if either X is TRUE *or* Y is TRUE *or* both.

$\neg X$ is TRUE if X is FALSE, and FALSE if X is TRUE.

$X \rightarrow Y$ is meant to be the propositional calculus form of the notion, 'If we can assume that X is true, then Y must be so'; that is, the truth of X implies that Y is true. In everyday speech this occurs in statements such as, 'If Tommy is six years old, then he can't do calculus.' The truth value of $X \rightarrow Y$ is defined to be TRUE if Y is TRUE or X is FALSE.

$X \equiv Y$ is TRUE if both X and Y are TRUE, or both X and Y are FALSE; $X \equiv Y$ is false if X and Y have different truth values.

The table on p.272 is a compressed truth table. It summarizes these definitions.

**prosodics,** *n*. rules describing fluctuation in STRESS and INTONATION across a sentence.

**PROSPECTOR,** *n*. an expert system that applies geological rules for forming models of ore deposits, along with a taxonomy of rocks and minerals to aid exploration geologists searching for ore deposits. The program takes as input field data about a geological region in order to estimate the prob-

| X | Y | X ∧ Y | X ∨ Y | X → Y | ¬ X | X ≡ Y |
|---|---|-------|-------|-------|-----|-------|
| T | T | T | T | T | F | T |
| T | F | F | T | F | F | F |
| F | T | F | T | T | T | F |
| F | F | F | F | T | T | F |

**Propositional logic**

ability of discovering particular types of mineral deposits in a given location. In doing so, the program assesses the potential for finding a variety of deposits, including massive sulfide, sandstone uranium, and porphyry molybdenum deposits. The program combines RULE-based KNOWLEDGE REPRESENTATION with a SEMANTIC NETWORK using CERTAINTY FACTORS and the propagation of PROBABILITIES associated with the data. Implemented in INTERLISP, PROSPECTOR was developed by SRI International.

**protection violation,** *n*. In PLANNING, the violation of previously achieved GOALS. In HACKER, these are treated as BUGS.

**protocol,** *n*. RULES that govern how computers exchange information. The scope of the rules includes how the units of data must be organized in order to transfer the data.

**protocol analysis,** *n*. a technique for isolating the procedures used by a human problem-solver (see HUMAN PROBLEM-SOLVING) on the basis of a record of selected aspects of his/her problem-solving behaviour. The form of the record may be verbal behaviour, such as a 'think-aloud protocol', or of non-verbal behaviour, such as eye-movements, or the sequence and timing of moves in a board game. A protocol analysis begins with the building of a Problem Behaviour Graph. The graph serves as a "rational reconstruction" of the solution steps. Regularities (patterns) are then identified and extracted, possibly in the form of a PRODUCTION RULE system.

**PROTOSYNTHEX,** *n*. a system that stores a REPRESENTA-

TION of a text in its DATA BASE and uses a variety of indexing schemes to retrieve material containing specific words or phrases.

**PROTOSYSTEM,** *n.* an AUTOMATIC PROGRAMMING system designed at the MIT laboratory for computer science. The system is part of a research project aimed at modelling, understanding, and automating the writing of a data-processing system (see DATA-PROCESSING SYSTEM, SYNTHESIS OF).

**prototype,** *n.* the initial version of a developing expert system. A prototype generally consists of between 25 to 200 RULES. The purpose of a prototype is to test the adequacy of the overall KNOWLEDGE REPRESENTATION and INFERENCE strategies being used.

**pruning,** *n.* a process in which one or more branches of a decision TREE are 'cut off' or ignored. In the case of EXPERT SYSTEMS, during an expert system consultation, HEURISTIC RULES reduce the SEARCH SPACE by determining that certain branches, or subsets of rules, can be ignored.

**pseudo-language,** *n.* the product of a technique for producing words, from randomly generated letters, with the same characteristics as actual English words.

**PSI,** *n.* a KNOWLEDGE-based PROGRAM SYNTHESIS system developed at Stanford and at Systems Control Inc. The design GOAL of PSI was the integration of the more specialized methods of AUTOMATIC PROGRAMMING into a total system. This system would, in turn, incorporate KNOWLEDGE ENGINEERING, model acquisition, program synthesis, efficiency analysis, and specification by examples, traces, or interactive NATURAL LANGUAGE dialogue. The research was directed toward determining the organization of such a system, the amount and type of KNOWLEDGE such a system would require, and the representation of this knowledge. The synthesis module consists of two major sub-systems: PECOS, the coding expert, is a set of refinement rules for program synthesis, which represents a range of knowledge about sets, mappings, arrays, etc.; LIBRA, the efficiency expert, consists of knowledge that enables the system to evaluate alternative implementations of a program. In PSI, a program is specified by means of an interactive, MIXED-INITIATIVE DIALOGUE, which may include partial specifications by examples of input/output pairs or by

traces. When the specification method is an INTERACTIVE DIA-
LOGUE, the user furnishes both a description of what the
desired program is to do and an indication of the overall control structure of the program. The PSI system deals with programs in the general class of symbolic computation, including
list processing, searching (see SEARCH) and sorting, data storage and retrieval, and CONCEPT FORMATION programs. It is a
knowledge-based system organized as a set of closely interacting modules, called EXPERTS. The complete PSI system has
synthesized the code for a simple version of a learning program.

**PSL,** *abbrev. for* Portable Standard LISP, a procedure-oriented
programming language that is a portable dialect of LISP (see
PROCEDURE-ORIENTED METHODS). Designed to run on a wide
variety of computers, PSL supplies all the features of standard
LISP along with extended language and INTERFACE features. It
features an integrated COMPILER, a DEBUGGING tool, and a
multi-window, full-screen editor allowing users to execute
expressions and display output in the windows. The INTER-
PRETER is written entirely in PSL. PSL was developed at the
University of Utah.

**PSYCO,** *n. acronym for* Production SYstem COmpiler, a
KNOWLEDGE ENGINEERING language for RULE-based representation which also permits FRAME-based representation. Initially
designed for building models of cognitive processes in human
decision making, PSYCO has been used as a more general-
purpose language. It features FORWARD CHAINING, and CON-
FLICT RESOLUTION based upon the importance of data.
Additionally, PSYCO can organize RULES and data into a network of frames. PSYCO was developed by the Imperial
Cancer Research Fund and Queen's Medical Centre.

**PTE (Prohibited Transaction Exceptions) Analyst,** *n.* an
expert system developed for Computer Law Systems to advise
lawyers on prohibited transaction exceptions.

**PTRANS,** *n.* **1.** a PRIMITIVE ACT in CONCEPTUAL DEPENDENCY
models that signifies the transfer of the physical location of an
object. For a person to 'go' is to PTRANS oneself. 'Putting'
an object somewhere is to PTRANS it to that place.

**2.** an expert system that helps control the manufacture and
distribution of Digital Equipment Corporation's computer

systems. The program uses customer order descriptions and information about plant activity to develop a plan for assembling and testing the ordered computer system, including when to build the system. PTRANS monitors the progress of the technicians implementing the plan, diagnoses problems, suggests solutions, and predicts possible impending shortages or surpluses of materials. PTRANS is designed to work with XSEL, a salesperson's assistant, so that once an order is made, the delivery date can be confirmed. The program is RULE-based using FORWARD CHAINING. Implemented in OPS5, PTRANS was developed jointly by Digital Equipment Corporation and Carnegie-Mellon University.

**PUFF,** *n.* an expert system that uses KNOWLEDGE of the test results different pulmonary (lung) disorders produce in order to diagnose the presence and severity of lung disease in a patient. The program interprets measurements from respiratory tests administered in a pulmonary function laboratory. The program is RULE-based using BACK-CHAINING. Implemented in EMYCIN, PUFF was developed at Stanford University and tested at the Pacific Medical Center in San Francisco.

**Pump Pro,** *n.* an expert system developed at Stone & Webster Engineering for aiding preventive maintenance and troubleshooting for centrifugal pumps. MAIDService is the development software.

**Purdue Grain Market Advisor,** *n.* an expert system developed at Purdue University for commercial use. It helps farmers determine the most favourable way to market the grain they produce. PERSONAL CONSULTANT is the development software.

**pyramid,** *n.* a set of arrays that is used to store a digitized image at different RESOLUTIONS; the highest resolution forming the base of the pyramid or resolution cone. Normally, a uniform relationship exists between adjacent levels of the pyramid. For example, a PIXEL intensity at a particular resolution is often the average value of the pixel intensities in the corresponding 2x2 pixel block at the next highest resolution. More generally, the concept of a regular hierarchical data structure has been extended to include processing elements within the structure, which is then called a processing cone.

## PUFF

Pyramids were originally used to explicate the relationship between the different image resolutions in a computer VISION system using PLANNING. For instance, the boundaries found at a low resolution might be used to refine the edge or boundary detection process at higher resolutions. This process can significantly improve the efficiency of the overall edge detection process. Image boundaries also occur over a wide range of scales, from sharp, step-like edges to fuzzy (see FUZZY LOGIC), blurred edges. One can use the relationships between corresponding edges occurring at different resolutions in order to make assertions about the scene boundary producing them. Since these regular hierarchical structures are inappropriate for non-spatial symbolic computations, their use is normally restricted to the early processing stage of a vision system.

# Q

**QA4,** *n.* the last in a series of PROBLEM-SOLVING languages in the QA-series developed at SRI from the mid-1960s to the early '70s. As an attempt to formalize the ideas in Raphael's SIR program, the problem-solving language QA1 had been developed by Green at SRI International in the mid-1960s. Immediately following this effort, QA2 was developed to apply the ideas of RESOLUTION THEOREM PROVING as the INFERENCE-making mechanism. QA2 introduced the method for extracting answers from the process of proving theorems with existentially quantified (see EXISTENTIAL QUANTIFICATION) variables (binding values to the variables that satisfy the theorem). QA3, which was used in STRIPS, was an improved implementation of QA2. With QA3, Green explored how to solve various types of problems with a resolution theorem prover, including PROGRAM SYNTHESIS, verification, and problem-solving QA4, developed in 1971, around the same time that MICRO-PLANNER was implemented at MIT, was intended to overcome certain problems with QA3, such as the difficulties in guiding the search to relevant facts and theorems in trying to derive a proof. It was necessary to specify PROCEDURAL KNOWLEDGE and DOMAIN-specific KNOWLEDGE about what facts to use and when to use them, in a way that a theorem prover – the underlying INFERENCE ENGINE – could use. Theorems or procedures needed to be indexed by their purposes, an idea that led to the implementation of PATTERN-directed invocation similar to that of PLANNER. QA4 was the first language to develop the idea of representing ASSERTIONS uniquely, so that properties can be associated with assertions.

**QLISP,** *n.* an implementation of QA4 embedded in INTERLISP in order to make QA4 more widely available and to take advantage of the new features in INTERLISP. Care was taken to preserve the extensive INTERLISP ENVIRONMENT while extending the language with QLISP constructs. When the spaghetti stack was implemented in INTERLISP, QLISP was modified to take advantage of it. Unlike MICROPLANNER and CONNIVER, which are interpreted languages on top of LISP, QLISP is basically a subroutine package for INTER-LISP, making it much easier to mix QLISP with INTERLISP in programming. In the same manner as the INTERLISP package CLISP, QLISP is implemented by means of an error-catching mechanism. When the INTERPRETER comes to a QLISP construct, it translates it into INTERLISP and executes it. It also stores the translated version, so that retranslation is not needed. Special features of QLISP include extra data types, such as sets, tuples, and bags, together with procedures for handling them, and QLISP's ability to use them in PATTERN MATCHING. Pattern matching is a prominent component of QLISP for use in tasks such as constructing data. In addition, QLISP makes the distinction between finding the truth of an ASSERTION by a simple lookup in the DATA BASE and finding it by deduction using consequent THEOREMS (this distinction is unclear in PLANNER). The notion of a TEAM OF PROCEDURES is introduced in QLISP, whereby the programmer can specify a team as worth considering anywhere that a PATTERN-directed procedure invocation might occur. (A team consisting of a single procedure corresponds to the traditional subroutine call. At the other extreme, a team consisting of all the goal-achieving procedures in the system corresponds to the non-deterministic style of PLANNER.) In programs, LISP and QLISP can be freely mixed. QLISP is thus a surface extension of INTERLISP, whereas PLANNER and CONNIVER are distinct language systems built on top of MACLISP. Implementing QLISP constructs through the error mechanism implies that execution of pure LISP constructs is not slowed down by the presence of QLISP. The NOAH systems and the DEDALUS systems were written in QLISP.

**quad tree,** *n.* a hierarchical image representation that is similar to a PYRAMID. Quad trees have NODES that correspond to the cells of a pyramid; each non-terminal node has four children. However, unlike a pyramid, a quad tree may be pruned and therefore become unbalanced. For example, when all nodes in a subtree have the same grey value, the subtree may be represented by its root without loss of information. Significant storage space can thus be obtained for many images. More importantly, quad trees allow some operations to be performed efficiently by recursive procedures (see RECURSION).

**quantification,** *n.* the ability to specify PROPERTIES of quantities of arbitrarily defined sets. There are two quantifiers, the universal quantifier ∀ (see UNIVERSAL QUANTIFICATION), meaning for all ... , and ∃, the existential quantifier, meaning there exists ....

**quantifier,** in PREDICATE CALCULUS, an indication of set membership. Specifically, there are two quantifiers, ∀, meaning for all ... , and ∃, meaning there exists.... The English-language sentence, 'All men are mortal', is thus expressed in predicate calculus, using the variable X, as:

$$\forall X. \, Man \, (X) \rightarrow Mortal(X),$$

which can be loosely translated as, 'For all individuals X, if X is a man (i.e., Man (X) is true), then X is mortal.'

**quantitative shape recovery,** *n.* the labelling of a line drawing in order to characterize a specific shape. For example, a trapezoidal block differs from a cube in its angle measurements, not in its qualitative labelling. Using gradients, quantitative shape recovery can be accomplished from line drawings; with this more complete specification of the scene, one is able to predict how a scene will look from different angles of view.

**query language,** *n.* a formal language used for querying a DATA BASE.

**query optimization,** *n.* the estimating of the cost of executing a particular query to a DATA BASE and reformulating the query automatically such that it will execute more quickly.

**question answering,** *n.* the process of a program that can give responses to questions in a NATURAL LANGUAGE. Examples of systems that feature question answering are SIR and SHRDLU.

**quiescence,** *n.* a state in a GAME-TREE SEARCH in which search is extended beyond the normal limit until all TIP NODES are relatively stable or until some absolute DEPTH BOUND has been reached.

**quiescent position,** *n.* a position in a game at which, when an EVALUATION FUNCTION is applied to that position, the

VALUES of all the terms are stable. This concept allows the SEARCH to continue beyond a predetermined limit from non-quiescent positions.

**QUIST,** *n.* a system using semantic–CONSTRAINT information available in the DATA BASE schema in order to improve the execution of queries. The AI techniques used in QUIST are not noticeable to the user but nevertheless result in an improvement in the behaviour of the system. For example, a typical piece of semantic-constraint information from a DATA BASE about shipping might be a statement like, 'The only ships over 600 feet are tankers.' Applying this constraint, QUIST can transform the question, 'Which ships are more than 700 feet long?' into 'Which tankers are more than 700 feet long?' The latter query might be much more efficient to process if, for example, the information about tankers were stored in a separate file in the data base. Quist contains a cost model enabling it to estimate the cost of executing a particular query (see COST (OF A RESOLUTION TREE)). Different, but semantically equivalent formulations of a query can therefore be compared with respect to the cost of processing them.

# R

**RABBIT,** *n.* an expert system that applies a process called 're-trieval by reformulation' in order to help DATA BASE users formulate data base queries. Retrieval by reformulation is a process of incrementally constructing a partial description of the data base items the user desires. This process is the actual form of the user's query. The program serves as an intelligent data base-assistant for users who have only a vague idea of what they want, or only possess limited knowledge of the content of the given data base. Implemented in SMALLTALK, RABBIT operates on a set of data bases represented in KL-ONE. RABBIT was developed at the Xerox Palo Alto Research Center.

**RADEX,** *n. acronym for* RADiology EXpert, an expert system that uses a conceptual model of relevant organs and organ abnormalities to help physicians and the MDX expert system diagnose the liver syndrome cholestasis. The program acts as a radiology consultant by taking summary descriptions of a patient's medical images and using them as a basis for answering questions about the patient's anatomical or physiological abnormalities. FRAME representations contain the descriptions, DEFAULT values, relationships, and attached procedures for four kinds of entity: the imaging procedures, such as liver scan ultrasonogram; major organs, such as liver and gallbladder; parts of organs, such as lumen and lobe; and abnormalities and deformities in the organs, such as tumour and stricture. Implemented in LISP, RADEX was developed at Ohio State University.

**RADIAL,** *n.* a KNOWLEDGE ENGINEERING language for RULE-based and procedural representation. It is the PROGRAMMING ENVIRONMENT used by the RULEMASTER system-building aid. RADIAL has its formal basis in finite automata theory. A program written in RADIAL consists of a set of modules. Each module contains a transition network of states, and each state contains a single rule in the form of a decision tree. The language is block-structured with scoped variables, argument – passing between modules, recursive module invocation, and conditional branching. RADIAL provides CERTAINTY handling and an EXPLANATION FACILITY for dealing with FUZZY LOGIC. Implemented in the C programming language, RADIAL runs on minicomputers, workstations, and microcomputers under the UNIX operating system. RADIAL was developed by the Radian Corporation.

**random–access memory,** *n.* a data storage device wherein the time required for obtaining data from or placing data into storage is independent of the location of the most recently obtained or placed data. A memory whose information media are organized into discrete locations, sectors, etc., each uniquely identified by an address. Data may be obtained from such memory by specifying the data address(es) to the memory (e.g., core, drum, disk, cards).

**random–access storage,** *n.* a storage device in which each record has a specific predetermined address that may be reached directly; access time in that type of storage is effectively independent of the location of the data. Such storage devices include VLSI chips and magnetic cores, disks, and drums.

**random–text generation,** *n.* a process of generating text (see TEXT GENERATION) using a random choice of possible RULES. It is used in GRAMMAR testing.

**range finder,** *n.* a VISION system that works from intensity images by inferencing three-dimensional structure from two-dimensional data (see INFERENCE).

**RBMS,** *abbrev. for* Rule-Based Modelling System, an expert system that uses a flight manifest to schedule the use of the Johnson Space Center FCRs (flight control rooms) over a period of months. The program takes as input the flight manifest, which contains flight numbers, launch dates, type of flight, duration, whether the flight is a space laboratory mission, and other data. RBMS then uses the input data to formulate a schedule of daily FCR activity that includes the number of hours required for each use of the facility, and computes the average number of hours per day the FCR will be used. Implemented in LISP and OPS5, RBMS runs on DEC VAX computers. The program was developed by Ford Aerospace for NASA.

**REACT,** *n.* an interactive program that aids chemists in the structure-elucidation task rather than in finding new synthetic routes.

**reactive learning environment,** *n.* ICAI programs in which the student is actively engaged with the instructional system and his or her interests and misunderstandings drive the tutorial dialogue.

**REACTOR,** *n.* an expert system that monitors the readings of nuclear reactor monitoring instruments, such as the feed-water flow and the containment radiation level, in order to identify deviations from normal operating conditions. The program aids reactor operators by first detecting a deviation and then evaluating the event in order to recommend appropriate action. KNOWLEDGE in the system includes the configuration of the reactor, the functional relations of the reactor's components, and knowledge about the expected behaviour of the reactor under known accident conditions. The program is RULE-based using both FORWARD CHAINING and BACK-CHAINING. Implemented in LISP, REACTOR was developed by EG&G Idaho.

**real-world problem,** *n.* a complex, practical problem that has a SOLUTION useful in some cost-effective way.

**reasoning,** *n.* the process of drawing INFERENCES or conclusions.

**reasoning by analogy,** *n.* a mode of reasoning that makes INFERENCES based on analogies drawn from past experience.

**recency,** *n.* a strategy of CONFLICT RESOLUTION favouring INSTANTIATIONS whose WORKING MEMORY elements were most recently created or modified. Recency contributes sensitivity to a PRODUCTION SYSTEM because subgoals (see SUBGOALING) can be spawned as soon as new data arrive.

**recognize-act cycle,** *n.* the cycle of events in a PRODUCTION SYSTEM or FORWARD-CHAINING SYSTEM. During the recognize phase, the RULES are examined in order to determine if their clauses are based on information currently stored in memory. During the act phase, one of the rules is selected and executed and its conclusion is stored in memory. Behaving as an iterative loop, each cycle consists of three successive phases: MATCH, CONFLICT RESOLUTION, and the firing of rules.

**record,** *n.* a collection of fields. The information relating to one area of activity in a data processing activity, e.g., all information on one inventory item. Sometimes called item.

**recursion,** *n.* defining an item in terms of itself. Recursive functions are functions that can call themselves. They involve operations that are defined in terms of themselves. For example, the factorial function, N!, on the positive integers is defined as 1 when N = 1 and otherwise as N(N - 1)!. The CONTROL structure of LISP, like the data structure, is uniform and based on a recursive definition.

**recursion formation,** *n.* the process of achieving a subgoal (see SUBGOALING) by computing via a recursive call. For example, in the construction of a program with the following specifications:

$$f(x) \lozenge \text{ compute } P(x) \text{ where } Q(x),$$

the system encounters a subgoal:

$$\text{Goal: compute } P(t),$$

which is an instance of the output specification, compute P(x). Because the program f(x) is intended to compute P(x) for any x satisfying its input specification Q(x), the recursion formation rule proposes achieving the subgoal above by computing P(t) with a recursive call f(t).

**recursion removal,** *n.* a process that transforms a recursive program into an iterative one, which is generally more efficient, avoiding the overhead of the stacking mechanism. Candidates for recursion removal are determined by performing PATTERN MATCHING of the parts of the program against a recursive-schema input pattern. If the MATCH is successful and if certain preconditions are met, the program is replaced by an iterative SCHEMA.

**recursive pattern matching,** *n.* the process of mapping a string of SYMBOLS onto a set of meaningful syntactic patterns.

**recursive transition network (RTN),** *n.* an extended FINITE-STATE TRANSITION DIAGRAM (FSTD) used in NATURAL LANGUAGE PARSING. A recursive transition network labels ARCS with both terminal symbols (a syntactic class such as noun) and nonterminal symbols (a syntactic construct such as noun phrase). If an arc labelled with a nonterminal SYMBOL is taken, then the construct is sent to a subnetwork for parsing. Because a subnetwork can call any other subnetwork, including itself, parsing proceeds recursively until the entire input string has been parsed.

**REDESIGN,** *n.* an expert system that assists engineers in the redesign of digital circuits to meet altered functional specifications. Given the redesign GOAL, the system generates plausible local changes to make within the circuit, ranks the changes based on IMPLEMENTATION difficulty and goal satisfaction, and checks for undesirable SIDE EFFECTS associated with the changes. The system provides design assistance by combining causal reasoning, analysing the cause–effect relations of circuit operation with functional reasoning, and analysing the purposes or roles of the circuit components. Circuit knowledge in REDESIGN is represented as a network of modules and data paths. The system was developed at Rutgers University.

**REDUCE,** *n.* a computer program for mathematical analysis.

**reducer,** *n.* an expression such as L $\rightarrow$ R applied to a formula or term by replacing an expression of the form L($\theta$), where ($\theta$) is a SUBSTITUTION, by the expression R($\theta$).

**REF-ARF,** *n.* one of the earliest general PROBLEM-SOLVING programs in AI. It was written in IPL and implemented some aspects of HEURISTIC SEARCH.

**referencing problem,** *n.* the problem of performance degradation due to increased knowledge. Increased knowledge expands the possible SOLUTION space, causing excess searching (see SEARCH).

**referential ambiguity,** *n.* the case where a referent in a sentence is not clear. The ambiguity is 'referential' when – determining the reference of, say, 'he' – there is more than one interpretation in the context.

**refinement of plan steps,** *n.* a process that involves replacing an ABSTRACT OPERATOR with a more specific one or replacing an abstract object with a more specific one. MOLGEN, for example, uses such a method.

**refinement of program specification,** *n.* a process of AUTOMATIC PROGRAMMING that proceeds via the repeated selection and application of TRANSFORMATIONAL RULES in the KNOWLEDGE BASE to parts of the program. Also referred to as GRADUAL REFINEMENT, this transformation process reduces the high-level specification to an IMPLEMENTATION within the target language. Each application of a RULE is said to produce a partial implementation, or refinement, of the program, and the transformation rules are called refinement rules.

**refinement–operator method,** *n*. is a data-driven learning method whereby special procedures (or PRODUCTION RULES) examine the set of TRAINING INSTANCES and decide how to refine the current set, H, of HYPOTHESES. A set of hypotheses develops via this method in a RULE SPACE separate from the INSTANCE SPACE. Refinement OPERATORS, which are selected by HEURISTICS that inspect the training instances, serve to modify the hypotheses. A general outline of these operator-based ALGORITHMS is the following: First, gather some training instances. Analyse these instances to decide which rule-space operator to apply. Then apply this operator to make some change in the current set, H, of hypotheses. Repeat these steps until satisfactory hypotheses are obtained. BACON, CLS, and AM are examples of systems using this technique.

**reflectance map,** *n*. a map that relates image intensities to surface orientation for a given reflectance function, viewpoint, and illumination direction. In general, it is possible to construct a reflectance map for a surface even under complicated illumination conditions, though it may be necessary to measure the intensities empirically as the relation is frequently too complex to be modelled analytically.

**refutation move,** *n*. in move ordering in games, a strong reply that may refute the proposed move.

**region,** *n*. a set of connected PIXELS that show a common property. For instance, the average GREY LEVEL, colour, or texture in an image.

**region analysis,** *n*. the grouping together of the PIXELS in an image that share some values of a feature. An image is represented as a two-dimensional array of pixels conveying image-feature values. For example, an image can be segmented into regions of similar colour, under the assumption that these regions correspond to surfaces in the scene that produced the image.

**region boundary,** *n.* the boundary between two adjunct RE-GIONS used in image analysis.

**region finding,** *n.* a method for producing a segmentation of the image in which the REGIONS (connected sets of PIXELS) found have a useful correspondence to projections of scene entities such as objects or surfaces. There are two main approaches. The first starts with the maximum number of regions (e.g., make every pixel a region) and merges adjacent regions based on some measure of similarity until a satisfactory segmentation has been achieved. The second starts with a few (possibly one) large regions and recursively splits them into smaller regions based on some measure of dissimilarity until a satisfactory segmentation has been achieved. Measures of similarity/dissimilarity have ranged from simple average intensities to complex methods incorporating SEMANTICS.

**region growing,** *n.* an approach to REGION SEGMENTATION starting with many tiny, trivial regions until the only regions that remain are uniform and no further merging is possible.

**region splitting,** *n.* an approach to REGION SEGMENTATION starting with a single, large region, such as the entire image, split into several pieces. The process continues splitting pieces until only uniform regions remain.

**regular grammar,** see TYPE 3 GRAMMAR.

**reinforcement,** *n.* a learning method in ACT, which reinforces productions by increasing or decreasing their strength.

**relation,** *n.* a link or ARC in a SEMANTIC NETWORK, which connects concept NODES.

**relaxation,** *n.* **1.** a technique for assigning globally consistent labels or VALUES to NODES in a network. The assignments are subject to local CONSTRAINTS, iteratively propagating the effects of constraints through the net. Relaxation has origins as a mathematical technique in numerical analysis for the solution of difference equations. A relationship has been shown between relaxation and various optimization techniques such as linear programming. In an application to the blocks world line-labelling domain, WALTZ'S FILTERING ALGORITHM provides the first significant use of relaxation to a vision problem. Looking at a problem of assigning labels to objects for the purpose of satisfying certain consistency requirements, unlike a

TREE representation where each context is explicitly a path, the space may be represented as a GRAPH in which each node carries a set of possible constraints. Generally, after an initialization stage in which each node has been assigned a list of labels and their associated confidence measures, the labels and confidences of neighbouring nodes are compared and, guided by the requirements to minimize local inconsistency (often a smoothness constraint), labels are deleted or their confidences adjusted. This process of comparison and adjustment iterates until it converges to some criterion of global consistency. Because both the assignment and updating processes can be done independently at each node, the computation is inherently parallel. Apart from Waltz's application, relaxation has been used to compute optical flow, the recovery of surface orientation from SHADING information, and the recovery of the orientation structure of images, stereopsis (see STEREO VISION) and structure from motion. The convergence properties of some relaxation operators are not always transparent. The most successful and scientifically useful applications have been when the theoretical analysis of a vision problem reveals a mathematical structure that can be exploited directly in the design of the relaxation algorithm rather than when a 'general operator' has been fitted in an ad hoc fashion to a vision labelling task.

**2.** a postprocessing technique in region segmentation. Instead of assigning a single label to each PIXEL, the probability $p_i$ that P belongs to class $C_i$ is estimated based on the distribution of IMAGE FEATURE VALUES. Then these probabilities are adjusted by some relaxation formula so that $p_i$ is revised iteratively using the previous values of its own and neighbouring pixels.

**RENDEZVOUS,** *n.* a system whose goal is interactive query-formulation. The program was designed to accept a partially specified query in rather rough form and to attempt to complete it by entering into a clarification dialogue with the user in order to resolve parts of the query that were unclear and attempting to fill in gaps in the initial query specification by initiating a dialogue. RENDEZVOUS operates by passing the initial query through a PARSER, which converts it to a logical form. The parser then initiates a clarification dialogue in order to resolve parts of the query that were ambiguous or unclear. The output from this phase is processed by a menu-driver, which offers a list of choices at each point in the dialogue, attempting to fill in any gaps in the query specification by interrogating the user. Finally, the completed query is passed to a GENERATOR, which prints out an English translation of the final form for the user's approval.

**Repair Diagnosis,** *n*. an expert system developed for Renault for diagnosing transmission faults in passenger cars.

**replacement,** *n*. a rule of INFERENCE where the connective 'implies' is interchangeable with its definition. So p ⊃ q can be replaced by ¬p ∨ q and vice versa.

**representation,** *n*. the way in which a system stores KNOWLEDGE about a DOMAIN.

**representation of programming knowledge,** *n*. the representation of the KNOWLEDGE of both the SEMANTICS of a programming language and such general computation mechanisms as GENERATORS, tests, loops, and hashing. Systems such as PROGRAMMER'S APPRENTICE, DEDALUS, LIBRA, and PECOS attempt to incorporate such knowledge in their systems.

**representation of programs,** see PROGRAM SPECIFICATION.

**Requirements Analysis, The,** *n*. an expert system developed by Computer Training Services for helping accountants choose appropriate SOFTWARE. Lotus 123 is the development software.

**resampling,** *n*. a process used in the PREPROCESSING of images by replacing a PIXEL value in a position in order to give an ideal image.

**RESEDA,** *n*. an expert system that helps a user retrieve biographical data from the field of medieval French history. The user initiates a query that is either satisfied by direct look up or results in a SEARCH for information implicit in the DATA BASE, making use of INFERENCE procedures. The data base of biographical data consists of frames built using a metalanguage based on CASE GRAMMAR. This data base includes all events in the public or private lives of the people of interest. The expertise required for retrieval of implicit information is embodied in RULES, which can perform simple inferences or automatically establish new causal links between FRAMES in the KNOWLEDGE BASE. Implemented in VSAPL, RESEDA was developed at the Centre Inter-Régional de Calcul Électronique (CIRCE) in France.

**resolution,** *n*. a rule of INFERENCE of PREDICATE CALCULUS for deducing a new formula from two old formulas. In automatic theorem proving, resolution has been used extensively because it is an efficient alternative to traditional rules of inference in mathematical logic. Of the three formulae involved, all must be in clausal form. If C and D are clauses and $P_i$ and $Q_j$ are atomic formulae, then the rule is:

$$C \vee P_i \vee \ldots \vee P_m$$
$$D \vee (not)\ Q_1 \vee \ldots \vee (not)\ Q_m$$
$$\overline{\phantom{xxxxxxxxxxxxxxxxxxxxxxx}}$$
$$(C \vee D)0$$

where 0 is the most general unifier of all the $P_i$ and $Q_j$ and is obtained by UNIFICATION. In its simplest form:

From $(A \vee B)$ and $(\neg A \vee C)$, infer $(B \vee C)$.

**resolution theorem proving,** *n*. a method used in AUTOMATIC DEDUCTION (mechanical theorem proving) based on the RESOLUTION method.

**resolvent,** *n*. a new clause derived from the union of the AXIOMS and the negated theorem in an AUTOMATIC DEDUCTION system based on RESOLUTION.

**response frame,** *n*. in HEARSAY, each KNOWLEDGE SOURCE looks at hypotheses posted on one level, called its STIMULUS FRAME, and in turn posts hypotheses on one or more levels, possibly the same one, which would be the response frame.

**response frame of a knowledge source,** *n*. a level in systems using a BLACKBOARD where hypotheses can be posted.

**response generalization,** *n*. a process in paired associate learning experiments in which, when two responses to a stimulus are similar, the wrong one may be given to that stimulus – that is, the response has been generalized to more than one stimulus (see STIMULUS GENERALIZATION).

**result,** *n*. a deep case in CASE GRAMMAR that indicates the ENTITY that comes into existence as a result of the action.

**Rete match algorithm,** *n*. an ALGORITHM for efficiently determining which RULES can be satisfied by the contents of WORKING MEMORY on each RECOGNIZE-ACT CYCLE. The algorithm computes bindings between PATTERNS and data. It exploits redundancy in production systems by saving partial results of the MATCH computation so they do not need to be recomputed at a later time. The name comes from an English word meaning 'network'.

**revision procedure,** *n.* a procedure for checking to see if a NODE in the JUSTIFICATION list of a DEPENDENCY network is active and, if so, making the node active along with all those dependent on it. This is also referred to as TRUTH MAINTENANCE and BELIEF REVISION.

**rewrite rules,** *n.* CONDITION-action pairs, demodulants; a set of ordered pairs of expressions (lhs,rhs) usually depicted as lhs → rhs. Generally, a similarity RELATION exists between the lhs and the rhs, such as equality, inequality, or double implication. Together with the rewriting rule of INFERENCE, a rewrite rule (as the pair is called) allows one expression to be 're-written' into another. A subexpression of the initial string is matched with the lhs of the rewrite rule yielding a SUBSTITUTION. The expression that results is the expression obtained by replacing the distinguished subexpression with the rhs of the rewrite rule after applying the substitutions. In sum, rewrite rules, or productions, specify the relations between certain strings of terminal and nonterminal NODES. The matching process may be full UNIFICATION or, more usually, a restricted form of PATTERN MATCHING where only the VARIABLES in the rewrite rule may be INSTANTIATED. Examples of uses of the rewrite rules are the restricted paramodulation inferences called demodulation, which are performed in THEOREM PROVING or in programming with abstract data types introduced by a series of equations.

**RI,** see XCON.

**Risch algorithm,** *n.* an ALGORITHM for evaluating various types of integrals incorporated into MACSYMA.

**RI-SOAR,** *n.* an expert system that uses some of the knowledge related to configuring VAX 11/780 computer systems embedded in XCON to perform a portion of the computer system configuration task. The program performs a SEARCH through a PROBLEM SPACE of possible SOLUTIONS in order to find an appropriate selection of components to add to the core system. Components are selected on the basis of their functional and spatial CONSTRAINTS. The customer's order supplies the initial data for the process. RI-SOAR extends from the SOAR general PROBLEM-SOLVING ARCHITECTURE. The GOAL for the program is to increase the understanding of how to reduce the limitations of both expert systems and general problem solvers. RI-SOAR was developed at Carnegie-Mellon University.

**RITA,** *n. acronym for* Rand Intelligent Terminal Agent, a KNOWLEDGE ENGINEERING language for RULE-based representation. It features FORWARD and BACK-CHAINING control schemes, and support for developing user agents, which are front ends to remote computing systems and networks. The SUPPORT ENVIRONMENT consists of TRACING, DEBUGGING, and EXPLANATION FACILITIES, a front end for the interactive creation and development of RULE sets, and a mechanism for accessing UNIX on PDP-11/45 and PDP-11/70 computer systems. RITA was developed by the Rand Corporation.

**RLL,** *n.* a KNOWLEDGE ENGINEERING language for FRAME-based representation. The language provides users with flexibility, permitting users to express a particular set of representations, INHERITANCE strategies, and control schemes in order to specify a DOMAIN-specific language. In addition, users can incorporate procedural attachment and general LISP structures as SLOTS of FRAMES. A sophisticated editor enables users to check both SYNTAX and SEMANTICS. Implemented in INTERLISP, RLL was developed at Stanford University.

**Roberts cross operator,** *n.* an OPERATOR devised to approximate the spatial first derivative of a picture function, the gradient in digital images. It computes the sum of squares of the differences between diagonal PIXELS in a 2x2 window:

$$R(i,j) = \{(f(i,j) - f(i+1,j+1))^2 + (f(i+1,j) - f(i,j+1))^2\}^{1/2}.$$

**ROBOT,** *n.* one of the first NATURAL LANGUAGE INTERFACES to DATA BASES.

**robot problem–solving,** *n.* that sub-area of PROBLEM-SOLVING involved in the locomotion of robots, especially in the development of WORLD MODELS and PLANNING.

**robot vision,** *n.* visual-sensing technology for industrial robots and anthropomorphic manipulators that allows them to operate in an unpredictable physical environment. Robotic VISION is especially useful in industrial applications, exploration of hazardous environments, and medical applications.

**robotics,** *n.* the branch of ARTIFICIAL INTELLIGENCE research concerned with enabling computers to 'see' and 'manipulate' objects in their surrounding environment. The search for solutions to the problem of controlling the physical actions of mobile robots. In the case of robots, the goal of artificial intelligence research is to develop the techniques necessary for developing robots capable of using HEURISTICS in order to function in a highly flexible manner while interacting within a constantly changing environment. The SOLUTIONS are complex and involve PLANNING at both high and low levels of abstraction. In order for a robot to function properly in its environment, for example, it is necessary for it to have information both about that environment in particular and about world states in general. The planning of action sequences and the monitoring of plan execution similarly involve both concrete and abstract knowledge. Optimal movements of a robot's arm or optimal sequencing of a robot's actions are typical problems in this .field. Most of the robots currently in use are not complex and perform repetitive tasks. The results of robotics research have provided a basis for many AI ideas.

**ROGET,** *n.* a TOOL for DOMAIN EXPERTS to use when designing a KNOWLEDGE BASE for a diagnosis–type expert system. The program acts as a system-building aid by querying the expert about the properties of the subproblems the expert must solve, the results or solutions the system must produce, the evidence or data required to solve the problem(s), and the relationships between the data or facts associated with a case and its solution – for example, what factors serve to confirm a solution or suggest other factors. It is implemented in a version of EMYCIN.

**roll,** *n.* the angular displacement around the principal axis of a body, especially its line of motion.

**root node,** *n.* **1.** The uppermost NODE in a TREE.
**2.** the point in a GRAPH, from which all ARCS emanate.

**root structure,** *n.* in INTERNIST, the conjunction of all the disease areas into which the DISEASE TREE is partitioned. The root structure is formally a set of subtrees of the disease tree, accounting for all the patient's manifestations.

**ROSIE,** *n. acronym for* Rule-Oriented System for Implementing Expertise, a KNOWLEDGE ENGINEERING language for RULE-based representation that also permits procedure-oriented representation. It features an English-like SYNTAX, a procedure-oriented structure allowing nested and recursive subroutines, powerful PATTERN-MATCHING facilities, and an INTERFACE to the local OPERATING SYSTEM, giving ROSIE control over remote jobs. In addition, the program supplies editing and DEBUGGING TOOLS. Implemented in INTERLISP, ROSIE has been converted to run in the C programming language. It was developed at the Rand Corporation.

**ROSS,** *n. acronym for* Rule-Oriented System for Simulation, a programming language for OBJECT-oriented representation and simulation. It permits INHERITANCE of ATTRIBUTES and behaviours from multiple parents and the free mixing of ROSS commands and LISP function calls. A display editor is included for objects and an abbreviation package aids the readability of programs. Implemented in FRANZ LISP, ROSS runs on DEC VAX systems under Unix. ROSS was developed by the Rand Corporation.

**Rotating Equipment Diagnostic System,** *n.* an expert system developed at Stone & Webster Engineering for troubleshooting various rotating equipment. Exsys is the development software.

**rote learning,** *n.* a form of learning where the ENVIRONMENT provides information exactly at the level of the performance task and, thus, no HYPOTHESES are needed.

**RPMS,** *abbrev. for* Resource Planning and Management System, a SOFTWARE TOOL that helps users with general PLANNING and scheduling of tasks, such as defining a schedule and minimizing resources like time, manpower, and materials. The schedule is represented graphically as a network containing tasks with bars indicating their durations and arrows pointing to successor and predecessor tasks. The user can define formal CONSTRAINTS between tasks, such as Task A must occur before Task B, by moving tasks (NODES) in the network itself, attempting to level out the use of resources. Implemented in ZETALISP and OPS5, RPMS uses the FLAVORS OBJECT-oriented features of ZETALISP. RPMS was developed by Ford Aerospace and has been applied to space shuttle reconfiguration at the Johnson Space Center.

**RTC,** *abbrev. for* Radar Target Classification system, an expert system that uses knowledge of models of ship classes in order to classify ships from its interpretations of radar images. The program compares features of the radar images with high-level models of possible ship classes stored in the program's KNOWLEDGE BASE. For each ship in the knowledge base, RTC stores one three-dimensional (3-D) model. In order to compare the radar image to the model, the program maps the 3-D model into the 2-D view appropriate for the given image. The program is a RULE-BASED PROGRAM. Implemented in FRANZ LISP, RTC was developed by Advanced Information & Decision Systems.

**RUBRIC,** *n. acronym for* Rule-Based Retrieval of Information by Computer, an expert system that helps users to access unformatted textual DATA BASES. The system performs conceptual retrieval; e.g., when the user names a single topic, RUBRIC automatically retrieves all documents containing text related to that topic. In RUBRIC, the relationships among topics, subtopics, and low-level word phrases are defined in RULE form. The rules also define alternative terms, phrases, and spellings for the same topic or CONCEPT. The user can formulate a query in the form of a rule that specifies retrieval criteria, e.g., a HEURISTIC weight that specifies how strongly the rule's pattern indicates the presence of the rule's topic. During retrieval, RUBRIC presents the user with documents that lie in a cluster containing at least one document with a weight above a user-provided threshold. This prevents an arbitrary threshold from splitting closely ranked documents. Implemented in FRANZ LISP, RUBRIC was developed at Advanced Information & Decision Systems.

**rule** or **production,** *n.* a formal manner of specifying a recommendation, directive, or strategy, which is expressed as IF premise, THEN conclusion; or IF condition, THEN action (see IF-THEN RULE). A conditional statement consisting of two parts. The first part, which consists of one or more IF clauses, serves to establish conditions that must apply if a second part, consisting of one or more clauses, is to be acted upon. A rule can support deductive processes such as BACK-CHAINING and FORWARD CHAINING. The clauses of rules are usually ATTRIBUTE-value pairs or OBJECT-ATTRIBUTE-VALUE TRIPLETS. In a formal grammar, rules specify the way in which sentences can be derived and parsed. In PRODUCTION SYSTEMS, rules are the units of production memory and are used to encode PROCEDURAL KNOWLEDGE.

**rule antecedent,** *n.* the left-hand side of a PRODUCTION RULE. Also called the condition or IF part of such a rule. Compare ACTION CLAUSE and CONSEQUENT.

**rule base,** *n.* that portion of a PRODUCTION SYSTEM containing the set of PRODUCTION RULES.

**rule-based methods,** *n.* programming methods using IF-THEN RULES to perform FORWARD or BACK-CHAINING.

**rule-based program,** *n.* a computer program that explicitly incorporates RULES or RULESET components. Similar in style to PRODUCTION SYSTEM programming, rule-based programming represents KNOWLEDGE explicitly via rules rather than by means of procedures. However, a rule-based program is not necessarily implemented in a general-purpose production system language and need not make exclusive use of the production system ARCHITECTURE.

**rule-based representation,** *n.* a KNOWLEDGE REPRESENTATION scheme utilizing some form of PRODUCTION RULES.

**rule-based system,** *n.* a program in which KNOWLEDGE is stored in the form of simple IF-THEN RULES or condition-action RULES.

**rule consequent,** *n.* the right-side of a PRODUCTION RULE. Also referred to as the ACTION CLAUSE or the THEN part of such a rule.

**RULEGEN,** *n.* a subprogram of META-DENDRAL that searches the RULE SPACE of bond environments in order from general to most specific. The ALGORITHM repeatedly generates a new set of HYPOTHESES, H, and tests it against positive TRAINING INSTANCES.

**RULEMASTER,** *n.* a TOOL for KNOWLEDGE ENGINEERS developing RULE-based expert systems. It acts as a system-building aid supplying an integrated set of tools, including RADIAL, an extensible language for expressing rules, and a rule INDUCTION system that creates rules from sets of examples. The language enables hierarchical structuring of generated rules. In addition, RULEMASTER can access external data and processes by way of any programs written in any UNIX-supported language. The program provides automatic generation of explanations as complete English sentences, and user-definable data types and operators. Implemented in C, RULEMASTER runs on minicomputers and microcomputers under the UNIX OPERATING SYSTEM. RULEMASTER was developed by Radian Corporation.

**RULEMOD,** *n.* in META-DENDRAL, a routine that conducts HILL CLIMBING SEARCHES in the portions of the RULE SPACE near the RULES located by RULEGEN. This is because the rules produced by RULEGEN are approximate and have not been tested against negative evidence.

**rule model,** *n.* In TEIRESIAS, empirical generalizations of subsets of RULES, indicating commonalities among the rules in that subset. For example, in MYCIN there is a rule model for the subset of rules that conclude affirmatively about organism category, indicating that most such rules mention the concepts of culture site and infection type in their premise. Another rule model notes that those rules that mention site and infection type in the premise also tend to mention the portal of entry of the organism.

**rule of generalization,** see GENERALIZATION.

**rule of inference,** see GENERALIZATION, RESOLUTION, THEOREM PROVING.

**ruleset,** *n.* a collection of RULES that constitutes a module of HEURISTIC knowledge.

**rule space,** *n.* the SPACE of possible general RULES.

**rule-space search algorithm,** *n.* a SEARCH ALGORITHM used in systems that include RULE form. Such ALGORITHMS include the CANDIDATE-ELIMINATION ALGORITHM, GENERATE AND TEST, and the $A^q$ ALGORITHM.

**RULEWRITER,** *n.* a TOOL that helps KNOWLEDGE ENGINEERS formulate RULES in the EXPERT language. It acts as a system-building aid by producing a model that correctly classifies training cases on the basis of their stored findings. To do so, the program uses knowledge about training cases, a taxonomy of plausible ASSOCIATIONS in the DOMAIN, and causal mechanisms. Associational and causal knowledge guides a rule induction process performed on the example of the training cases. Classification rules learned from training cases are expressed directly in EXPERT. Implemented in LISP, RULE WRITER was developed at Rutgers University.

**run–length,** *n.* a technique of coding for image processing that minimizes the amount of memory and processing required. For a line image of n PIXELS, a straightforward binary connectivity analysis requires on the order of $n^2$ operations, while the ALGORITHM using run–length coding requires on the order of n operations. In general, run–length coding is an effective technique for reducing the amount of information processing and storage.

**runtime version** or **runtime system,** *n.* that version of a program that results when an expert system building TOOL is modified to incorporate one or more specific KNOWLEDGE BASES and to deactivate certain programming features. Knowledge system building tools permit users to create and run various knowledge bases. A user might create a dozen knowledge bases using a single tool. In the case of a given problem the user is facing, the user would load an appropriate knowledge base and undertake a consultation. Users can easily modify a knowledge base with such a tool.

**RX,** *n.* an expert system that automates the process of both HYPOTHESIS generation and exploratory analysis in order to help users perform studies on large, nonrandomized, time-oriented, clinical DATA BASES. The KNOWLEDGE the program contains includes a tree-structured KNOWLEDGE BASE representing a TAXONOMY of relevant aspects of medicine and statistics. The program also includes DOMAIN KNOWLEDGE about systemic lupus erythematosus along with limited areas of general internal medicine. The program generates lists of hypothesized (see HYPOTHESIS) relationships using nonparametric correlations to generate them. Using appropriate statistical methods, the program tests the hypotheses and incorporates the positive results into the data base. RX has been used to find causal relationships within the American Rheumatism Association Medical Information System (ARAMIS) data base. Implemented in INTERLISP, RX was developed at Stanford University.

# S

**S Set,** *n*. the set of specific elements in some HYPOTHESES. The set H of plausible hypotheses can be represented by two subsets: the set of most general elements in H, the G SET and the set of most specific elements in H, the S set.

**SACON,** *n*. an expert system that engineers can use in co-operation with MARC, a program that uses finite-element analysis methods to simulate the mechanical behaviour of objects. The SACON system helps determine analysis strategies for particular structural analysis problems. MARC is used to implement the SACON-generated strategy of choice. The SACON program serves to identify the analysis class of the problem and recommends specific features of the MARC program to activate when performing the analysis. SACON's knowledge of STRESSES and deflections of a structure under different loading conditions serves as a basis to determine an appropriate structural analysis strategy. The program is RULE-based using BACK-CHAINING. SACON can analyse structures such as aircraft wings, reactor pressure vessels, rocket motor casings, and bridges. Implemented in EMYCIN, SACON was developed at Stanford University.

**SADD,** *n*. *acronym for* Semi-Automatic Digital Designer, an expert system that assists engineers in the design of digital circuits. The program takes as input a functional description of the proposed circuit in English and uses it to build an internal model of the circuit. To do so, the program uses knowledge about the model, component characteristics, and circuit behaviour to design a plausible circuit, which it tests for correctness by simulating its operation. SADD uses a FRAME-based representation of knowledge about circuit components. Implemented in LISP, SADD was developed at the University of Maryland.

**SAD-SAM,** *n*. *acronym for* Syntactic Appraiser and Diagrammar-Semantic Analyzing Machine, a program that accepts English sentences about kinship relations, and builds a

DATA BASE, and answers questions about the facts it has stored. It was written in IPL-V.

**SAIL,** *n.* a programming language for procedure-oriented RE-PRESENTATION that is derived from the block-structured programming language ALGOL 60. Unlike most AI LANGUAGES, SAIL is a COMPILER based language. Originally designed with robotics in mind, SAIL incorporates LEAP, a fast, associative facility. An associative memory capability and a large set of low-level input and output and data manipulation functions serve to extend SAIL with respect to ALGOL 60. SAIL is further extended with flexible linking to hand-coded assembly language procedures, a compile-time macro system, record, set, and list data types, and ITEMS. An item is indexed off each of three positions, thus making the retrieval process very efficient. A well developed MULTIPROCESSING facility enables communication between processes being handled by a message queuing system. Any process may 'sprout' another process, thus inheriting the ALGOL-60 scoping rules so that the child process shares the same DATA BASE as the parent. A control PRIMITIVE 'join' suspends one process until another has terminated in order to aid synchronization. PATTERN MATCH-ING is used only for data base retrieval. The package also supplies users with a high-level DEBUGGER and user-modifiable error handling, backtracking, and interrupt facilities. Sail was originally designed to run on PDP-10 computers under the TOPS-10 and TENEX operating systems. It was developed at the Stanford University artificial intelligence laboratory.

**SAINT,** *n. acronym for* Symbolic Automatic INTegrator, a program that solves elementary symbolic INTEGRATION PROBLEMS, especially those concerning indefinite INTEGRATION, with the accuracy of a college freshman. It was written in LISP.

**SAL,** *n. acronym for* System for Asbestos Litigation, an expert system that uses knowledge about damages, defendant liability, plaintiff responsibility, and case characteristics in order to help attorneys and claims adjusters evaluate claims related to asbestos exposure. The program estimates the sum of financial compensation the plaintiff in an active case should be awarded in order to promote a rapid settlement. SAL currently handles the class of diseases called asbestosis, and one class of plaintiffs, insulators. The program is RULE-based using FORWARD CHAINING. It has been implemented in ROSIE, at the Rand Corporation.

**SAM,** *n. acronym for* Script Applier Mechanism, a computer program developed at Yale University to demonstrate the use of SCRIPTS and PLANS in understanding simple stories. SAM understands stories by fitting them into one or more scripts. After this MATCH is completed, the program makes summaries of the stories.

**Samuel's Checkers Player,** *n.* a program that was used for experiments with three different learning methods – ROTE LEARNING, POLYNOMIAL EVALUATION FUNCTIONS, and SIGNATURE TABLES. The experiments showed that significant improvement in playing checkers (draughts) could be obtained. Among the earliest investigations of MACHINE LEARNING, these studies were some of the most successful both in terms of improved performance and in terms of lessons for AI.

**SARA,** *n.* an expert system that helps lawyers analyse decisions governed by discretionary norms. Given the facts of a case and the decision reached, the lawyer identifies factors deemed relevant to the decision; for example, the rent paid for an apartment may be a relevant factor in granting social aid. The lawyer then indicates to SARA the factors (and their values) relevant to a particular decision. On the basis of examples like these, SARA assigns weights to each factor, adjusted to explain as many of the specified decisions as possible. Factors assigned high weights are deemed important with respect to the discretionary norm under consideration. Factors and decisions are represented as FRAMES, and an iterative correlation method is employed for weight calculation. SARA was developed at the Norwegian Research Centre for Computers and Law.

**satisfice,** *n.* a process during which one pursues a SOLUTION that satisfies a set of CONSTRAINTS. It is a PROBLEM-SOLVING strategy that terminates with success when a potential solution satisfies specified minimal criteria of acceptability. In contrast to optimization, a process that pursues the best possible solution, satisfice simply seeks a solution that will work. The solution is not necessarily optimal since in the case of many problems, finding the optimal solution is unnecessary and costly in terms of time. Many managers seeking solutions to solving practical problems are satisfied with identifying a tenable solution and do not continue to search for the best possible solution.

**SAVOIR,** *n.* a KNOWLEDGE ENGINEERING language for RULE-based representation. It features BACK and FORWARD CHAINING, a KNOWLEDGE BASE COMPILER, built-in CERTAINTY FACTOR handling routines, support for FUZZY LOGIC, and DEMON control structures. Also included is an on-line help facility, a menu-oriented user INTERFACE, and an EXPLANATION FACILITY. SAVOIR runs on a wide range of computers and operating systems including the IBM PC, Sirius, Apricot, SAGE II and IV, VAX 11 series, and PDP 11. It was developed by the British company ISI.

**scaling problem,** *n.* the difficulty associated with attempts to apply PROBLEM-SOLVING techniques developed for a simplified version of a problem to the actual problem itself.

**SCENARIO-AGENT,** *n.* an expert system for military application that supplies a model of nonsuperpower behaviour in strategic conflict situations in order to aid war game participants. The program supplies information about the likelihood of the nonsuperpowers granting access rights to the superpowers, including the use of military bases, and the likelihood of the nonsuperpowers contributing forces to the main conflict. The program is rule-based (see RULE-BASED PROGRAM) encoding RULES that describe the behaviour of nonsuperpowers in various conflict situations. In addition, the program uses FORWARD CHAINING and PROCEDURE-ORIENTED inferencing. Implemented in ROSIE, SCENARIO-AGENT was developed at the Rand Corporation.

**scene analysis,** *n.* the process of seeking information about a three-dimensional scene from information derived from a two-dimensional image. Generally, the process involves the transformation of simple features into abstract descriptions.

**scene domain,** *n.* in VISION studies, the physical, three-dimensional aspects of a scene, such as occlusion of one surface by another or the concavity or convexity of edges.

**scene feature,** *n.* an aspect of a scene inferred from image features. Scene features include tilt, reflectivity, and smoothness of surfaces. Vertex, edge and surface are also scene features. (Compare IMAGE FEATURE.)

**scheduler,** *n.* the part of the INFERENCE ENGINE that decides when and in what order to apply different pieces of DOMAIN KNOWLEDGE.

**scheduling,** *n.* determining the order of activities for execution in a fashion generally based on CONTROL HEURISTICS. Developing a time sequence to follow in order to achieve GOALS.

**schema,** *n.* any formalism for representing information about a single CONCEPT in terms of properties related to it. Usually, the properties are represented as SLOTS as in frames and can consist of attached procedures for computing properties that are not immediately available. An example is a frame-like representation formalism in a KNOWLEDGE ENGINEERING language such as SRL. In a system such as TEIRESIAS, when the expert has identified a deficit in the KNOWLEDGE BASE of the performance program, TEIRESIAS questions the expert in order to correct the deficit by filling in slots.. This process relies heavily on META-level KNOWLEDGE about the performance program, which is encoded in RULE MODELS and schemas. In effect, TEIRESIAS uses these data structures to represent knowledge about what the performance program knows. The meta-level knowledge about OBJECTS in the DOMAIN can include both structural and organizational information and is specified in such data structure schemas. Acquisition of knowledge about new objects can take place as a process of INSTANTIATING a schema. Instantiating a schema creates the required structural components with which to build the new data structure, and take care of its interrelations with other data structures. By querying in a simple form of English about the VALUES of the schema's components, this KNOWLEDGE ACQUISITION process is made to appear to the expert as a natural, high-level inquiry about the new concept. The process is, naturally, more complex, but the key component is the system's description of its own REPRESENTATION. (See also FRAME).

**schema instantiation,** *n.* a method for SEARCHING RULE SPACE. It uses a set of RULE SCHEMAS to provide general CONSTRAINTS on the form of plausible rules. The method attempts to INSTANTIATE these schemas from the current set of TRAINING INSTANCES. The instantiated schema that best fits the training instances is considered the most plausible rule.

**SCHOLAR,** *n.* the first intelligent tutoring system, developed to simulate the behaviour of an experienced TUTOR. It engaged the user in a dialogue concerning the geography of the countries of South America. The dialogue was MIXED-INITIATIVE (see MIXED INITIATIVE DIALOGUE) in the sense that students could interrupt the questioning by the system in order to ask questions of their own. As an expert system, SCHOLAR incorporated many of the features of a good tutor based on observations of human dialogues. The tutorial features that SCHOLAR incorporates include an ability to communicate with the student in NATURAL LANGUAGE; an ability to set priorities for depth versus breadth; and an ability to pose questions, evaluate and monitor responses, explain incorrect answers, present new information, review old material, and answer questions. The program was unique in incorporating four important features of human tutorial interaction: the selection of topics, the interweaving of questioning and presentation, reviewing, and error correction. Knowledge of geography in the program was represented as a SEMANTIC NETWORK containing ATTRIBUTES (e.g., geographical features, cities, climate) and VALUES of the attributes (e.g., Andes Mountains, Santiago, temperate). Within the KNOWLEDGE BASE, each entry has a fixed importance tag ranging from 0 signifying most important to 6 signifying least important. Each high-level topic in the net is allowed a set of nested subtopics. In order to provide extensive cross referencing, information can be represented at multiple points in the net. For explaining incorrect answers and answering user-initiated questions, the program also contains knowledge of generic terms, such as city and capital. The program can make plausible INFERENCES from its SEMANTIC NETWORK about information that is not specifically stored. The organization of the knowledge base in terms of nested topics permits both breadth and depth of coverage. The tutor can cover topics at the highest level or it can trace through all of its nested subtopics. In tutorial mode, SCHOLAR adopts what is called a web strategy, covering all important topics on the first pass through the material and then pursuing topics in increasingly more detail on subsequent passes.

**Schooner,** *n.* an expert system developed by Hewlett-Packard for troubleshooting asynchronous datacom links. PERSONAL CONSULTANT Plus is the development software.

**scope of knowledge representation,** *n*. that portion of the external world that can be represented by a KNOWLEDGE REPRESENTATION system.

**scope of variable,** see VARIABLE SCOPING.

**scoring of a hypothesis,** *n*. the computing of a VALUE if the logical decision criteria are insufficient to confirm or deny a HYPOTHESIS. The scoring of a hypothesis can be computed by combining the value of a FUNCTION that measures the fit of observed findings and typical (expected) findings and the value of a function that is the ratio of the number of findings.

**scripts,** *n*. a FRAME-like structure specifically designed for representing sequences of events. Adopted primarily as a support for NATURAL LANGUAGE UNDERSTANDING, a script is a structure for use in the large-scale organization of KNOWLEDGE, and is related to CONCEPTUAL DEPENDENCY, a primary form of KNOWLEDGE REPRESENTATION. The standardized sequence of events of scripts describes some stereotypical human activity, such as going to a restaurant or visiting a doctor. The underlying assumption is that people know many such scripts and use them in order to establish the context of events. A script is functionally similar to a frame or a SCHEMA in the sense that it can be used to anticipate aspects of the events it represents. For example, a RESTAURANT script involves going to a restaurant, being seated, consulting the menu, and so on. People who are presented with an abbreviated description of this activity, for example, the sentence 'John went out for dinner', infer from the knowledge they possess about restaurants that John ordered, ate, and paid for the food at the restaurant. Moreover, people anticipate from a sentence that fills part of the script (e.g., 'John was given a menu') what sort of sentences are likely to follow (e.g., 'John ordered steak'). Scripts attempt to capture the kind of knowledge that people apply to make the above INFERENCES.

**SCSIMP,** *n*. a HILL-CLIMBING ALGORITHM guaranteed to produce the smallest answer. SCSIMP is a search–oriented simplifier provided in MACSYMA for those applications in which the user desires the smallest possible form for an expression. When given an expression and a set of RULES,

SCSIMP applies each of the rules to the expression, in turn, and retains the smallest result. If any such substitution leads to an expression smaller than the original, the process is repeated.

**SDC Speech System,** see SRI/SDC SPEECH SYSTEM.

**search,** *n*. PROBLEM-SOLVING, using such methods as DEDUC-TION, INFERENCE, PLANNING, HEURISTICS and THEOREM PROV-ING. The process of looking through the set of possible SOLU-TIONS to a problem in order to find an acceptable solution. Most AI applications, whether in the field of ROBOTICS, NATURAL LANGUAGE UNDERSTANDING, games, or expert systems, employ search as a TOOL for finding a solution to a problem. (See also PROBLEM-SOLVING.)

**search algorithm,** *n*. an ALGORITHM used in searching. (See A* ALGORITHM, ALPHA/BETA PRUNING, BANDWIDTH SEARCH, BEAM SEARCH, BEST-FIRST SEARCH, BIDIRECTIONAL SEARCH, BLIND SEARCH, BREADTH-FIRST SEARCH, DEPTH-FIRST SEARCH, FULL-WIDTH SEARCHING, GENERATE-AND-TEST, HEURISTIC PATH ALGO-RITHM, HIERARCHICAL SEARCH, LENGTH-FIRST SEARCH, NEGMAX, ORDERED SEARCH, UNIFORM-COST SEARCH.)

**search graph,** *n*. a GRAPH or TREE that is constructed as a SEARCH proceeds from where the NODES and ARCS are re-presented by explicit data structures.

**search space,** *n*. the set of all possible SOLUTIONS to a problem. A GRAPH or TREE that is constructed before a SEARCH proceeds, which includes all states that are theoreti-cally possible. Many problem DOMAINS have large or even in-finite search space. It is possible to measure the search space by estimating the number of NODES it encompasses. (See also PROBLEM SPACE.)

**search tree,** see SEARCH GRAPH.

**secondary search,** *n*. in games, a SEARCH that is carried out after a best move has been found, to confirm the evaluation. Such a search usually is carried out for an additional two PLY.

**SECS,** *n. acronym for* Simulation and Evaluation of Chemical Synthesis, an expert system that assists chemists in synthesiz-ing complex organic molecules. The chemist presents the structure of a target molecule, and the system generates a PLAN to create the target molecule from basic building block molecules. The plan is basically a series of chemical reactions applied to functional groups of atoms. The system, with the help of the chemist, systematically works backward from the target toward simpler molecules until a synthesis route is found from the target to the building blocks. Implemented in FORTRAN, SECS was developed at the University of California, Santa Cruz.

**SEE,** *n.* in IMAGE UNDERSTANDING, a program developed to analyse scenes without prestored models of OBJECTS. The program begins with a line drawing and identifies all the separate objects in it, even if they are not completely visible.

**SEEK,** *n.* a TOOL for KNOWLEDGE ENGINEERS that provides advice about RULE refinement for diagnostic-type expert systems. It acts as a system-building aid helping to refine rules represented in the EXPERT language but expressed in a tabular format. The program looks for regularities in the rules' performance on a body of stored cases with known conclusions in order to suggest approaches for generalizing or specializing the rules. It engages users interactively by first suggesting the type of change (generalization or specialization) and what components to change. Users in turn decide how to specifically generalize or specialize the components. SEEK's refinement method produces the best results when the expert knowledge is accurate and when small changes in the KNOWLEDGE BASE cause significant improvement in the performance of the expert system. Implemented in FORTRAN, SEEK was originally designed to run on a DEC-20 system and was developed at Rutgers University.

**segment variable,** *n.* a variable appearing in a PATTERN that can match a subpart of a list.

**segmentation,** *n.* the extraction of such features of an image as lines and REGIONS.

**segmented lattice,** *n.* in the HWIM system, lattice representation of different pronunciations embedded in a TREE-like dictionary. In this dictionary any two words that could be spoken in sequence were linked by an ARC representing any contextual effect on pronunciation.

**selection sort,** *n.* the enumerating of OBJECTS according to a particular ordering RELATION.

**selective attention,** *n.* a process whereby humans attend to areas of high information and ignore less interesting areas.

**selective forgetting,** *n.* a procedure allowing a system to determine empirically which items of information are most frequently reused. In this approach the system decides whether or not to forget information it has stored.

**self-description,** *n.* a process used in the AUTOMATIC PROGRAMMING system CHI that is used for self-compilation and in modifying and extending its ENVIRONMENT. It uses the language V.

**self-organizing system,** *n.* LEARNING SYSTEMS that modify themselves in order to adapt to their ENVIRONMENT.

**semantic ambiguity,** *n.* the AMBIGUITY that arises from the fact that a word or sentence may have more than one sense or INTERPRETATION.

**semantic analysis,** *n.* the conversion of some input sentence to a NATURAL LANGUAGE processing system and constructing an internal, semantic REPRESENTATION of it.

**semantic component,** *n.* that part of a TRANSFORMATIONAL GRAMMAR that gives one or more SEMANTIC INTERPRETATIONS to the DEEP STRUCTURE REPRESENTATION of a sentence.

**semantic data model (SDM),** *n.* an approach to DATA BASE modelling that allows more precise specification of semantic information. The SDM was designed to promote the representation of information about the DOMAIN of application in addition to that of the data base itself.

**semantic decomposition,** *n.* see SEMANTIC PRIMITIVE.

**semantic grammar,** *n.* a type of GRAMMAR used in LANGUAGE UNDERSTANDING systems, where the use of general grammatical KNOWLEDGE is replaced by grammars that are very specific to the task requirements. In contrast with conventional grammars, semantic grammar relies predominantly on semantic rather than syntactic categories. For example:

MESSAGE → PATIENTTYPE HAVE DISEASETYPE

In some cases, the semantic categories and structures are re-labellings of conventional syntactic categories and structures or have a mixture of syntactic elements. Semantic grammars are especially effective for language processing in limited DOMAIN CONTEXTS such as interpreting DATA BASE queries, where syntactic PARSING is unnecessarily costly, but general-purpose semantic grammars are not. A connection exists between the semantic grammars, SEMANTIC PRIMITIVES and semantic CASE FRAMES. However, systems making heavy use of general-purpose semantics are not conventionally described as relying on semantic grammars.

**semantic interpretation,** *n.* **1.** a method of producing an application-dependent scene description from a feature set derived from the image.

**2.** the analysis of the meaning of a sentence, phrase, or word.

**semantic marker,** *n.* DATA BASE definitions contain semantic markers that can be used by the syntactic programs to rule out grammatical but similarly incorrect sentences, such as 'The table picks up blocks.' In Winograd's SHRDLU, these markers are calls to semantic procedures that check for restrictions, for example, the restriction that only animate objects pick up things.

**semantic memory,** *n.* that part of a model of COGNITION where KNOWLEDGE of the meanings of words and concepts is stored. (See SEMANTIC NETWORK).

**semantic network** or **semantic net,** *n.* a psychological model of human associative memory. It is a principle for large-scale organization of knowledge that emphasizes the multiple associations of individual concepts. A net is a type of KNOWLEDGE REPRESENTATION consisting of both the NODES and links between the nodes that combine to form a linked graph. The nodes represent objects, concepts, and events. The links between the nodes represent interrelations between the nodes forming labelled ARCS. The following is an example of a simple semantic net:

birds ——————————→ wings
has-part

**Semantic network**

BIRD and WINGS are nodes representing sets or concepts and HAS-PART is the name of the link specifying their relationship. Among the many interpretations of this net fragment is the statement:

All birds have wings.

A wide range of network structure types is possible. A semantic net should properly be based on definitions of the net structure, namely, the SYNTAX and SEMANTICS of nodes and links, and configurations of these and the net structure (the syntax and semantics of node-to-node transitions).

**semantic primitive,** *n.* a primitive ATTRIBUTE of a DOMAIN that is used to build up facts in the DATA BASE. In the design of an AI system, a major question surrounds the vocabulary to be used within the FORMALISM set forth by the given representation technique – in a LOGIC-based representation, for example, what predicates are to be used in a semantic network, what NODE and link types should be provided. Research on semantic primitives is concerned with this problem of establishing the representational vocabulary. One can think of a PRIMITIVE as any SYMBOL that is used but not defined within the system. A second and narrower usage takes semantic primitives as elements of meaning into which words are to be broken down.

**semantics,** *n.* the study of the meaning, intention, or significance of a symbolic expression (see SYMBOL), as opposed to its form. Semantics can be viewed as a constraint on a language understander because not all grammatically legal sentences have a meaning, e.g., 'the snow was loud'. The term contrasts with SYNTACTIC, which refers to the formal pattern of the expression. In the case of SYNTAX, computers can determine the accuracy of an expression, but in the case of semantics, computers have trouble making accurate judgments about the semantic content of an expression. For example, 'Mary had a little drink', is a grammatically correct sentence; its syntax is correct, but its semantic content is very ambiguous (see AMBIGUITY). As we alter the context in which the sentence occurs, the meaning can change.

**sentential connective,** *n.* truth-functional PREDICATES used to combine simple PROPOSITIONS. The five most commonly used connectives are:

| | |
|---|---|
| And | ∧ or & |
| Or | ∨ |
| Not | ¬ |
| Implies | → or ⊃ |
| Equivalent | ≡ |

**SEQ,** *abbrev. for* SEQuence analysis system, an expert system that helps molecular biologists perform several types of nucleotide sequence analysis. The system can store, retrieve, and analyse nucleic acid sequences, and it can provide a statistical analysis of structural homologies and symmetries. SEQ's searching routines can be customized by manipulating a set of DEFAULT parameters; for example, the biologist may vary the weights for penalties and size of gap results during a Needleman-Wunch alignment. Implemented in LISP, SEQ was developed as part of the MOLGEN project at Stanford University and then further developed by Intellicorp.

**sequential diagnosis,** *n.* in medical applications involving more complex programs, a program that performs diagnoses in order when sufficient information is not available. To get more information, the program determines the next test to be given the patient. This process is accomplished via a sequential strategy, which selects the best test based on three factors: the cost of the test, the danger to the patient, and the amount of discriminating information the test would supply.

**sequential processing,** *n.* the computer technique of performing actions one at a time in sequence.

**set-of-support strategy,** *n.* a RESOLUTION strategy in which at least one parent of each RESOLVENT is chosen from the negation of the THEOREM or from the set of clauses that are derived from it. This strategy restricts the number of clauses that can be resolved at any given time. It is usually more efficient than BREADTH-FIRST SEARCH.

**S-expression,** *n.* a symbolic expression. In LISP, a sequence of zero or more ATOMS or S-expressions enclosed in parentheses.

**shading,** *n.* an unintensional large-area brightness gradient in a display. The term is also used to describe graphics SOFTWARE ALGORITHMS that establish the appearance of solid-object surfaces.

**shadow,** *n.* a line label used in interpreting line images.

**shape description,** *n.* the statement of the shape of an object in a scene involving constructing a description of objects from sensed data and then matching (see MATCH) the description with stored object models. Shape descriptions of models and objects must be represented by similar terms for range-data analysis and must describe the relative positions of elements of a scene.

**shape from shading,** *n.* the process of extracting three-dimensional shape information from smooth gradations of reflected light intensity. If certain assumptions are made concerning the reflectance function and illumination of a surface, it is possible to formulate and solve equations relating surface shape to the measured intensities in an image of the surface.

**shape from texture,** *n.* the process by which the three-dimensional structure of a surface is determined from the spatial distribution of surface markings. Projecting into the image plane distorts the geometry of surface textures in a manner dependent upon the shape of the underlying surface. As a surface recedes from the viewer its markings appear smaller due to the effects of perspective, and as a surface is inclined away from the frontal plane its markings appear compressed in the direction of the inclination. By isolating these projective distortions it is possible to recover the shape of a textured surface.

**shape recovery,** *n.* the recovery of shapes from images. It includes the use of reflectance, illumination, orientation of the surface, and shadowing (see SHADOW).

**shape-from method,** *n.* is a method used in recovering shape in monocular images. These methods include shape from SHADING, TEXTURE, and contours (see CONTOUR LINE).

**sharpening,** *n.* also called deblurring, a technique used in image processing to improve the quality of blurred images. The simplest methods include SPATIAL DIFFERENTIATION and HIGH-EMPHASIS FREQUENCY FILTERING.

**shelf,** *n.* in INTERNIST, a list of illness's manifestations, which a diagnosis cannot account for. At the beginning of a consultation, a list of manifestations is entered. As each manifestation is entered, it evokes one or more NODES of the DISEASE TREE. A model is created for each evoked disease node. The model consists of four lists of which the first is called the shelf, containing the observed manifestations that this disease does not account for.

**shell,** *n.* a DOMAIN-independent expert systems 'framework,' i.e., an INFERENCE ENGINE with EXPLANATION FACILITIES etc., but without any DOMAIN-specific KNOWLEDGE. In the event the framework is a suitable one for a given problem, adding domain-specific knowledge to build a new expert system may be possible without committing the effort necessary to start building a system from the beginning. The disadvantages of using shells stem from the way shells impose design decisions, including the form in which knowledge is represented (generally only as RULES), the approach for handling reasoning with uncertain knowledge, etc. Such constraints can considerably reduce the range of application of a particular shell.

**shortfall density,** *n.* an ordering metric developed for the HWIM system. One important issue in the control of the recognition process is determining which HYPOTHESIS about the contents of the signal should be attended to at each instant. In the HEARSAY and SDC/SRI systems (see SDC SPEECH SYSTEMS), hypotheses are not ordered by their scores alone, because it is recognized that all hypotheses should not necessarily compete. In particular, two hypotheses about different parts of the utterance should both be examined and a bridge formed between them if possible. An ordering metric called the SHORTFALL DENSITY was developed based on these considerations.

**short-term memory,** *n.* the portion of human memory that people actively use when thinking about a problem. Short-term memory is analogous to the RANDOM-ACCESS MEMORY (RAM) of computers. Random-access memory contains all the data that are instantly available to the system. The content of human short-term memory is usually conceptualized in terms of CHUNKS. Most cognitive theories hold that human short-term memory can contain and manipulate about four chunks at one time (see COGNITIVE SCIENCE).

**short-term memory buffer,** see CONTEXT.

**SHRDLU,** *n.* a NATURAL LANGUAGE processing system written at MIT. The design of the system was based on the belief that to understand language, a program must deal in an integrated way with SYNTAX, SEMANTICS, and REASONING. The program was written in LISP and MICRO-PLANNER, which is a LISP-based programming language. The assumption guiding the implementation was that meanings (those of words, phrases, and sentences) can take the form of procedural structures, and in addition, language is a way of activating appropriate procedures within the hearer. Terry Winograd thus embodied the knowledge in SHRDLU in pieces of executable computer code instead of representing KNOWLEDGE about syntax and meaning as RULES in a GRAMMAR or as PATTERNS to be matched against the input. For example, the context-free rule saying that a sentence is composed of a noun phrase and a verb phrase,

$$S \rightarrow NP\ VP,$$

is embodied in the MICRO-PLANNER procedure:

```
(PDEFINE SENTENCE
(((PARSE NP) NIL FAIL)
((PARSE VP) FAIL FAIL RETURN)))
```

When called, this program uses independent procedures for PARSING a noun phrase followed by a verb phrase. These, in turn, can call other procedures. The process fails if the required constituents are not found.

**SIAP,** *abbrev. for* Surveillance Integration Automation Project, an expert system that uses digitized acoustic data from hydrophone arrays in order to detect and identify various types of ocean vessel. The program attempts to identify the vessels and then to classify them into higher-level units, such as fleets. The acoustic data is transmitted in the form of sonogram displays, which are analog histories of the spectrum of received sound energy. The program uses KNOWLEDGE about the sound signature traits of different ship classes to interpret the data. In addition, the program analyses data and updates its findings for continually arriving data in real-time. Knowledge in the program is represented as RULES within a BLACKBOARD ARCHITECTURE and organized into a HIERARCHY for CONTROL. Implemented in INTERLISP, SIAP was developed through a joint effort by Stanford University and Systems Control Technology.

**signal processing,** *n.* complex analysis of wave forms in order to extract information.

**signal-to-noise ratio (S/N),** *n.* the ratio between the level of signal (or meaningful information) and the level of NOISE.

**signature table,** *n.* an n-dimensional array wherein each dimension of the array corresponds to one of the measured board features of a game board.

**simplex algorithm,** *n.* an ALGORITHM used to decide sets of linear inequalities over the real numbers.

**simulation,** *n.* an AI technique that uses a model of intelligent human behaviour in order to determine if the computer will exhibit the same intelligent behaviour as a human.

**simulation program,** *n.* a program for simulating a process. One of the earliest such systems was NLPQ, which was used for simulating queuing.

**simultaneous–goal principle,** *n.* a principle that states that to satisfy a GOAL of the form:

$$\text{Achieve } P_1 \text{ and } P_2,$$

a program F is first constructed in order to achieve $P_1$, and then F is modified in order to achieve $P_2$ while protecting $P_1$ at the end of F. A special protection mechanism ensures that no modification is permitted that destroys the truth of the protected condition $P_1$ at the end of the program.

**SIN,** *n. acronym for* Symbolic INtegrator, the Symbolic integration program that aimed at simulating behaviour comparable to expert human behaviour.

**single–representation trick,** *n.* the use of the same RE-PRESENTATION scheme for RULES and INSTANCES. A factor relating to the difficulty of SEARCHING the rule and instance spaces is the difference between the representation used for the RULES and the representation used for the TRAINING INSTANCES. If the representations for the RULE SPACE and the INSTANCE SPACE are different from each other, then the searches of the two spaces must be coordinated by complex interpretation and some experimentation. One trick used to avoid this problem is to choose the same representation for both spaces.

**single–step task,** *n.* a task in which one RULE, or a set of independent rules, can be applied in one step in order to accomplish the performance task.

**SIR,** *n. acronym for* Semantic Information Retrieval, a prototype understanding machine that accumulates facts and then makes deductions about them in order to answer questions. It was developed at MIT and was written in LISP.

**skeletal knowledge engineering language,** *n.* a computer language designed for building expert systems. The language is derived by removing all DOMAIN-specific KNOWLEDGE from an existing expert system. (See also SHELL.)

**skeletal plan,** *n.* an abstract PLAN that contains the basic steps for some modelled behaviour. When scientists invent an experimental design, they find a strategy, called a skeletal plan, which is useful for some related experimental GOAL, and then INSTANTIATE it with the proper laboratory methods for their specific goal and laboratory conditions. The skeletal plan may be very specific if the goal is similar to one for which a very good experiment has already been designed. It may be very general.

**skeletal system,** see SKELETAL KNOWLEDGE ENGINEERING LANGUAGE.

**skewed symmetry heuristic,** *n.* a HEURISTIC for shape interpretation. Symmetry in a two-dimensional picture has an axis for which the opposite sides are reflective: The symmetrical property is found along the transverse lines perpendicular to the symmetry axis. The concept of skewed symmetry relaxes this condition slightly, referring to the class of two-dimensional shapes in which symmetry is found along lines not necessarily perpendicular to the axis but at a fixed angle to

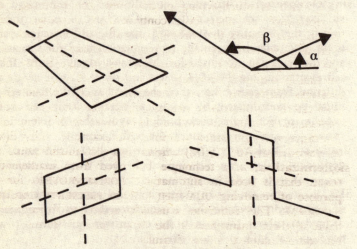

**Skewed symmetry heuristic**

it. The figure opposite shows a few examples. Formally, these shapes are defined as two-dimensional, linear transformations of real symmetries. A skewed symmetry defines two directions, called the skewed-symmetry axis and the skewed-transverse axis, as shown in the figure opposite. The skewed-symmetry heuristic is: A skewed symmetry in the image depicts a real symmetry in the scene viewed from some (unknown) viewing angle. One can transform this heuristic into CONSTRAINTS in the GRADIENT SPACE. Let $\alpha$ and $\beta$ denote the directional angles of the skewed-symmetry axis and the skewed-transverse axis, respectively, as in the figure. Let G = (p,q) be the gradient of the plane that includes the skewed symmetry. The heuristic demands that the two three-dimensional space vectors corresponding to the skewed-symmetry axis and the skewed-transverse axis be perpendicular.

**skill,** *n.* the efficient and effective application of KNOWLEDGE in order to produce SOLUTIONS in some problem DOMAIN.

**skill acquisition,** *n.* a type of LEARNING. Researchers in AI and cognitive psychology have sought to understand the kinds of KNOWLEDGE that people need to perform skilfully. Psychologists have noted that long after people are told how to do a task, such as touch-typing or computer programming, their performance on that task continues to improve through practice. It appears that although people can easily understand verbal instructions on how to perform a task, they must still do much work to turn that verbal knowledge into efficient mental or muscular operation.

**Skolem function,** *n.* a FUNCTION used whenever an EXISTENTIAL QUANTIFIER occurs within the scope of a UNIVERSAL QUANTIFIER. Its VARIABLE is replaced with a function of the universally quantified variable. For example, AxEy P(x,y) be rewritten as Ax P(x,f(x)) where f is a skolem function.

**skolemization,** *n.* a technique borrowed from mathematical LOGIC that is used in automatic THEOREM PROVING for the purpose of removing QUANTIFIERS from PREDICATE CALCULUS FORMULAE. The technique is usually applied to formulae that have all their quantifiers at the front (prenex normal form), but can be adopted to any formula.

**SLIP,** *n. acronym for* Symmetric List Processor, the programming language in which ELIZA was written.

**slot,** *n.* the place where KNOWLEDGE fits within the larger CON-TEXT created by a FRAME. In the form of a NODE, a slot is a feature or component description of an OBJECT in a frame, and corresponds to such intrinsic features as the object's name, definition, or information about the frame's creator. Slots may also represent derived ATTRIBUTES such as VALUE, RULES to determine values (significance), and pointers to related frames (analogous objects).

**small knowledge systems,** *n.* systems that generally contain under 500 RULES. Such systems are designed to help in-dividuals solve difficult analysis and decision-making problems without needing the equivalent degree of EXPERTISE of a human expert.

**small knowledge system building tools,** *n.* a TOOL that can run on personal computers.

**SMALLTALK,** *n.* a programming language for OBJECT-oriented REPRESENTATION. It permits users to organize objects hierarchically (see HIERARCHY) into classes. Each subclass in-herits (see INHERITANCE) the instance storage requirements and message PROTOCOLS of its superclass. Additionally, the sub-classes can add new information of their own and override in-herited behaviours. An interactive user INTERFACE displays high-resolution graphics and operates with a mouse or other pointing device. SMALLTALK runs on Xerox 1100 and other WORKSTATIONS. It was developed by the Palo Alto Research Center during the 1970s and early 1980s.

**smoothing,** *n.* the process of fitting together curves and sur-face to produce a smooth, continuous geometry. The aim of smoothing in image processing is to remove the NOISE from an image. The image taken by an IMAGING DEVICE is often contaminated by noise, the simplest kind of which is additive noise. Since smoothing techniques tend to blur the image, the main problem for smoothing methods is to remove noise without introducing undesirable blurring of details such as edges.

**SNAP,** *n.* an expert system developed by Boeing Computer Services for Infomart (Dallas) to assist new Infomart visitors in determining their computer needs. PERSONAL CONSULTANT is the development software.

**SNIFFER,** *n*. a network deduction system constructed around a matching PARADIGM. SNIFFER has the general power of a THEOREM PROVER for making deductions from the network DATA BASE. It can also take advantage of HEURISTIC KNOWLEDGE embedded (see EMBEDDING)in procedures called selector FUNCTIONS, which provide advice about which network elements should be matched (see MATCH) first and about how to match the selected element. These heuristics allow the system to proceed in a direct and sensible way when the amount of information in the data base becomes very large and blind retrieval strategies, like SPREADING ACTIVATION or systematic matching, are useless because they take too long.

**SOAR,** *n*. a general PROBLEM-SOLVING ARCHITECTURE for RULE-based REPRESENTATION of HEURISTIC, SEARCH-oriented problem-solving. The system provides a means for viewing a problem as a search through a PROBLEM SPACE, a set of states representing solutions and a set of OPERATORS that TRANSFORM one state into another. The principal FEATURES of SOAR include the automatic creation of a HIERARCHY of subgoals (see SUBGOALING) and problem spaces and a parallel rule INTERPRETER. Although SOAR is designed for generality, it has been applied to a KNOWLEDGE-intensive expert task. SOAR was originally implemented (see IMPLEMENTATION) in XAPS2, which has a parallel PRODUCTION SYSTEM architecture, and was reimplemented in a modified version of OPS5 with extensions for parallel execution. SOAR was developed at Carnegie-Mellon University.

**Sobel operator,** *n*. a convolution OPERATOR for detecting edges (see EDGE DETECTION). It is similar to other difference operators such as the Prewitt Operator. The 3x3 operators shown in the figure overleaf also compute first derivatives, and they are often referred to as the Sobel operators. In these WINDOWS, larger weights are given to the PIXELS close to the central point (i,j). This makes Sobel operators less sensitive to NOISE.

**Socratic style of tutoring,** *n*. a TUTOR that first attempts to diagnose the student's misconceptions and then presents material that will force the student to see his own errors. An important part of the SCHOLAR research has been an emphasis

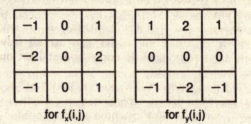

for $f_x(i,j)$       for $f_y(i,j)$

**Sobel operator**

on the nature of TUTORIAL DIALOGUE, in particular, this style of tutoring.

**software,** *n.* the programs, languages, procedures, RULES, and associated documentation used in the operation of a data processing system.

**software, levels of,** *n.* a continuum for describing SOFTWARE. Beginning at the lowest level, with MACHINE LANGUAGE, the levels of software extend up through a continuum of low-level languages and TOOLS, and progress to systems that USERS can use actually to solve problems (see PROBLEM SOLVING).

**software engineer,** *n.* a person who designs computer SOFTWARE. In the development of a conventional software program, the role of a software engineer is similar to that of the KNOWLEDGE ENGINEER.

**Soldier,** *n.* a differential equation solver developed at MIT.

**solution,** *n.* for a STATE SPACE problem, a finite sequence of applications of OPERATORS, which changes an initial state into a GOAL STATE.

**solution graph,** *n.* a subgraph that demonstrates that the start NODE of a SEARCH SPACE or SEARCH TREE can be solved. To demonstrate that the node is solvable (see SOLVABLE NODES), it is sufficient to determine that the node is a TERMINAL NODE; or it is a nonterminal node whose successors are AND nodes that all are solvable; or if its successors are OR nodes, then at least one of them is solvable. Conversely, to demonstrate that the start node is unsolvable, it is necessary to determine that it is a nonterminal node with no successors (see SUCCESSOR NODES); or if its successors have AND nodes, at least one of them is an UNSOLVABLE NODE; or if its successors have OR nodes, all of them are unsolvable.

**solvable node,** *n.* a TERMINAL NODE, or a NODE whose SUCCESSOR NODES are AND nodes that are all solvable, or a node whose successors are OR nodes and at least one of them is solvable.

**S.1,** *abbrev. for* System 1, a KNOWLEDGE REPRESENTATION LANGUAGE for RULE-based representation, which also permits FRAME-based and procedure-oriented representation. It features BACK-CHAINING, built-in CERTAINTY handling, and CONTROL blocks that support procedure-oriented representation and programming methods. Also included are GRAPHICS-oriented DEBUGGING TOOLS for TRACING and breaking during consultations and an EXPLANATION FACILITY. Implemented in INTERLISP, S.1 runs on Xerox 1100 and 1108 WORKSTATIONS. It was developed by Teknowledge.

**SOPHIE,** *n. acronym for* SOPHisticated Instructional Environment, an expert system that teaches students how to troubleshoot electrical circuits. The program demonstrates how to locate a circuit fault by enabling the student to select a fault in a simulated circuit and to proceed through the steps necessary to find the fault. At each step the program asks the student to predict the qualitative behaviour of the test instrument, e.g., whether the measured voltage is correct. When the student makes the error, the program shows the measurement and explains it. For the student's review, the program provides a printed history of the diagnosis session. The circuit simulator in SOPHIE contains a mechanism for modelling and portraying causal fault propagation, i.e., how the failure of one component can cause others to fail. Implemented in INTERLISP and FORTRAN, the latter being used for the circuit simulation package, SOPHIE was developed at Bolt, Beranek, and Newman.

**sort,** *n.* a type, kind, or set. A one-place PREDICATE defines a set or sort. For any one-place predicate P, all individuals X can be sorted into two disjoint groups: Forming one group are OBJECTS that satisfy P, i.e., for which P(X) is true. Forming the other group are those objects that do not satisfy P. Some sorts include other sorts; for example, all men are animals, and all knaves are playing cards.

321

**soundness,** *n.* the measure of a LOGIC system, which states that a logic is sound if it is impossible to prove a false statement.

**SOUP,** *n. acronym for* Semantics Of User Problem, FUNCTION in NOAH that contains KNOWLEDGE about the problem DOMAIN.

**source,** *n.* **1.** a deep case in CASE GRAMMAR that indicates the place from which something moves.
**2.** the language from which the TARGET LANGUAGE is translated.

**Source Rock Advisor,** *n.* an expert system developed by Phillips to assist geologists in the evaluation of the oil potential of rock. M.1 is the development SOFTWARE.

**space in a partitioned network,** *n.* a technique used to represent ASSERTIONS. A typical space asserts the hypothetical (see HYPOTHESIS) existence of physical entities having specific PROPERTIES and participating in specific RELATIONS.

**space–planning task,** *n.* the problem addressed in many PLANNING SYSTEMS concerned with arranging things in a space subject to given CONSTRAINTS that must be satisfied.

**SPADE-O,** *n.* in the CONTEXT of a LOGO-GRAPHICS programming TUTOR, a system which explores the relation between expert KNOWLEDGE and student modelling (see STUDENT MODEL). Since a complete expert module for programming tasks is beyond the state of the art, SPADE-O focuses on providing an instructional programming ENVIRONMENT in which an articulate programming-planning dialogue can take place.

**SPAM,** *n. acronym for* System for Photo interpretation of Airports using MAPS, an expert system that interprets high-resolution airport scenes where the image SEGMENTATION has been performed in advance. The system labels individual regions in the image (e.g., hangars) and interprets the collection of those regions as major functional areas of an airport model. SPAM has three major components: (a) an image/map DATA BASE called MAPS that stores facts about feature existence and location; (b) a set of image processing TOOLS that includes an interactive segmentation system and a linear feature extraction and 3-D junction analysis program; and (c) a RULE-based INFERENCE system that guides scene INTERPRETATION by providing the image processing system with the best next task to perform. KNOWLEDGE of spatial constraints comes from a body of literature on airport planning. Implemented in OPS5, SPAM was developed at Carnegie-Mellon University.

**SPARC,** *n.* a system that attempts to solve a LEARNING PROBLEM that arises in the card game ELEUSIS. Eleusis is a card game in which players attempt to discover a secret RULE invented by the dealer. The secret rule describes a linear sequence of cards. In their turns, each player attempts to extend this sequence by playing additional cards from his or her hand. The dealer gives no information except for indicating whether or not each play is consistent with the secret rule. Players are penalized for incorrect plays by having cards added to their hands. The game ends when a player empties his or her hand.

**spatial differentiation,** *n.* a method for shaping images; it is used to intensify edges. It involves subtracting the second derivative of a function from the function itself. Since an image is represented by discrete PIXELS, the derivative of the picture function at a pixel is approximated by the difference in intensity between adjacent pixels, and the higher order differences from the first-order pixels.

**spatial domain,** *n.* in image processing, the distribution of intensities on the image plane that varies as a function of x and y (compare FREQUENCY DOMAIN).

**SPE,** *abbrev. for* Serum Protein Electrophoresis diagnostic program, an expert system that distinguishes among various causes of inflammatory conditions in a patient (e.g., cirrhosis of the liver or myeloma) by interpreting waveforms (serum protein electrophoresis patterns) from a device called a scanning densitometer. The system makes its interpretations by applying knowledge about how the instrument readings and patient data relate to disease categories. SPE, a FORWARD CHAINING, RULE-BASED SYSTEM, was first implemented in EXPERT and then translated into the assembly language for the Motorola 6809 microprocessor. The program was developed at Rutgers University and has been incorporated into CliniScan, a scanning densitometer marketed by Helena Laboratories.

**specialist,** *n.* **1.** an expert in a narrow problem DOMAIN.

**2.** one of the several expert subsystems that cooperate in a HEARSAY-II ARCHITECTURE.

**specialization,** *n.* a characteristic of a RULE, such as having the ability to contact or restrict the DOMAIN and range of a CONCEPT.

**specialization of fragmentation rules,** *n.* the characteristic of rules of fragmentation in META-DENDRAL. The function IN-TSUM provides accounting for a single fragmentation process in the CONTEXT of a single molecule.

**specification of programs,** see PROGRAM SPECIFICATION.

**speech act,** *n.* a theory of NATURAL LANGUAGE that focuses on the PRAGMATICS of the communicative process; in particular, how intentions are communicated to a reader or listener.

**speech recognition,** *n.* recognition by a computer of spoken words or sentences.

**speech signal,** *n.* the input to a SPEECH UNDERSTANDING system.

**speech understanding,** *n.* the use of ARTIFICIAL INTELLIGENCE methods to process and interpret audio signals representing human speech.

**SPEECHLIS,** *n.* a speech system developed by BBN under contract from ARPA. It was succeeded by HWIM.

**spelling graph,** *n.* a technique for representing the different pronunciations possible for a word in the SRI/SDC speech understanding system (see SRI/SDC SPEECH SYSTEM).

**SPERIL-I,** *n.* an expert system that uses the DOMAIN KNOWLEDGE of civil engineers to perform structural damage assessments of existing structures subjected to earthquake excitation. It considers relations among such factors as structural damping, stiffness, creep, and buckling. The program takes as input accelerator and visual inspection data in order to determine the damage state of structures. The program is RULE-based using FORWARD CHAINING and uses CERTAINTY FACTORS combined with FUZZY LOGIC to calculate the damage class of a structure. Implemented in the C programming language, SPERIL-I was developed at Purdue University's department of civil engineering.

**SPERIL-II,** *n.* an expert system that uses KNOWLEDGE taken from case studies to evaluate the general safety and damageability of an existing structure. During an earthquake, the program first analyses inspection data and instrument records of structural responses such as acceleration and displacement at certain locations in the structure. It then evaluates the damage-ability of the structure's elements according to relevant safety characteristics incorporated into a structure (e.g., interstorey drift, stiffness, and damping). The program is rule-governed using both FORWARD and BACK-CHAINING. CERTAINTY FACTORS are combined using the Dempster-Shafer ALGORITHM. Implemented in a dialect of PROLOG, SPERIL-II was developed at Purdue University.

**SPEX,** *n. acronym for* Skeletal Planner of EXperiments, an expert system that assists scientists in PLANNING complex laboratory experiments. The scientist describes the objects to be manipulated (i.e., the physical ENVIRONMENT of the experiment and the structure of the experimental OBJECTS) and the system assists in developing a SKELETAL PLAN for achieving the experimental GOAL. The system then refines each abstract step in the PLAN, making the steps more specific by linking them to techniques and objects stored in the system's KNOWLEDGE BASE. Although the system has been tested exclusively in the DOMAIN of molecular biology, it contains no built-in molecular biology mechanisms; thus it could be applied to other problem areas. SPEX is implemented in UNITS, a FRAME-based language for REPRESENTATION. The system was developed at Stanford.

**Spin Pro,** *n.* an expert system developed by Beckman Instruments to help scientists perform ultracentrifugation operations. The program is implemented in GC LISP.

**spreading activation,** *n.* a process by which two NODES in a SEMANTIC NETWORK are activated. In turn, all of the nodes connected to each of the two nodes are activated, forming an expanding sphere of activation around each of the original CONCEPTS.

**SRI CBC,** *abbrev. for* Computer Based Consultant, a system that contains specialized KNOWLEDGE about a particular task DOMAIN and makes that knowledge available to users working in that domain. In particular, the first application was designed to help a novice mechanic work with electromechanical equipment. The GOAL of this research was to build a system that approximates a human consultant in its communication and perceptual skills, as well as in its reasoning and problem-solving skills. The consultant was designed to answer the user's spoken questions and to monitor the user's progress on the task, offering advice and reminders where necessary. To fit the needs of a particular user, it is essential that the system be able to provide advice about the task at several levels of detail. To determine the appropriate level of detail, the CBC must form a model of the user, monitor performance as the user executes the task, and update internal models (see MODEL BUILDING) to reflect the current state of the task ENVIRONMENT.

**SRI Vision Module,** *n.* a MACHINE-VISION system developed by SRI International. The techniques include connectivity analysis with RUN-LENGTH coding, numerical shape descriptors, and recognition of parts with a nearest-neighbour method. The principal components of the vision module are a solid-state TV camera with 128x128 resolution, an interference unit for digitizing the video signal, and an LSI-11/2 micro-computer. The system is a package of useful programs with all necessary hardware for many visual sensing and inspection tasks.

**SRI/SDC Speech System,** *n.* an ARPA speech understanding project undertaken jointly by SRI International and Systems Development Corporation (SDC). The low-end portions of the system (SIGNAL PROCESSING, acoustics, and PHONETICS) were developed at SDC from earlier work done there on SPEECH RECOGNITION systems. SRI provided the top-end of the system (PARSING, SYNTAX, SEMANTICS, PRAGMATICS, and discourse-analysis). The SRI speech understanding research extended earlier work in NATURAL LANGUAGE UNDERSTANDING and KNOWLEDGE REPRESENTATION. The top-end system was developed and tested with simulated output from the SDC bottom-end. The important features of the SRI speech under-standing research included concern with the nature of real man-machine discourse, a LANGUAGE DEFINITION SYSTEM for specifying the input language to be understood, techniques for focusing the system's attention on certain aspects of the dialogue (see DIALOGUE MANAGEMENT), top-down process control stressing phrase-level hypothesizing, knowledge representation using partitioned SEMANTIC NETWORKS, and experimental evaluation of system design parameters.

**SRL,** *abbrev. for* Schema Representation Language, a KNOW-

LEDGE ENGINEERING language for FRAME-based REPRESENTATION. It features automatic and user-definable INHERITANCE relationships and multiple CONTEXTS. Users select a set of PRIMITIVES to define relations and their inheritance SEMANTICS, including SEARCH specification parameters to modify the inheritance search procedure. Each frame can be associated with a metalevel of knowledge (see METAKNOWLEDGE) about how SRL uses its DOMAIN KNOWLEDGE. The multiple contexts permit revision management of models and REASONING in alternative worlds. A dialect of SRL, SRL/1.5, implemented in FRANZ LISP, runs on a DEC VAX under UNIX. SRL was developed at the Robotics Institute of Carnegie-Mellon University.

**SRL+,** *abbrev. for* Schema Representation Language +, a KNOWLEDGE ENGINEERING language for FRAME-based REPRESENTATION, which also permits LOGIC-based, RULE-based, and OBJECT-oriented representation. It features user-definable INHERITANCE RELATIONS, PROCEDURAL ATTACHMENT, an AGENDA mechanism, a discrete SIMULATION language, and a user-definable error (see ERROR (IN TRAINING INSTANCES)) handling facility. SRL+ supplies a user INTERFACE based on the PLUME NATURAL LANGUAGE parser together with an embedded DATA BASE management system. The SRL+ ENVIRONMENT also permits two-dimensional GRAPHICS and business graphics. Implemented in COMMON LISP and FRANZ LISP, SRL+ runs on Carnegie Group workstations, DEC VAX's, and Symbolics 3600 workstations. It was developed by the Carnegie Group.

**SSL,** *n.* a high-level language used to specify abstract relations in PROTOSYSTEM.

**stability of the environment,** *n.* a factor in the development of LEARNING SYSTEMS. In particular, in a rapidly changing ENVIRONMENT, ROTE LEARNING is not very helpful or effective. One important assumption underlying rote learning is that information stored at one time will still be valid later. If, however, the information changes frequently, this assumption can be violated. A rote learning system must be able to detect, in a manner which makes stored information invalid, when the world has changed. This is an instance of the FRAME PROBLEM.

**stack frame,** *n.* a construct that is used to represent a process.

It can contain the process state and links indicating from where control was passed and where to obtain the VALUES of the free VARIABLES.

**start symbol,** *n.* typically denoted <SENTENCE> or S, the distinguished nonterminal SYMBOL in a TREE or GRAPH. Applying sequences of productions in order to derive the set of strings of TERMINAL SYMBOLS from the start symbol is called the language generated by the GRAMMAR.

**starting state,** *n.* the first STATE examined by a problem-solver (see PROBLEM-SOLVING).

**state,** *n.* a data structure in a STATE-SPACE REPRESENTATION, which gives a description of the problem at a particular point in the SEARCH process.

**state description compiler,** *n.* a program that performs PROGRAM SYNTHESIS from examples. The program being synthesized is defined by specifying input/output conditions on the memory cells that it affects. The difference between the current state and the desired state is looked up in a table that specifies which OPERATORS to apply in order to transform appropriately the contents of the cells.

**state of the world,** *n.* the structure of a problem DOMAIN at a given time in the execution of a program.

**state space,** see SEARCH SPACE.

**state–space representation,** *n.* a PROBLEM-SOLVING program in which a set of OPERATORS is applied sequentially to the problem in its INITIAL STATE(s), thereby transforming it so that it is consistent with the GOAL STATE(s). This FORWARD REASONING system can also be thought of as a directed GRAPH whose NODES are states and whose arcs are operators.

**state–space search,** *n.* a formalism developed for PROBLEM-SOLVING and game-playing programs. As perhaps the earliest representation formalism used extensively in AI, the SEARCH SPACE is not a REPRESENTATION of KNOWLEDGE per se; it represents the structure of a problem in terms of the alternatives available at each possible STATE of the problem. An example is the problem where alternative moves are available on each turn of a game. The search proceeds from a given STATE in a problem, and all possible subsequent states are determined with a small set of rules called TRANSITION OPERATORS (or LEGAL-MOVE GENERATORS in game-playing programs). For example, in the game of chess, the original state is the board position at the beginning of the game. The legal-move generators within the program correspond to the RULES for moving each piece. For all the subsequent states of the game, that is, the board configurations after each of White's possible first moves, the legal move generators can supply a move. Similarly, all possible states can be generated after Black's first move.

**static evaluation function,** *n.* a FUNCTION that assigns a VALUE to the TIP NODES of a partial SEARCH TREE in order to determine the most valuable OPERATOR or best move. In a game, the function does not usually estimate the distance between the current state (position) and the GOAL, but rather compares the features of the position with features that are known to be advantageous for the program.

**statistical learning algorithm,** *n.* the use of statistics in learning by example. In particular, in PATTERN RECOGNITION, and sometimes in CONTROL, it is possible to view the unknown system as making a decision to assign the input, x, to one class, y, out of m classes. By defining a loss function that penalizes incorrect decisions (i.e., decisions in which $\bar{y}$ differs from y), a minimum-average-loss Bayes classifier can be used to model the unknown system. The problem of identifying the unknown system then reduces to the problem of estimating a set of parameters for certain probability density functions.

**stative predicate,** *n.* one of four classes of PREDICATES recognized in the LNR MEMOD system. This type of predicate indicates that a STATE OF THE WORLD holds over some time period. LOC, for example, is a stative predicate incorporated in the surface verb 'locate'.

**status of hypothesis,** *n.* a CONFIDENCE FACTOR for a NODE in a CASNET causal net. It is derived from a diagnostic session, beginning with the program's asking the user, a physician, a series of questions about the patient. The physician answers with VALUES for any tests, signs, and symptoms, or he answers UNKNOWN. These values, together with the confidences (see CONFIDENCE FACTOR) associated with the tests and the weights associated with the causal arcs, are used to compute the status.

**STEAMER,** *n.* an expert system that uses a mathematical simulation of a steam propulsion plant together with a graphical INTERFACE displaying animated colour diagrams of plant subsystems to instruct Navy propulsion students in the operation of a steam propulsion plant for a 1078–class frigate. The program monitors the student's performance in executing the boiler light–off procedure for the plant. It acknowledges appropriate actions the student takes and corrects inappropriate actions. Students manipulate simulated components, including valves, switches, and pumps, and then observe the effect of their actions on plant parameters such as changes in pressure, temperature, and flow. The program uses an OBJECT-oriented representation scheme supported by ZETALISP'S FLAVORS. Implemented in ZETALISP, STEAMER was developed by the Naval Personal Research and Development Center in co-operation with Bolt, Baranck and Newman.

**step edge,** *n.* the ideal form of the change in intensity across an edge profile. An ideal step edge profile is illustrated below.

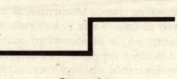

**Step edge**

**stereo vision,** *n.* the use of triangulation in IMAGE UNDER-STANDING. In image understanding, a central problem is to recover the three-dimensional form of an OBJECT that produced a two-dimensional image. One approach to the problem is to measure quantitatively the distance from a camera to each point of interest in a scene. If views of the same object from two different positions are available, one can measure the distance from camera to object by triangulation. This technique is known as stereo or binocular VISION; it is a primary source of information for humans about three-dimensional objects in their ENVIRONMENT.

**stereotype,** *n.* a FRAME-like structure. For example, it is used in PREFERENCE SEMANTICS to indicate the typical constructions that a word can be used in. This is implemented in a MACHINE TRANSLATION system to choose translational equivalents.

**stimulus frame,** *n.* a FRAME in the HEARSAY BLACKBOARD PARADIGM. In HEARSAY, each KNOWLEDGE SOURCE looks at HYPOTHESES posted on the BLACKBOARD on one level, called its stimulus frame, and then posts hypotheses on one or more other levels, possibly the same one, the RESPONSE FRAME.

**stimulus generalization,** *n.* a characteristic of paired–associate learning whereby overt errors in recall are attributable to similar stimuli being confused and their responses becoming interchanged.

**stochastic automaton,** *n.* an automaton that is a MODEL of LEARNING, having a random transition matrix for each possible input SYMBOL. Reinforcement techniques are then applied to adjust the transition probabilities.

**stochastic learning model,** *n.* a MODEL that models the probability that a student will give a specific response to a stimulus. In general, knowing the probability of a response has little diagnostic power. It is not the same as knowing what a student understands. Mathematical stochastic learning models were used in some early FRAME-ORIENTED CAI systems.

**storage allocation,** *n.* the allocation of space to data storage. The two contrasting types of allocation are static and dynamic. In the former, each VARIABLE or ARRAY has a fixed amount of storage reserved for it before the program is executed. In the latter, for example in LISP, list structures are allowed to grow unpredictably.

**Storage System Test,** *n.* an expert system developed at IBM for managing final manufacturing tests for storage systems. E.S. Dev. Env/VM is the development software.

**store–versus–compute trade–off,** *n.* a consideration made in deciding whether to store or compute KNOWLEDGE. In ROTE LEARNING it is important that processing does not decrease the efficiency of the system, since the primary GOAL of rote learn-ing is to improve the overall performance of the system. For example, it is conceivable that the cost of storing and retriev-ing the memorized information is greater than the cost of re-computing it. This is certainly the case with the multiplication of two numbers. All computers recompute the product of two numbers rather than store a large multiplication table. There are two basic approaches to the store-versus-compute trade-off. One is to decide at the time the information is first available whether or not it should be stored for later use. A cost-benefit analysis can be performed that weighs the amount of storage space consumed by the information and the cost of re-computing it against the likelihood that the information will be needed in the future. A second approach is to go ahead and store the information and later decide whether or not to forget it. This procedure, called SELECTIVE FORGETTING, allows the system to determine empirically which items of information are most frequently reused.

**story grammar,** *n*. a GRAMMAR that refers to the structure of a story. Story grammars that are SYNTACTIC in nature describe a story as a collection of parts, such as setting, characters, GOAL introduction, and PLANS. In such story grammars, the story parts are determined by their sequential position in the story rather than by their meaning. In the more semantic orientations there is an underlying semantic representation of each phrase in a story that is based on some KNOWLEDGE representation FORMALISM. Among such formalisms are SCRIPTS, plans, goals, and THEMES.

**story understanding,** *n*. a task in NATURAL LANGUAGE processing that focuses on the SEMANTIC INTERPRETATION of long text. An example of a system that focuses on this task is SAM.

**strategy for control,** see CONTROL STRATEGY.

**strategy space,** *n*. the top layer of MOLGEN, used for PLAN-NING strategy. The strategy space includes four very general OPERATORS that decide planning strategy. These are FOCUS and RESUME, which together propose new planning steps and reactivate old ones that have been put on a wait list, and GUESS and UNDO, which make planning decisions heuristically (see HEURISTIC) when there is not sufficient information to focus on or to resume.

**stress,** *n*. the comparative increase in force assigned to a syllable needed to be recognizable in a SPEECH UNDERSTANDING system.

**STRIPS,** *n. acronym for* Stanford Research Institute Problem Solver, a STATE-SPACE REPRESENTATION program that searches for a PLAN (a sequence of OPERATORS) that will enable a robot to achieve a GOAL within a controlled ENVIRONMENT. It is a PROBLEM-SOLVING METHOD designed to solve the PLANNING problems faced by a robot involved with rearranging objects and navigating in a cluttered environment. In the case of representing the large number of facts concerning the positions of the robot, objects, open spaces etc., simpler methods commonly used for solving puzzles or games are not adequate. STRIPS uses the first-order PREDICATE CALCULUS as a REPRESENTATION scheme. The program operates by seeking a MATCH between one of the world models stored in the DATA BASE and a given GOAL.

**STRIPS assumption,** *n.* the assumption that performed actions change none of a program's BELIEFS about the world except those explicitly listed in the description of an action. For example, a description of a robot's action of moving from one location to another would list only changes in beliefs about the robot's position. When the robot moves, the STRIPS assumption DEFAULT leaves its belief about world geography intact.

**STROBE,** *n.* a programming language for OBJECT-oriented representation that augments the INTERLISP environment. STROBE permits structured objects in INTERLISP much the way FLAVORS does for ZETALISP. The language features multiple resident KNOWLEDGE BASES, support for generalization HIERARCHIES, a flexible PROPERTY INHERITANCE mechanism, PROCEDURAL ATTACHMENT, and indirect procedure invocation. STROBE also permits nonobject NODES in its knowledge base, such as S-EXPRESSIONS, LISP functions, bit maps, and ARRAYS. Implemented in INTERLISP, STROBE was developed by Schlumberger-Doll Research.

**structural description,** see STRUCTURAL LEARNING.

**structural learning,** *n.* a form of learning used primarily in situations in which the OBJECTS to be classified have important substructure. Parametric lineardiscriminant approaches (see LINEAR DISCRIMINANT FEATURES) can represent only the global features of objects. However, by employing PATTERN GRAPHS and GRAMMARS, important substructures, such as the pen strokes that make up a character and the PHONEMES that make up a spoken word, can be learned.

**structural presentation,** *n.* a technique employed by PATTERN

RECOGNITION researchers in order to aid GRAMMATICAL INFERENCE. The program is given some information about the DERIVATION TREE of the sample sentences. The derivation tree presents a move-by-move, or a RULE-by-rule, performance standard along with each TRAINING INSTANCE.

**structured growth,** *n.* a programming style in which an initial program with a simple structure is written, tested, and then allowed to grow by increasing the ambition of its modules. The process continues recursively (see RECURSION) as each module is rewritten. The principle applies to the flexibility of the data handled by the program, the sophistication of deduction (see DEDUCTION, NATURAL), and the number and versatility of the services provided by the system.

**structured programming,** *n.* the practice of organizing a program into modules that can be designed, prepared, and maintained independently of each other. Organizing programs into modules makes them easier to write, check, and modify.

**structure–from–motion theorem,** *n.* a theorem that states that three separate views of four noncoplanar points on a rigid OBJECT uniquely define the three-dimensional structure and motion of the object.

**structure–generation algorithm,** *n.* an ALGORITHM used in CONGEN, an off-shoot of DENDRAL, to generate an exhaustive and non-redundant list of structures.

**STUDENT,** *n.* a PATTERN MATCHING program that solves algebra problems. Written at MIT, STUDENT can read and solve high-school-level algebra word problems.

**student model,** *n.* in ICAI, a model indicating what the student does and does not know.

**stylistics,** *n.* the part of a TEXT GENERATION program focusing on the structure of output sentences based on aesthetic criteria.

**STYRENE,** *n.* an expert system developed for Badger (LMI) for simulating (see SIMULATION) the manufacture of styrene. PICON is the development software.

**subgoal** *n.* part of a SEARCH GRAPH representing a subproblem. If a subgoal can be reached in a search graph, a recurrence of it elsewhere in the graph means that it may not have to be recomputed. It may also serve as a PARTIAL SOLUTION to a larger problem which cannot be solved.

**subgoaling,** *n.* the division of a task into smaller GOALS. In many planning systems using a backward SEARCH of the space that is defined by the available OPERATORS, a goal is split into SUBGOALS, and then the system recursively tries to satisfy those subgoals. A major problem with this method is that the subgoals may be independent. To achieve subgoal G1 it may be necessary to apply an operator that makes it impossible to achieve subgoal G2.

**substitution,** *n.* a RULE of INFERENCE in which the replacement of a VARIABLE by an expression takes place in all its occurrences throughout the THEOREM. For example, substituting the expression p V q for the variable p transforms:

$$p \supset (q \lor p)$$

into

$$(p \lor q) \supset [q \lor (p \lor q)]$$

(Compare REPLACEMENT).

**substitution instance,** *n.* the particular SUBSTITUTION used in a UNIFICATION.

**successor node,** *n.* in a SEARCH TREE, a new state generated from the initial state by the application of a single OPERATOR. (See FIXED ORDERING OF SUCCESSOR NODES.)

**sum cost,** see COST.

**summarization,** *n.* a set of procedures in EXCHECK that analyses a proof (see PROOF THEORY) into parts and isolates the mathematically important steps. The program keeps track of what is to be established at each point, which terms are relevant, and how the current part fits into the whole structure.

**support environment,** *n.* the facilities, associated with an EXPERT SYSTEM-building TOOL, that help users interact with the expert system. Examples of these aids include sophisticated DEBUGGING aids, editing programs, and advanced graphic devices.

**support hypothesis,** *n.* in IMAGE UNDERSTANDING, to calculate depth, the assumption that each object must be supported in some way, either by another object or by the ground.

**support relation,** *n.* a relation between an object and the object that supports it in a VISION system.

**surface knowledge,** *n.* KNOWLEDGE acquired from experience and used to solve practical problems. Surface knowledge usually involves specific facts and theories about a particular DOMAIN or task and a large number of rules-of-thumb.

**surface structure,** *n.* the structure mapped by the TRANSFORMATIONAL RULES of a GENERATIVE GRAMMAR.

**SWIRL,** *n. acronym for* Simulating Warfare In The ROSS Language, an expert system that uses KNOWLEDGE of SIMULATION analysis abilities and offensive and defensive battle strategies and tactics in order to aid military strategists supplying an air penetration simulation of offensive forces attacking a defensive area. The program provides users with interactive simulations of air battles and an ENVIRONMENT in which to develop and to debug (see DEBUGGING) strategies and tactics. The simulations depict penetrators entering an airspace with a preplanned route and bombing mission. The defensive forces must counter and eliminate the enemy before the enemy can reach its targets. The program displays the animated simulations via a colour graphics output device. An OBJECT-oriented KNOWLEDGE REPRESENTATION scheme permits objects such as offensive penetrators, defensive radars, and SAMs to communicate via the transmission of messages. Implemented in ROSS, SWIRL was developed at the Rand Corporation.

**Switch Diagnoser,** *n.* an expert system developed by Bell Communications Research for troubleshooting telephone switching equipment. S.1 is the development SOFTWARE.

**syllable,** *n.* a basic unit in SPEECH UNDERSTANDING systems. It consists of a vocalic sound preceded and/or followed by one or more consonants.

**syllabus,** *n.* in WUMPUS, the developmental path that a learner takes in acquiring new skills.

**symbol,** *n.* any character string used to represent a label, MNEMONIC, data constant, OBJECT, operation (see OPERATOR), relationship (see RELATION). A string of characters that stands for some real-world concept. A LISP data object used to name a VARIABLE, a functional definition, or a LISP object with PROPERTIES.

**symbol manipulation,** *n.* the fundamental idea of AI that the computer can be used not only to manipulate numbers but also to manipulate arbitrary SYMBOLS.

**symbol-manipulation language,** *n.* a computer language

designed expressly for representing and manipulating complex CONCEPTS, e.g., LISP and PROLOG.

**symbolic algorithm,** *n.* an ALGORITHM for manipulating SYMBOLS. The term is usually used in the context of algebraic manipulation.

**symbolic execution,** *n.* the execution of a program description to see if it can account for a given protocol in AUTOMATIC PROGRAMMING.

**symbolic integration,** *n.* a DOMAIN of AI dealing with the manipulation of symbolic rather than numerical expressions, in particular, expressions representing the problem of integration. Early examples of such programs are SAINT and SIN.

**symbolic reasoning,** *n.* PROBLEM SOLVING based on the application of strategies and HEURISTICS in order to manipulate SYMBOLS representing problem concepts.

**symbolic versus numeric programming,** *n.* the two primary uses of computers. Such tasks as data reduction, DATA BASE management, and word processing are examples of numerical programming. KNOWLEDGE SYSTEMS on the other hand depend on symbolic programming for manipulating strings of SYMBOLS with logical (see LOGIC) rather than numerical OPERATORS.

**SYN,** *abbrev. for* circuit SYNthesis program, an expert system that assists engineers in synthesizing electrical circuits. The engineer inputs partially specified circuit diagrams and CONSTRAINTS on particular circuit components, and the system combines this information with KNOWLEDGE about constraints inherent in the circuit structure to specify the circuit completely, e.g., to fill in the impedance of resistors and voltages of power sources. The system combines constraints by using symbolic (see SYMBOL) algebraic manipulation of the formulae describing the circuit components. The system was developed at MIT.

**SYNCHEM,** *n.* an expert system that uses knowledge about chemical reactions to synthesize complex organic molecules automatically. From a set of given starting molecules, the program creates a PLAN to develop the starting molecule without the aid of USER interaction. Working backward from the target molecule to the starting materials, the program tries to determine which reactions could produce the target molecule and what materials (molecules) would be required in the process. As the process continues, the program establishes a synthesis route from the target to the starting materials. Implemented in PL/1, SYNCHEM is the predecessor of SYNCHEM2 and was developed at the State University of New York at Stony Brook.

**SYNCHEM2,** *n.* an expert system that synthesizes complex organic molecules without assistance or guidance from a chemist. It tries to discover a plausible sequence of organic synthetic reactions that will turn a set of available starting materials into the desired target molecule. SYNCHEM2 uses KNOWLEDGE about chemical reactions to generate a PLAN for creating the target molecule from basic building block molecules. The system attempts to find an optimal synthesis route from the starting materials to target compound by applying HEURISTICS that limit the SEARCH to pathways satisfying the problem CONSTRAINTS. These constraints may include information about toxic reaction conditions and the quality and yield of the desired product. The system is implemented in PL/1. It is the successor to SYNCHEM and was developed at the State University of New York at Stony Brook.

**SYNCOM,** *n.* a COMPILER that translates ALCHEM statements into machine readable form before SECS reads the KNOWLEDGE BASE.

**syntactic,** *adj.* pertaining to the form or structure of a symbolic expression, as opposed to the expression's meaning or significance (see SYMBOL). Refers to the formal pattern of an expression. Contrasts with semantic.

**syntactic analysis,** *n.* recognizing images or structures by a PARSING process as being built up of PRIMITIVE elements.

**syntactic category,** *n.* a non-terminal SYMBOL in the GRAMMAR of language. In NATURAL LANGUAGES, syntactic categories include noun and verb.

**syntactic component,** *n.* the part of a TRANSFORMATIONAL GRAMMAR that generates the SYNTACTIC structure of a language.

**syntactic method,** *n.* an approach in VISION systems that applies GRAMMAR-like constructs to the analysis of scenes. In this method patterns are regarded as sentences in a language defined by a formal grammar.

**syntactic query optimization,** *n.* the optimization of the SYNTACTIC (versus semantic) analysis of a query.

**syntactic symmetry,** *n.* an aspect of geometry THEOREM PROVING systems that is used to reduce the SEARCH needed to find a proof. For example, if $d(X,Y)$ is the distance from x to y, $d(A,B)=d(C,D)$ is obviously symmetric with $d(D,C) = d(A,B)$.

**syntax,** *n.* the RULES of GRAMMAR in any language, including computer languages. A set of rules describing the structure of statements allowed in a computer language. To make grammatical sense, commands and routines must be written in conformity to these rules.

**Syscon,** *n.* an expert system developed at Honeywell for configuring the DPS 90 Mainframe. OPS5 and MACLISP are the development software.

**system identification,** *n.* a method in system theory that attempts to construct a model (see MODEL BUILDING) by observing the system in operation and finding an empirical relationship between the inputs and the outputs.

**SYSTEM-D,** *abbrev. for* SYSTEM for Diagnostic PROBLEM SOLVING, an expert system that uses case-specific and diagnostic DOMAIN KNOWLEDGE of the potential causes of dizziness in order to aid physicians diagnosing a patient complaining of dizziness. The program handles cases where multiple causes of dizziness may be present simultaneously. Physicians respond to the program's prompts, entering their findings and describing any manifestations. Based on the physician's input, the program generates a diagnosis and ranks competing alternative diagnoses. The diagnostic knowledge the program contains is taken from a distribution of various medical specialities corresponding to the numerous potential causes of dizziness. The program uses a FRAME-based KNOWLEDGE REPRESENTATION scheme together with a sequential GENERATE-AND-TEST INFERENCE routine. Implemented in KMS, SYSTEM-D was developed at the University of Maryland.

**systemic grammar,** *n.* a theory within which linguistic structure is studied, as it relates to the FUNCTION or use of language (which is often termed PRAGMATICS). The systemic grammar approach to an account of linguistic structure contrasts with that of TRANSFORMATIONAL GRAMMAR. Transformational grammar has been concerned with the structure of an utterance apart from the intended use of the utterance. According to Halliday, an account of linguistic structure that ignores the functional demands made on language is an account lacking in perspicacity, since it offers no principles for explaining why the structure is organized one way rather than another. In systemic grammar the act of speech is viewed as a simultaneous selection from among a large number of inter-related options. These options represent the 'meaning potential' of the language. If system networks representing these options are suitably combined and developed to enough detail, they provide a way of writing a GENERATIVE GRAMMAR quite distinct from that proposed by transformational grammar (see NETWORK REPRESENTATION). For use in NATURAL LANGUAGE UNDERSTANDING programs in AI, the systemic grammar formalism has been found to be readily adaptable (see, for example, SHRDLU). This model of a grammar has four PRIMITIVE categories:

(a) The units of language, which form a HIERARCHY. In English, these are the sentence, clause, group, word, and morpheme (see MORPHEMICS). The rank of a unit refers to its position in the HIERARCHY.

(b) The structure of units. Each unit is composed of one or more units at the rank below, and each of these components fills a particular role. The English clause, for example, is made up of four groups, which serve as sub-ject, predicator, complement, and adjunct.

(c) The classification of units, as determined by the roles to be filled at the levels above. The classes of English groups, for instance, are the verbal, which serves as a predicator; the nominal, which may be a subject or complement; and the adverbial, which fills the adjunct function.

(d) The system. A system is a list of choices representing the options available to the speaker. Since some sets of choices are available only if other choices have already been made, the relation between systems is shown by combining them into networks, as in the example opposite:

The INTERPRETATION is that each clause is independent or

dependent; if independent, then it is either declarative or interrogative. In general, system networks can be defined for units of any rank, and entry to a system of choices may be made to depend on any Boolean combination of previous choices.

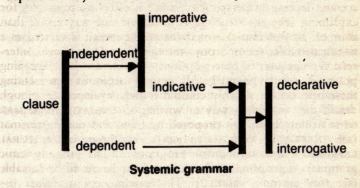

**Systemic grammar**

# T

**table of connections,** *n.* a DOMAIN–dependent data structure in GPS that lists the operators relevant to reducing each difference type in a set of objects.

**tag,** *n.* a data type used for jumping from one process to another in CONNIVER's generalized control structure.

**TALIB,** *n.* an expert system that uses KNOWLEDGE about sub-circuit interconnection characteristics and the propagation of CONSTRAINTS between subcircuits to synthesize automatically integrated circuit layouts for nMOS cells. The program takes as input a description of the circuit components to be laid out on the silicon wafer, their interconnections, and the topological and geometric requirements around the outside boundary of the circuit. Based on the input, the program creates cell layouts that are correct and compact. The program is RULE-based using FORWARD CHAINING. Implemented in OPS5, TALIB was developed at Carnegie-Mellon University.

**tapered forward pruning,** *n.* a SEARCH strategy whereby the number of moves retained during PRUNING is a function of the depth at which they are generated.

**target language,** *n.* **1.** the language in which the AUTOMATIC PROGRAMMING system writes the finished program. Examples of target languages include high-level languages such as GPSS, LISP, and PL/1. A user of an automatic programming system, possibly using examples of what he or she wanted the program to do, would expect the system to produce a program in, for example, LISP that would do the right thing based on the examples used.
**2.** the language to be output in machine translation.

**TATR,** *abbrev. for* tactical Air Target Recommender, an expert system that helps an air force tactical air targeter develop a PLAN for attacking enemy airfields. The system, under the interactive guidance of the targeter, produces a preferential ordering of enemy airfields, determines the target elements to attack on those airfields, and identifies the weapons systems that would be most effective against those target elements. The system projects the effects of implementing the plan over a period of days so the targeter can revise the plan if it fails to meet the attack objectives. TATR is a FORWARD CHAINING, RULE-BASED SYSTEM implemented in ROSIE. It was developed at the Rand Corporation.

**tautology,** *n.* a sentence that is true no matter what PROPOSITIONS are substituted for the sentential constants X, Y, and Z. For example, the sentence:

$$(X \text{ IMPLIES } (Y \text{ AND } Z)) \equiv ((X \text{ IMPLIES } Y) \text{ AND } (X \text{ IMPLIES } Z))$$

expresses a tautology. It states, 'Saying X implies Y and Z is the same as saying that X implies Y and X implies Z'.

**TAXADVISOR,** *n.* an expert system that uses both DOMAIN KNOWLEDGE and general knowledge taken from textbooks to aid attorneys in tax and estate planning for clients with estates larger than $175,000. The program takes as input client data in order to infer actions clients must take to settle their financial profile; including purchases, retirement actions, transfer of wealth, and modifications to gift and will provisions. The program is RULE-based using BACK-CHAINING. Implemented in EMYCIN, TAXADVISOR was developed at the University of Illinois, Champaign–Urbana.

**TAXIS,** *n.* a language for the design of information systems such as DATA BASES. It uses a SEMANTIC NETWORK representation FORMALISM and also applies the principles of data-abstraction and exception handling from programming language research.

**TAXMAN,** *n.* an expert system that assists in the investigation of legal reasoning and legal argumentation using the DOMAIN of corporate tax law. The system provides a framework for representing the legal concepts and a transformation methodology for recognizing the relationships among those concepts. Transformations from the case under scrutiny to related cases create a basis for analysing the legal reasoning and argumentation. The KNOWLEDGE contained in TAXMAN is represented using FRAMES and includes corporate tax cases, tax law, and transformation principles. TAXMAN I originally used a FRAME-like, logical TEMPLATE representational FORMAL-

ISM. Later versions employ a PROTOTYPE-plus-deformation model, describing concepts in terms of their differences from certain prototypical legal concepts. Implemented in AIMDIS, TAXMAN was developed at Rutgers University.

**taxonomic net,** *n.* a network that keeps track of important element–subset RELATIONS among terms in a PARTITIONED SEMANTIC NETWORK.

**taxonomy,** *n.* a hierarchical (see HIERARCHY) classification of OBJECTS.

**Teachable Language Comprehender (TLC),** *n.* a system of NATURAL LANGUAGE UNDERSTANDING based on the SEMANTIC NETWORK REPRESENTATION of KNOWLEDGE.

**teacherless learning,** *m.* an expression used to refer to ICAI learning ENVIRONMENTS.

**team of procedures,** *n.* a set of PROCEDURES that a programmer can specify in QLISP as worth considering anywhere that a pattern-directed procedure invocation might occur (see PATTERN PROCEDURE RETRIEVAL).

**technology transfer,** *n.* in the context of expert systems, the process by which KNOWLEDGE ENGINEERS turn over an expert system to a USER group. Because expert systems require continual updates, the knowledge engineers must train users to maintain a system before it is delivered to the user. In effect, some users must learn how to do knowledge engineering.

**TED,** *n.* a system that functions similarly to LADDER with the exception that the NATURAL LANGUAGE INTERFACE is derived semi-automatically. Instead of requiring extensive programming in order to build the NATURAL LANGUAGE interface, the TED system uses the DATA BASE SCHEMA and a dialogue it conducts with the user; the result of this process is a GRAMMAR similar to the one used by LADDER.

**TEIRESIAS,** *n.* a TOOL for KNOWLEDGE ENGINEERS that helps transfer KNOWLEDGE from a DOMAIN EXPERT to a KNOWLEDGE BASE (named for the blind seer Teiresias in the Greek tragedy, *Oedipus the King*). Within a restricted subset of English, the program interacts with users in order to acquire new rules about a given problem domain. In addition, the program acts as a system-building aid by providing explanations and consistency checking for DEBUGGING the knowledge base. Systems that attain expert-level performance in PROBLEM-SOLVING derive their power from a large store of task-specific knowledge. As a result, the creation and management of large knowledge bases and the development of techniques for the informed use of knowledge are central problems of AI research. TEIRESIAS was written to explore some of the issues involved in these problems. Most expert programs embody the knowledge of one or more experts in a field (e.g., infectious diseases) and are constructed in consultation with these experts. Typically, the computer scientist mediates between the experts and the program he or she is building in order to model the expertise of the expert. The computer scientist's task is difficult and time-consuming because the scientist must learn the basics of the field in order to ask good questions about what the program should actually do. The GOAL of TEIRESIAS is to reduce the role of the human intermediary in this task of knowledge acquisition by assisting in the construction and modification of the system's knowledge base. The human expert communicates, via TEIRESIAS, with the performance program (e.g., MYCIN), so that he or she can discover, with TEIRESIAS's help, what the performance program is doing and why. Via TEIRESIAS, the human expert can 'educate' the program just as he or she would tutor a human novice who makes mistakes. The core of TEIRESIAS's success stems from ideas about how this 'debugging' process is best carried out. TEIRESIAS can be viewed as a learning program, since it incorporates advice from the human expert. Implemented in INTERLISP, TEIRESIAS was developed on the MYCIN project at Stanford University.

**template,** *n.* a PROTOTYPE skeleton that can be used directly to MATCH image characteristics for OBJECT recognition or inspection and SPEECH RECOGNITION.

**term selection,** *n.* a partial solution to the problem of a LEARNING SYSTEM discovering the appropriate terms for representing its acquired KNOWLEDGE. In term selection, a learning program for chess, for example, is provided with a list of 38 possible terms. Its learning task is to select a subset of 16 of these terms to include in the EVALUATION POLYNOMIAL. Using a rather straightforward selection process, the program starts with a random sample of 16 features. For each FEATURE in the polynomial, a count is kept of how many times that feature has had the lowest weight (i.e., the weight nearest zero). This count is incremented after each move by Alpha. When the count for some feature exceeds 32, that feature is removed from the polynomial and replaced by a new term. At all times, 16 features are included in the polynomial, and the remaining 22 features form a reserve queue. New features are selected from the top of the queue, while features removed from the polynomial are placed at the end of the queue. Viewed in the context of credit assignment, such a program assigns blame to features whose weights have values near zero, since those features are making no contribution to the evaluation function.

**terminal node,** *n*. a final leaf NODE emanating from a branch in a TREE or GRAPH REPRESENTATION.

**terminal symbols,** *n*. the SYMBOLS that appear as leaves in a TREE REPRESENTATION, such as the words in a language, e.g., the words in English. These are concatenated into strings called sentences (if the terminals are words). A language is then viewed as a subset of the set of all the strings that can be formed by combining the terminal symbols in all possible ways.

**termination in rule–based deduction systems,** *n*. in forward and backward RULE-based deduction systems, a condition in which there is a symmetric abutment between the NODES of a GOAL GRAPH and those of a fact graph. This symmetric relationship, sometimes called CANCEL, is said to exist between two nodes (n,m) if one is a fact node and the other a goal node and if n and m are labelled by unifiable (see UNIFICATION) literals or n has an outgoing k–connector to a set of successors $\{s_i\}$, such that CANCEL $(s_i,m)$ holds for each member of the set. The graph that demonstrates that the nodes of the goal graph and fact graph cancel each other is called a candidate CANCEL graph and is an actual solution if all the most general unifiers in it are consistent.

**texel,** *n*. a small TEXTURE element that corresponds to a PIXEL. Close parallels can be drawn between SHAPE FROM SHADING and SHAPE FROM TEXTURE. Just as the intensity at a pixel changes with surface orientation, so does the appearance of a texel in the image; its appearance includes its shape and its local density.

**text generation,** *n*. the process of using computers to construct text (phrases, sentences, paragraphs) in a NATURAL LANGUAGE.

**text-based NL system,** *n*. a NATURAL LANGUAGE system that relies on a textual DATA BASE for understanding.

**textual function,** *n*. in SYSTEMIC GRAMMAR, that FUNCTION that reflects the need for coherence in language use (e.g., how a given sentence is related to preceding ones). (See also IDEATIONAL FUNCTION and INTERPERSONAL FUNCTION.)

**texture,** *n*. a local variation in PIXEL VALUES that repeats in a regular or random way across a portion of an image or OBJECT. In images, textures are fine-grained patterns of small elements, arranged with a certain structure. REGIONS of texture appear homogeneous. Texture thus provides important cues for distinguishing objects and natural scenes.

**theme,** *n*. the background information upon which one bases one's predictions that an individual will have a certain GOAL. Themes, in their situation–action quality, are similar to PRODUCTION SYSTEMS.

**theorem,** *n*. a PROPOSITION, or statement, to be proved based on a given set of PREMISES.

**theorem proving,** *n*. the proving or disproving of a THEOREM. This involves both deductive reasoning, which can be formalized by the language of PREDICATE LOGIC, and intuitive leaps, which are based on the specialized knowledge of a system. (See also DETACHMENT.)

**theorem-proving representation,** *n*. an approach to PROBLEM REPRESENTATION that normally uses FORWARD REASONING and applies OPERATORS to conjunctions of OBJECTS in the DATA BASE.

**theory formation,** *n*. an area of AI that centres on understanding how scientists build theories to describe and explain complex phenomena.

**theory of conclusions,** *n*. a theory of DEFAULT reasoning based on classical DECISION THEORY. Classical decision theory analyses how the strength of each of one's HYPOTHESES about the world should be revised with each new evidential fact. The intent of conclusion theory is to avoid the continual re-evaluation of all hypotheses, and instead to accept certain strong hypotheses as conclusions, and to hold these conclusions unless and until the introduction of very strong contrary evidence.

**THINGLAB,** *n.* the CONSTRAINT-resolving extension of the message-passing SMALLTALK.

**THNOT,** *n.* a PRIMITIVE in PLANNER used to specify DEFAULTS. For example, (THNOT PARAPLEGIC (X) ASSUME WALKS (X)), which means unless it can be shown that X is a paraplegic, assume X can walk.

**3-D sketch,** *n.* a level of REPRESENTATION in VISION systems that makes explicit information about OBJECT shapes.

**thresholding,** *n.* **1.** the process of quantizing PIXEL brightness to a small number of different levels. A threshold is a level of brightness at which the quantized image brightness changes.
**2.** a numerical score of a HYPOTHESIS; if it exceeds a certain preset value as defined by the expert who builds the KNOWLEDGE BASE, the hypothesis is believed to be true.

**THYROID MODEL,** *n.* an expert system that combines KNOWLEDGE of RULES of diagnostic reasoning with a TAXONOMY of thyroid function and thyroid pathology in order to help physicians diagnose disorders of the thyroid. The program takes as input an initial set of patient findings; including demographic information, symptoms, and laboratory test results. The program then prompts for any additional data needed for a diagnosis. The program is rule-based using FORWARD CHAINING. An EXPLANATION FACILITY displays the decision rules and the associated certainty factors the program used to arrive at a given HYPOTHESIS. Implemented in EXPERT, THYROID MODEL was developed at Rutgers University.

**tick list,** *n.* a convenient declarative REPRESENTATION used in INTERPLAN; it allows protection violations to be detected.

**tilt,** *vb.* to rotate in the vertical plane.

**time frame,** *n.* in HEARSAY, an indicator of when a sentence unit was hypothesized (see HYPOTHESIS).

**time-of-flight,** *n.* a type of system that measures the time required for a waveform to propagate to an object and reflect back.

**TIMM,** *n. acronym for* The Intelligent Machine Model, a tool for KNOWLEDGE ENGINEERS that helps DOMAIN EXPERTS construct expert systems. The USER first enters a list of all possible decisions the system should make along with the

VALUES of factors the system should consider when arriving at a decision. The program then queries the user for examples of factors and associated values in order to use the examples to infer a set of IF-THEN RULES that capture the reasoning process involved. The program also enables the use of CERTAINTY VALUES for representing probabilistic information. Implemented in FORTRAN, TIMM runs on the VAX 11/780. The program was developed by General Research Corporation.

**TIMM/TUNER,** *n.* an expert system that assists system managers in tuning a VAX/VMS operating system. The program helps to reduce performance problems that arise due to a constantly changing computer environment. System managers respond to queries the program uses to base recommendations about adjusting system parameters or user authorization VALUES, redistributing or reducing user demand, changing user SOFTWARE design, or purchasing new hardware. A RULE-based representation scheme operates within TIMM, a commercial system for automated KNOWLEDGE ACQUISITION. Implemented in TIMM, TIMM/TUNER was developed by General Research Corporation.

**tip node,** *n.* in solution GRAPHS, any NODE that does not yet have SUCCESSOR NODES.

**TITAN,** *n.* an expert system developed for Radian to assist technicians in troubleshooting Texas Instrument's 990 minicomputer. RULEMASTER is the development software.

**TOGA,** *n.* an expert system developed at Radian for diagnosing faults in large utility transformers, based on gas chromatograhic analysis of insulating oil. RULEMASTER is the development software.

**token,** see INSTANCE.

**T.1,** *n.* a TOOL in the form of a tutorial package that introduces basic KNOWLEDGE ENGINEERING CONCEPTS to technical professionals and managers. It supplies USERS with videotape lectures, laboratory exercises, reading materials, and SOFTWARE that demonstrates knowledge engineering concepts. The demonstration software incorporates a modified version of the Teknowledge M.1 language. T.1 runs on IBM PCs under DOS 2.0 and was developed by Teknowledge.

**TOME,** *n. acronym for* Table Of Multiple Effects, a table in

NOAH that summarizes changes at each level in a PROCEDUR-
AL NET. It contains an entry for every PROPOSITION asserted or
derived by more than one NODE at that level in the net.
TOMEs are used to check for interactions between GOALS.

**tool,** *n*. **1.** a short-hand notation for EXPERT-SYSTEM-BUILDING
TOOL. As a computer SOFTWARE package, tools are designed to
simplify the effort involved in building an expert system.
Most often, tools contain an INFERENCE ENGINE, various USER
INTERFACE and KNOWLEDGE ACQUISITION aids, and lack a
KNOWLEDGE BASE. Expert system tools tend to incorporate restrictions that make the tools easy to use for certain purposes
and difficult or impossible to use for other purposes. Thus,
when selecting a tool for use in building a particular expert
system, care must be taken to select an appropriate tool.
Defined more broadly, a tool is a SHELL allowing users to
rapidly develop a system that contains specific data. In this
sense, an electronic spreadsheet program is a tool. By entering
financial data to the spreadsheet, the user creates a system that
will perform specific projections. A KNOWLEDGE ENGINEER, in
the same manner, uses a tool to create an expert system that
will supply advice about a specific type of problem.
**2.** something mounted on the end of a robot arm; for
example, a hand, a simple gripper, or an arc welding torch.

**tool builder,** *n*. the individual who designs and builds the
EXPERT-SYSTEM-BUILDING TOOL.

**top-down,** see BACKWARD REASONING.

**top-down parser,** *n*. a parser that begins by looking at the
RULES for the desired top-level structure (sentence, clause, etc.)
(see PARSING). Then it looks up rules for the constituents of
the top-level structure and progresses until a complete sentence
structure is built up. If the sentence it builds matches the input
data, the parse is successfully completed; otherwise, it starts
back at the top again, and generates another sentence
structure.

**TORUS,** *n*. a system based on a SEMANTIC NETWORK RE-
PRESENTATION used to provide NATURAL LANGUAGE access to a
DATA BASE MANAGEMENT SYSTEM.

**totally dependent, uniform game tree,** *n*. a TREE that
demonstrates that every move in a game is critical. That is,
one of the multiple successors of a NODE will always produce

descendants whose value is greater than the descendants of the other successors. See SUCCESSOR NODE.

**Tower Of Hanoi,** *n.* a recursive PROBLEM SOLVING puzzle. A tower is formed by transferring a stack of disks on a peg onto another peg, for example, from peg A onto peg B, moving only one disk at a time and never placing a larger disk on top of a smaller one. In the figure below, peg C may be used for temporary storage.

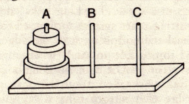

**Tower Of Hanoi**

A recursive SOLUTION to the problem begins with noticing that to move a tower of just two disks, one would move the smaller disk from peg A to peg C, and then move the big disk from peg A to peg B. The general problem of moving a tower of N disks can now be reduced to three steps as shown in the figure above: Transfer the subtower of disks 1 through N - 1 from peg A to peg C, move the biggest disk, N, from peg A to peg B, and then transfer the subtower back from peg C to peg B.

**toy problem,** *n.* an artificial problem, such as a game, or an unrealistic adaptation of a complex problem.

**TQA,** *n.* a NATURAL LANGUAGE INTERFACE to DATA BASES.

**TQMSTUNE,** *abbrev. for* Triple-Quadrupole Mass Spectrometer TUNEr, an expert system that interprets signal data from a triple quadrupole mass spectrometer (TQMS) in order to fine-tune the instrument. Analysing signal data such as spectral peak ratios, widths, and shapes, the program applies KNOWLEDGE about how varying the TQM's instrument control settings can affect sensitivity and spectral configurations. TQMSTUNE was developed by Intellicorp using KEE.

**trace,** *n.* **1.** the history of RULES and VARIABLE VALUES during the execution of a program.
**2.** scanning path of the beam in a raster display.

**trace interval,** *n.* the time during which a visible raster line is scanned.

**tracing facility,** *n.* a mechanism in a programming or KNOWLEDGE ENGINEERING language that can display the RULES or subroutines executed, including the VALUES of VARIABLES used.

**tracking,** *n.* a method of processing sequences of images in real time in order to derive a description of the motion of one or more OBJECTS in a scene. Tracking links edges into a larger contour by visiting the neighbouring elements one after another. A typical method is to scan the edge–element image left to right and top to bottom and, when an edge element is found, check whether any of its eight neighbours are edge elements. If one is, mark it and move to it, and repeat the process. The edge elements that have been visited must be marked as such, so that no duplicate tracking occurs. If two or more neighbours are edge elements, remember their positions in a stack as branch points. If there is no neighbouring edge element, the present position is the terminal of a contour, and processing continues from the last branch point. If there are no more branch points, the image is scanned for another starting point. This process will eventually visit all edge elements.

**Train Braking Advisor,** *n.* an expert system developed by Hitachi to control locomotive braking for accuracy and comfort.

**Train Travel Advisor,** *n.* an expert system developed by Thomas Cook that helps travel agents plan train itineraries. ESI Prolog-2 is the development SOFTWARE.

**training instance,** *n.* an example used by a LEARNING SYSTEM. For example, in META-DENDRAL, the rules to be learned constitute a REPRESENTATION of the relevant fragmentations in the mass spectrometer. In order to learn rules, META-DENDRAL is presented with many examples of actual input-output pairs from the mass spectrometer. Each pair represents a molecular GRAPH structure, together with a single data point from the mass spectrum for that structure. Typically, the program starts with a training set of 6 to 10 related molecules and their associated spectra, each containing 50 to 150 data points, which are peaks marking the masses of recorded fragments (and the relative abundance of fragments at those masses). These are the training instances.

**transfer of expertise,** *n.* the acquisition of KNOWLEDGE from human experts by a system and the explanation of REASONING to human users.

**transform,** *n.* PRODUCTION RULES of the condition-action form. The left-hand side of each RULE represents a sub-structure pattern to be matched in the target structure or intermediate structure and the right-hand side is a description of precursors that will produce the GOAL structure under specified reaction conditions.

**transformation, obligatory and optional,** see OBLIGATORY TRANSFORMATION and OPTIONAL TRANSFORMATION.

**transformation of programs,** see AUTOMATIC PROGRAMMING.

**transformational grammar,** *n.* a term that refers to a theory of GRAMMAR. The theory proposes that an utterance denotes the surface manifestation of a deeper structure, which represents the meaning of the sentence (see SURFACE STRUCTURE). This 'deep structure' of a sentence can undergo a variety of 'transformations' of form (word order, endings, etc.) on its way to a surface structure, and still retain its essential meaning. (See also TYPE O GRAMMAR.)

**transformational rule,** *n.* a rule of a GENERATIVE GRAMMAR that rearranges the strings and adds or deletes morphemes in order to form REPRESENTATIONS of the full variety of sentences that are generable from some input TREE representation of a sentence.

**TRANSISTOR SIZING SYSTEM,** *n.* an expert system that uses KNOWLEDGE of the relationship between speed and power for nMOS circuits in order to perform part of the refinement process from a schematic circuit diagram to an nMOS layout. The program assists circuit designers designing integrated circuits by first considering the designer's GOALS of speed and power consumption. It then analyses the circuit to determine critical paths with respect to delay and produces a trade-off curve based on simple delay models. The designer finally selects a goal point on the curve, and the program re-sizes the transistors according to the designated goal. The KNOWLEDGE REPRESENTATION scheme is both FRAME-based and OBJECT-oriented. Implemented in LOOPS, the program operates within the PALLADIO ENVIRONMENT. TRANSISTOR SIZING SYSTEM was developed at Stanford University.

**transition operator,** see LEGAL-MOVE GENERATOR.

**transition tree grammar,** *n*. a simplified form of the AUGMENTED TRANSITION NETWORK used in LIFER.

**transitivity system,** *n*. that part of a SYSTEMIC GRAMMAR that focuses on the relations of ACTORS, GOALS, etc., and PREDICATES.

**transparency,** *n*. a characteristic of the performance element of a LEARNING SYSTEM. For the learning element to assign credit or blame to individual rules in the KNOWLEDGE BASE, it is useful for the learning element to have access to the internal actions of the performance element. If the learning element is given a TRACE of all the moves that were considered by the performance element (rather than only those moves that were actually chosen), the CREDIT-ASSIGNMENT PROBLEM becomes easier to solve.

**tree,** *n*. a GRAPH in which there is exactly one path between any two distinct NODES.

**tree structure,** *n*. the organization of information in the form of a connected GRAPH, wherein each NODE can branch into other nodes deeper in the structure.

**triangle table,** *n*. in STRIPS, a data structure that stores a PLAN (a sequence of OPERATORS) and represents the preconditions for and effects of each operator in the plan.

**triangulation,** *n*. in STEREO VISION, a process that finds corresponding points in two images and infers (see INFERENCE) lines extending from these points, through the centres of their respective lenses, and out into space to where the lines intersect. The intersecting lines and the baseline between the two lenses constitute a triangle.

**trigger,** see PROCEDURAL ATTACHMENT.

**trihedral world,** *n*. a world that is made up of objects that have exactly three surfaces meeting at any vertex (see VERTEX TYPE). Many important issues for VISION research have first been proposed and explored in the context of a trihedral blocks world, because they are simplified by explicit assumptions about the physical structure of this world.

**trivial language,** *n*. the most specific language that contains all of the strings in a language.

**Trouble Shooting Aid for F6502,** *n.* an expert system developed by Textronix for assisting technicians in diagnosing and repairing an F6502 instrument. The development SOFTWARE is Detektr (Tektronix's electronics troubleshooting tool).

**truth maintenance,** *n.* the task of preserving consistent BELIEFS in a REASONING system whose beliefs change over time.

**Truth Maintenance System (TMS),** *n.* a system used to record justifications for ASSERTIONS for purposes such as generating explanations and to track down the underlying assumptions of assertions. In RUP, every justification is a disjunctive clause of sentential (propositional) ATOMS and any such clause can be treated as a JUSTIFICATION. RUP's TMS takes as input a set of such propositional clauses (see PROPOSITION) and performs propositional CONSTRAINT propagation to ensure that every assertion with a valid justification is in fact believed by the system and therefore ensuring a deduction invariant. In addition, RUP's TMS ensures that for every propositional clause whose atoms are false, there is an entry on a contradiction queue.

**truth value,** *n.* one of the two possible VALUES – true or false – associated with a PROPOSITION in LOGIC.

**TURBOMATIC,** *n.* an expert system developed at Radian for aiding in diagnosis of vibration problems in large turbomachinery. RULEMASTER is the development software.

**Turing machine,** *n.* a universal, nonnumerical model of computation. It can recognize the language generated by a TYPE O GRAMMAR.

**turtle geometry,** *n.* a type of geometry that starts from the notion of curvature instead of points and straight lines (Euclidean geometry) or coordinate systems (analytic geometry) and results in a geometry enabling one to gain relatively quickly an intuitive notion of such important underlying ideas as number theory and topology.

**tutor,** *n.* **1.** the teaching component of an ICAI system.
**2.** a module in the WUMPUS ICAI system that uses explanation RULES to select the appropriate topic and choose the form of EXPLANATION. These rules include rules of simplification and of rhetoric.

**tutorial dialogue,** see DIALOGUE MANAGEMENT.

**tutorial goal,** *n.* a GOAL for a tutorial dialogue (see DIALOGUE MANAGEMENT) such as refining a student's causal structure strategy with the most important factors and gradually incorporating more subtle factors.

**tutorial program,** *n.* an AI program for teaching.

**tutorial rule,** *n.* a RULE used in a tutorial, such as the dialogue for presenting diagnostic rules and for constructing a student model.

**tutoring module,** *n.* the component of an ICAI program that selects the strategies for presenting tutorial information to a student.

**tutoring strategy,** *n.* in ICAI, a strategy that specifies how the system presents material to the student.

**TWIRL,** *n. acronym for* Tactical Warfare In the ROSS Language, an expert system that uses KNOWLEDGE of offensive and defensive battle tactics to provide military tacticians with interactive SIMULATIONS of ground combat engagements between two opposing military forces. The program uses a hasty river-crossing simulation as a test for exploring issues in command, control, communications countermeasures, electronic warfare, and electronic combat. TWIRL users can also develop and debug (see DEBUGGING) military tactics within an ENVIRONMENT including a colour graphics facility that produces an animated display of the simulation. The program is OBJECT-oriented using RULES to define the behaviour of objects. Implemented in ROSS, TWIRL was developed at the Rand Corporation.

**2½-D sketch,** *n.* a level of REPRESENTATION in image analysis that makes information about the surface explicit.

**two-space view,** *n.* a way of LEARNING from examples as a simultaneous, cooperative SEARCH of the INSTANCE SPACE and the RULE SPACE.

**TYPE,** *n.* in INTERNIST, a measure of how expensive it is to test for a manifestation, in terms of both financial cost and physical risk to the patient. TYPE is used to order the questions asked by the consultation program. In particular, questions about less expensive manifestations are asked first.

**type O grammar,** *n.* a set of productions over a given vocabulary of SYMBOLS with no restrictions on the form of the productions. It has been demonstrated that a language can be generated by a type O grammar if and only if it can be recognized by a TURING MACHINE. A TRANSFORMATIONAL GRAMMAR is an example.

**type 1 grammar,** *n.* a type of GRAMMAR in which the form of the REWRITE RULES is restricted so that, for each production X → Y of the grammar, the right-hand side, Y, contains at least as many symbols as the left-hand side, X. Type 1 grammars are also called CONTEXT-SENSITIVE GRAMMARS. An alternate definition for context-sensitive grammars is that the productions must be of the form: uXv → uYv.

**type 2 grammar,** *n.* a GRAMMAR in which each production must have only a single nonterminal symbol on its left-hand side. Also called CONTEXT-FREE GRAMMAR.

**type 3 grammar,** *n.* a GRAMMAR in which every production is of the form:

$$X \rightarrow aY \text{ or } X \rightarrow a,$$

where X and Y are single variables and a is a single terminal. Also called REGULAR GRAMMAR.

# U

**uncertainty,** *n.* in the context of expert systems, uncertainty refers to a VALUE of a piece of KNOWLEDGE that cannot be determined during a consultation. Most expert systems can accommodate uncertainty. They allow a user to indicate if he or she does not know the answer. In the event the user does not know the answer, the system either relies on DEFAULT values or uses its other rules in order to try to establish the value by other means.

**understandability of a knowledge representation,** *n.* that feature of a KNOWLEDGE REPRESENTATION scheme that allows a human user to easily comprehend what the system is trying to capture.

**unification,** *n.* in RESOLUTION, a process for determining if two expressions of the PREDICATE CALCULUS will match. In predicate calculus, terms of an expression may be of one of three forms: a constant, a VARIABLE, or a FUNCTION. The function consists of a function symbol applied to a number of terms. A SUBSTITUTION is a set of ordered pairs in which the first element of each pair is a term and the second element is a variable. When such a substitution is applied to a FORMULA, a matching term (see MATCH) replaces each variable appearing in the set of ordered pairs. Two expressions are unifiable (see UNIFICATION) if a substitution (the unifier) serves to make both expressions identical when the substitution is applied. A unification ALGORITHM determines if a given set of expressions are unifiable, and, if they are unifiable, proceeds to find a unifying substitution. In resolution-based systems, it is common to specify that the substitution that is to unify two expressions is the most general such substitution in order that the expressions lose as little generality as is necessary to make the resolution occur.

**uniform game tree,** *n.* a GAME TREE in which every TIP NODE has the same depth and the same number of SUCCESSOR NODES.

**uniform scoring policy,** *n.* a system for calculating VALUES to be assigned to HYPOTHESES. For example, in HWIM the internal TEMPLATE REPRESENTATION of a proposed sound or sound sequence is compared with a segment (see SEGMENTATION) of the actual speech signal, and the similarities and differences are noted and a number is calculated representing the likelihood that the proposed sound exists at that point. The sound templates stored in the system's DATA BASE never exactly MATCH segments of the acoustic signal, so that the hypotheses about individual speech sounds are scored.

**uniform–cost search,** *n.* a type of breadth–first ALGORITHM in which a nonnegative cost is associated with every OPERATOR and the cost of a SOLUTION can be measured by adding the costs of the operators applied. If all operators have equal cost, then the search becomes a BREADTH-FIRST SEARCH.

**unique termination,** *n.* a PROPERTY of certain sets of reducers such that, for every expression t, all irreducible forms of t are identical.

**unit,** *n.* in MOLGEN, a KNOWLEDGE structure used to represent bacteria, drugs, and laboratory operations.

**Unit Commitment Advisor,** *n.* an expert system developed for helping schedule power plant fire up and shutdown to meet demand. MAIDService is the development software.

**UNITS,** *n.* a system-building aid for KNOWLEDGE ACQUISITION that is FRAME-based and used for REPRESENTATION and manipulation. KNOWLEDGE is stored in 'units,' which may be divided into possibly overlapping partitions. Units have SLOTS, and procedures may be attached to slots and units. The procedures can be written in LISP or in a specially provided pseudo–English procedural language. Built-in PROPERTY INHERITANCE mechanisms and PATTERN matchers (see PATTERN MATCHING) are included in UNITS, yet most of the INFERENCE must be provided by application of specific methods. Also included are mechanisms for automatically documenting KNOWLEDGE BASES, and transferring information within and among knowledge bases. UNITS was developed at Stanford University as part of the MOLGEN project, and UNITS has subsequently been used by several other projects. It is implemented in INTERLISP and runs under the TENEX and TOPS20 operating systems.

**unity path,** *n*. the resulting path involved in the search through a TREE where the RULES have a CERTAINTY FACTOR of 1. In MYCIN, for example, this increases an INFERENCE ENGINE's efficiency. Before the entire list of rules for a subgoal (see SUBGOALING) is retrieved, the program attempts to find a sequence of rules that would establish the GOAL with certainty, based only on what is currently known. Since this is a search for a sequence of rules with CF = 1, the result is termed a unity path.

**universal language,** *n*. a language that contains all possible strings of the TERMINAL SYMBOLS in a language.

**universal quantification,** *n*. the process in PREDICATE CALCULUS to convey the meaning that the clause is true for all OBJECTS.

**universal specialization,** *n*. a form of ∀-elimination. Universal specialization states that, for any well-formed expression Φ that mentions a variable X, if we have:

$$\forall\ X.\ \Phi(X)$$

we can conclude:

$$\Phi(A)$$

for any individual A. In other words, if we know:

$$\forall\ X.\ Man\ (X) \rightarrow Mortal\ (X),$$

we can apply this to the individual Socrates, using the ∀-elimination rule, to get:

$$Man(Socrates) \rightarrow Mortal(Socrates).$$

**unsolvable node,** *n*. **1.** a NODE that is not a TERMINAL NODE and has no successors.
**2.** a node whose SUCCESSOR NODES are AND nodes and at least one of them is unsolvable; or a node whose successors are OR nodes and all of them are unsolvable.

**user,** *n*. an individual who uses an expert system. A user is conventionally understood as an END-USER, a DOMAIN EXPERT, a KNOWLEDGE ENGINEER, or a clerical staff member.

**user interface,** *n*. the bidirectional communication module that permits communication between the expert system and the USER.

# V

**V,** *n.* a very high-level, wide-spectrum language used in the AUTOMATIC PROGRAMMING system CHI for specifying both programs and programming knowledge and for interacting with the PROGRAMMING ENVIRONMENT. The V language includes constructs for sets, mappings, RELATIONS, PREDICATES, enumerations, state-transformation sequences, PROGRAM-SYNTHESIS RULES, and control META-RULES.

**validation,** *n.* the assessment of the accuracy, utility, and dependability of a system.

**value,** *n.* a quantity or quality that can be used to describe an ATTRIBUTE. When considering an attribute such as colour, the possible values of colour are all the names of colours that can be used. When considering a particular OBJECT, assigning a specific value to the observed attribute might involve saying, 'That house is painted bright red.'

**variable,** *n.* a term in data or processing structure that can assume any VALUE from a set of values. The values become part of the DOMAIN of the value, which can be determined by SYNTACTIC or semantic PROPERTIES.

**variable domain array,** *n.* a direct REPRESENTATION scheme in the GENERAL SPACE PLANNER with respect to the properties of size, shape, and position.

**variable scoping,** *n.* the extent of the assignment of a VALUE to a VARIABLE. (See DYNAMIC SCOPING.)

**verification of synthesized code,** *n.* the VALIDATION of code in AUTOMATIC PROGRAMMING by evaluating the program on the example set, or by generating new examples for the program.

**verification trees,** *n.* a TREE of FORMULAS generated from the original statement of a problem. Such trees are called verification trees. The verification tree for a problem constitutes a reduction of the original, usually not directly verifiable, condition to a collection of directly verifiable conditions, the formulas at the leaves. These trees have the PROPERTY that the failure of the formula at a NODE in the tree explains the failure of formulas at any of its ancestors. Similarly, the failure of a formula at a node is explained by the failure of formulas at any of its descendants.

**version space,** *n.* **1.** a method developed for representing all versions of the left-hand side of a RULE that are consistent with the observed data for all iterations made thus far. This representation is referred to as the version space of the rule. By examining the version space of a rule R one can discover which of the recommended changes to R will preserve its performance on past instances. This is usually any changes that yield a version of the rule contained in the version space. Version spaces avoid selecting a single, intractable modification to R and therefore eliminate the need for backtracking. For example, all the elements of the version space that MATCH some negative instance S are eliminated. Similarly, when new data are encountered in which a situation S' is found to correctly trigger R, only those elements of the version space that match S' are retained.

**2.** a technique for learning CONCEPT rules from instances that are presented sequentially. When given a description language on which a partial generality ordering is defined, along with a series of instances, a rule is found that can classify instances as belonging to a concept or not. The method consists of maintaining two boundary sets (see BOUNDARY LINE) that are defined in terms of that generality ordering; first, a maximally specific set of descriptions, which are instances that fit one of these descriptions, or a more specific set that are more positive instances of the concept, and then, a minimally general set, which are instances that do not fit those descriptions that are negative instances of the concept. The space below the upper boundary, containing all possible rules, is called the version space. There is a method for maintaining the boundaries. For positive instances, a new specific boundary consists of the descriptions that fit the set union of instances covered by the previous boundary and the new instance. For negative instances, a new general boundary consists of the descriptions that fit the set covered by the previous boundary minus the new one. This method is only useful if there exists a representation for the boundary sets.

**vertex type,** *n.* a type of intersection produced from the combination of convex and concave edges. There are four vertex types:

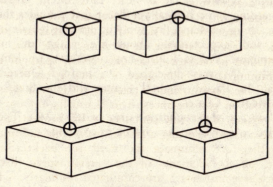

**Vertex type**

**viewpoint,** *n.* a specified WINDOW on a display surface that marks the limits of a display.

**vision,** *n.* in ROBOTICS, the use of TV cameras to input visual information into a system. In other applications, research has made it possible for systems to recognize OBJECTS and SHADOWS or identify minute differences between similar pictures, as in aerial reconnaissance.

**VISIONS,** *n.* an expert system that provides artificial VISION.

**vision study,** *n.* any project where the focus of research is on understanding a scene from its projected image(s).

**VL$_1$,** *n.* a REPRESENTATION language used to represent DISCRIMINATION RULES. It is an extension of the PROPOSITIONAL CALCULUS.

**VLSI,** *abbrev. for* Very Large Scale Integration, the design of the layout and construction of extremely complex electronic circuits that can be put on small chips. VLSI technologies are instrumental in the design of large computers that fit in small containers. VLSI design work is an application DOMAIN for expert systems.

**VM,** *abbrev. for* Ventilator Manager, an expert system that provides diagnostic and therapeutic suggestions about post-surgical patients in an intensive care unit (ICU). The system identifies possible alarm conditions, recognizes spurious data, characterizes the patient state, and suggests useful therapies. The system interprets quantitative measurements from an ICU monitoring system, such as heart rate, blood pressure, and data regarding a mechanical ventilator that provides the patient with breathing assistance by applying knowledge about patient history and expectations about the range of monitored measurements. VM is a RULE-BASED SYSTEM. Implemented in INTERLISP, VM was developed at Stanford University and tested at the Pacific Medical Center and the Stanford University Medical Center.

**voice chess,** *n.* the application area of HEARSAY-I. The system responded to moves spoken into a microphone.

# W

**Waltz filtering,** *n.* a procedure used in image understanding that applies CONSTRAINT satisfaction. It is based on the Huffman-Clowes principle that each line in the picture must be assigned a single label along its entire length. The Waltz ALGORITHM tries to label all junctions uniquely and usually does converge on a single INTERPRETATION.

**Warehouse Planner,** *n.* an expert system developed by Hitachi for assisting in automated warehousing.

**Water Permit Review System,** *n.* an expert system developed at Software Architecture and Engineering Inc. for the EPA. It helps review water use permit applications. KES is the development software.

**Waterman's Poker Player,** *n.* a computer program that learns to play draw poker.

**WAVES,** *n.* an expert system developed by Teknowledge for helping geologists choose the appropriate process for seismic data. The development software is KS 300.

**web grammar,** *n.* a GRAMMAR whose atomic elements are restricted to pieces of a labelled, directed GRAPH.

**weight space,** *n.* the space of all possible weight vectors.

**Weld Defect Diagnosis System,** *n.* an expert system developed at Stone & Webster for helping to determine causes of welding defects. Exsys is the development software.

**Weld Procedures Selection System,** *n.* An expert system developed at Stone & Webster Engineering for advising welders on procedures, materials, and electrolyte type. Exsys is the development software.

**Weld Selector,** *n.* **1.** an expert system developed by the Colorado School of Mines for the American Welding Institute to help welding engineers choose proper weld procedures. PERSONAL CONSULTANT is the development software.
**2.** an expert system developed by Intellicorp for Babcock and Wilcox to help welding engineers choose proper weld procedures. KEE is the development software.

**Welder Qualification Test Selection System,** *n.* an expert system developed at Stone & Webster for helping managers choose appropriate qualification tests for welders. Exsys is the development software.

**well-formed program,** *n.* a program that satisfies a set of CONSTRAINTS.

**well-founded relation,** *n.* a RELATION that admits no infinitely decreasing sequences.

**WEST,** *n.* an expert system from which students learn by interacting with a coach.

**wff,** *abbrev. for* a well-formed formula. An expression that is created with syntactically allowed combinations of CONNECTIVES, PREDICATES, constants, VARIABLES, and QUANTIFIERS (see SYNTAX).

**Wheat Counselor,** *n.* an expert system developed by ICI (Imperial Chemicals) to aid in the diagnosis of wheat diseases.

**WHEEZE,** *n.* an expert system that diagnoses the presence and severity of lung disease by interpreting measurements of pulmonary function tests. The program uses clinical laboratory test results, such as total lung capacity, patient history, and history of smoking, as the basis for the diagnosis. WHEEZE's EXPERTISE consists of a translation of the RULES used by PUFF into a FRAME-based REPRESENTATION. The frames contain two types of CERTAINTY FACTOR, one indicating the likelihood of an ASSERTION when its manifestations are believed, and the other indicating the degree to which the assertion is believed to be true during a particular consultation. WHEEZE's control mechanism provides a kind of BACK– and FORWARD CHAINING, implemented by using an AGENDA, with each suggested assertion placed on the agenda according to a specified priority. Implemented in RLL, WHEEZE was developed at Stanford University.

**WHISPER,** *n.* a system designed to reason exclusively by ANALOGICAL KNOWLEDGE REPRESENTATION. The program operates in a simplified BLOCKS-WORLD ENVIRONMENT, solving problems such as the following: Given four blocks in some two-dimensional representation, what will happen when block X tumbles down onto block Y? The system has three components:

(a) Diagram: an ARRAY that represents the 2-D scene.

WHY

(b) Retina: a set of parallel receptors arranged in concentric circles, with each receptor viewing a small part of the diagram.

(c) High-level reasoner: the DOMAIN-dependent part of the system that contains qualitative physical knowledge such as information regarding the behaviour of rigid bodies when acted upon by gravity.

The significance of the diagram component to WHISPER resides in the fact that there are two types of analogue – analogues between static states of the diagram and the world and also between dynamic behaviour of OBJECTS in the diagram and of objects in the world. The correspondence between the diagram and the world is simple and well defined; no complicated processes are required to map from one to the other: A number of PROPERTIES, such as position, orientation, and size of blocks, are represented analogically. For those properties, it is not necessary to perform complicated deductions, since the desired information 'falls out' of the diagrams. For example, to test whether or not a particular area of the world is empty (i.e., not occupied by any block), the system has only to look at the corresponding area of the diagram. With most propositional representations, it would be necessary to examine each block individually, testing whether or not that block overlapped the space in question.

**WHY,** *n.* a system that is an extension of SCHOLAR; it teaches students about rainfall. WHY was an outgrowth of the SCHOLAR project and, like SCHOLAR, engages students in a tutorial discussion based upon the Socratic method. It went beyond previous work in attempting to teach about a complex process, namely, the causes of rainfall. In order to acquire an understanding of the factors that influence rainfall, the student had to learn to make predictions, distinguish between necessary and sufficient conditions, and evaluate HYPOTHESES, in addition to mastering new facts. KNOWLEDGE in the program was represented as SCRIPTS. The main script consisted of a set four major events occurring in chronological order: absorption of moisture by warm air mass, movement of air mass, cooling, and precipitation. These steps were linked by relationships (e.g., 'precedes' or 'causal'). The scripts were

367

hierarchically (see HIERARCHY) organized, with subscripts under each of the major events that expanded on those events. For example, a subscript on evaporation expanded on the first major event, the absorption of moisture. Each script had a set of roles associated with it, such as AIR MASS or BODY OF WATER, that could be instantiated (see INSTANTIATION) for different cases, such as Oregon or Ireland. The WHY tutor conversed with the student in simple English and asked questions designed to uncover errors and omissions in the student's understanding. The dialogue was conducted by applying PRODUCTION RULES.

**WILLARD,** *n.* an expert system that helps meteorologists forecast the likelihood of severe thunderstorms occurring in the central United States. The system queries a meteorologist about pertinent weather conditions for the forecast area and then produces a complete forecast with supporting justifications. The user may specify a particular geographical area for WILLARD to consider. The program characterizes the certainty of severe thunderstorm occurrence as 'none,' 'approaching', 'slight', 'moderate', or 'high', and each is given a numerical probability range. WIILARD's expertise is represented as RULES generated automatically from examples of expert forecasting. Implemented using RULEMASTER, WILLARD was developed at Radian Corporation.

**window,** *n.* a partition of the screen on a terminal. Window SOFTWARE permits information drawn from different DATA BASES to be displayed in different windows. Conventional computer terminals, on the other hand, use the entire screen to present information drawn from one data base. A user can have a word processing program running in one window and a graphics program running simultaneously in a second window. Much expert system research is conducted on computers that allow the user to display different views of the system's activity simultaneously. Windows are an example of a technique originally developed by artificial intelligence researchers that has now become part of conventional programming technology.

**Winston's ARCH program,** *n.* a system for structural learning. The task of the program is to learn CONCEPT descriptions that characterize the construction of arches. Input is a set of line drawings that the program interprets into a SEMANTIC NETWORK description.

**word island,** *n.* a HYPOTHESIS about the identification of a word in the HWIM system.

**word template,** *n.* a REPRESENTATION of the acoustic signal produced by a speaker uttering a single word. In the form of word TEMPLATES, phonetic (see PHONETICS) knowledge was used in early ISOLATED-WORD RECOGNITION systems. The word templates were matched (see MATCH) against the signal to be recognized.

**working memory,** *n.* the dynamic portion of a PRODUCTION SYSTEM's memory. Working memory contains the DATA BASE of the system, which changes as RULES are executed. In expert systems, working memory consists of all of the ATTRIBUTE-VALUE relationships which are established while the consultation is in progress. Because expert systems continuously check rules and seek values, all values that are established must be kept immediately available until all the rules have been examined. This is done in working memory. (See SHORT-TERM MEMORY, DYNAMIC KNOWLEDGE BASE.)

**workstation,** *n.* the configuration of computer equipment designed to be used by one person at a time. In general, a workstation consists of an input device, a display device, memory, and an output device such as a printer or plotter. Workstations may have a terminal connected to a larger computer, or may stand alone having local processing capability. Generally, workstations refer to computer systems that help a USER perform his or her job. For example, large financial institutions currently have trading rooms where individuals constantly monitor currency or stock prices and conduct trades by means of computers arranged in front of them.

**world** *n.* the PROBLEM AREA that is being modelled by the computer system.

**world coordinate system,** *n.* a device-independent three-dimensional Cartesian coordinate system in which two- and three-dimensional objects are described to a viewing system.

**world knowledge,** *n.* general KNOWLEDGE about the world or a DOMAIN of interest.

**world model,** *n.* in ROBOTICS, a set of statements that describe the physical ENVIRONMENT of the ROBOT.

**WUMPUS,** *n.* an expert system that teaches LOGIC, PROB-ABILITY theory, DECISION THEORY, and geometry.

**WUSOR,** *n.* one of three generations of computer coaches for WUMPUS.

# X

**XCON,** *abbrev. for* eXpert CONfigurer of VAX computer systems, an expert system that configures VAX computer systems. From a customer's order it decides what components must be added to produce a complete operational system and determines the spatial relationships among all of the components. XCON outputs a set of diagrams indicating these spatial relationships to technicians who then assemble the VAX system. The program handles the configuration task by applying KNOWLEDGE of the constraints on component relationships to standard procedures for configuring computers. The system is noninteractive, RULE-based, and uses a FORWARD CHAINING CONTROL scheme. Implemented in OPS5, XCON was developed through a collaboration between researchers at Carnegie-Mellon University and Digital Equipment Corporation.

**X-ray Diffractometer Asst.,** *n.* an expert system developed by Westinghouse Electric Co. for assisting in identifying crystallographic structures of metals. PERSONAL CONSULTANT is the development software.

**XSEL,** *abbrev. for* eXpert SELling assistant, an expert system that helps a salesperson select components for a VAX computer system and assists in designing a floor layout for them. XSEL selects a central processing unit, primary memory, SOFTWARE, and peripheral devices, such as terminals and disk drives, and then passes it to XCON to be expanded and configured. XSEL contains DOMAIN KNOWLEDGE about the relations among components and the various applications a customer might have and knowledge about how to lead a USER through a selection process. The system is interactive, RULE-based, and uses a FORWARD CHAINING control scheme. Implemented in OPS5, XSEL was developed through a collaboration between researchers at Carnegie-Mellon University and Digital Equipment Corporation.

**XSITE,** *n.* an expert system developed by Digital Equipment

## XSITE

Corporation to prepare a site layout plan for a customer's computer room. OPS5 is the development SOFTWARE.

# Y

**YES/MVS,** *abbrev. for* Yorktown Expert System for MVS operators, an expert system that helps computer operators monitor and control the MVS (Multiple Virtual Storage) OPERATING SYSTEM, the operating system most widely used in large mainframe IBM computers. YES/MVS addresses six major categories of tasks: maintaining adequate JES (Job Entry System) queue space, handling network communications between computers on the same site, scheduling large batch jobs off prime shift, responding to hardware errors, monitoring subsoftware systems, and monitoring overall system performance. YES/MVS runs in real time, directly interpreting MVS messages and sending either commands to the operating system or recommendations to the console operator. The program is RULE-based using FORWARD CHAINING and is implemented in an extended version of OPS5 by an expert system group at the IBM T.J. Watson Research Center in Yorktown Heights, New York.

# Z

**zero–crossing,** *n.* a point at which a mathematical FUNCTION changes its sign, i.e., passes through zero. Technically, a zero-crossing is defined as the intersection of the zero plane $(z=0)$ with a surface $(z=f(x,y,))$. Convolving a grey-level image (see GREY-LEVEL CORRECTION) with a difference of gaussians and then finding zero crossings in the output is one way of looking for edge points. The detection of zero-crossings is also used in SPEECH RECOGNITION.

**ZETALISP,** *n.* a programming language for PROCEDURE-ORIENTED REPRESENTATION. It is a dialect of LISP based on MIT's MACLISP, but substantially extended and improved. It provides all of the standard LISP features, a large number of extensions (e.g., FLAVORS), and a sophisticated support ENVIRONMENT. The support environment includes a high-resolution, bit map graphics display, a WINDOW system, an integrated program/text editor, and a display-oriented DEBUGGER. ZETALISP runs on Symbolics' LM-2 and 3600 computer systems and on LMI's Lambda and Lambda/Plus machines. It was developed at MIT as a research system and is available commercially.

# COLLINS DICTIONARY OF ELECTRONICS

*Ian R. Sinclair*

The *Collins Dictionary of Electronics* is a completely new and up-to-date guide to the science and technology of electronics. Containing over 2,000 entries, from *aberration* to *zero error,* the Dictionary also includes over 100 diagrams, together with lists of symbols used in electronics.

The Dictionary is intended for anyone who needs a source book providing clear, helpful definitions of electronic terms, including advanced school students and those embarking on higher-education courses, as well as technicians and hobbyists. The Dictionary will also prove useful to anyone whose work or study involves the use of electronic devices — which now have become vital tools in areas as diverse as music, archaeology and medicine.

The Dictionary guides the reader through the various fields within electronics such as microprocessor technology, digital electronics, telecommunications, hi-fi, radio, and television. The emphasis throughout is on the practical application of concepts and devices, although the theoretical background is also well covered, and the reader will find entries on such topics as the *superposition theorem*, the *Biot–Savart law,* and the *permeability* and *permittivity of free space.* Where appropriate, the mathematical aspects of a topic is introduced, although this is generally avoided.

Ian R. Sinclair is a professional technical author. He has written many books on computing for Collins, including the *Collins Dictionary of Computing.*

'. . . the dictionary should prove useful.' — *What's new in Electronics.*

ISBN 0 00 434345 X

# COLLINS DICTIONARY OF COMPUTING

*Ian R. Sinclair*

Aimed primarily at those using microcomputers as a tool — whether it be at university, school or college, or in the home or office — rather than the professional computer expert, the Dictionary will also prove invaluable to anyone whose work is related in any way to computers, be they micro, mini or mainframe.

Far too many computer manuals assume that even the beginner knows the meaning of a vast array of specialized jargon, leaving the user in a state of near despair. Although not a handbook to particular machines, *Collins Dictionary of Computing* contains definitions and explanations of over 2,000 of the terms that the average user is most likely to come across, from *access* to *zero compression*. Written with a clarity and precision that will be welcomed by all computer users, the entries are augmented by nearly 100 diagrams and explanatory captions.

Comprehensive without indulging in unnecessary padding, and of course completely up-to-date, the Dictionary includes such basic terms as *BASIC, bit* and *binary*, as well as those strange terms that computer buffs have made peculiarly their own, such as *blow, bomb* and *bubble*. Fields covered range through hardware, software, programming, computer logic, data and word processing, languages, systems, and graphics, to those areas of information technology in which computers play such a vital role.

Ian R. Sinclair, a full-time technical author, has written numerous best-selling computer books for Collins, and is also author of the *Collins Dictionary of Electronics*.

'. . . excellent value for money.' — *Computer Weekly*.

ISBN 0 00 434349 2